"Dannefer's ground-breaking book places the life course at the heart of our understanding of ageing and old age, and boldly integrates social, biological and hermeneutic frameworks into an exciting new theoretical perspective. This compelling work combines an impressively wide range of analyses, from child development psychology to the political economy of old age, by way of the sociology of science, epigenetics and much more. It is rich in both historically grounded arguments and state of the art sociological ones. Building on this solid foundation Dannefer concludes with a sharp political message focusing on the continuing cumulative growth of advantage and disadvantage, which underpins increasing intracohort inequalities, and the huge life course risks associated with rampant individualism."

Alan Walker, *University of Sheffield*

"In this insightful and comprehensive book, the prominent social gerontologist, Dale Dannefer, draws upon research from the social and behavioral sciences as well as biology, history and economics to debunk myths about aging and highlight key debates in research on aging. *Age and the Reach of Sociological Imagination* is beautifully written, rich in theory, comprehensive in coverage and replete with lively anecdotes. Among the topics Dannefer covers are the ways the organization of age has changed over time and the persistence of ageism, and his discussion of the factors leading to cumulative disadvantage over the life course is especially helpful. This book should be required reading in every graduate and advanced undergraduate course in gerontology."

Jill Quadagno, *Author of Aging and the Life Course*

"As told by one of the field's most original social theorists, *Age and the Reach of Sociological Imagination* is a brilliant intellectual history of thinking on age, aging, and the aged. Drawing on compelling insights ranging from NASCAR aerodynamics to feral children to skills learned on the 19th Century shop floor, Dannefer directs our attention away from the developmental paradigms that homogenize human experience and toward the social structures that account simultaneously for its standardization and diversity."

Judith Treas, *University of California, Irvine*

"In this wide-ranging and ambitious book, Dale Dannefer takes us through the paradigmatic approaches and arguments of aging research, throwing light on the shortcomings of the functionalist-developmental nexus and using his sociological imagination to delineate more fruitful alternatives. A thoughtful statement by an eminent sociologist of aging."

Martin Kohli, *European University Institute*

"A major contribution to the study of ageing from one of the leading theorists in the field. The book is unusual in combining work across a range of social science disciplines, as well as being historically grounded in the development of ageing societies. The unique strength of the book is its sophisticated grasp of the nature of human development, drawing on a detailed reading of life course and related literature. The importance for the reader is the critical perspective which is brought to the analysis, notably in relation to the problem of reductionism, and the failure to address the full range of social structural issues influencing the life course."

Christopher Phillipson, *Manchester University*

Age and the Reach of Sociological Imagination

The dominant narratives of both science and popular culture typically define aging and human development as self-contained individual matters, failing to recognize the degree to which they are shaped by experiential and contextual contingencies. Our understandings of age are thereby "boxed in" and constricted by assumptions of "normality" and naturalness that limit our capacities to explore possible alternative experiences of development and aging, and the conditions—both individual and social—that might foster such experiences.

Combining foundational principles of critical social science with recent breakthroughs in research across disciplines ranging from biology to economics, this book offers a scientifically and humanly expanded landscape for apprehending the life course. Rejecting familiar but false dichotomies such as "nature vs nurture" and "structure vs. agency", it clarifies the organismic fundamentals that make the actual content of experience so centrally important in age and development, and it also explores why attention to these fundamentals has been so resisted in studies of individuals and individual change, and in policy and practice as well.

In presenting the basic principles and reviewing the current state of knowledge, Dale Dannefer introduces multileveled social processes that shape human development and aging over the life course and age as a cultural phenomenon—organizing his approach around three key frontiers of inquiry that each invite a vigorous exercise of sociological imagination: the Social-Structural Frontier, the Biosocial Frontier and the Critical-Reflexive Frontier.

Dale Dannefer is the Selah Chamberlain Professor of Sociology and Chair, Department of Sociology at Case Western Reserve University.

AGING AND SOCIETY

Edited by Carroll L. Estes and Assistant Editor Nicholas DiCarlo

This pioneering series of books creatively synthesizes and advances key, intersectional topics in gerontology and aging studies. Drawing from changing and emerging issues in gerontology, influential scholars combine research into human development and the life course; the roles of power, policy, and partisanship; race and ethnicity; inequality; gender and sexuality; and cultural studies to create a multi-dimensional and essential picture of modern aging.

Aging A – Z: Concepts toward Emancipatory Gerontology (2019)
Carroll L. Estes with Nicholas DiCarlo

The Privatization of Care: The Case of Nursing Homes (2020)
Pat Armstrong and Hugh Armstrong

Age and the Research of Sociological Imagination: Power, Ideology, and the Life Course (2021)
Dale Dannefer

When Strangers Become Family: The Role of Civil Society in Addressing the Needs of Aging Populations (2021)
Ronald Angel and Verónica Montes-de-Oca Zavala

For more information about this series, please visit: https://www.routledge.com/Aging-and-Society/book-series/AGINGSOC

Age and the Reach of Sociological Imagination

POWER, IDEOLOGY, AND THE LIFE COURSE

DALE DANNEFER

Routledge
Taylor & Francis Group

NEW YORK AND LONDON

First published 2022
by Routledge
605 Third Avenue, New York, NY 10158

and by Routledge
2 Park Square, Milton Park, Abingdon, Oxon, OX14 4RN

Routledge is an imprint of the Taylor & Francis Group, an informa business

Library of Congress Cataloging-in-Publication Data
A catalog record for this book has been requested

ISBN: 978-0-367-19088-0 (hbk)
ISBN: 978-0-367-19089-7 (pbk)
ISBN: 978-0-429-32367-6 (ebk)

Typeset in Bembo
by Apex CoVantage, LLC

**To the memory of
Elaine Frances Dannefer**

*My loving partner, my wise teacher, my brilliant critic,
and so much more*

CONTENTS

ACKNOWLEDGMENTS

If one of the themes of this project is the importance of social interaction and relationships in productive human activity, that theme could scarcely have a better illustration than in the production of this work itself. In writing it, I have drawn directly on perspectives, knowledge and insights gained from discussions, debates and challenges from so many valued colleagues across multiple disciplines that it would be impossible to enumerate all those to whom I'm intellectually indebted. I will limit myself here to mentioning the relatively few pivotally important or sustained collegial relationships that have been especially valuable in constructing the argument of this book.

For the ideas and the understanding of social-system dynamics and their human elements brought together in this work, the foundation was provided by my first real teachers in social theory, Eugene V. Smith at Indiana State, where I began my graduate work, and Peter Berger at Rutgers. They could not have been more different in the paradigms of social thought they represented, and in some ways the argument set forth here attempts to integrate the modern systems approach I learned from Smith with the phenomenological principles and dialectical dynamics of consciousness, interaction and structure explicated in Berger's work. For stimulating and supporting my efforts to integrate these perspectives with the framework of critical theory, I am indebted to my longtime colleagues Jan Baars, George Gonos, Chris Phillipson and Philip Wexler. For help in applying these perspectives to the study of age and life-course processes, I had the great benefit of Matilda Riley's mentorship and colleagueship, and of the intellectual stimulation of many colleagues, especially Vern Bengtson, Glen Elder, Gunhild Hagestad, Martin Kohli, Peter Uhlenberg and Alan Walker. My early efforts to integrate cumulative dis/advantage with the study of the life course were catalyzed by Jim Rosenbaum's pioneering work on tournament mobility and by subsequent discussions with Ralph Sell and especially with Gunhild Hagestad, and with respect to the methodological questions posed by challenges of CDA, especially to Jessica Kelley.

For my understanding of new social possibilities across social settings, from preschool to nursing homes, I am indebted to Barry Barkan, RoseMarie Fagan, Bill Thomas, Peter and Cathy Whitehouse, Carter Catlett Williams and my collaborators from whom I learned much when they were nominally my students—Robin Shura, Rebecca Siders and especially Paul Stein.

The arguments in this book have also been profoundly shaped by interdisciplinary exchange with colleagues from other disciplines, and especially with psychology. This includes explorations with progressive and critical theorists such as John Broughton, Laurence Parker and Anna Stetsenko, but I have learned equally as much in the process of vigorous debate with those with whom I have sometimes had profound disagreements, especially Paul Baltes, Richard Lerner, Daniel Levinson, Marion Perlmutter and Warner Schaie. I owe a special word of thanks to Glen Elder and Warner Schaie, pioneers of the life-course and life-span perspectives respectively, both of whom generously gave of their time to be interviewed concerning their foundational work and the establishment of these two fields.

With regard to the discussion of gene-environment interactions, I have greatly benefited from collaboration with my coauthor Kathryn Douthit and from conversations with Gerry Maclearn and Neil Pendleton, and to my lifelong friendship and colleagueship with biochemist Michael Gresser.

For the production of the book itself, I am particularly grateful to Jan Baars, Carroll Estes and Alan Walker who read multiple chapters of the manuscript, with special thanks to Chris Phillipson, who read the entire manuscript multiple times. Andy Achenbaum generously read and critiqued several drafts of Chapter 4, devoted to historical perspectives on aging. Tim Black, George Gonos, Paul Hill, Anna Stetsenko and Peter Whitehouse also read and critiqued key passages of the book. My special thanks to my dedicated and able student assistants—Micah Arafah, Luma Al Masarweh, Chengming Han, Anvitha Ravipati, Ananya Sarker and Reema Sen—for their work on various chapters, and especially to Wenxuan Huang for her thorough and perceptive reading of the manuscript. I also want to thank Michelle Corcoran and Caitlin O'Connor for their excellent clerical assistance. I am deeply grateful to my Routledge editor, Dean Birkenkamp, for his wise counsel, patience and tireless support throughout the project, and to series editor Carroll Estes for both her critique and encouragement.

In acknowledging those to whom I'm indebted, one person is in a class of her own, and that is my late wife Elaine Frances Dannefer, who we lost to cancer in 2016. Elaine, herself an accomplished family therapist, sociologist and an internationally known reformer in medical education, was my wonderful life partner and more. She was a sounding board and critic for ideas, a regular source of fresh perspectives and creative insights as well as needed caution, a wellspring of common sense, wisdom and discernment, as well as personal encouragement, affirmation and inspiration, and I dedicate this book to her.

CHAPTER 1
SOCIOLOGICAL IMAGINATION AND HUMAN AGING

As a senior citizen was driving down the freeway, his cell phone rang. Answering, he heard his wife's urgent voice warning him, "Herman, I just heard on the news that there's a car going the wrong way on Interstate 77. Please be careful!"

"Hell!" said Herman, "It's not just one car. It's hundreds of 'em!"

Three old guys were out walking.
First one said, "Windy, isn't it?"
The second one said, "No, it's Thursday!"
The third one said, "So am I. Let's go get a beer!"

During John McCain's presidential campaign, he visited a senior community in Florida. He was surprised that two women residents he encountered at a community center did not seem to recognize him. "Do you know who I am?" he asked.

One of the women answered, "No, but if you check with that nurse at the desk, she can tell you".

You know you're getting old when you get that one candle on the cake. It's like, "See if you can blow this out."

Jerry Seinfeld

"No one reached out to me and said, 'As a senior citizen, are you willing to take a chance on your survival in exchange for keeping the America that all America loves for your children and grandchildren?'" But if they had? "If that is the exchange, I'm all in."
Texas Lt. Governor Dan Patrick speaking about COVID risk, on Fox TV News, 3/23/2020

AGE CONSCIOUSNESS AND AGEISM IN CULTURE AND SCIENCE

Although we live in an era in which political correctness and basic civility and respectfulness inhibit jokes and stereotypical commentary across multiple domains including race, religion, ethnicity and gender, the subject of age remains fair game. The manifestations of ageism in popular culture are wide-ranging, from the open season on old age of late night comedians to well-documented practices of discrimination in the workplace or other settings, which often continue unchecked even when they are subject to legal sanction.

A decided lack of attention to ageism as a research problem in the social and behavioral sciences has been well documented by several scholars (Nelson 2005; North and Fiske 2012; Palmore 1999). In the US, where age discrimination is illegal, older scientists who submit grant proposals through peer-review processes that claim to be purely objective and meritocratic encounter an unapologetic and often overt ageism (Kahana, Slone, Kahana, Langendoerfer, and Reynolds 2016). At least one leading expert has recently presented a strong case that ageism in general, as a standard component of contemporary popular culture, is actually on the increase (Gullette 2011).

Neither the cultural impulses that generate ageism nor the ease with which it is popularly accepted can be reduced to any single cause. Yet one force that clearly provides a legitimating framework for such ideas is a largely unquestioned inclination to subscribe to the idea that development and aging are self-contained matters of the individual—anchored in time-bound, chronometrically governed processes working themselves out within the organism, within each human body.

Reinforcing such notions is the counterpart belief—so deeply rooted that it typically goes unquestioned and unremarked—that aging is a largely inevitable process that pervades the body, driven by imperatives of physical change with the passage of time. Indeed, that is how it typically appears in everyday life, as we observe family members or other longtime acquaintances going through gradual but seemingly predictable long-term patterns of physical and social change. And if so, perhaps there is nothing to do but accept it—and joke about it.

SOCIOLOGY, LIFE-SPAN DEVELOPMENT AND THE LIFE-COURSE FALLACY: A FIRST WAVE OF CONCEPTUAL TRANSFORMATION

For gerontologists and other scientists studying age-related phenomena, the idea that aging inevitably entails a one-way process of pervasive and multidimensional decline and adverse change was largely rejected several decades ago in an intellectual revolution that transformed the scientific study of aging in the 1960s and 1970s. A key factor in this revolution was the discovery that people who are born at different times grow up and grow older in dramatically different ways with regard to functioning, health and cognitive performance, and also with regard to lifestyle, attitudes, activities, social relationships and even longevity. How people age and how people change with age was found to be, in considerable measure, historically contingent.

Until this realization, it was common practice to assume that patterns of aging could be inferred "cross-sectionally"—that is, by comparing individuals of different ages at a single point in time—just by looking at the differences between, for example, 25-year-olds and 65-year-olds. A classic example of the extent to which this broad-based discovery called into question the then-current "established wisdom" concerning age and aging is provided by Warner Schaie and Sherry Willis's (1986) comparison of cross-sectional and longitudinal data on cognitive performance (see Figure 1.1). In contrast to the

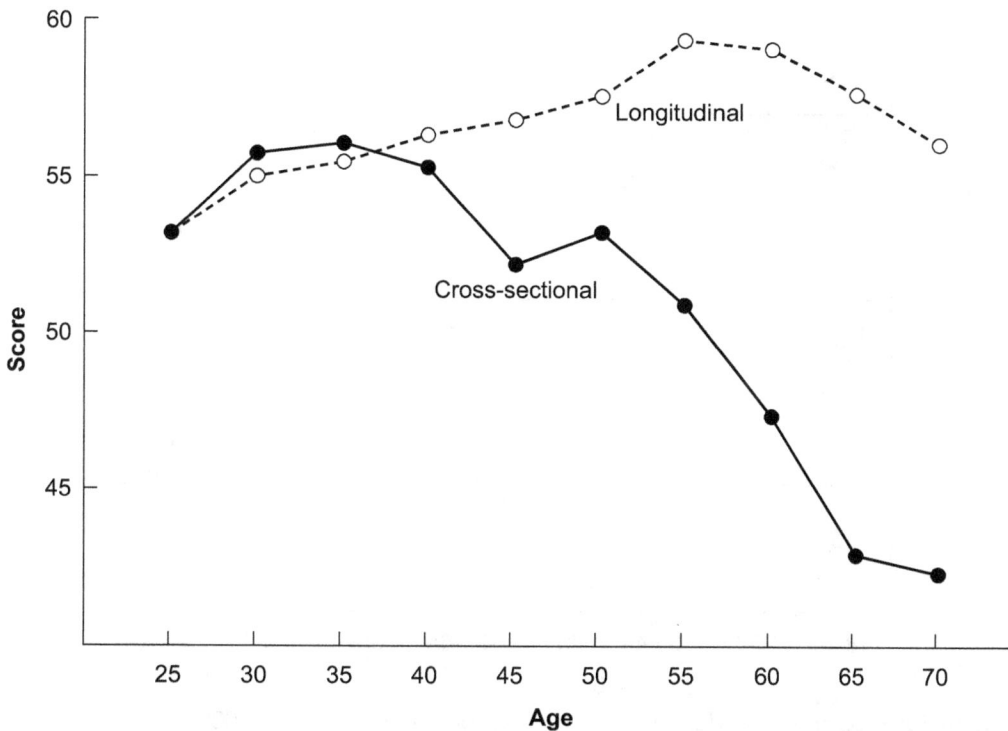

Figure 1.1 Cognitive performance by age, comparing cross-sectional and longitudinal data

Source: Adapted from Schaie and Willis 1986:298

dramatic declines suggested by a cross-sectional analysis, longitudinal data follow the same individuals over time, and present a dramatically different picture: A relatively high degree of stability, with a long-term gradual trend of increase, followed after age 60 followed by an equally gradual decline. In this work, Schaie and Willis (1986) highlighted the risk of reaching erroneous conclusions about aging (as has indeed often has been done) based on evidence from cross-sectional data (see Figure 1.1).

If the contrast between the two lines in Figure 1.1 initially appears puzzling, a key to understanding it can be found by considering trends in education over the same time period. The plummeting cross-sectional line in Figure 1.1 representing an age-related cross-sectional decline in cognitive performance is mirrored by the historical trend of educational attainment in the US over the same time period, as can be seen in Figure 1.2. However, since educational attainment is not a reversible characteristic, it quickly becomes apparent that the age-related decline in education requires a conceptual recalibration. It is factually correct, yet it is obvious that it cannot be interpreted as an effect of age, since graduating from high school cannot be undone. Thus, this figure reveals nothing whatever about the process of aging; it reflects instead the dramatic expansion of mass education in the US (and elsewhere) across the decades of the 20th century, It is an artifact of the long-term 20th-century historical trend of educational expansion, just as is the cross-sectional pattern of cognitive performance.

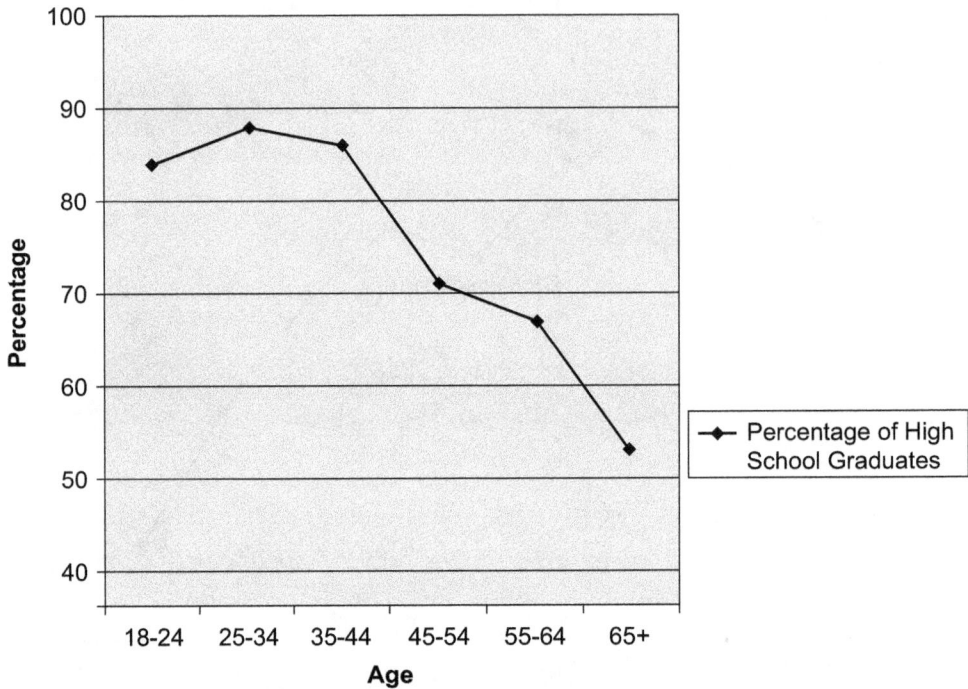

Figure 1.2 Proportion graduating from high school in the US, 1920–2000
Source: Derived from Table 223, Statistical Abstract of the United States, 1992, p. 145

Figure 1.1 thus illustrates the dangers of the *life-course fallacy* (Riley, Johnson, and Foner 1972; Riley 1973), which is the practice of assuming that cross-sectional comparisons can be relied upon to represent biographical, life-course patterns. It demonstrates dramatically the difference between how individuals of different ages appear at a particular point in time compared with the actual experience of individuals as they move through the life course.

With a proliferation of such discoveries across a range of characteristics and throughout the life course in the 1960s and 1970s, longstanding assumptions about aging were suddenly subjected to unprecedented scrutiny. Along with a recognition of the dangers of the life-course fallacy came a compelling new set of insights, a fresh sense of intellectual and existential possibilities with respect to aging and several new principles to guide research: First, that understanding how people change with age requires *tracing individuals and cohorts over time*, and cannot be inferred from "cross-sectional" comparisons of old and young people at a single point in time, immediately rendering suspect the longstanding research practice of making pronouncements about the effects of age based on such cross-sectional comparisons. Second, that an accurate understanding of how people change as they age could not be inferred from age alone but required data *on what specifically happens to them* as they age. This principle, in turn, compelled a recognition of the essential need for longitudinal data as a basis for an adequate characterization of patterns of aging. Finally, it compelled the recognition of the methodological centrality of cohort analysis (Alwin 1991; Riley et al. 1972; Riley 1973; Ryder 1965; Uhlenberg 1988). The discovery of the importance of cohort analysis was not limited to a single discipline. While its basic logic and the associated techniques are derived from demography (Ryder 1965), its importance was recognized in psychology (Baltes 1968; Schaie 1965), sociology (Riley and Foner 1968), epidemiology (Breslow 1985) and other social science fields (e.g., Cline 1980).

As the life-course fallacy became recognized in the scientific specializations that study aging and human development, its insights and implications had a cataclysmic impact, prompting a paradigm change that spread rapidly across disciplines. It fueled the development of the contemporary field of the *sociology of age* (see, e.g., Matilda White Riley's landmark paper, "Aging and Cohort Succession" [1973]), and the establishment of the *life-course perspective* (Cain 1964; Clausen 1972; Elder 1975), which was launched to prominence by the publication of Glen Elder's classic monograph, *Children of the Great Depression* ([1974]1999)—the study which provided a foundational introduction to the importance of life-course circumstances and experiences in shaping subsequent patterns of aging.

In psychology, parallel developments were also occurring, with the emergence of life-span psychology in the late 1960s similarly deriving from a recognition of the dangers of inferring biographical, life-course patterns from cross-sectional data (Schaie 1965; Baltes and Schaie 1976). On this basis, reviewing at the end of the 1970s what he then accurately called the "explosion" of life-span work, Paul Baltes wrote that life-span research had demonstrated that traditional views of human development were "unduly restrictive". He argued that an adequate conceptual framework for approaching human development and aging must include "multidimensionality, multidirectionality, and discontinuity" (1979:263) as integral features of human aging. While such arguments were not readily embraced in psychology (Baltes and Schaie 1974, 1976; Horn and Donaldson 1976, 1977; Horn, Donaldson, and Engstrom 1981), their evidentiary grounding combined with an expanding interest in adulthood and aging earned them growing respect and interest. Thus, the traditional views and established organismic approaches to age and human development were being rapidly supplanted across multiple disciplines.

These major theoretical breakthroughs were soon accompanied by advances in the domains of data, methods and techniques of analysis based on the establishment of large-scale longitudinal data sets. In 1988, the National Institute on Aging convened a panel that led to the Health and Retirement Study (HRS), a large-scale longitudinal study of 50+-year-olds that began in 1992, which was designed to facilitate the study of longitudinal life-course change and cohort differences. The HRS study design has been replicated in other nations, which include the *English Longitudinal Study of Aging* (ELSA), the *Study of Health, Aging, and Retirement in Europe* (SHARE) and the China Health and Retirement Longitudinal Study (CHARLS) with further longitudinal studies continuing to be launched elsewhere, including in developing countries such as India and Mexico. In the US, other studies with similar designs and purposes quickly followed, some focusing on younger participants, including the *National Longitudinal Study of Adolescent to Adult Health* (Add Health) and the *National Longitudinal Survey of Youth*. Newly developing riches in multi-cohort panel data also led to the refinement of relevant analytic techniques (e.g., event history analysis) and the development of new ones (e.g., latent growth curve modeling, sequence analysis) (Collins and Sayer 2001; Singer and Willett 2003; Yang and Land 2016).

In sociology, the initial theoretical developments paralleled and stimulated scholarly development of work on aging from other theoretical traditions—interactionist, constructivist and critical—that also challenged the traditional approach to human development and aging. Working from an interactionist approach, Vern Bengtson (1973) demonstrated the potentials for applying labeling theory to aging, and Jay Gubrium (1976) demonstrated how aging in nursing homes and medical settings could be usefully viewed as a constructed social reality as well as a biomedical one.

Early examples of a critical approach were introduced soon thereafter. Carroll Estes (1979) posed a challenge to the normative and "natural aging" assumptions of the biomedical model and its ideological underpinnings with her monograph *The Aging Enterprise*, and Victor Marshall and Joseph Tindale (1979) introduced the potentials of a "radical" approach in correcting the normative biases inherent in the field. Estes' analysis was soon followed by further articulations of the political economy critique (Phillipson 1982; Walker 1981). At the same time, historians and demographers began to focus on age and old age with a new scrutiny, examining how the *meaning* of age—from the childhood and teenage years to old age—has changed historically, in response to demographic shifts, technological developments and broader changes in social structure (Achenbaum 1978, 2015; Demos 1978; Haber 1983; Hareven 2013 [1978]; Laslett 1965; Uhlenberg 1974, 1978).

Taken together, these contemporaneous efforts had a powerful effect. They posed a serious challenge to adherents to the traditional dogma that treated age as a uniform and inevitable process of decline largely unaffected by social and environmental variation, and prompted a period of intellectual reflection and paradigmatic ferment. They offered a fresh array of contextualist perspectives to the scholarly discourse on aging, each proposing fresh approaches to understanding age-related change, from childhood to old age.

One result of this theoretical expansion was that commonly observed patterns of aging—long assumed to result from the inevitabilities of human nature from birth to death—began to be scrutinized as situational and conditional, as potentially modifiable and as influenced in previously unrecognized ways by experience and by an array of social forces. Thus, the subject matters of human development and aging were interrogated with new levels of energy and intellectual rigor and scrutiny—opening a new and exciting field of inquiry across and beyond the disciplines of the social and behavioral sciences. In such times of paradigmatic turbulence, it is especially important to think clearly and proactively, and to exercise a lively intellectual and sociological imagination.

SCIENCE—AS LONG AS IT'S NOT TOO MUCH SCIENCE!

One of the most perplexing and unfortunate elements of the intellectual history of age and life course studies is the record of the *reactions* of researchers to this initial flurry of intellectual energy and theoretical ferment. Given the developments just reviewed, there was clearly both an ample evidentiary basis and an emerging set of theoretical tools to challenge and rethink longstanding assumptions about the causal mechanisms underlying human development and shaping the life course. If patterns of age-related characteristics and trajectories of aging vary significantly across historical time, cohorts and context, they obviously are not fixed by imperatives of physical change over the life course. Clearly, then, the age trajectories of many key characteristics respond to the social setting and the specifics of individual experience, and cannot be reduced to intraindividual, ontogenetic factors.

Fresh questions about human nature and human possibility were logically compelled by these insights into the dynamic and contingent nature of individual change across the life course. What are the *characteristics of human beings* that allow for such a multiplicity of outcomes? What are the *forces that shape such a diversity* of life-course patterns and trajectories? What, if any, *are the limits of changing* how human beings develop and age? And why is it that life-course development often seems to be *in many ways orderly and predictable, yet can assume such very different forms*, within as well as across social and historical contexts? And what is the role of that wild card (Dannefer and Perlmutter 1990) in social life, *intentional human action*—sometimes called *agency*—in producing such predictable societal life-course patterns?

Another line of questions derived from contrasts with what we know of the aging processes undergone by other life forms. The recognition of historically and culturally diverse patterns of human aging appeared to be largely a human phenomenon—not so applicable to other species. What is it about *homo sapiens* that gives the species such a seemingly wide array of age-related possibilities? What do these discoveries imply for the basic paradigmatic assumptions that should guide our understanding of human development and aging? Why are human beings so variable in the patterning of development and aging? And, if traditional notions about the causality related to patterns of aging are fundamentally incorrect, what known explanatory principles and intellectual perspectives are most promising for the task of accounting for age-related outcomes?

Such questions cried out for attention. Clearly, a vista of new explanatory potentials and intellectual possibilities that could place the fundamental understanding of aging on a more contextual and social foundation awaited to be developed—seemingly, a wide and newly opened door for the exercise of sociological imagination.

Remarkably, however, the mobilization of intellectual energies to pursue such questions *did not happen*. Looking back over the history of research and theorizing on aging and the life course in sociology (and in life-span psychology as well) over the past few decades, one of the most remarkable things to note is that after a brief initial flurry of intellectual excitement and ferment, these questions *received almost no attention* by most researchers and scholars interested in these areas. The obviously logical "next steps" were not taken. Instead, behavioral and social science research on aging took more cautious directions, turning back to familiar and more conventional paradigmatic formulas for posing questions and designing studies. Rather than intellectual expansion, the body of developing research on aging and the life course was marked by a disinclination to probe too deeply into such questions, and by tending to limit inquiry to a few areas close to the comfort zone of established theoretical assumptions. Instead of viewing the newly discovered importance of cohort differences as a clue—as just one category of factors in a broader matrix of social forces—researchers sought to "control" for those forces simply by controlling for cohort—with the assumption and hope that the "true pattern of normal aging" might yet manifest itself (see, e.g., Dannefer 1984a; Broughton 1987; Maddox 1987; Morss 1995).

Thus, rather than recognizing the *dangers* of reductionism, researchers across disciplines tended to resurrect it, hastening back to the safety of traditional, individual-level explanations. What we see time and again is that each time a new set of insights about the importance of social factors is introduced into the discourses of human development and aging, a tendency to resist the implications of the discovery regularly surfaces. In general, this resistance takes the form of attempting to reframe of the discovery of age-related outcomes attributable to social forces as individual-level phenomena. Or, alternatively, they are regarded as diffuse and random in their origins. Since we will see this "seduction of reduction" occurring again and again throughout the history of developmental and life-course studies and of life-span development as well over the past several decades, it is worth considering in detail from whence these impulses come.

This broad reaction allowed some key conceptual restraints on attention to social and environmental effects that had been there from the beginning to remain undisturbed and to go uninterrogated. Why? Given the evidence of the need for a new approach, this is an important question. It is a question that does have an answer, an answer that reveals how the intricacies of logical, paradigmatic assumptions can end up having consequences far removed from their origins.

One key part of the answer concerns a paradox surrounding the concept of social change. The intellectual developments in question cannot be understood without considering the special position of social change and its effects on patterns of aging. As evident in cohort-based and historical comparisons, social change has of course been central to the discovery of the importance of cohort analysis. The rapidity of educational expansion and technological change across the 20th century produced marked differences in the patterns of aging manifest in successive human cohorts, and thus benchmarked the effects of social change on patterns of aging, as illustrated in the work of Schaie and associates.

Inevitably, such trends prompted a strong conceptual focus on issues of history and the impact of social change. Yet the emphasis on change as a source of variation in the patterns of aging outran itself because researchers across disciplines tended to equate "change" and "context"—thus creating a spurious equivalence between social change and the entirety of the social environment. This equivalence had the very costly effect of obscuring attention to other forms of contextual influence besides those prompted by social change.

THE CONFLATION OF SOCIAL FORCES AND SOCIAL CHANGE

It is clearly true that social change is crucially important in generating conditions that lead to novel developments and variation in patterns of aging, and that much can be learned by studying the resultant cohort differences. As noted previously, the seminal idea that cohorts born at different times have quite different kinds of life experiences leading to contrasting patterns of aging was tightly bound up with historical comparisons and trends of change, and with an emphasis on cohort analysis not only in sociology but in psychology and other disciplines. Thus, the attention given to social change was indeed understandable as a first logical step in advancing the study of aging and the life course.

Yet this discovery of historical change and the resultant cohort differences is really only the beginning of attention to the broad and vast arena of context, and logically raises more questions about the scope of the interrogation. Why do history and social change matter? What is it about *homo sapiens* that makes human individuals so responsive to change? In reality, of course, historical change is only one of many axes of social variation upon which social and contextual effects operate and need to be analyzed. And across disciplines and across fields, one thing that is evident is a remarkable *absence of attention to the implications* of the discovery that "change matters" for considering the impact of social context and experience on how people age. If change is so important (and clearly it is), why should that be? Such questions, while important, received scant attention.

Symptoms of this problem are evident from the beginning, in the earliest formulations of the new "social paradigm" of aging and development. Ironically, such symptoms are contained within the formulations of the pioneers whose work stimulated the paradigmatic challenge in the first place. For example, consider the paradigmatic schemes that were initially introduced to characterize the fields of sociology of age and life-span psychology, reproduced in Figures 1.3 and 1.4.

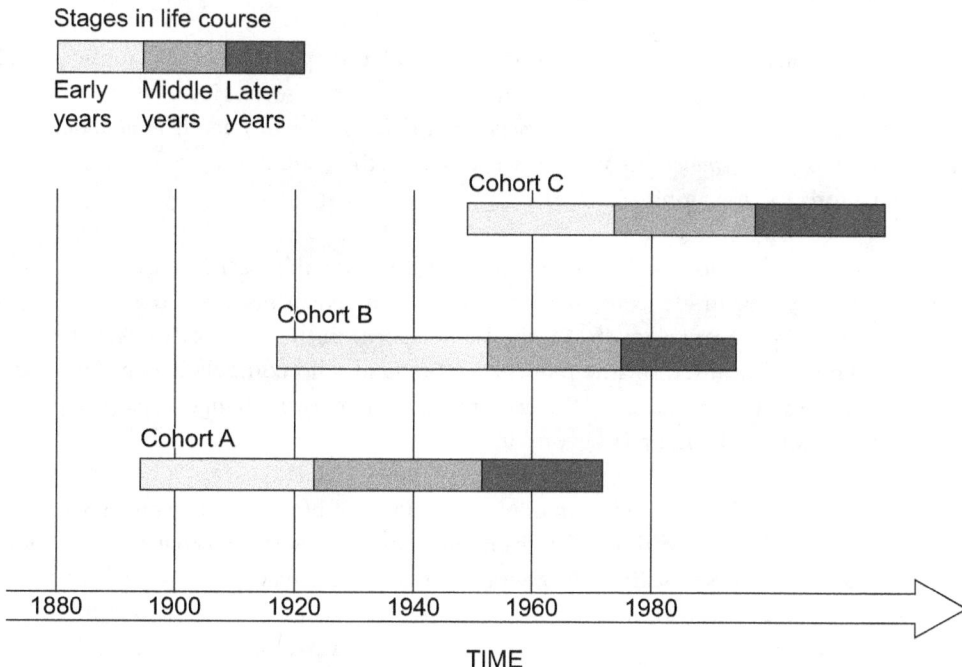

Figure 1.3 Processes of cohort flow and aging showing selected cohorts over time
Source: Riley 1973

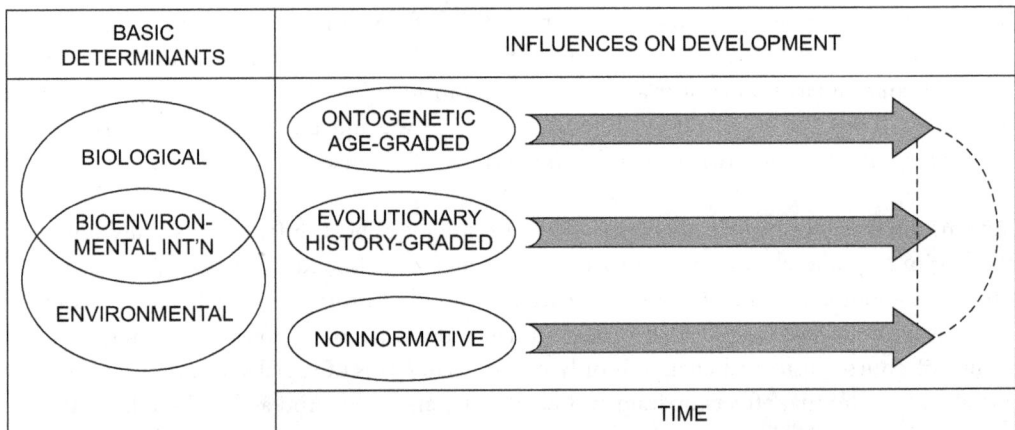

BASIC DETERMINANTS	INFLUENCES ON DEVELOPMENT
BIOLOGICAL / BIOENVIRON-MENTAL INT'N / ENVIRONMENTAL	ONTOGENETIC AGE-GRADED / EVOLUTIONARY HISTORY-GRADED / NONNORMATIVE
	TIME

Figure 1.4 Three systems of influences regulate the nature of life-span development

Source: Baltes and Brim 1979

Figure 1.3 presents the well-known figure from Matilda Riley's (1973) groundbreaking formulations. This figure demonstrates the intersection of cohort location, age and history—biographical time and historical time. This is a paradigmatic figure to capture the logic of cohort analysis, but at the same time it is a framework from which all other contextual variables are omitted. Figure 1.4, a similarly foundational paradigmatic scheme introduced in life-span psychology by Paul Baltes, provides for systematic consideration of only "history-graded" environmental effects, relegating all other environmental effects to the "nonnormativity", which in effect meant relegating them to the error term.

These paradigmatic approaches are important to consider; they are canonical, foundational formulations, and they continue to inform and guide research (see, e.g., Gerstorf et al. 2020). *Yet in neither of these models is there room for explicit consideration of any kind of contextual influence other than social change.* As we will see, however, there are many other ways in which social forces shape aging.

The pervasiveness of the inclination to equate social forces with social change can also be seen in the emphasis in life-course work on the specificity of historical events and change (e.g., the Great Depression, 9/11, the Baby Boom) in this body of work, extending across disciplines. Ironically, the same pioneers of the field who compelled a challenge to the traditional dogma by pointing to the importance of historical change, thus lacked a framework that could take matters beyond it.

Thus, despite what Paul Baltes called an explosive "surge of life-span thinking" (Baltes 1979:256–7) to challenge traditional developmental approaches, studies that took any note of social-structural factors that impact development and aging *other than those related to societal change* were very few in number. In those rare cases when they were included, the results were promising. For example, Gribbin, Schaie and Parham's (1980) longitudinal investigation of cognitive performance suggested an effect of "lifestyle" factors related to social class (education- and occupation-related variables) over a period of 14 years. Although such studies deserve credit for encouraging at least a modestly broader view of context, their discoveries have seldom been elaborated or pursued in subsequent research. In sociology, the life course as a field of study was, as noted earlier, launched to prominence by Elder's *Children of the Great Depression* (1999 [1974]). Similar to the life-span approach, the life-course perspective placed great emphasis on the importance of cohort location in historical time and the crucial intersection of age and historical events and change. This emphasis is especially telling in the case of the life-course perspective, since in many analyses presented in this classic work and subsequent research, Elder and colleagues document the effects of contextual variables, including social-structural variables such as social class and family configuration. Thus, the effects of social structure are often evident in the patterns of findings reported by Elder and his associates. Without question, *Children of the Great Depression* stands as the classic American cornerstone of empirical research in the sociology of the life course, contributing a wide-ranging and provocative set of findings and initiating a long and flourishing research tradition. At many turns, the findings reported are intricate and ingenious—for instance, by attending carefully to the intersection of age, gender, family resources and varieties of hardship experience brought by the Great Depression in accounting for later-life outcomes. As one example, boys in deprived households aspired to enter adult roles earlier and showed little evidence of persistent disadvantage from the Depression, whereas girls who assumed domestic responsibilities while their mothers sought out work were more vulnerable to psychological disturbances and frequently stopped working after marriage or childbirth. A major difference in late-life outcomes was also attributed to the timing in which the Great Depression was experienced with dependent children born a decade later experiencing financial deprivation that left them more vulnerable to family instability and conflicts than those born earlier (Elder 1999 [1974]:239, 279; see also Dannefer and Settersten 2010:7–8).

Thus, it is noteworthy that—despite the inherently interactive nature of these patterns— the primary thematic interpretation for which Elder's work is known has remained heavily focused on the social change side of the interaction. Work in this tradition has emphasized what can be learned from social change and comparing cohorts who develop and age under different circumstances, and stops short of developing a detailed analysis of the enduring and stable aspects of social structure through which individual life-course patterns and aging are constituted on a daily basis in everyday social interaction. Indeed, throughout his scholarly career, Elder has consistently emphasized the importance of "changing social contexts", "history and the life course", "aging and social change" and so on. He has singled out the omission of consideration of social change and related issues as a major limitation in the work of other scholars—whether sociologists of the stature of C. Wright Mills or child psychologists (Elder and Shanahan 2007). In one sense, the preoccupation with change is clearly warranted, as it has been a crucially important source of evidence for variation in life-course patterns and the contextual factors accounting for such variation. Yet it is also more than ironic, given Elder's numerous findings that demonstrate dramatic effects of social class or economic deprivation in which social change is itself *incidental*, except for providing the opportunity to observe varying contextual conditions (e.g., Elder 1994:11, 1984:187). As we will see, such socially structured effects are robust and have been demonstrated for the parents as well as the children of the Great Depression (e.g., Elder and Liker 1982). Although many of Elder's findings and contributions demonstrate the importance of such socially structured variation in distributing age-related resources at a given point in time, he positions it as secondary to change: "[E]ven more valuable is a focus on exposure to a particular contextual or historical change" (Elder and Shanahan 2007:676).

Thus, paradoxically, one of the places where the tendency *to limit social investigation can be clearly seen has been in the pursuit of cohort analysis itself.* Although cohort analysis had rightly compelled attention to the importance of social context by calling attention to the effects of social change upon individuals' life-course patterns, the intense focus of researchers upon the impact of "historical events", "cohort differences" and "intercohort comparisons" had the consequence of obscuring from view some of the most challenging implications of the initial discovery of cohort differences—implications concerning the broader and more general power of social forces to create variation and diversity, and shape patterns of human development and aging.

The potential explanatory cost involved in the problem of equating and conflating the significance of social context with social change can be seen by considering a counterfactual question: *What if there were no change?*

Imagine a society that existed for many generations in a state of great cultural, technological and demographic stability, instead of the marked long-term trends of social change with which we are all familiar. In such a case, would we expect that social forces play any role at all in shaping age-related patterns and outcomes? If the observed patterns of aging in this hypothetically stable society also manifested a high degree of stability and predictability in cohort after cohort, could we then assume that the observed pattern of aging represented true human nature, and dispense with the notion that social forces play a role in the shaping of life course and developmental patterns?

Obviously, the answer to this last question is an unequivocal and resounding "no"! For if *homo sapiens* is a species in which individuals develop, change and age differently under different social conditions (which we now know to be the case), one would fully expect stable and repeated patterns of development and aging as a direct result of conditions of high contextual stability. Stability in patterns of individual aging is no less contingent on social stability than are changes in patterns of aging contingent on social change. Thus, the observation that historical change produces cohort differences and cohort effects should not be construed as the grand finale of social science insight or the primary fulcrum on which to leverage an understanding of the impact of the social world on aging. Rather, it is simply a starting point—again, a *clue* to the broader set of underlying forces and processes that require attention.

In this context, the significance of change is simply that it provides some of the variable conditions of an experiment of nature or "social technique", as Thomas and Znaniecki put it (1927:75; see Elder and Shanahan 2007:667), thereby making visible the reality that variation in social circumstances and experiences are related to varying patterns of human development and aging over the life course. This is clearly a major heuristic benefit of making intercohort comparisons in age-specific circumstances and life-course trajectories. Yet at the same time, what the conflation of social forces and social change does is to *block from view a consideration of types of social forces that operate regularly*, in stable societies as well as changing ones, and *within* each cohort as well as *between* them.

Thus, as we will see, one of the primary consequences of researchers' obsession with social change has been to allow scholars collectively to avoid confrontation with anything like the full scope of the implications of social structure for aging, and with attention to the mechanisms by which, and the depths to which, social forces shape the life course. Again, this is paradoxical because it was the discovery of the effects of social change, deriving from cohort analysis and cohort comparisons, that pried open the closed organismic paradigm that assumed universal patterns of normal aging. The point that has been steadfastly unnoticed is that the effects of change are not the only way to see the effects of social forces on the life course but simply one window through which those effects can be observed.

COHORT EFFECTS, CONTEXT EFFECTS AND SOCIOLOGICAL IMAGINATION

Perhaps it was that the "Pandora's Box" of possibilities of social and contextual explanation opened up by the discoveries of the 1960s and 1970s were overwhelming, or even frightening. Perhaps they brought too close to home C. Wright Mills' observation that a rigorously applied sociological imagination is "in many ways . . . a terrible lesson . . . as well as a magnificent one" (1961:5). Perhaps it was due to bewilderment in the face of the complexity of a continuously interacting array of powerful contextual forces, prompting researchers to retreat to the security of familiar ways of thinking about human development, human aging and human nature—limiting, yet also comforting—without implications that necessitate a radical rethinking of, perhaps, existential as well as theoretical assumptions. Perhaps it was, for some, the ontological angst involved in taking seriously the implications of having to confront the power of social forces in organizing human experience and what is often thought of as "human nature".

Despite the relevance of such concerns, such worries do not appear to have been the primary factors. The sources of denial appear to be intellectually deeper and more systemic than a mere "fear reaction" would suggest. For in order to be frightened by the possibilities implied by a confrontation with the social dimensions of aging, one has to operate from a perceptual field that allows one to glimpse those possibilities in the first place. And it is clear that—despite their foundational achievements—the early leading figures of both the sociology of age and of life-span psychology operated, with few exceptions, within conceptual paradigms that inhibited or precluded their thinking from coming fully to terms with the reality they had discovered: *the reality that aging and human development are not reducible to the individual level and can never be adequately understood as individual-level phenomena.* Instead of embracing the implications of this discovery, they—perhaps inadvertently in many cases—resisted those implications.

Thus, the key to understanding the resistance to a thoroughgoing sociological analysis across these areas is to be found not primarily in anxiety about Mills' "terrible lessons", but in the theoretical underpinnings of the mainstream approaches to age taken in both psychology and sociology. Especially as applied to human development and aging, sociology and psychology have each had their own governing paradigm: structural-functionalism in sociology and the organismic paradigm of developmental theory in psychology. And in both cases it is probably not an accident that these paradigms resonate with the reigning cultural ethos of Western individualism. They also have a remarkable compatibility with each other.

With the growth of recognition of the importance of interdisciplinarity in efforts to understand human development and aging, the default intellectual approach in each discipline was provided by the intellectual resonance of these two paradigmatic approaches. These approaches share several key (albeit largely unexplicated) assumptions, which have enabled scholars across disciplines to rely on each other's work in a synergistic interdependence based on shared but largely invisible paradigmatic assumptions.

REDUCTIONISM AND THE FUNCTIONAL-ORGANISMIC NEXUS: A HEURISTIC OF "CONTAINMENT"

Beyond their continuing influence within their respective disciplines, these two paradigms—structural-functionalism and the organismic paradigm—intellectually complement each other (Dannefer 1984a, 2008; Estes, Binney, and Culbertson 1992). They have supported each other in a relationship of symbiotic co-dependence, with a logic that resists evidence demonstrating the relevance of social and experiential contingency, social causation and the invisible force of naturalized power. Constrained by conventional paradigmatic assumptions, such insights are neutralized—contained within peripheral spaces of discourse where they do not intrude upon the reductionist comforts of mainstream thought. I call this symbiotic relationship the *functional-organismic nexus*. It will be important to examine carefully the contribution of each of these two perspectives to the heuristic logic of these multidisciplinary impulses of containment.

THE ORGANISMIC PARADIGM IN PSYCHOLOGY

In psychology, the organismic paradigm is premised on the idea that basic maturational processes are an enduring part of human nature and, hence, effectively universal. Within psychology and the field of human development, the claim or hypothesis of universality has been challenged and discredited (e.g., Broughton 1987; Dannefer 1984a; Dannefer and Perlmutter 1990; Lave and Wenger 1991; Lerner 2002; Rogoff 2003; Stetsenko 2012, 2016), yet those committed to it continue to pursue efforts to sustain their claims and arguments (e.g., Arnett 2016; Baltes 1979; Carstensen 1992, 2006; Gutmann 1987; Levinson 1994). But the claim of universality is not merely a contentious point to be resolved with more data on larger samples. It is symptomatic of an underlying paradigmatic preference that logically entails a specific form of inquiry.

It is instructive to consider the sweep of presumption with which such assumptions have often been pursued. For example, Daniel Levinson (1978, 1994) advanced an influential hypothesis of a universal sequence of adult stage development in his best-selling and still-influential volumes *Seasons of a Man's Life*, and *Seasons of a Woman's Life*. *Seasons of a Man's Life* was based on interviews conducted with a sample of 40 men, ages 35 to 45 (10 novelists, 10 managers, 10 biologists and 10 blue-collar workers) in the Boston-New York corridor in the late 1960s and early 1970s. This volume was criticized on a number of grounds including, unsurprisingly, his small, unrepresentative and all-male sample. Yet it sparked widespread debate in the academic study of human development and had an impact in related disciplines and professional fields. Given the sustained interest it generated, Levinson and associates addressed the gender critique in *Seasons of a Woman's Life*, published 16 years later, in which women were the subject and the sample size was increased by 50% (from 40 to 60). Based on these interview data, Levinson proposed that he had discovered a reliably discernible and universal pattern of human development that he expected would hold up transculturally and transhistorically:

> We energetically offer the following hypothesis: this sequence of eras and periods exists in all societies, throughout the human species, at the present stage of human evolution. The eras and periods are grounded in the nature of man as a biological, psychological and social organism, and in the nature of society as a complex enterprise extending over many generations.
>
> (1978:322)

By almost any standard, this has to be regarded as a remarkably reckless contention, when one considers that this claim is based on such small and unrepresentative samples. What logic would justify such a claim?

Other researchers operating from similar premises sought to strengthen claims of universality by expanding the scope of their sampling. For example, David Gutmann (1987) proposed a different but also putatively universal and gender-differentiated pattern based on small samples drawn from five societies, claiming a "gender crossover" in midlife (with an increase in instrumental and agentic action for women, and the reverse for men). Although Gutmann's own data did not unequivocally support his claims of universality, his work also garnered considerable positive interest and attention.

But the more fundamental issue with such a work, as noted previously, is not a matter of methods or samples. Rather, it is an issue of fundamental paradigmatic assumptions (Dannefer 1984a, 1984b).

To illuminate this theoretical preference, we must again ask: Why would one expect that the universals of human development could be discovered based on the lives of 40 men in New England in the early 1970s, and a few dozen women interviewed a few years later or, in Gutmann's case, on the lives of a handful of respondents from each of a few 20th-century societies? And even more fundamentally, why should a universal pattern have been a theoretically expected claim to make in the first place? What mode of inquiry and what kinds of assumptions would lead one to expect such an invariance? The answer to such questions lies in the underlying paradigmatic assumptions that guide such thought. Those assumptions began with a core conception of development and aging as rooted in essentialist processes of maturational unfolding. The individual's life structure and changes in that structure—physically, mentally, socially—are seen as *contingent on the age of the organism*, as in biological models of clearly delineated age-graded stages as are observed, for example, in the life cycles of frogs, moths or opossums. Thus, it follows the traditional paradigm of developmental change, which typically assumes the following characteristics: sequentiality, unidirectionality, an end state, irreversibility, qualitative-structural transformation, as well as universality (Lerner 2002; Baltes 1979:262–3; Lerner 2002; Reese and Overton 1970).

Given these premises, the organismic paradigm has strong implications for the structuring of inquiry. Specifically, it dictates the following sequence: 1) identify and define a sequence of age-based progression, 2) describe the "normal" (nomothetic, normative) character of each stage (and in some cases the exact age at which the respective stages emerge) and 3) establish the claim of universality by denying the existence of alternative ones—attributing them to errors of measurement or individual pathology. Such organismic theories include stage theories like those in the traditions of Erikson, Freud, Piaget, or Kohlberg, and in adulthood, Erikson and Gilligan together with the notions of Levinson and Gutmann referenced earlier.

In gerontology, the paradigm of disengagement theory rests on just such assumptions (Cumming and Henry 1961; Hochschild 1975). Such age-based theories of decline have traditionally been in good paradigmatic company. As neuropsychiatrist Norman Doidge describes the "common wisdom" of medicine and science, it has been generally taken for granted that "after childhood the brain changed only when it began the long process of decline" (2007:xvii). The fact that such common wisdom is now debunked has, at least to date, done little to reduce its influence. As we will see later, nuanced forms of such approaches, including disengagement, continue to flourish as part of a heuristic logic that continues to delimit inquiry.

Even if not explicitly adopted, the influence of the organismic model of individual development remains influential, within and beyond the discipline of psychology. As will be discussed in Chapter 8, it continues to shape thinking across disciplines, even among some who regard themselves as its critics. Its essential features encourage researchers to think of the study of human development, change and age as, even if more qualified than formerly imagined, still having as its goal the identification of transhistorical, transcultural universals and, therefore, to organize research agendas around the task of describing the essential developmental or age-based pattern that remains after cohort-based or other socioenvironmental variation is taken into account. This practice raises a number of problems.

SOCIOLOGICAL STRUCTURAL-FUNCTIONALISM

Like developmental theory, the idea of society as a functioning system also rests on an organismic metaphor in the works of classical sociological thinkers, especially Emile Durkheim. Durkheim's core ideas—society as a reality *sui generis*; societal relations as *systemic, social facts* having obdurate *"thingness"* (*choseite*)—are foundational to the discipline of sociology and are of enduring importance. A significant problem arises, however, in Durkheim's view of the social system as analogous to a biological organism.

The very idea of a system as a healthy, functioning organism implies its inherent integrity and legitimacy and is not conducive to thinking in terms of structural change, nor of recognizing conflict, exploitative power and struggle as inherent to social relations, and as sometimes leading to humanly destructive consequences. Like a bacterial infection in a physical organism, social conflict is instead implicitly assumed to be aberrant, unusual, pathological and outside the paradigm of a smoothly functioning system or "organism". Despite its impressive scope and illumination of some systemic aspects of social organization, Talcott Parsons' framework (e.g., 1951) similarly avoided dealing with conflict and power dynamics and is thus characterized by the same limitation.

Structural-functionalism is known for having difficulty incorporating into its framework such centrally important social phenomena as power, innovation conflict, and change. For this and other reasons, it has long been recognized as a fundamentally inadequate paradigm in social theory generally and has long since been abandoned by many substantive arenas of sociological inquiry. Nevertheless, it has remained alive and well—although often implicit and unremarked—in some less rigorously theorized areas of sociology, including the study of aging and life course.

Given functionalism's inclination to accept and naturalize existing social arrangements and especially in a context where microfication and a tendency to return to the individual are underlying intellectual impulses, one can perhaps see the interlocking appeal of the functional and organismic paradigms. Both of these frameworks are intuitively appealing in their seemingly straightforward simplicity and elegance. Each offers a self-contained closed system that, under the guise of established paradigmatic science, authoritatively claims to systematize the descriptive realities in which we live—offering immediate "face validity" to what Berger and Luckmann (1967) called the world-taken-for-granted, the "normality" of human existence as we know it and of the familiar social practices and arrangements of late modernity. The familiarity of such ideas gives them a plausibility that makes it easy to accept them uncritically. And the perspectives they are offered are generally comforting, both existentially and politically. It is "not for nothing" that researchers find them appealing.

This plausibility also includes a taken-for-granted acceptance of the power differentials and relations that underlie the social arrangements that end up shaping individual lives. Power relations in every everyday form—whether youth or age, patriarchy, or White privilege— can easily remain entirely unnoticed when one begins by thinking of dominant social institutions as beneficently arranged systems designed to accommodate individual needs and address their limitations, rather than as possibly suppressing their needs or contributing to their limitations. Functionalism "is committed to making things work"—as Gouldner put it—"despite wars inequities, scarcity, and degrading work, rather than to finding a way out" (1970:281). The issue of "imbalanced flows of power" and their institutionalization (Schwalbe 2008:26), which in reality pervade all social life, never arises as a problem to be directly addressed.

More generally, the functional-organismic nexus often makes it easy to overlook the diversity of individuals in a society. Instead of recognizing such diversity, the focus is on searching for what is "normal" in the course of human development. It is thus no accident that functionalists have no difficulty embracing the premises of the organismic paradigm. It is noteworthy that Talcott Parsons (1961) wrote the preface to Cumming and Henry's treatise advancing disengagement theory, an organismic theory of "old age" (1961; see also, e.g., Smelser and Erikson 1980).

Social normality has often been equated with statistical normality, thereby justifying statistical averaging and characterizing populations based on means or other measures of central tendency. Of course, it is now increasingly recognized that such characterizations, equating central tendency with what is normal across entire populations, are themselves a form of symbolic violence (Bourdieu 1986; Burawoy 2019). They legitimate and reinforce assumptions of "normality" that disrespect the subject matter under study and often serve to lay the foundation for "othering", ignoring that many of us do not conform to dominant or normative depictions of "healthy development", "normative aging" and "age-appropriate conduct" that the nexus expects.

Specifically with respect to aging, this logic has made it easy to overlook that many social institutions based on assumptions about aging are taken-for-granted fixtures of common knowledge and everyday life. Such institutions are assumed to be legitimate, even when they are humanly restrictive and sometimes destructive, as in the case of the conventional nursing homes in the US. Consider this paradox: The daily lives of individuals in many indigenous cultures, judged by habits and expectations comfortable to late modern citizens are also not "normal" (and certainly not generally regarded as desirable or "ideal"). Yet immigrants from such societies who work in low-paying jobs in US nursing homes often comment with alarm and even outrage upon what they regard as the barbarism of these institutions in their treatment of the elders that they are intended to serve. Such reactions were already offering a challenge to the modern "normality" of forced social disengagement and warehousing of frail elders long before the currently prominent issues of "culture change" became fashionable and before gerontologists took up the cause.

In sum, the symbiotic relationship between sociological functionalism and the organismic paradigm allows a cross-disciplinary view of aging that shares assumptions of a benign social order that has been designed to accommodate individual needs, and to which individuals are best served by adjusting, and of the "naturalness" of the world within which mainstream researchers tend to operate. Within such a cultural and intellectual framework, the idea of interrogating the constitutive force of social systems and the stratification of interests served by this benign social order cannot arise.

Understandably, those who pursue what Thomas Kuhn (1962) calls "normal science" within these paradigms are made somewhat uncomfortable by the growing traces of a different and much deeper order of social causation revealed by a rigorously social paradigm of aging. These are, of course, traces that point to the actual and empirically documented state of affairs, which is that social forces shape human growth, development and aging much more deeply than has generally been imagined, and likely more deeply than is yet understood by any of us. Even if challenging, the science of aging nevertheless requires a paradigm that can apprehend this actual state of affairs, which means one that is open to heretofore unrecognized dimensions of societal effects on individual patterns of development and aging.

What is needed is a paradigm that displaces the stability and predictability of the functional-organismic nexus with what Berger and Luckmann (1967) call the "world-openness" of the human organism and the human species. World-openness recognizes the uncertainties and the possibilities that are part of open-ended change and unconstrained potentiality. However, neither Berger and Luckmann nor others who have explicated this important characteristic of *homo sapiens* have extended their analysis to consider its specific implications for human development and aging. That will be the task of the next two chapters.

CHAPTER SUMMARY AND PLAN OF THE BOOK

The great contributions of late 20th-century scholarship provided the insights upon which to found a comprehensive approach to theorizing age and the life course—an approach which acknowledges that aging is not fixed but contingent, and that opens a new horizon along which the relentless yet largely unrecognized power of social forces in shaping processes of aging can be explored. Yet to date, those potentials have been explored only to a limited extent because research on age and the life course has been effectively contained by the heuristic logic of outdated theoretical assumptions that are premised on paradigmatically rigid and limited views both of individual development and aging and of social structure.

As a field, we have yet to interrogate the constricting assumptions underlying the functional-organismic nexus. In the chapters that follow, I will propose a foundation for a critical and scientific alternative, and I will also review the intellectual, explanatory and practical human costs of the symbiotic relationships of these two paradigms—costs deriving from their effectiveness in blocking developmental and life-course thought from an accurate and realistic assessment of the magnitude of the influence of social forces in shaping aging. This can be seen again and again in different domains of research. It can be seen in the reluctance to confront intracohort diversity and inequality. It can be seen in the uncritical response to an increasingly medicalized approach to aging in the professions and in the society as a whole. It can be seen in the unwarranted alliance between the age and family as academic areas of study, and it can be seen in the astructural microfication of some ethnographic research and in other micro-interactional studies of aging. It can be seen in the approach initially adopted by gerontologists as by other social scientists in approaching the topic of gene-environment interactions.

NASCAR auto racing has faced the problem that redundantly powerful and aerodynamic race cars can generate so much speed that on the superspeedways they can too easily become airborne. To prevent this dangerous possibility, restrictor plates are placed between the carburetor and intake manifold to limit the flow of fuel to the engine and reduce its performance. In science, paradigmatic assumptions can sometimes perform a similar function—controlling the scope of inquiry by directing it along established, well-ordered lines that remain "under control" and squelching unfamiliar questions and novel observations that may open one's assumption to fundamental challenge and threaten to launch inquiry beyond the established paradigmatic boundaries of permissible research topics. That is, there is a desire to do science in a way that allows for empirical inquiry and the testing of ideas, so long as it doesn't go so deep and wide as to overpower the comfortable and entrenched daily operations of normal science. The heuristic of containment, produced by the functional-organismic nexus, serves to protect the normal science assumptions of the study of human development, aging and the life course from such a danger. Analogous to Herbert Marcuse's (1955) notion of "surplus repression", we may consider the result to be a kind of *surplus individualization* in the conduct of normal science.

In the quest for knowledge, however, there is no warrant for the kind of limits on performance that are permissible in auto racing. For in the enterprise of science, no basis exists for restricting inquiry even if the challenge calls into question paradigmatic assumptions that are not only taken-for-granted and unquestioned but cherished. Unlike in NASCAR, science is not entitled to the safety and comfort of "throttling back" the questions that confront us even if they sometimes are, as Mills puts it, "terrifying" and even if they threaten, like an overly powerful V-8 engine, to send us "over the wall" into an unfamiliar domain of intellectual exploration. As we will see, that may be the case when one understands that both human beings and social systems are under human control (and not nature's control) to a remarkable extent, giving the matter of "how we age" both existential and political dimensions that we could avoid dealing with, if only the functional-organismic view were correct and most of the contours of human existence were fixed and largely out of human and social control.

As will become clear, many features of human development and aging are not out of human control at all, and for human beings to fail to recognize the power and capacities of their own actions for control and change is a form of alienation in the most classic and fundamental sense, just as is our failure to recognize their power in shaping our own existence. In this regard, it will also be necessary to visit the paradox that the potential magnitude of human possibility and human change is obscured by the familiar and rather glib emphasis on "agency" and "choice" that adduces both of these terms to explain residual variance but offers an analysis of neither (Dannefer 1999; Dannefer and Huang 2017; Marshall and Clarke 2010).

Despite such ongoing issues and challenges for the field and despite the restrictor-plate assumptions of past work, great credit must be given to the intellectual pioneers—Baltes, Birren, Cain, Elder, Neugarten, Riley, Schaie and numerous others—who forged openings within which such questions and issues can be raised. When the discovery of cohort differences cracked open the "closed system" of the static and reductionist organismic model, it created tasks for social science inquiry in at least three major domains of sociological investigation—three frontiers along the explanatory potentials of social forces for shaping the realities of individual aging warrant careful investigation. These frontiers are 1) the *social-structural* frontier, 2) the *biosocial* frontier and 3) the *reflexive-critical* frontier. The *social-structural* frontier deals with the role of macro-, meso- and microstructural forces in organizing aging and will be the focus of Chapters 4 through 6. The *biosocial* frontier links these social-structural dynamics to the physical body—how do life-course experiences interact with and impact the physical bodies of aging individuals? This is the question of Chapter 7, and it is a matter that is also addressed in Chapters 2 and 3. The *reflexive-critical* frontier, considered in Chapters 8 through 10, examines age as a product of the meaning-making processes of science itself, and by its interaction with political and economic as well as cultural forces within that context. These broader social forces impose constraints on inquiry, further limiting sociological imagination. Chapter 10 offers some examples of what is humanly and socially possible when such constraints are interrogated and deconstructed by offering some actual examples of the potentials of sociological imagination to rehumanize everyday personal and institutional practices that shape the life course.

However, before turning to an examination of these three frontiers, it is necessary to clarify the basic anthropological and developmental features of the human species responsible for the remarkable diversity of patterns of human development, aging and the life course. Why is it that we see such variation and environmental contingency in human development and aging? The internally guided structuring of aging and development into universal stages or trajectories that is assumed by the organismic approach does indeed appear in many respects to be applicable for many other forms of life. That is an understandable part of the reason why scholars from multiple disciplines have expected them to be applicable in the human case as well. So why aren't they? What is it about the character of *homo sapiens* as a species that means the organismic assumptions do not apply in the same way? And what is it about *homo sapiens* that causes human environments to be so dynamic and variable? These foundational questions are the subjects of the next two chapters.

REFERENCES

Achenbaum, W. Andrew. 1978. *Old Age in the New Land: The American Experience Since 1790.* Baltimore, MD: Johns Hopkins University Press.

Achenbaum, W. Andrew. 2015. "Delineating Old Age: From Functional Status to Bureaucratic Criteria." Pp. 301–19 in *Age in America: The Colonial Era to the Present,* edited by C. T. Field and N. L. Syrett. New York: New York University Press.

Alwin, Duane F. 1991. "Family of Origin and Cohort Differences in Verbal Ability." *American Sociological Review* 56(5): 625–38.

Arnett, Jeffrey Jensen. 2016. "Life Stage Concepts across History and Cultures: Proposal for a New Field on Indigenous Life Stages." *Human Development* 59(5): 290–316.

Baltes, Paul B. 1968. "Longitudinal and Cross-Sectional Sequences in the Study of Age and Generation Effects." *Human Development* 11(3): 145–71.

Baltes, Paul B. 1979. "Life-Span Developmental Psychology: Some Converging Observations on History and Theory." *Life-Span Development and Behavior* 2: 255–79.

Baltes, Paul B., and Orville G. Brim. 1979. *Life-Span Behavior and Development.* Vol. 2. Cambridge, MA: Academic Press.

Baltes, Paul B., and K. Warner Schaie. 1974. "The Myth of the Twilight Years." *Psychology Today* 40: 35–8.

Baltes, Paul B., and K. Warner Schaie. 1976. "On the Plasticity of Intelligence in Adulthood and Old Age: Where Horn and Donaldson Fail." *American Psychologist* 31(10): 720–5.

Bengtson, Vern. 1973. *The Social Psychology of Aging*. Indianapolis, IN: Bobbs-Merrill.

Berger, Peter L., and Thomas Luckmann. 1967. *The Social Construction of Reality: A Systematic Treatise in the Sociology of Knowledge*. New York: Anchor.

Bourdieu, Pierre. 1986. *Distinction: A Social Critique of the Judgement of Taste*. New York: Routledge.

Breslow, Norman E. 1985. "Cohort Analysis in Epidemiology." Pp. 109–43 in *A Celebration of Statistics*, edited by Anthony C. Atkinson and Stephen E. Fienberg. New York: Springer Publishing Company.

Broughton, John. 1987. *Critical Theories of Psychological Development*. New York: Springer Publishing Company.

Burawoy, Michael. 2019. *Symbolic Violence: Conversations with Bourdieu*. Durham, NC: Duke University Press Books.

Cain, Leonard. 1964. "Life Course and Social Structure." Pp. 272–309 in *Handbook of Modern Sociology*, edited by R. E. L. Faris. Chicago: Rand McNally.

Carstensen, Laura L. 1992. "Motivation for Social Contact Across the Lifespan: A Theory of Socioemotional Selectivity." *Nebraska Symposium on Motivation* 40: 209–54.

Carstensen, Laura L. 2006. "The Influence of a Sense of Time on Human Development." *Science* 312(5782): 1913–15. doi: 10.1126/science.1127488.

Clausen, John A. 1972. "The Life Course of Individuals." Pp. 454–574 in *Aging and Society: Vol. III: A Sociology of Age Stratification*, edited by M. W. Riley, M. E. Johnson, and A. Foner. New York: Russell Sage.

Cline, Hugh F. 1980. "Criminal Behavior Over the Lifespan." Pp. 641–74 in *Constancy and Change in Human Development*, edited by O. G. Brim, Jr. and J. Kagan. Cambridge, MA: Harvard University Press.

Collins, Linda M., and Aline G. Sayer, eds. 2001. *New Methods for the Analysis of Change*. Washington, DC: American Psychological Association.

Cumming, Elaine, and William E. Henry. 1961. *Growing Old: The Process of Disengagement*. New York: Basic Books.

Dannefer, Dale. 1984a. "Adult Development and Social Theory: A Paradigmatic Reappraisal." *American Sociological Review* 49(1): 100–16.

Dannefer, Dale. 1984b. "The Role of the Social in Life-Span Development Psychology, Past, Present and Future: Rejoinder to Baltes and Nesselroade." *American Sociological Review* 49(6): 847–50.

Dannefer, Dale. 1999. "Freedom Isn't Free: Power, Alienation, and the Consequences of Action." Pp. 105–31 in *Action & Development: Origins and Functions of Intentional Self-Development*, edited by J. Brandstadter and R. Lerner. New York: Springer Publishing Company.

Dannefer, Dale. 2008. "The Waters We Swim: Everyday Social Processes, Macro-Structural Realities and Human Aging." Pp. 3–22 in *Social Structure and Aging: Continuing Challenges*, edited by K. Warner Schaie and Ronald P. Abeles. New York: Springer Publishing Company.

Dannefer, Dale, and Wenxuan Huang. 2017. "Precarity, Inequality, and the Problem of Agency in the Study of the Life Course." *Innovation in Aging* 1(3): 1–10.

Dannefer, Dale, and Marion Perlmutter. 1990. "Development as a Multidimensional Process: Individual and Social Constituents." *Human Development* 33: 108–37.

Dannefer, Dale, and Richard Settersten, Jr. 2010. "The Study of the Life Course: Implications for Social Gerontology." Pp. 3–19 in *Sage Handbook* of *Social Gerontology*, edited by D. Dannefer and C. Phillipson. London: Sage.

Demos, John. 1978. "Old Age in Early New England." Pp. S248–87 in *Turning Points*, edited by J. Demos and S. S. Boocock. Chicago: University of Chicago Press.

Doidge, Norman. 2007. *The Brain That Changes Itself: Stories of Personal Triumph from the Frontiers of Brain Science*. London: Penguin.

Elder, Glen H., Jr. 1999 (1974). *Children of the Great Depression*. Chicago: University of Chicago Press.

Elder, Glen H., Jr. 1975. "Age Differentiation and the Life Course." *Annual Review of Sociology* 1(1): 165–90.

Elder, Glen H., Jr. 1984. "Families, Kin, and the Life Course: A Sociological Perspective." Pp. 80–136 in *Review of Child Development Research: The Family*, edited by R. D. Parke. Chicago: University of Chicago Press.

Elder, Glen H., Jr. 1994. "Time, Human Agency, and Social Change: Perspectives on the Life Course." *Social Psychology Quarterly* 57(1): 4–15.

Elder, Glen H., Jr., and Jeffrey K. Liker. 1982. "Hard Times in Women's Lives: Historical Influences Across Forty Years." *American Journal of Sociology* 88(2): 241–69.

Elder, Glen H., Jr., and Michael J. Shanahan. 2007. "The Life Course and Human Development." Pp. 665–715 in *Handbook of Child Psychology: Theoretical Models of Human Development*, Vol. 1, 6th ed, edited by W. Damon and R. M. Lerner. Hoboken, NJ: John Wiley & Sons Inc.

Estes, Carroll L. 1979. *The Aging Enterprise*. San Francisco: Jossey-Bass.

Estes, Carroll L., Elizabeth A. Binney, and Richard A. Culbertson. 1992. "The Gerontological Imagination: Sociological Influences on the Development of Gerontology, 1945–Present." *International Journal of Aging and Human Development* 35(1): 49–65.

Gerstorf, Denis, Gizem Hueluer, Johanna Drewelies, Sherry L. Willis, K. Warner Schaie, and Nilan Ram. 2020. "Adult Development and Aging in Historical Context." *American Psychologist* 75(4): 525–39. doi: 10.1037/amp0000596.

Gouldner, Alvin. 1970. *The Coming Crisis in Western Sociology*. New York: Basic.

Gribbin, Kathy, K. Warner Schaie, and Iris A. Parham. 1980. "Complexity of Lifestyle and Maintenance of Intellectual Abilities." *Journal of Social Issues* 36(2): 47–61.

Gubrium, Jaber F. 1976. *Living and Dying at Murray Manor*. Charlottesville, VA: University of Virginia Press.

Gullette, Margaret M. 2011. *Agewise: Fighting the New Ageism in America*. Chicago: University of Chicago Press.

Gutmann, David. 1987. *Reclaimed Powers: Toward a New Psychology of Men and Women in Later Life*. New York: Basic Books.

Haber, Carole. 1983. *Beyond Sixty-Five: The Dilemmas of Old Age in America's Past*. New York: Cambridge University Press.

Hareven, Tamara K. 2013 (1978). "The Historical Study of the Life Course." In *Transitions: The Family and the Life Course in Historical Perspective*, edited by T. K. Hareven. New York: Academic Press.

Hochschild, Arlie R. 1975. "Disengagement Theory: A Critique and Proposal." *American Sociological Review* 40(5): 553–69.

Horn, John L., and Gary Donaldson. 1976. "On the Myth of Intellectual Decline in Adulthood." *American Psychologist* 31(10): 701–29.

Horn, John L., and Gary Donaldson. 1977. "Faith is Not Enough: A Response to the Baltes-Schaie Claim That Intelligence Does Not Wane." *American Psychologist* 32(5): 369–73.

Horn, John L., Gary Donaldson, and Robert Engstrom. 1981. "Apprehension, Memory, and Fluid Intelligence Decline in Adulthood." *Research on Aging* 3(1): 33–84.

Kahana, Eva, Michael R. Slone, Boaz Kahana, Kaitlyn Barnes Langendoerfer, and Courtney Reynolds. 2016. "Beyond Ageist Attitudes: Researchers Call for NIH Action to Limit Funding for Older Academics." *Gerontologist* 58(2): 251–60. doi: 10.1093/geront/gnw190.

Kuhn, Thomas S. 1962. *The Structure of Scientific Revolutions*. Vol. 2. Chicago: The University of Chicago Press.

Laslett, Peter. 1965. *The World We Have Lost: England before the Industrial Age*. London: Methuen.

Lave, Jean, and Etienne Wenger. 1991. *Situated Learning: Legitimate Peripheral Participation*. London: Cambridge University Press.

Lerner, Richard M. 2002. *Concepts and Theories of Human Development*. 3rd edition. Mahwah, NJ: Lawrence Erlbaum Associates.

Levinson, Daniel J. 1978. *The Seasons of a Man's Life*. New York: Random House Digital, Inc.

Levinson, Daniel J. 1994. *Seasons of a Woman's Life*. New York: Knopf.

Maddox, George L. 1987. "Aging Differently." *The Gerontologist* 27(5): 557–64.

Marcuse, Herbert. 1955. *Eros and Civilization: A Philosophical Inquiry into Freud*. Boston: Beacon Press.

Marshall, Victor, and Phillipa Clarke. 2010. "Agency and Social Structure in Aging and Life-Course Research." Pp. 294–314 in *The SAGE Handbook of Social Gerontology*, edited by C. Phillipson and D. Dannefer. London: Sage.

Marshall, Victor W., and Joseph A. Tindale. 1979. "Notes for a Radical Gerontology." *International Journal of Aging and Human Development* 9(2): 163–75.

Mills, C. Wright. 1961. *The Sociological Imagination*. New York: Grove Press.

Morss, John. 1995. *Growing Critical: Alternatives to Developmental Psychology*. New York: Routledge.

Nelson, Todd D. 2005. "Ageism: Prejudice Against Our Feared Future Self." *Journal of Social Issues* 61(2): 207–21. doi: 10.1111/j.1540-4560.2005.00402.x.

North, Michael S., and Susan T. Fiske. 2012. "An Inconvenienced Youth? Ageism and Its Potential Intergenerational Roots." *Psychological Bulletin* 138(5): 982–97.

Palmore, Erdman. 1999. *Ageism: Negative and Positive*. 2nd edition. New York: Springer Publishing Company.

Parsons, Talcott. 1951. *The Social System*. New York: Free Press.

Parsons, Talcott. 1961. "Preface." In *Growing Old: The Process of Disengagement*, edited by Elaine Cumming and William E. Henry. New York: Basic Books.

Phillipson, Christopher. 1982. *Capitalism and the Construction of Old Age*. London: Macmillan.

Reese, Hayne W., and Willis F. Overton. 1970. "Models of Development and Theories of Development." Pp. 115–45 in *Life-Span Developmental Psychology*, edited by W. F. Overton and R. M. Lerner. Cambridge, MA: Academic Press.

Riley, Matilda White. 1973. "Aging and Cohort Succession: Interpretations and Misinterpretations." *Public Opinion Quarterly Spring* 37(1): 35–49.

Riley, Matilda White, and Anne Foner. 1968. *Aging and Society, Vol. I: An Inventory of Research Findings*. New York: Russell Sage Foundation.

Riley, Matilda White, Marilyn Johnson, and Anne Foner. 1972. *Aging and Society, Vol. III: A Sociology of Age Stratification*. New York: Russell Sage Foundation.

Rogoff, Barbara. 2003. *The Cultural Nature of Human Development*. New York: Oxford University Press.

Ryder, Norman B. 1965. "The Cohort as a Concept in the Study of Social Change." *American Sociological Review* 30(6): 843–61.

Schaie, K. Warner. 1965. "A General Model for the Study of Development Problems." *Psychological Bulletin* 64(2): 92–107.

Schaie, K. Warner, and Sherri Willis. 1986. *Adult Development and Aging*. 2nd edition. Boston: Little Brown.

Schwalbe, Michael. 2008. *Rigging the Game: How Inequality Is Reproduced in Everyday Life*. New York: Oxford University Press.

Singer, Judith D., and John B. Willett. 2003. *Applied Longitudinal Data Analysis*. New York: Oxford University Press.

Smelser, Neil J., and Erik H. Erikson. 1980. *Themes of Love and Work in Adulthood*. Cambridge, MA: Harvard University Press.

Stetsenko, Anna. 2012. "Personhood: An Activist Project of Historical Becoming through Collaborative Pursuits of Social Transformation." *New Ideas in Psychology* 30: 144–53.

Stetsenko, Anna. 2016. *The Transformative Mind: Expanding Vygotsky's Approach to Development and Education*. Cambridge, UK: Cambridge University Press.

Thomas, William I., and Florian Znaniecki. 1927. *The Polish Peasant*. Boston: Gorham Press.

Uhlenberg, Peter. 1974. "Cohort Variations in Family Life Cycle Experiences of U.S. Females." *Journal of Marriage and the Family* 36: 284–92.

Uhlenberg, Peter. 1978. "Changing Configurations of the Life Course." Pp. 65–97 in *Transitions: Family and the Life Course in Historical Perspective*, edited by T. K. Hareven. New York: Academic Press.

Uhlenberg, Peter. 1988. "Aging and the Societal Significance of Cohorts." Pp. 405–25 in *Emergent Theories of Aging*, edited by J. E. Birren and V. L. Bengtson. New York: Springer Publishing Company.

Walker, Alan. 1981. "Towards a Political Economy of Old Age." *Ageing & Society* 1(1): 73–94.

Yang, Claire (Yang), and Kenneth C. Land. 2016. *Age-Period Cohort Analysis: New Models, Methods and Empirical Applications*. Boca Raton, FL: Chapman & Hall/CRC.

26

CHAPTER 2
SOCIOMATICS: THE SOCIAL STRUCTURING OF HUMAN DEVELOPMENT AND AGING

I would really like to see J.J. Rousseau here, with all his rantings against the social state!

—Jean-Francois de la Harpe (quoted in Wairy 1830)

THE STATUE AT ST. SERNIN

Those who have occasion to take the drive from Toulouse to Roquefort in Southern France, through the wonderfully rustic farm country of the foothills of the Midi Pyrenees, will unavoidably pass through the vintage farming village of St. Sernin, nestled on a steep hillside just above the valley floor of the Rance River. Since the highway makes a sharp turn on a hillcrest right at the center of town, passing motorists from both directions are unlikely to notice the small statue that gazes at them from inside the arc of the curve, in the town square (Figure 2.1).

Those who do happen to notice the statue, however, are likely to take a second look, for it is jolting—eerie, even—in its intensity and ambiguity. On first glance, it resembles a lion (given its stance and its large mane of hair), until one notices it has no tail. Thus it is often guessed to be a griffin or other mythic being—given its mane, its seemingly human limbs and facial features, combined with an aggressive, quadruped stance.

The identity of the statue is revealed by the plaque beneath it. It reads: "Victor, ENFANT SAUVAGE de l'Aveyron, capture a St. Sernin Rance, 8 Janv 1800". It is a statue of the "Wild Child", the "Wild Boy of Aveyron," who after living for years—summer and winter, day and night—naked in the nearby forests was, at the approximate age of 12, finally captured and coerced to commence living in human company in this village, St. Sernin, in the January of 1800.

Googling "Victor of Aveyron" immediately generates links to keywords like "werewolf", "sasquatch", "occultism", "goblin" and "wolf boy". The last association, in particular, is more than coincidence or fancy. The hills south of St. Sernin that were Victor's habitat have been described as "wolf-infested", and it is possible that animals provided Victor in early childhood with nurturing or with clues that he used to develop critical strategies and skills for survival. Surely he had not learned the skills that had enabled him to survive in the woods from a human teacher, for his strategies included almost none of the practices that are generally considered "normal" for a human being. Indeed, Victor evidenced no trace of recognition of the basic features of

Figure 2.1 Statue of the "Wild Boy of Aveyron," created in 1985 by Remi Coudrain. St. Sernin, Toulouse, France

Source: Photo by author

human interaction and communication. As described by his teacher and guardian, Dr. Jean-Marc Itard, Victor was:

> A disgustingly dirty child affected with spasmodic movements, and often convulsions who swayed back and forth ceaselessly like certain animals in a zoo, who bit and scratched those who opposed him; and who showed no affection for those who took care of him; and who was, in short, indifferent to everything and attentive to nothing.
>
> (Itard 1802:17)

Victor had no recognizable sensibilities of sociability, modesty or even comfort. Upon his capture, he was completely uninterested in people unless they directly offered him food. According to the detailed accounts of his behavior, he resisted wearing any clothes regardless of temperature and weather conditions and without adverse health effects, and he had no discernible language, grasp of language, or interest in language. He was reported as interested only in food, sleep and the freedom to return to the familiar out of doors.

This did not change when he was relocated from the Pyrenees to Paris, disappointing the expectations of the Parisians:

> Many curious people anticipated great pleasure in beholding what would be his astonishment at the sight of all the fine things in the capital. On the other hand, many persons eminent for their superior understanding . . . thought that the education of this individual would be the business of only a few months, and that they should very soon hear him make the most striking observations concerning his past manner of life.
>
> (Itard 1802:16–17)

However, Victor showed no ability to offer any such observations on his past life. Indeed, he showed no interest whatever in "normal" human comforts such as warmth or a soft bed; in the period after his capture he loved to escape and, naked, to run back into the woods, or even roll in the snow. He was especially excited, in fact, by new snowfall: "There, he exhibited the utmost emotions of pleasure; he ran, rolled in the snow and, gathering it up by the handful, devoured it with incredible avidity" (Itard 1802:4).

Globally, more than 300 cases of feral children have been reported, in accounts strewn over the last several hundred years of recorded history. Often, details are sketchy and evidence uncertain. These include accounts of imperial experiments of forced isolation of children designed to discover the "essential" or "socially unspoiled" character of human language and human nature.

Of these, Victor of Aveyron was, until recently, perhaps the most carefully documented and researched. As soon as he was captured, Victor's features and behavior became the subject of intense curiosity and prompted extensive study and observation. In Paris, he was placed under the care of Itard, resident physician at the National Institute for Deaf Mutes, who spent extended time periods with him daily for nearly seven years. Itard's work with Victor was subsidized by the French government, and he kept a detailed diary that was subsequently published.

At least partly because of his work with Victor, Itard came to be regarded as a founder of special education, and his work with Victor can be considered the first "individualized education program" (see, e.g., Bayat 2017:6). Some indication of the success of Itard's efforts in enabling Victor to learn is provided by the widespread subsequent influence of his methods. Edouard Seguin, a student of Itard's, set out to prove that persons then labeled as "idiots" were capable of education, and lectured on Itard's teaching methods at the Hospital for Incurables. He emigrated to the US in 1850, where he continued his work and teaching, influencing Maria Montessori. Montessori extended Itard's method and applied it to the education of preschool children and the mentally challenged, incorporating some of its elements into the Montessori movement. The approach has also been used in developing methods for the teaching of the deaf (Montessori 2004; Musiek 2006).

In Europe, several cases of feral children had been reported before the case of Victor. The first record of such cases in France is actually found in the works of Jean-Jacques Rousseau, who detailed six examples of wild children, most over the prior century. In line with the vision of his writings, Rousseau had hoped that such children, uncorrupted by civilization, would provide new insights into the essence of pure, unspoiled human nature.

It was in response to this Rousseauian agenda that the playwright Jean-Francois de La Harpe offered the observation that serves as this chapter's epigraph, as a comment on Victor's outrageous and wildly disruptive behavior at a French dinner party in 1801, hosted by an elegant socialite, Madame Juliette Recamier. It was apparently quite a dinner, with a highly distinguished guest list that included nobility, celebrities, and other members of the cultural elite, and the challenges of Itard's project were made manifest in a dramatic way. Seated next to Madame Recamier, Victor made a startling impression from the beginning of dinner. According to her biographer, Eduard Herriot, Victor was "too occupied with the abundant things to eat, which he devoured with startling greed as soon as his plate was filled". During dessert, Victor abruptly left the table after he had "adroitly filled his pockets with all the delicacies he could filch". Next, Victor was "glimpsed running across the lawn with the speed of a rabbit" as he tore off his clothes, climbed a tree and "leapt from branch to branch and from tree to tree, until there were neither trees nor branches in front of him and he reached the end of the avenue. The gardener then had the idea of showing him a basket full of peaches" (Lane 1976:108–9).

Victor's origins are unknown. In Aveyron and Toulouse, speculations about his history fueled folk songs and even a play, in which Victor's birth results from the ravaging of a "farm girl" by a local lord. In the area of St. Sernin, the small town in which he was first captured, it was long speculated that he was the unwanted offspring of an aristocrat. In this strongly Catholic region in which illegitimate pregnancy comprised a crushing stigma, it is unsurprising that Victor was not the first abandoned and wild forest child to be reported in the region. As is the case with abandoned infants throughout history and today, there is no certain way to assess the actual number of such cases, especially since survival—and even the survival of a corpse—is improbable.

It is impossible to know Victor's age or condition at the time of his separation from human society. Experts then and since have believed that a large scar on his neck was humanly inflicted, adding support to the idea that Victor was deliberately abandoned early in his life, and fueling speculations of illegitimacy. Of course, such ideas remain in the realm of conjecture. What can be said with certainty is that Victor lived much of his childhood in the wild—at minimum several years. He had been observed from a distance by hunters, digging for roots and turnips for nearly three years before his capture in 1800. Although it cannot be established, most who have studied the case, then and since, believe he was abandoned in infancy (e.g., Itard 1807; Lane 1976; Malson 1970; McCrone 1993).

Although Victor never developed linguistic competence, under Itard's tutelage he demonstrated a sharp intelligence in nonlinguistic areas, both abstract and practical. He mastered a range of tasks, such as preparing vegetables for cooking and setting the table for dinner. Although many such tasks were simple, it appears that he not only performed them competently, but with remarkable attention to organization, and with a high level of motivation. More significantly, it appears that he also developed an acute sense of empathy, a sense of justice and a sense of aesthetics (e.g., valuing neatness and orderliness). In contrast to his initial disinterest in sociability, he came to place great emphasis on his relationships with others, despite his continuing and profound linguistic limitations.

As Victor was developing these skills and sensibilities, his body was also gradually becoming habituated to cultural routines. Itard's journals record how Victor gradually developed an interest in conventional comforts such as a warm bath and soft bed. Although he had initially spent much time crouched under his bed, and slept under it, he eventually began to prefer to sleep on it. Initially, Victor seemed indifferent to the aftermath of bed-wetting, but this behavior also stopped. He also came to appreciate a wider range of foods (Lane 1976:66), including both meat and desserts. Yet without language, Victor's integration into social life remained dramatically limited, despite the strong desire for human sociality that he gradually developed as Itard worked with him.

Despite the documentation of Victor's case, it has often been regarded as suspect because of the many unknowns, about such matters as his origins and about the actual structure of his brain. How much can be said from a sample size of one? Numerous other such cases have been either found to be hoaxes (Armen 1974; Dombrowski, Gischlar, Mrazik, and Greer 2011; Lane and Pillard 1978) or have involved arguably even more terrible and possibly disabling childhood conditions than being abandoned to the wild (such as Genie, who was tied to a chair and isolated in one room for her entire childhood [Curtiss 1977]), and hence cannot be considered comparable. Obviously, such questions cannot be pursued experimentally, separating infants into treatment and control groups. However, it has often been remarked that it could be telling if such cases could be investigated with recently developed brain scan technologies.

CONTEMPORARY EVIDENCE OF THE DEVELOPMENTAL LESSONS OF FERALITY

For the most tragic of reasons, such opportunities are presenting themselves in the contemporary world. Growing precarity in many parts of the world has created circumstances in which feral children may be increasing in number. Political turbulence, social upheaval and economic crises around the planet have aggravated conditions that put children at risk of severe neglect or even abandonment. Contributing factors include the extra strain placed by government cutbacks on already burdened child welfare agencies in many societies, sometimes accompanied by a more general disintegration of infrastructures and social life, especially in remote areas.

For a few individuals who are known to have endured feral conditions and to have survived the complete or near-complete deprivation of human company, human neglect has been compensated by the companionship of dogs, leading in some cases to canine-like behavior. Some of these children have been located and brought into society, treated and studied. One of the best-known such cases, Oxanna Malaya, has been featured in numerous documentaries and journalistic accounts. While Oxanna Malaya as a child lived on the land of her Ukrainian family, the family's dysfunctionality, neglect and rejection led her from a young age to socialize with dogs, and apparently, literally to live in the doghouse, and to develop remarkably canine behavioral patterns. As an apparent result, her body—in a testament to the developmental flexibility of *homo sapiens*—became habituated to doglike routines of quadruped running and slurping from troughs or brooks and barking, and her cognitive and linguistic capabilities are described as impaired. However, some such children have been rescued before passing critical points of brain development when language learning is no longer possible, and have become well-functioning human beings.

With recent and contemporary cases, unlike in Victor's case, brain scans can be and in some cases have been conducted (Perry 2002). The results provide powerful evidence in support of the primary interpretation of Victor's experience, as described earlier. One well-documented North American example can be found among the remarkable case studies provided through the work of Bruce Perry, a child trauma specialist, and reported in his book *The Boy Who Was Raised as a Dog*, coauthored with Maia Szalavitz (2006). The book's title refers to a boy called Justin who, due to an extraordinarily unfortunate confluence of circumstances, had been isolated from human company for the first six years of his life. After his initial rescue, Justin was diagnosed as suffering from "static encephalopathy", which meant that

> he had severe brain damage of unknown origin and was unlikely to improve . . . he was unable to walk or even say a few words by the time most children are actively exploring toddlers who have begun to speak in sentences . . . his brain had been scanned, revealing atrophy . . . of the cerebral cortex and enlargement of the fluid-filled ventricles in the center of the brain . . . his brain looked like that of someone with advanced Alzheimer's disease.
>
> (Perry and Szalavitz 2006:128–9)

It turned out that Justin had spent most of the first six years of his life in a dog cage, raised by a dog breeder who "was very limited himself, probably with mild mental retardation" and while presumably not intending to be cruel, had no understanding of parenting or the needs of children (Perry and Szalavitz 2006:130). His frame of reference for offering nurture derived from his interactions with dogs. Rescued at the age of 6, Justin was able to develop physically (he learned to stand and developed motor skills and strength), socially (including developing a sense of humor and learning to be affectionate, and not to sniff inappropriately, something he had apparently learned to do from his six years with dogs). Very importantly, he was able to develop cognitively: he began to learn language and speech. Perry and Szalavitz state that "his once dormant, undeveloped neural networks began to respond to these new repetitive patterns of stimulation. His brain seemed to be like a sponge, thirsty for the experiences it required, and eagerly soaking them up" (Perry and Szalavitz 2006:133).

While Justin's story ends happily, it is clear that not all children who have had such tragically horrific experiences find the support they need to become fully functional human beings before it is too late developmentally. Despite their deeply tragic aspects, such cases afford a modern confirmation of the lessons drawn from Victor's case, of the malleability and plasticity of human developmental processes over the life course, and their limits.

Of course, the experiences of Justin, Oxanna and Victor occurred during early childhood. Moreover, they are extremely rare experiences. Thus, the reader may well be wondering why they warrant such detailed treatment in a discussion of a general approach to age and the life course. Yet upon reflection, the reason should be clear: it is to ensure that we begin with a clear understanding of the very broad range of possibilities open to the human organism that have been empirically documented for its development and aging. It must be recognized that the consciousness of scientists no less than other citizens is typically both ethnocentric and cohort-centric, and we all have a *nomizing* tendency to normalize and naturalize what we see around us (Berger 1969:22). The implications of ferality for understanding the unexplored range of human possibilities have yet to be articulated in developmental and life-course theory.

FERALITY AND THEORETICAL PARADIGMS OF AGING AND DEVELOPMENT

Taking time to consider in detail how members of our species respond and adapt under extremely "asocial" circumstances puts us in a position to come to terms with the profound depth to which human bodies and minds are subject to shaping by the environment. This is clearly true in childhood, and as we will see later, it clearly remains true to a greater extent than generally realized, throughout the life course.

The experience of feral human beings makes clear that without contact and interaction, human organisms who survive to the teenage years are unable to become functional members of society because they have not developed and cannot develop language. Their condition demonstrates, from the beginning of the life course onward, the radical dependence of each individual human being upon stable patterns of social interaction and linguistic communication for the very structuring and development of her own body and mind, of her perceptual apparatus, of her physical capabilities and of her aesthetic sensibilities. No preformed or self-contained homunculus, every human individual and each member of every new cohort of newborns can become a functional human being only in the course of experience with other human beings, a process that Berger and Luckmann term *habitualization* (1967). Every human individual will develop habituated rhythms of speech, action and taste, as well as innumerable physical as well as cognitive characteristics, based on what she learns from the specific experiences of those who teach her, and will continue to be shaped in interaction with context throughout the life course. This general set of dynamics is close to what Bourdieu (1977) refers to as *habitus*.

Yet a self-contained homunculus is precisely the conception of the human individual that has been encouraged by the functional-organismic nexus. Acknowledgment of the centrality of experience in the constitution of human characteristics and developmental patterns has been woefully absent in the traditional and currently dominant approaches to both human development and life-course processes.

The traditional organismic paradigm is the anchoring point for human developmental theory. The established versions of theorizing about human development offered by organismic theorists from Freud onward—including Piaget, Kohlberg, and even the more critical and more contextually attuned research of scholars such as Carol Gilligan and Gilbert Gottlieb all fall within the organismic paradigm with the kinds of constricting assumptions described in Chapter 1 (see, e.g., Lerner 2002; Overton 1991, 2002). And these theories have served as the template for organismic theories of adulthood and aging such as disengagement theory, some elements of Carstensen's socioemotional selectivity theory, and the theories of such scholars as Erikson, Levinson, Gutmann and Pascual-Leone. In relying on these assumptions, these scholars have been in good company. Such an organismically anchored and rigid view of development and decline was until recently a longstanding premise of medicine generally and of cognitive neuroscience specifically—

although it is a view that is rapidly being supplanted with growing evidence of the remarkable scope of neuroplasticity throughout adulthood (Doidge 2007).

I will return to the issue of contemporary discoveries that bear upon human plasticity in more detail later, but as a brief way of appreciating its relevance for human development and aging, consider the case of disengagement theory. As many readers will know, disengagement theory, introduced by Elaine Cumming and William Henry in 1960, remains a highly influential, yet controversial, paradigm in social gerontology. The theory posits that disengagement from activity and social life is an integral part of aging into later life, and is an essential and inevitable stage of human development that bears precisely the features of the organismic model of development described previously (universality, sequentiality, unidirectionality, qualitative-structural transformation). Although it has been repeatedly debunked empirically and theoretically, on both logical and empirical grounds (e.g., Achenbaum and Bengtson 1994; Dannefer 1984; Ekerdt 1986; Hockschild, 1975; Quadagno 2005:25–8), its influence remains significant, and it is a powerful demonstration of the resilience of the functional-organismic nexus.

What is needed, then, is a paradigmatic foundation that explicitly recognizes the fundamental features of human anthropology that account for the lack of determinacy in human development and aging. Although this need has received limited attention, suggestions about how to develop it can be found in the work of some thoughtful social and behavioral scientists. For example, in a little-remarked-upon but pivotally important early section of their classic treatise *The Social Construction of Reality*, Peter Berger and Thomas Luckmann (1967) observed human beings are born, as they put it, "curiously unfinished"—unformed and "open", compared to other species. In psychology, Barbara Rogoff (2003) emphasizes that human beings are constitutionally *hard-wired for flexibility*. Plasticity (e.g., Lerner 1984, 2002) has become a fashionable term in psychology and related fields. In conversations with contemporary social and behavioral scientists, it is not unusual to hear such characteristics of human nature and human development casually acknowledged. Few actively dispute them, yet few also acknowledge the challenge they pose. The questions they raise about the potentials of human development logically entail relatively open-ended possibilities that compel us to push our thinking about the possibilities for aging, the life course and human development beyond the comfort zone of the functional-organismic nexus.

DISTINCTIVES OF HUMAN AGING AND DEVELOPMENT

Broad terms such as plasticity and malleability have frequently been used by developmentalists to signal a recognition that human development is not entirely a "hard-wired" phenomenon. Yet what specifically such terms imply for our fundamental understanding of human development often goes unspecified. Often, it seems, they suggest that there is some measure of "wiggle room" on the margins of the fixed contours of development, and hence a need for some minor tinkering or qualification— some "soft edges" to the organismic paradigm where the homunculus is malleable. Individual characteristics may not be "entirely" a matter of inborn characteristics, such as temperament, yet the core remains undisturbed.

Others have even contended that developmental plasticity can also be understood as something more akin to resilience—as something like "the newer plastics"—that may be capable of flexing back into shape after taking a hit (e.g., Scarr 1982). If such possibilities are present, however, the extent to which an individual is capable of realizing them will depend in substantial part on her own earlier internalizations.

As the cases of feral children dramatically demonstrate, plasticity and malleability go much deeper than this. They point to the profound degree to which human development and aging are dependent upon daily experience, and are actually constituted through such everyday processes (Baars 1991). This is a circumstance that implies the need for a more fundamental rethinking of paradigmatic assumptions. It draws attention to specific and identifiable features of human anthropology that have generally been overlooked, and that must be carefully considered. More than that, it points to the need to start with a conceptual framework for apprehending such organismic flexibility throughout the life course, beginning with its embryological and developmental base. They constitute the organismic foundation for human malleability. Thus understood, such knowledge does not pose a threat of disorder, but it does require a reframing of thought about the bases of order.

I begin by focusing on three such principles, *exterogestation*, *neoteny* and *world-construction*. These principles have rarely been made explicit in social and behavioral science research. This is more than remarkable because, despite their neglect by the mainstream study of development and aging, they accurately describe paradigmatically important features of *homo sapiens* and comprise the starting point for understanding the developmental plasticity of "human nature".

It can also be noted that these characteristics provide the developmental and physiological basis for the rapidly developing body of historical and critical work that acknowledges the embodiment of human experience, and depicts the human body as having a history, as having been lived differently, brought into being within widely dissimilar material cultures, subjected to various technologies and means of control, and incorporated into different rhythms of production and consumption, pleasure and pain (e.g., Gallagher and Laqueur 1987; Lancy 2020; Rogoff 2003). These processes also provide the physiological and developmental scaffolding that organically shapes the habitus, both individually and collectively (e.g., Bourdieu 1977).

These facts fundamentally challenge the commonsense, taken-for-granted assumptions about human development and aging in both scientific and popular discourse. This challenge comes at several levels, beginning with what they reveal about the depth and breadth of human malleability in processes of aging and development. To use Victor again as an example, it is clear that the homeostasis of his body as well as his psychic processes had been shaped by a life of almost unimaginable harshness, entailing remarkable physical and cognitive adaptations that produced in his body a trajectory that diverged radically from anything remotely resembling "normal" child development. It is equally well documented that subsequent exposure to and engagement with humans in social interaction altered many aspects of Victor's habituated physiology and patterns of behavior. His tastes and sensibilities, which at first prioritized free-range roaming through virgin forests and a diet of roots and nuts, were gradually but radically recalibrated when he was placed within a matrix of stable and caring human relationships, and concomitantly subjected to the rhythms and routines of a human society. Similar observations have been made about Justin, the boy "raised with dogs".

With the benefit of electronic brain imaging as well as added information from this and other recent cases, we now know that such conditions dramatically and adversely impact physical brain development, yet it is an impact that can be remedied if proper ameliorative measures are taken in time (Doidge 2007; Perry 2002; Perry and Szalavitz 2006).

The extraordinary flexibility of the developing person to adapt and interact in a generative fashion in most any setting is a distinctly human capability, one that is responsible for the fact that human beings have learned to survive by developing and creating highly diverse modes of interaction with the physical environment, from the equator to polar regions of the planet, even as diverse modes of daily action in an environment are internalized, embodied and habitualized to create highly diverse human beings.

This capacity is bound up with a number of physiological and developmental characteristics that appear to be largely unique to *homo sapiens* including the three developmental features I identified earlier. In the remainder of this chapter, I discuss the first two of these, exterogestation and neoteny. I will turn to world-construction in Chapter 3.

The lives and developmental dynamics of feral children are especially useful in revealing some of the dimensions of the first of these characteristics, *exterogestation*. Exterogestation is a condition that has been well recognized in developmental biology and physical anthropology, but has, as noted, been steadfastly overlooked by social and behavioral scientists interested in development and aging. Yet a grasp of its dimensions illuminates some of the essential elements in the organismic base of human beings' "hard-wiring for flexibility", to use again Barbara Rogoff's term. The same can be said for the second characteristic, neoteny. Therefore, I now turn to these two concepts.

EXTEROGESTATION

Although it is seldom noticed as forming a biological foundation for constructivist approaches to human development and aging, Peter Berger and Thomas Luckmann emphasize the implications of exterogestation for sociological analysis in *The Social Construction of Reality*, their classic treatise of the sociology of knowledge and social constructivism. Drawing on the work of Adolf Portmann and Arnold Gehlen, they use the term *extrauterine fruhjahr* to describe the "unfinished" condition of the human infant (Berger and Luckmann 1967:48). As they note, the flexibility in development afforded by this unfinished state accounts for the fact that the human species is virtually alone in its capacity to live in any and all ecological climates existing on planet earth. This is one of several ways in which *homo sapiens* are "unspecialized" as a species, compared with other species. It has sometimes been suggested that a primary human specialization is precisely a lack of specialization.

The meaning of exterogestation is effectively summarized in the title of Stephen Jay Gould's lucid essay on the subject, "Human Babies as Embryos". The term refers specifically to the entry of every human being into the world in a state of extraordinary prematurity, relative to the circumstance of other species (Montagu 1989:75). Indeed, the maturity evidenced

by newborns of other primate species is evidenced by humans at about 21 months after
conception (Gould 1977b:72, 1977c:369; Montagu 1989), leading to the notion of a
"postnatal *fruhjahr*" of exterogestation (Buytendijk 1958; Portmann 1962, 1990).

The significance of this circumstance for the initial months of individual development can be
seen in numerous ways. For example, about 75% of human brain growth occurs postnatally,
compared with only about a third for chimpanzees (Coqueugniot, Hublin, Veillon, Houët,
and Jacob 2004; Gould 1977c). This means that the organization of neural networks in the
human brain is something that occurs within—and relies directly upon interaction within—a
social environment. As Norman Doidge has recently made clear in his debunking of what he
calls the "theory of the unchanging brain" (2007:xviii), brain growth and change continue to
occur not only throughout childhood but in adulthood as well.

Beyond the neuronal level, exterogestation can be seen in numerous other kinds of
physiological indicators, some of which are familiar to anyone who has been a parent
or cared for an infant. The neonate skull's "soft spot" reflects a general delay in the
calcification of the skull. "[T]he sutures between our skull bones do not fully close until
well after adulthood" (Gould 1977b:65). By contrast, the skulls of other species including
primates are nearly fully ossified at birth.

The issue of skeletal formation applies not only to the skull but to the rest of the body as well.
The long bones and digits of the human infant are still cartilaginous, a condition that may
explain why Victor's fingers had formed with an extraordinary joint structure that allowed
them to rotate "upward", bending back so the nail could touch his wrist—illustrating that
bone and joint structures are among the features of development that are environmentally and
socially shaped: "the flexibility of his fingers in all directions is astonishing, one would even say
they were dislocated" (Bonaterre 1834 as translated in Lane 1976:35).

For every human being, the impact of social context upon the physical flexibility of these
early potentials is consequential in numerous ways. The human brain grows at a significant
rate after birth, compared to other primates who experience the majority of their brain
growth during gestation (Gould 1977b:365–7). For humans, by contrast, cranial capacity at
the end of the neonatal stage is approximately 25%, which doubles by the end of the first
year and reaches 90% by the end of the fifth year (Coqueugniot et al. 2004; Robson, van
Schaik, and Hawkes 2006).

The importance of the phenomenon of exterogestation can be seen not only in that the
size the organism attains at the end of the "postnatal *fruhjahr*", but also because at around
21 months, a key change occurs in the natal developmental rate, which for other species
happens about the time of birth (Gould 1977c:368–75).

Such characteristics also permit the differential development of physiologically based skills.
A well-known example comes from the world of dance, where it is generally believed
that professional-level performance requires that training start no later than age 7 or 8,
so that it can become an integral part of the development of strength and muscle groups
(e.g., Paskevska 2016). More generally, such physical flexibility accounts for cultural and
subcultural variations in the development of posture, gait, and patterns of gestural and facial

expressiveness. Without denying the importance of ontogenetically fixed characteristics that have been adapted by selection to specific aspects of both physical and cultural environments, the structural changes in skeletal development brought by disciplined ballet training signal a potentially wide range of culturally produced patterns of physiological development.

Structural variation in musculoskeletal development can also result from health challenges or disease processes that frequently have an environmental source or component. For example, "long face syndrome", which involves mandibular extension (the length of the jaw) and dental occlusion in childhood, can result from untreated allergies or asthma (Fialho, Pinzan-Vercelino, and Gurgel 2014; Linder-Aronson 1970; Ngan and Fields 1997:6; Sharma, Bansal, and Asopa 2015:2). Especially in early childhood, the respiratory difficulties resulting from such health conditions produced strained breathing and a high frequency of breathing through the mouth, which can have the result of altering dental bite patterns, lengthening the lower jaw and extending the entire facial structure. Of course, the allergies themselves and the organism's response to them are influenced by external and cultural factors including climate, diet, treatment and also the demands for exertion placed upon the body.

Although it is located at the very beginning of the life course, exterogestation comprises a foundational component for approaching age, human development and the life course because of what it reveals about the nature of *homo sapiens*. It provides an empirically grounded, organismic anchorage for understanding why human development and aging proceed on a foundation of "hard-wiring for flexibility". It refers to a set of decidedly underdetermined, open-ended growth processes.

These physical and developmental features of human development map onto a number of relevant sociological perspectives. Some of these growth processes may set parameters for lifelong aging, as the "long arm of childhood" studies propose, while others shape early skill development, patterns of conduct and social practices that impact opportunity structures or more generally the responses of others (e.g., codes of language [Bernstein 1981; Silva, Shimpi, and Rogoff 2015]). Again, this constitutes the anthropological foundation for the internalization and embodiment of the socially organized world, similar in Bourdieu's terminology to habitus (1977).

As we shall see in subsequent chapters, the contemporary expansion of knowledge in domains ranging from brain imaging to epigenetics suggests the dramatic degree to which experience shapes the structuration of neural networks. Such effects can now be evidenced by metrics of physical development and change, much more now than was the case when these facts were first emphasized several decades ago.

Of course, this relatively premature period of extrauterine development would not have evolved as it has and would not carry the significance it does if it were not for the specially evolved capability of human infants to capitalize on this circumstance with a mind that is simultaneously undergoing continued rapid growth and becoming organized in response to experience over a sustained period of years. It is a mind that is preprogrammed for flexibility and learning and generative action through experimentation and symbolic communication, rather than one that is preprogrammed by instincts that would restrict activity to specialized patterns of behavior. Thus, the social organization of neural networks is not just a matter of becoming habituated to cultural practices, programs and routines that are shaped in the beginning of the life course. Beyond such habituation, hard-wiring for flexibility also is the basis for realizing the generative potentials of human action, through which human beings develop capacities for imagination and innovation as they act in the world (Dannefer and Perlmutter 1990; Doidge 2007; Donald 2001). I will return to this crucially important topic in several subsequent sections.

NEOTENY

If exterogestation is captured in the phrase *human babies as embryos*, neoteny may be described in a parallel phrase—*human adults as children. Young* children, in fact. According to Ashley Montagu, the term "neoteny" was first applied to human beings by the pioneering sexologist Havelock Ellis, who in 1894 observed the relative similarity of fetal and adult human forms, compared with the sharp divergence evident in other species, including other primates (Ellis 1894:25). Neoteny, also called paedomorphism, is defined as the retention of fetal or juvenile characteristics into adulthood through the "deceleration" of the ontogenetic pace and rate of physical development (Gould 1977c:483; Montagu 1989:1–15, 251). The phenomenon of decelerated development has both temporal and structural aspects.

Temporally, neoteny refers to a reduction in the chronological rate of change, and to the lengthy and protracted period of childhood that characterizes human development. It refers to "the process whereby . . . fetal or juvenile traits are retained into later stages of individual development" (Montagu 1989:8). *Homo sapiens* have "absolutely the most protracted period of infancy, childhood and juvenility of all forms of life" (Krogman 1972). Primates in general grow to maturity more slowly than other life forms, but humans are inordinately "retarded" in their developmental rate, even among primates (Gould 1977b:67).

The Dutch anatomist Louis Bolk (1926) coined the term "fetalization", referring to the retarded rate of physical development of human beings from infancy to adulthood. Bolk's initial conceptualization had an impact in psychiatric as well as evolutionary circles, notably influencing Jacques Lacan, and stimulating considerable debate about evolutionary processes (Kranich 1999; Levivier 2011; Verhulst 1993).

Extending the world-openness with which humans enter the world, neoteny means that humans continue to be characterized by malleability and flexibility, even after the crucial structuring experiences of the first few years of life. It describes the basis for extending into adulthood and even later life, of many dimensions of the responsiveness and flexibility that are embedded in the processes of exterogestation. The circumstances and experiences of middle and later adulthood continue to affect physical as well as mental states of individuals through the life course. Thus, human beings remain relatively youth-like— "juvenescent"—throughout their adult lives.

Structurally, neoteny refers to the retention of the morphological features of the childhood form of the organism. Several pioneering scholars who focused carefully on the details of human development have made similar observations, often independently. As Ashley Montagu characterized Bolk's work:

> Adult human beings show many physical traits that are also features of the human fetus"…. (Such characteristics) change in other animals but … in human beings persist into adulthood…. In short, said Bolk … 'Man, in his bodily development, is a primate fetus that has become sexually mature.'
>
> (1989:6)

Similarly, pioneering evolutionary biologist J.B.S. Haldane demonstrated that human evolution had proceeded not by evolving new characteristics but rather by "the preservation of embryonic and infantile traits" (Haldane 1932:81; see also Montagu 1989:7). This distinctly human characteristic—of being an adult fetus—obviously has profound implications for social and behavioral dimensions of human development and aging. Before turning to those implications, it will be useful to review briefly their ontogenetic foundations.

Structural aspects of human physiology reflecting neoteny include numerous "infantile" features of the human body. Going back to Haldane and Bolk, a number of scholars have catalogued a range of such anatomical characteristics (Ghadially 2012; Montagu 1989:40ff). Table 2.1 presents a list of the features published by Montagu in his important treatise on neoteny, *Growing Young*. Like exterogestation, neoteny has both physiological

Table 2.1 Neotenous physical traits in humans

Cranial flexure	Nonrotation of big toe
Retarded closure of cranial sutures	Relative hairlessness of body
Head situated over top of spine	Lack of pigment in some groups
Forward position of foramen magnum	Curvature of pelvic axis
Forward position of occipital condyles	Lack of pronounced physical differences
Lack of heavy brow ridges	
Orbits under cranial cavity	Caudal flexure of pelvic organs
Flatness of face (orthognathy)	Anterior position of vagina
Contact between sphenoid and ethmoid bones in anterior cranial cavity	Persistence of labia majora
	Persistence of hymen
Large braincase	Large size of brain
Small teeth	Round-headedness (fetal head index 72–82)
Late eruption of teeth	
Prominent nose	Small jaws
Absence of cranial crests	Small face
Thinness of skull bones	Gently curved hard palate
Gracile skeleton	Erect posture
Thin nails	Persistence of penile prepuce

Source: Montagu 1989:255

and psychological aspects. Its physiological aspect is reflected in how unusually childlike the adult human is in overall shape, compared to other species (Lorenz 1971:180). Several scholars have focused on a graphing of structural and anatomical comparisons of fetal and adult forms of multiple species to illustrate the significance of neoteny. The fetal forms of many species—notably including the higher primates—share many physiological features and characteristics with each other, but only in the human case are these characteristics retained in adulthood. All other species "outgrow" them.

In addition to Montagu, influential scholars who have emphasized neoteny include Stephen Jay Gould (1977b) and Arnold Gehlen (1993 [1940/1950]). Gehlen's work is of particular significance for those concerned with the connection between these distinctive anthropological fundamentals and social processes. Berger and Luckmann rely heavily on his insights into the implications for human social life of both physical anthropology and his theory of institutions in their classic framework introduced in *The Social Construction of Reality* (1967).

These two features of human development—exterogestation and neoteny—make clear the fundamental "category error" of trying to force-fit our understanding of human development into a theory of fixed and universal theory of stages of development (Dannefer and Perlmutter 1990; Morss 2017). These distinctly human potentials for flexibility and growth throughout the human life course have functional implications. Some of these concern communication and interaction. Many aspects of human physiology are designed to facilitate interpersonal connection and complex communication, both emotional and cognitive, arguably including even the forward positioning of the sex organs in the pelvic area which enables eye contact, thus facilitating intersubjective communication during intimate activity (Bromhall 2004:25–8).

In sum, the "lack of specialization" involved in neoteny is decisive for human development in multiple respects. Instead of developing specialized instincts to organize perception and channel behavior, human beings must figure out how to order their lives and actions as they encounter reality on a day-by-day, indeed moment-by-moment, basis. The resultant quest for order—*nomos*—is the basis for Peter Berger's observation that human beings are a *nomizing* species. *Nomization*, according to Berger, is "the most important function of society" (1969:22). It makes explicit that human beings must seek and rely upon coherent (and hence patterned and ultimately institutionalized) communication with others in order to direct human activity.

This set of conditions also implies physical vulnerability of the lone individual, which extends beyond the simple need for order, or nomos. It has also been noted, for example, that maturing human beings do not develop specialized features for predation or defense (e.g., deadly claws or teeth). Instead, for *homo sapiens* defense entails knowledge, which in turn requires interaction with others. Thus, in both of these respects, human beings require interaction with and influence of others to structure and provide order to their daily existence and define their location within the coordinates of both space and time. This is why *anomie* is an ever-present risk for human beings, in a way that is not the case, or is much less central, in other species (although work on baboons and other species may suggest some significant costs of social marginality; see, e.g., Sapolsky 2004, 2017).

But if the risk of anomie is always present, so are the potentials for learning, innovation and growth. Some research suggests that human growth during adulthood, even later adulthood, is possible in ways that even proactive gerontologists have not anticipated. Some of these have to do with recent discoveries about the generation of new brain cells in response to environmental stimulation, extending throughout the life course. As noted earlier, the idea of such new brain growth was considered laughable a few decades ago but has now become the basis for a wide array of new research initiatives in neuroscience (e.g., Doidge 2007; Woollett and Maguire 2011). I will consider the implications of related discoveries for studying aging and the life course in more detail in Chapter 7.

Beyond its implications for the cognitive domain, human neoteny can also be seen in research indicating the potential of aging human beings for physical growth. Psychologist Ellen Langer conducted a remarkable experiment in which she demonstrated that experimental conditions simulating different kinds of everyday life environments have the potential to stimulate growth and change not only in the mind but also in the physical body—ranging from measured height and finger length to visual acuity (Langer 2009; see also Langer et al. 1990).

This unusual experiment focused on potentials for change in physical and psychological characteristics of men in their early seventies. The control group was invited to spend five days at a remote country retreat, and to spend their time reminiscing about their lives from decades earlier, specifically in 1959 (Langer 1989:102–3). The experimental group, by contrast, was placed in a simulated time travel situation. For their experience, the retreat setting was set up differently: it was decorated and equipped with furniture, magazines and artifacts, records and even television programs, in an effort to replicate the environment of 1959. And the participants were instructed to try to interact as though it were 1959 (when they would have been perhaps in their late forties), and to avoid any reference to post-1959 events, technological developments, etc. Both physical and psychological measurements were taken pre- and posttest, and both groups responded well to these apparently pleasant experiences. Both improved on a number of measures, ranging from performance on a memory test to hand strength and other physical measures. Beyond those shared similarities, however, the experimental group grew taller, grew longer fingers, gained significantly more near-point vision and performed better on numerous psychological tests (Langer 1989:132–3). Langer emphasized the lessons contained in this experiment for the untapped reserves of power in the human mind for influencing various dimensions of the individual's physiology, but it is also instructive in revealing the power of context on both mind and body. These findings clearly point to the potentials for physical growth and change in later life, and to the contingency on physical as well as cognitive change of the content of daily experience. While costly and difficult to replicate, the implications of this project were later elaborated into a book-length treatment (Langer 2009).

As discussed earlier in relation to feral children, recent developments in neuroimaging have also been used by researchers to link daily experience to observed changes in the brain in adulthood, including functional growth in response to environmental cues. As an example, consider the work of Eleanor Maguire and associates, who documented substantial hippocampal growth in individuals who were studying and memorizing the map of

London in preparation for taking the test to become London cabbies (Maguire et al. 2000; Woollett and Maguire 2011).

Thus, *hard-wiring for flexibility* applies not just to children and teenagers but also to a lack of *predetermination* of a trajectory of change with age across the life course—through adulthood and even into later life. Such evidence makes clear why theories that seek to define general patterns of age-specific change, including age-related declines, often turn out not to be universal after all.

NEOTENY, SOCIAL FORCES AND ONTOGENY

While the principles of exterogestation and neoteny mean that there is a level of indeterminacy and contingency in human development, they do not mean that human developmental outcomes are unpredictable. It is true that *lack of specialization* and *hard-wiring for flexibility* mean that we cannot conjure any sort of gyroscope or metronome within the developing human being to direct its activity. Lacking such instinctual guidance, we must construct our species-being through operations of cognitive imagination and performative ingenuity. Yet we know from the experience of feral children and other evidence that imagination and ingenuity do not flourish in isolation. Young human beings require human interaction to develop language and useful cognitive skills. And we also know from simple empirical observation that age and development, like human conduct more generally, does not proceed in random and chaotic fashion. It is remarkably orderly. From whence comes the orderliness?

Clearly, these facts and principles about human development suggest that it will be fruitful to look at factors in the environment rather than to the internal programming of the organism itself (as expressed in ideas like "stages", "normal aging" or "internal clocks") in order to find the ordering principles that account for age-related outcomes. Of course, the "environment" is for humans a *social* environment, composed in social settings of multiple levels of complex structures and processes. Very importantly, the social environment is an environment that is not pregiven in nature but is created and exists only in and through human activity. In the chapters that follow, we will begin the task of identifying how some of those structures affect the organization of human development, aging and the life course.

Before turning to that task, one last point of clarification is in order. Thoughtful readers of the foregoing pages have likely already been asking questions like these: Is there no place for "hard-wiring" of some aspects of development of aging? Are there no domains of ontogenetic change, defined as change processes or characteristics that can be interpreted as genetically fixed within each phenotype? If one acknowledges the "curiously unfinished" state of the human neonate and the importance of social forces in organizing the life rhythms of individuals and their patterns of development and aging, does this imply a claim of complete organismic relativism? Within this view, can it be acknowledged that *any* universals of development and aging exist?

The answer to such questions is a clear "yes". Some features of development and aging do indeed reflect universally fixed organismically based sequences and processes (Dannefer and Perlmutter 1990). For example, the development of secondary sex characteristics and fecundity are obviously necessary for the species to survive. These characteristics emerge through a well-defined, effectively universal sequence, even though the timing of sexual maturation (not to mention the specific forms of sexual interest and activity) may vary considerably. Menopause is another obvious example, although its meaning and interpretation as well as its timing and associated physical health events can vary dramatically by social context (see. e.g., Locke 1994).

A second class of ontogenetic characteristics refers not to universal features of development but to specific adaptive characteristics evolutionary selected over a long period of time for their survival advantage in a given climatic environment. One obvious example is pigmentation of skin (Sturm and Duffy 2012). A second example is offered by high-altitude populations such as those living in the mountains in Tibet or the Andes: "populations living in these high-altitude regions for thousands of years have adapted and thrived, with varying physiological adaptations to hypoxic environment" (Fan, Hansen, Lo, and Tishkoff 2016:56; see also Beall 2006, 2007).

To return to a central point of Chapter 1, then, the point is not to claim that nothing is ontogenetic, or "hard-wired" (Dannefer and Perlmutter 1990). Clearly, some aspects of development (e.g., critical periods of brain formation, pubertal change, musculoskeletal and brain maturation) appear to have an organismically programmed sequencing. Rather, it is to alert us all to the degree to which the functional-organismic nexus has too often led researchers to a *containment* of such questions—to a premature foreclosure of inquiry that encourages an easy acceptance of organismic, individual-level interpretations of age-correlated patterns without a thoughtful consideration of aspects of development and aging that might not be so fixed, and of the actual causal processes underlying such patterns and outcomes. The question, thus, is the intellectual stance with which one approaches a research question or problem. Relying on the implicit assumptions of the functional-organismic nexus and operating with a heuristic logic of containment, the history of our field is a history of microfication, of privileging of familiar and taken-for-granted individual-level explanations and expending little intellectual energy to consider the possible role of social forces and of risking an ontogenetic fallacy (Dannefer 1984).

In the previous sections I have emphasized the consequences of *world-openness*—how the nature of *homo sapiens* as a species includes a physical and developmental flexibility that opens the species to the importance of lived experience social factors in shaping the contours of development, both structurally and temporally. I turn now to *world-construction*. As noted earlier, world-construction—a third distinctive of human development—is anchored in consciousness—in the cognitively generative (Dannefer and Perlmutter 1990) and consciously intentional processes that are the wellspring of human action (often called agency) and through which social relations, institutions and practices are constituted.

REFERENCES

Achenbaum, Andrew W., and Vern L. Bengtson. 1994. "Re-engaging the Disengagement Theory of Aging: On the History and Assessment of Theory Development in Gerontology." *The Gerontologist* 34(6): 756–63. https://doi.org/10.1093/geront/34.6.756.

Armen, Jean-Claude. 1974. *Gazelle-Boy: A Child Brought Up By Gazelles in the Sahara Desert*. London: Bodley Head.

Baars, Jan. 1991. "The Challenge of Critical Gerontology: The Problem of Social Constitution." *Journal of Aging Studies* 5(3): 219–43.

Bayat, Mojdeh. 2017. *Teaching Exceptional Children: Foundations and Best Practices in Inclusive Early Childhood Education Classrooms*. New York: Routledge.

Beall, Cynthia M. 2006. "Andean, Tibetan and Ethiopian Patterns of Adaptation to High-Altitude Hypoxia." *Integrative and Comparative Biology* 46(1): 18–24.

Beall, Cynthia M. 2007. "Two Routes to Functional Adaptation: Tibetan and Andean High-Altitude Natives." *Proceedings of the National Academy of Sciences of the United States of America* 15(1): 8655–60.

Berger, Peter L. 1969. *The Sacred Canopy: Elements of a Sociological Theory of Religion*. New York: Anchor.

Berger, Peter L., and Thomas Luckmann. 1967. *The Social Construction of Reality: A Systematic Treatise in the Sociology of Knowledge*. New York: Anchor.

Bernstein, Basil. 1981. "Codes, Modalities, and the Process of Cultural Reproduction: A Model." *Language in Society* 10(3): 327–63.

Bolk, Louis. 1926. *Das Problem der Menschwerdung*. Jena, Germany: Gustav Fisher.

Bourdieu, Pierre. 1977 (1972). *Outline of a Theory of Practice*. Cambridge, UK: Cambridge University Press.

Bromhall, Clive. 2004. *The Eternal Child: How Evolution Has Made Children of Us All*. London: Ebury Press.

Buytendijk, Frank F. 1958. *Mensch und Tier*. Hamburg, Germany: Rowohlt. (as cited in Peter L. Berger & Thomas Luckmann, *The Social Construction of Reality: A Systematic Treatise in the Sociology of Knowledge*. New York: Anchor).

Coqueugniot, Helene, Jean-Jacques Hublin, Francis Veillon, Francis Houët, and Teuku Jacob. 2004. "Early Brain Growth in Homo Erectus and Implications For Cognitive Ability." *Nature* 431(7006): 299–302.

Cumming, Elaine, and William E. Henry. 1961. *Growing Old: The Process of Disengagement*. New York: Basic Books.

Curtiss, Susan. 1977. *Genie: A Psycholinguistic Study of a Modern-Day of 'Wild Child'*. New York: Academic Press Inc.

Dannefer, Dale. 1984. "Adult Development and Social Theory: A Paradigmatic Reappraisal." *American Sociological Review* 49(100–116).

Dannefer, Dale. 1987. "Aging as Intracohort Differentiation: Accentuation, the Matthew Effect, and the Life Course." *Sociological Forum* 2(2): 211–36.

Dannefer, Dale. 1999a. "Freedom Isn't Free: Power, Alienation, and the Consequences of Action." Pp. 105–32 in *Action & Development: Origins and Functions of Intentional Self-Development*, edited by J. Brandstadter and R. Lerner. New York: Springer Publishing Company.

Dannefer, Dale. 1999b. "Neoteny, Naturalization and Other Constituents of Human Development." Pp. 67–93 in *Self and Society of Aging Processes*, edited by C. Ryff and V. Marshall. New York: Springer Publishing Company.

Dannefer, Dale. 2008. "The Waters We Swim: Everyday Social Processes, Macro Structural Realities and Human Aging." Pp. 3–22 in *Social Structures and Aging Individuals:*

Continuing Challenges, edited by K. W. Schaie and R. P. Abeles. New York: Springer Publishing Company.

Dannefer, Dale, and Marion Perlmutter. 1990. "Development as a Multidimensional Process: Individual and Social Constituents." *Human Development* 33(2–3): 108–37.

Dannefer, Dale, and Ralph R. Sell. 1988. "Age Structure, the Life Course and 'Aged Heterogeneity': Prospects for Research and Theory." *Comprehensive Gerontology: Section B, Behavioural, Social, and Applied Sciences* 2(1): 1–10.

Doidge, Norman. 2007. *The Brain That Changes Itself: Stories of Personal Triumph from the Frontiers of Brain Science*. New York: Penguin Press.

Dombrowski, Stephen C., Karen Gischlar, Martin Mrazik, and F. W. Greer. 2011. "Feral Children." Pp. 81–93 in *Assessing and Treating Low Incidence/High Severity Psychological Disorders of Childhood*, edited by S. C. Dombrowski and K. L. Gischlar. New York: Springer Publishing Company.

Donald, Merlin. 2001. *A Mind So Rare: The Evolution of Human Consciousness*. New York: Norton.

Ekerdt, David J. 1986. "The Busy Ethic: Moral Continuity between Work and Retirement." *The Gerontologist* 26(3): 239–44. https://doi.org/10.1093/geront/26.3.239.

Fan, Shaohua, Matthew E. B. Hansen, Yancy Lo, and Sarah A. Tishkoff. 2016. "Going Global by Adapting Local: A Review of Recent Human Adaptation." *Science* 354(6308): 54–9.

Fialho, Melissa Proença Nogueira, Célia Regina Maio Pinzan-Vercelino, Rodrigo Proença Nogueira, and Júlio de Araújo Gurgel. 2014. "Relationship between Facial Morphology, Anterior Open Bite and Non-Nutritive Sucking Habits during the Primary Dentition Stage." *Dental Press Journal of Orthodontics* 19(3): 108–13. doi: 10.1590/2176-9451.19.3.108-113.oar.

Gallagher, Catherine, and Thomas Laqueur, eds. 1987. *The Making of the Modern Body: Sexuality and Society in the Nineteenth Century*. Berkeley, CA: University of California Press.

Gehlen, Arnold. 1993 (1940, 1950). *Der Mensch: Seine Natur und seine Stellung in der Welt*. Frankfurt, Germany: Klostermann.

Ghadially, Ruby. 2012. "25 Years of Epidermal Stem Cell Research." *Journal of Investigative Dermatology* 132(3): 797–810.

Gould, Stephen J. 1977a. "The Child as Man's Real Father." Pp. 63–69 in *Ever Since Darwin: Reflections on Natural History*, edited by S. J. Gould. New York: Norton.

Gould, Stephen J. 1977b. "Human Babies as Embryos." Pp. 70–5 in *Ever Since Darwin: Reflections on Natural History*, edited by S. J. Gould. New York: Norton.

Gould, Stephen J. 1977c. *Ontogeny and Phylogeny*. Cambridge, MA: Harvard University Press.

Haldane, J. B. 1932. "A Method for Investigating Recessive Characters in Man." *Journal of Genetics* 25(2): 251–5.

Hochschild, Arlie R. 1975. "Disengagement Theory: A Critique and Proposal." *American Sociological Review* 40(5): 553–69.

Itard, Jean M. 1802. *An Historical Account of the Discovery and the Education of a Savage Man, of the First Developments, Physical and Moral of the Young Savage Caught in the Woods near Averyon in the Year 1798*. London: Richard Phillips.

Kranich, Ernst-Michael. 1999. *Thinking Beyond Darwin: The Idea of a Type as Key to Vertebrate Evolution*. Hudson, NY: Lindisfarne Books.

Lancy, David F. 2020. *Child Helpers: A Multidisciplinary Perspective*. New York: Cambridge.

Lane, Harlan. 1976. *The Wild Boy of Aveyron*. Cambridge, MA: Harvard University Press.

Lane, Harlan, and Richard Pillard. 1978. *The Wild Boy of Burundi: A Study of an Outcast Child*. New York: Random House.

Langer, Ellen J. 1989. *Mindfulness*. Boston: Addison-Wesley.

Langer, Ellen J. 2009. *Counterclockwise: Mindful Health and the Power of Possibility*. New York: Ballantine.

Langer, Ellen J., Benzion Chanowitz, Mark Palmerino, Stepen Jacobs, Mark Rhodes, and Philip Thayer. 1990. "Non-Sequential Development and Aging." Pp. 114–36 in *Higher Stages of Human Development: Perspectives on Adult Growth*, edited by C. N. Alexander and E. J. Langer. New York: Oxford University Press.

Lerner, Richard M. 1984. *On the Nature of Human Plasticity*. Cambridge, UK: Cambridge University Press.

Lerner, Richard M. 2002. *Concepts and Theories of Human Development*. Mahwah, NJ: Psychology Press.

Levivier, Marc. 2011. "The Fetalization of Louis Bolk." *Essaim* 1(26): 153–68.

Linder-Aronson, S. 1970. "Their Effect on Mode of Breathing and Nasal Airflow and Their Relationship to Characteristics of the Facial Skeleton and the Denition: A Biometric, Rhino-Manometric and Cephalometric-Radiographic Study on Children with and without Adenoids." *Acta-Otolaryngologica Supplement* 265: 1–132.

Locke, Margaret M. 1994. *Encounters with Aging: Mythologies of Menopause in Japan and North America*. Berkeley, CA: University of California Press.

Lorenz, Konrad. 1971. *Studies in Animal and Human Behavior*. Cambridge, MA: Harvard University Press.

Lorenz, Konrad, and Robert Martin. 1971. "Studies in Animal and Human Behaviour." *British Journal for the Philosophy of Science* 22(1): 81–2.

Maguire, Eleanor A., David G. Gadian, Ingrid S. Johnsrude, Catriona D. Good, John Ashburner, Richard S. J. Frackowiak, and Christopher D. Frith. 2000. "Navigation-Related Structural Change in the Hippocampi of Taxi Drivers." *Proceedings of the National Academy of Sciences* 97(8): 4398–4403. doi: 10.1073/pnas.070039597.

Malson, Lucien. 1970. *Wolf Children*. New York: Monthly Review Press.

Montagu, Ashley. 1989. *Growing Young*. New York: McGraw-Hill.

Montessori, Maria. 2004. *The Discovery of the Child: Revised and Enlarged Edition of the Montessori Method*. Delhi, India: Aakar Books.

Musiek, Frank E. 2006. "Auditory Training and CAPD: A Short History." *The Hearing Journal* 59(8): 52. doi: 10.1097/01.HJ.0000286378.15174.f9.

Ngan, Peter, and Fields, Henry W. 1997. "Open Bite: A Review of Etiology and Management." *Pediatric Dentistry* 19(2): 91–8.

Overton, Willis F. 1991. "The Structure of Developmental Theory." Pp. 1–37 In *Advances in Child Development and Behavior*. Vol. 23, edited by H. W. Reese. New York: Academic Press.

Overton, Willis F. 2002. "Development Across the Life Span." Pp. 13–42 in *Handbook of Psychology: Developmental Psychology*. Vol. 6, edited by R. M. Lerner, M. A. Easterbrooks, and J. Mistry. New York: Wiley.

Paskevska, Anna. 2016. *Getting Started in Ballet: A Parent's Guide to Dance Education.* New York: Oxford University Press.

Perry, Bruce D. 2002. "Childhood Experience and the Expression of Genetic Potential: What Childhood Neglect Tells Us about Nature and Nurture." *Brain and Mind* 3(1): 79–100. doi: 10.1023/A:1016557824657.

Perry, Bruce D., and Maia Szalavitz. 2006. *The Boy Who Was Raised as a Dog: And Other Stories from a Child Psychiatrist's Notebook: What Traumatized Children Can Teach Us about Loss, Love and Healing.* New York: Basic Books.

Portmann, Adolf. 1962 (1956). *Zoologie und das neue Bild des Menschen: Biologische Fragmente zu einer Lehre vom Menschen.* Reinbek, Hamburg: Rowohlt.

Portmann Adolf. 1990. *A Zoologist Looks at Humankind.* New York: Columbia University Press.

Quadagno, Jill. 2005. *Aging and the Life Course: An Introduction to Social Gerontology.* New York: McGraw-Hill.

Robson, Shannen L., Carel P. van Schaik, and Kristen Hawkes. 2006. "The Derived Features of Human Life History." Pp. 17–44 in *The Evolution of Human History*, edited by K. Hawkes and R. R. Paine. Santa Fe: School of American Research.

Rogoff, Barbara. 2003. *The Cultural Nature of Human Development.* New York: Oxford University Press.

Sapolsky, Robert. 2004. "Social Status and Health in Humans and Other Animals." *Annual Review of Anthropology* 33(1): 393–418.

Sapolsky, Robert. 2017. *Behave: The Biology of Humans at Our Best and Worst.* New York: Penguin.

Scarr, Sandra. 1982. "Development is Internally Guided, Not Determined." *Psychological Critiques* 27(11): 852–3.

Sharma, Shantanu, Ayushi Bansal, and Kirti Asopa. 2015. "Prevalence of Oral Habits among Eleven to Thirteen Years Old Children in Jaipur." *International Journal of Clinical Pediatric Dentistry* 8(3): 208–10. doi: 10.5005/jp-journals-10005-1314.

Silva, Katie D., Priya M. Shimpi, and Barbara Rogoff. 2015. "Children's Attention to What's Going On: Cultural Differences." Pp. 207–27 in *Advances in Child Development and Behavior*, edited by M. Correa-Chávez, R. Mejía-Arauz, and B. Rogoff. New York, NY: Elsevier.

Sturm, Richard A., and David L. Duffy. 2012. "Human Pigmentation Genes under Environmental Selection." *Genome Biology* 13(9): 248–60. doi: 10.1186/gb-2012-13-9-248.

Verhulst, Jos. 1993. "Louis Bolk Revisited II: Retardation, Hypermorphosis and Body Proportions of Humans." *Medical Hypotheses* 41(2): 100–14.

Wairy, Louis Constant. 1830. *Memoires sur le Privie de Napoleon: sa Familie, et sa Cour.* Paris: Ladvocat. (as cited in Harlan Lane, *The Wild Boy of Aveyron.* Cambridge, MA: Harvard University Press).

Woollett, Katherine, and Eleanor A. Maguire. 2011. "Acquiring 'the Knowledge' of London's Layout Drives Structural Brain Changes." *Current Biology* 21(24): 2109–14.

CHAPTER 3
AGENCY, INTENTIONALITY AND WORLD-CONSTRUCTION

A spider conducts operations that resemble those of a weaver, and a bee puts to shame many an architect in the construction of her cells. But what distinguishes the worst architect from the best of bees is this, that the architect raises his structure in imagination before he erects it in reality.

Marx, *Capital*, Vol. 1:174

This simple observation succinctly conveys a key aspect of a third distinctively human feature of development and aging, which can be called *world-construction*. It should be clear from the foregoing chapter that human species-being represents a highly distinctive and unusual form of life—plastic and malleable, yet agentic and imaginative. Human development, as we have seen, is *hard-wired for flexibility* (Rogoff 2003), highly responsive to environmental cues. Its neotenous character means that it is also unusually decelerated in its pace of maturation so that youthful "juvenescent" features are preserved. With this continuously interactive set of processes, physical and experiential openness and growth potential are maintained throughout the life course.

At the species level and at the individual level, it is a dynamic and contingent mode of operating, and it is abundantly clear that the fixed developmental and age-related sequences that work well in describing earthworms, weaverbirds or even many mammals cannot be extrapolated to *homo sapiens*. Yet this picture does not exhaust the ways in which human beings are distinctive. Exterogestation, neoteny and "hard-wiring for flexibility" can take us only part of the distance required if we are to apprehend the core aspects of human experience that underlie the constitution of human development over the life course.

I anticipate, based on many conversations and written exchanges with students and colleagues on this topic, that some readers will recoil from the notions of malleability and plasticity implied by exterogestation and neoteny because they seem to imply a socially imposed determinism and a passivity for individuals that is intellectually and existentially troubling. I therefore wish to assure readers that such a predicate does not follow from the fact of the extraordinary flexibility of the human organism. It is not the view of contemporary social theory (e.g., Archer 2017; Burawoy 2019; Giddens 1984, 1991; Wacquant 2005), and it is certainly not my view. Indeed, such a negative and naïve view of malleability itself reflects a failure to consider systematically and fully the character of *homo sapiens*, both as a species and as individuals.

In fact, the same cluster of human characteristics responsible for malleability are also responsible for the uniquely human potentials for ingenuity, creativity and innovation.

While the developmental processes of individual members of other species may often be less shaped by their environments than are humans, those other species are also less able to change their circumstances or environments in order to control their own existence, or to change themselves, because they are preprogrammed by developmental sequences and instincts that allow them to function only within a very narrow range.

These fundamental differences are the reason that the hermeneutic tradition recognizes the subject matters of the natural and social sciences as "radically discrepant" (Giddens 1984:1; see also Berlin 1939:39; Mcauley 2019:36). Indeed, it is difficult to see how anyone who takes empirical evidence seriously could fail to recognize that neither human *species-being* nor human developmental processes can be reduced to physical, ontogenetic and evolutionary mechanisms governing the natural order. It is, irreducibly, a wild card in nature (Dannefer and Perlmutter 1990:122).

Compared to humans, most other species are not only rigid in their own phenotypic developmental sequences; they also have a quite rigid relation to their environments. As Berger and Luckmann put it, they live "in closed worlds whose structures are predetermined by their biological equipment" (Berger and Luckmann 1967:42). This is true even when structural change occurs phenotypically in response to environmental inputs (as when individual locusts develop stronger wings and change color based on ecological circumstances) because those changes occur in biologically regulated, predetermined ways (Gilbert and Epel 2008; see also Gluckman and Hanson 2005). Such, phenotypic flexibility notwithstanding, each such species becomes adapted to its habitat by selection pressures, and it survives in that habitat primarily thanks to innate behavior patterns that are adapted to it.

"NATURE'S ENGINEER": PREPROGRAMMED SKILLS AND ABILITIES

This general point is well illustrated by considering a species often singled out by humans for its extraordinary skills and industriousness—*Castor canadensis*, commonly known in the English-speaking world as the beaver. Not uncommonly, natural history museums feature displays that credit beavers' enterprise and building skills with appellations such as "nature's #1 engineer" or "nature's most talented builders" (Goldfarb 2018:1060). "Tim the Beaver" has long been the mascot of the Massachusetts Institute of Technology, in recognition of the species' technical prowess.

It is certainly true that beavers are fascinating creatures with admirable traits and unique and highly impressive construction skills (Amery 1892; Wilsson 1971). Moreover, their constructions have had a major impact on the lives of other species (e.g., providing habitat for salmon [Goldfarb 2018:1059]), and contrary to some views, possibly even benefiting humans: sediment trapped in beaver ponds is claimed to have "produced the rich farm land . . . of the northern half of North America" (Ruedemann and Schoonmaker 1938).

However, what accolades such as "nature's master builder" seldom acknowledge is that as an engineer, the beaver has—so far as is known—brought no innovative ideas to improve upon or change its modus operandi in the last several millennia. The dam- and lodge-building programs implemented by beavers are theirs by instinct, and remain constant across centuries and continents. While some learning may occur as young beavers grow to adulthood and their skills develop, learning from others is not necessary for them to embark upon a lifetime of tree-cutting and hydro construction projects, so long as they are exposed to essential materials during their own critical period of development, which occurs in the first few months of their lives (Richard 1983; Zurowski 1992). As a result, innovation, change and accumulation of knowledge are relatively absent in the species-being of *Castor canadensis*.

In a recent effort to reintroduce beavers into areas from which they have been displaced and where they can be ecologically advantageous, humans have carefully simulated the rudiments of beaver dam-building in "beaver dam analogs"—efforts that have apparently been quite successful (Goldfarb 2018:1058–61). Beavers have joined humans in this fascinating cross-species collaboration. However, it must be noted that, while this effort has required imagination, creativity and learning on the part of the humans involved, there is no indication that *Castor canadensis* has changed at all their instinct-driven building program, or has contributed a single innovative idea to the collaboration. The collaboration has been entirely dependent on one species, the human species, with its capabilities of finding ways to create the habitat of the other species—despite lacking the latter's physiological equipment.

The processes underlying the activity of beavers are thus fundamentally different from human action. These comments are not intended to diminish the beauty, significance and value of beavers, a species no less fascinating than admirable. Yet, their impressive productivity notwithstanding, imagination and creativity are in short supply for them.

This example calls again to mind Marx's simple yet provocative contrast that serves as the epigraph for this chapter, comparing spiders and architects. Marx's observation succinctly conveys at least two key aspects of the distinctiveness of *homo sapiens*. First is the central role of consciousness—of intentionality in guiding human activity; the second is imagination, relating to the uniquely human capabilities of creativity and productive, spontaneous new ideas and synthetic formulations.

There is yet a third aspect of this distinctly agentic feature of human activity that is equally fundamental. This feature can be called world-construction. *World-construction* builds on these features and amplifies them in action and interaction with other human beings. It concerns the human actors' constitutive role in the generation and maintenance of the shared reality of social relations and, simultaneously, in the life of each human being and in the constitution of the self. It is only through intentional human activity in interaction with others that social systems are created, and through those same interactive processes and in the context of social relationships, that the self is created. Each of these three features—intentionality, imagination and world-construction—warrants discussion.

HUMAN ACTIVITY ORIGINATES IN CONSCIOUS INTENTIONALITY, NOT INSTINCT

This general point recalls Weber's classic formulation of social action by reference to its meaning: "action is social insofar as its subjective meaning takes into account the behavior of others and is thereby oriented in its course" (Weber 1964:4). For present purposes, human action can be defined as subjectively meaningful and intentional social conduct. In addition to its indebtedness to Weber, recognition of the central importance of intentionality and purposefulness is present in the work of other classical theorists such as Du Bois (1994 [1903]), Simmel (1950 [1908]), Marx (1978 [1932], 2015 [1867]) and Mills (1940). It is consistent with interactionist (Blumer 1969; Mead 1934), phenomenological (Shutz 1971) and critical (Broughton 1987; Wexler 1996) traditions, with Vygotskian activity theory (Stetsenko 2004, 2016; Vygotsky 1978) and with social theory generally (Berger and Luckmann 1967; Bourdieu 1986; Collins 2004; Giddens 1984, 1991; Parsons 1951). As Giddens puts it, "to be a human being is to be a purposive agent" (1984:3). The degree to which such action represents a distinctly human mode of operation in the world can hardly be overemphasized.

The breadth of this definition indicates the pervasiveness of action in human experience. At the same time, it also implies some clear definitional boundaries: human action cannot be equated with the movement of the body. For example, "holding still" for the dentist is action; it is the product of disciplined intent, even though one's muscles and joints remain inert. On the other hand, dramatic physical movements do not necessarily qualify as action. Many readers will not need to be reminded of Weber's (1964:113) classic example of this point—an accidental collision of two bicycles which, despite the noticeable physical movement of both riders' bodies, does not count as action because the collision event entirely unintended.

Because the sources of intentional action reside in the meanings held in consciousness, they are irreducibly social. The centrality of language here can scarcely be overestimated. Subjective meaning and intention are experienced and expressed in linguistic or other symbolic terms. As dramatically illustrated by the feral children we visited earlier, language is only acquired through learning in interaction with others, and is thus inherently social.

Obviously, language gives the actor enormous power to understand the actions of others and to communicate plans of action. If I intend to do something, I can explain to myself and to others what I intend to do or, alternatively, I can intend not to tell others. Even physiologically motivated activities (e.g., eating, elimination) involve social meaning, as human variation across time and culture in taste, etiquette and norms of privacy attest (see, e.g., Elias 2000 [1939]). Action is thus a property of the self, and the self has its genesis in social interaction (Berger and Luckmann 1967; Mead 1934; Staudinger 1996). For present purposes, we can leave aside the parallel question of whether some classes of intentional human acts may not be considered social (see Dannefer 1999; Dawe 1978; Meacham 1984).

The externalization of conscious intentions in action is the exercise of what sociologists of age and the life course are fond of calling agency. Yet in the life-course and gerontological literatures (and in other literatures as well), the concept of agency is overused and often misused. It is often mobilized to account for "unexplained variance" and, simultaneously, to happily declare that individuals have a measure of existential freedom of choice that defies prediction (Dannefer and Huang 2017; Giddens 1984, 1991; Marshall 2005; Marshall and Clarke 2010). In fact, the philosophical question of freedom has no direct relation to agency, which becomes clear when we consider that what agency most fundamentally represents is the externalization of conscious intent in action. Intentionality is something that is continuously experienced in human consciousness, and is orthogonal to the number of degrees of freedom the actor perceives that she has. It is possessed equally by the nomad and the prisoner, the gig economy jockey and the artist. To assume that agency somehow amounts to "freedom of choice" is to misunderstand this fundamental condition (Dannefer 1999).

Similarly, it is important to recognize that agency is not something that individuals exercise on special and remarkable occasions (as in "deciding" to marry, look for a new job or join the military) any more than breathing is something one exercises only when singing a solo or pacing oneself in a yoga class or marathon. Rather, agency represents the constant and continuous expression of conscious intentions of action in everyday life. Often, intentionality is subordinated to habituated routines that do not require the full attention of conscious awareness, allowing for multitasking and subordinating some activities to habituated routines. Such complexity testifies further to the power of human cognition but does not change the reality of conscious intent and control over action.

HUMAN ACTIVITY ENTAILS IMAGINATION AND INNOVATION

Imagination and creativity are also continuous potentials of human activity. Creativity can be defined as the "ability to produce new ideas" (Russ and Fiorelli 2010). From a sociological perspective, a key word in this definition is "new". Whether or not something is "new" depends upon the stock of knowledge available to those in a given social world. Innumerable examples exist of "new" ideas that actually consist of the rediscovery or adoption of practices long taken-for-granted in another cultural setting.

If one considers what is required of the actual cognitive procedures involved in the creative process, that circumstance in which an invention already patented but unknown to the actor in question makes it no less creative. For some isolated hermit who has never seen one, "re-inventing the wheel" would be a creative act. It may not be a particularly socially valued act, but it would obviously be an exercise of creative human potential.

As a general activity of conscious effort, what scholars of creativity call "little-c creativity" (e.g., Merrotsky 2013), the creative process occurs all the time, in children as well as adults. While the great majority of creative activity thus goes unnoticed and unremarked, the human world is filled with the products of human creative endeavor—whether in spontaneously developing a new foxhole survival strategy in wartime or a new parenting tactic when confronted with a challenging teenager, or for the teenager, an innovative response to what she regards as restrictive parenting.

Despite the popular inclination to associate creativity with innovations of socially recognized value, doing so misunderstands the creative process in a way that seriously underestimates the creativity that pervades everyday life. Confronting those who "decry (little-c) creativity as a ridiculous democratization of the ideology of the genius", Hans Joas (1996:72) rightly notes that "a more obvious interpretation would be to consider the ideology of the genius as an undemocratic distortion of the idea of creativity".

More generally, the products of imagination and creativity can readily be seen in the ingenuity humans have deployed in devising ways to survive and thrive across the spectrum of physical environments, from the equator to the poles. This is why, as noted earlier, *homo sapiens* "has no species-specific environment, no environment firmly structured by its own instinctual organization" (Berger and Luckmann 1967:47). Human beings have established societies over much of the earth's surface—over more diverse conditions than any other species. Thus it is that, except perhaps for some human parasites and others who enjoy human company (such as the cockroach), humans are unique in establishing habitats from equatorial climates to the poles of the planet.

Variation in climatic conditions has its own sociosomatic effects. Mild versions of this can be seen in something as benign as the habituation of residents to climatic variation. For example, it is not uncommon to see residents of Los Angeles bundled up in wintry coats when the temperatures dips to 55 degrees Fahrenheit, while in Liverpool such a temperature may offer reason to sit outside one's favorite pub in short shirtsleeves. Such variations presumably reflect, to a large extent, habituated expectations and acclimatization of one's own body. At the same time, much more enduring and consequential effects of climatic variation upon the physical body also occur, including enduring long-term effects. As noted earlier, the physical demands of these divergent climatic and ecological conditions are argued to have led, through selective pressures, to environment-specific genetic adaptations that may in some cases influence aging and development (e.g., Beall 2000, 2007; Beall and Goldstein 1982).

Such conditions comprise one form of gene-environment interaction, a topic to which I return in Chapter 7. For the moment, it should be noted that such consequential and well-ordered variation in human response to different environmental conditions does nothing to change the commonly shared universals of human potentials. Individuals who have grown up in equatorial tribes in the Amazonian rain forest can live and function in Canada, and Northern Europeans can live out their lives in tribal rain-forest villages, as demonstrated by anthropologists who have "gone native" and decided to join societies they initially intended to study, whether isolated indigenous tribes like the Yanomama (Good and Chanoff 1991) or Japanese Geisha culture (Tedlock 1991).

THE CO-CONSTITUTION OF THE SELF AND SOCIAL RELATIONS

While the possibilities of human activity are distinguished from those of other species in that human action originates in conscious intent, that fact hardly exhausts the significance of human action. The discussion so far has assumed the operation of two fundamental and interrelated sets of processes that require explication.

Two primary effects of human action (paradoxically, they are largely unintended effects) are the co-constitution of self and of society. As Berger and Luckmann formulated it half a century ago, this co-constitutive process consists of three continuously occurring, dialectical moments: "man (sic) is a social product; society is a human product; society is an objective reality" (Berger and Luckmann 1967:61). It is only through human activity that society is created, and through this same set of interactional processes a sense of self develops within each human being. However, each of these processes involves its own distinct dynamics, and each warrants discussion.

Although it is frequently unnoticed by individuals in the world of everyday life, a central fact of human experience is that human beings must "exercise agency", must externalize their intentions in action in order for society to exist at all. Externalizing thought in action is necessary to communicate, and communication of some sort is necessary to create and sustain relations with others. Any society, however large or small, is based on the fact that its members are in interaction with one another, and communicating meaningfully with one another. If members of a social system stop interacting, the system will break down.

In acts that are so familiar that they occur without awareness of their effects, humans constantly produce and reproduce social relations while enacting the routines of everyday life, and those relations are patterned, and bounded. They comprise micro-level social systems. Irreducibly, those relations depend on purposeful human action and communication, and will not be sustained without it. It is through those relations that the most fundamental elements of social structure are constituted. Popular acknowledgments of this fundamental principle can be seen in the frequent allusions to the importance of continuous communication in maintaining relationships such as friendship or marriage (for a classic example, see Berger and Kellner's essay on marriage and the construction of reality [1964]). Events that suddenly impose a pause in social relations, such as the COVID pandemic, provide a real-time glimpse into the extent to which the actor's sense of reality depends on regular interaction, especially for individuals trapped or constricted in complete isolation—as indexed by the toll of such events on mental health (Banerjee and Rai 2020; Holt-Lunstad 2020; Pfefferbaum and North 2020).

Although every viable human society, however large or small, takes on the character of objective reality, societies actually are comprised of nothing but the material and social products of human activity and interaction patterns. When interaction patterns become established as stable, habitualized routines that make interaction relatively predictable and commonly typified and understood by multiple actors, they comprise *social institutions*. Thus, through acting purposefully in the world, the individual constitutes not only her own biography but also the social relations and established formations of social life that comprise a crucial part of her environment (Berger and Luckmann 1967; Dannefer 1999).

The ongoing processes that produce this sense of objectivity and taken-for-grantedness of social reality is to a large extent a massive enterprise of intricately interconnected self-fulfilling prophecies. Since human beings are deeply enmeshed in these activities in the course of daily life, they tend to go unnoticed. As Marshall McLuhan (1966:20) and others have noted, "We don't know who discovered water but we're pretty sure it wasn't a fish" (see Dannefer 2008:6). So it is with the force of social life in human development and aging. Everyday social relations are the invisible and unnoticed waters in which we are immersed.

In the course of pursuing the most mundane of daily activities and tasks, a concomitant effect is to reinforce the patterns of social interaction and structures of belief and "knowledge" that constitute society. One's action conveys an expectation for the other, and the other responds in a way that reinforces the expectations. Habitualized patterns of interaction develop and are sustained, and when these are broadly shared and regularly reproduced, we can say they have become institutionalized (Berger and Luckmann 1967). Such patterns of interaction are both part of, and are also the mechanism of transmission of, what Berger and Luckmann term the "social stock of knowledge" that brings order to the experience of interaction in everyday life and underlies a sense of the taken-for-granted reality in any society.

The operation of processes of world-constitution can be readily discerned at the level of face-to-face interaction. There, it is possible to trace the formation and disintegration of the power of groups through the structure and content of members' interactions. Family therapists, professional coaches, organizational consultants and other such "human process" professionals are analysts and facilitators of such micro-level processes of "reality production"—although of course such processes do not depend at all on such professionals. In sum, actions intended only to meet one's mundane daily needs and fulfill one's daily obligations—whether punching a time clock or preparing dinner for children— pervasively and continuously sustain existing social relationships and sometimes create new ones. Society is, as Berger and Luckmann put it, a human product. The failure of human beings to recognize social forms and relationships as a product of their own activities is perhaps the most profound of several meanings assigned to the term alienation: an inability to recognize the products of one's own activity as having been produced by the actor in question (Marx 1978 [1932]:85). However, it is not only the social system itself that is constituted through the interaction process; so is the self and personhood of the individual, and so are the individual developmental trajectories of system members. The examples of feral children reviewed in Chapter 2 demonstrate dramatically, albeit tragically, the Meadian principle of the social genesis of the self (Mead 1934).

Such cases demonstrate the fundamental requirement of a social and linguistic environment for children to become human beings. Similarly, cross-cultural work demonstrates the power of the social world in constituting its members as persons, and in determining their trajectories of development and aging (see, e.g., Fernandez 2015; Rogoff 2011; Rogoff, Mejia-Arauz, and Correa-Chavez 2015).

The constitution of the self through action and in social interaction has been extensively detailed in social theory (see, e.g. Baars 1991; Berger and Luckmann 1967; Bourdieu 1977; Brandstädter 1998; Dannefer and Perlmutter 1990; Giddens 1984; Mead 1934). A general consequence of action in a social system is the actor's formation and sustenance of a sense of identity and selfhood, not just as an actor, but as an objective component—a member, a role occupant—of the system of social relations that her action is co-constituting.

This consequence thus entails the role of the self as object in relation to the self as agent, or, in Mead's (1934:173–6) classic discussion, the me in relation to the I. Taking oneself as an object means seeing the self as the actor imagines that others see her, as indicated by Mead's famous phrase, "taking the role of the other" (1934:152–9). This is a definitional characteristic of having a self. To have a self is to be able to reflect upon one's own being in the world—to stand outside of oneself, to converse with oneself. To varying degrees, humans engage in this recursive process whether acting in complete isolation or interacting with and constituting social relations with others. Thus, the human actor's sense of her own position within the system of social relations that she is co-constituting is an integral moment—arguably the critical moment—in the dialectic of action. It defines her sense of where she stands in relation to others, and it is in that relation that the actor continuously defines and redefines herself.

Whether or not by intent, other group members unavoidably make appraisals of each member's characteristics and abilities. Inclusion or exclusion from activities or future opportunities may be based on those appraisals; and the self-appraisal of every aspect of the member in question is likely to be influenced by the informal and formal messages offered by other members. Often, age—whether one is 6 or 11, whether one is 31 or 101— becomes a component in the appraisals of an actor made by both by herself and by others. As we will see, the relevance of age to an actor's sense of self is something that varies enormously across different social systems.

In sum, actions intended only to meet one's mundane daily needs and fulfill one's daily obligations—whether punching a time clock or preparing dinner for children—have the concomitant effect of sustaining both one's sense of self, and the social systems within which one participates. One does not have to be preoccupied with age, nor even vaguely aware of it, for the regular processes of a given social system to shape one's sense of age identity, nor one's age-related life-course opportunities. In subsequent sections, we will draw on research literatures in the sociology of education, work, medicine and long-term care, all of which contain examples of how age is utilized by the social organizations that define the context of everyday life—schools, work organizations, hospitals and nursing homes—to shape both socially structured opportunities and internal appraisal of those opportunities.

The foregoing discussion has emphasized the centrality and power of human intention and action, and the dynamic, processual and conditional aspects of reality construction. This should not be taken to mean—as those with a superficial understanding of constructivism have sometimes done—that individual actors are somehow free to create or remake their social worlds in just the way they would like. This is in part because actions generally have unintended consequences (Giddens 1984; Merton 1968) but that is not the primary reason. Much more important is the fact that action can never proceed from any kind of existential *tabula rasa*. Rather, human intentions are deeply shaped by the social world in which the actor is located, and thus the expression of those intentions in action primarily serve to reproduce the contours of the world. Thus, the self-society relation is always and necessarily asymmetrical (Dannefer 1999).

For this reason, intentional human action under reasonably stable, everyday social conditions has as a primary effect the *reproduction* of the social reality, knowledge and structures that governs those conditions. If everyday life operates as a giant, symphonic self-fulfilling prophecy, it is a process not easy to derail. This is precisely the understanding of reproduction theory. It is core to Bourdieu's notion of habitus, which is both *structured* (by the internalized and embodied practices, routines and knowledge governing daily experience) and *structuring* (by the externalization of actions which reinforce and reproduce the shared social realities; see Bourdieu 1977, 1986; Wacquant 2005). This is generally consistent with Berger and Luckmann's dialectical framework, including a shared emphasis on embodiment—that is, on physical as well as psychological aspects of internalization. Habitus entails both "the externalization of internality and the internalization of externality" (Wacquant 2005:318); it is both a "structured structure" (structured by the internalized of the social world) and a "structuring structure" (structuring by organizing intentions, activity and interaction in a way that contributes to the ongoing reproduction of the existing social world [Pallas and Jennings 2009:218]). These circumstances ensure further that intentional action and human agency will always be asymmetrically subordinate to the social circumstances in which they are expressed (Dannefer 1999).

Since the world that is internalized is a world-taken-for-granted, objectified and largely naturalized—assumed to be part of the natural order of things—everyday life consciousness operates within the frame of that world and can scarcely question it or recognize its features. This adds to the reasons that social change, especially intentionally conceived and desired change, can be so difficult to achieve.

Thus, while the constructivist (Berger and Luckmann 1967) and social constitutionalist (Baars 1991) perspectives that articulate human processes of world-construction offer a framework and analysis that departs radically from the unreflective assumptions of the functional-organismic nexus, they nevertheless describe processes and social dynamics that are, in stable social orders, highly resilient and by definition conservative—operating to legitimate and reproduce dominant institutions and practices and the interests that maintain them (e.g., Bourdieu 1986; Erdmans 2004:79; Giddens 1984:8).

SUMMARY: FOUR QUESTIONS

Why begin a book on human aging and development with discussions of ferality and fetalization and with other perhaps esoteric-sounding and arcane terms and concepts? The answer is that if, as Herbert Blumer (1969:48) rightly reminds us, "the genuine mark of an empirical science is to *respect the nature of its empirical world*" and "to fit its problems . . . its concepts and its theories to that world", then such a beginning is unavoidable and necessary. It entails a stripping away of the largely unquestioned and unspoken paradigmatic assumptions of the "normal science" of development and aging, which have too often been imported from other disciplines and fields (see, e.g., Morss 1990, 1995;

Shapin 2010) and that conform scientific work to the unreflected assumptions of scientists' daily life and culture.

The principles of exterogestation, neoteny and world-construction describe elemental aspects of the nature and dynamic potentials of the organisms on which human development is based. Although these principles must therefore be acknowledged as foundational, such acknowledgment hardly solves the problem of developing a sound approach to development and aging; rather, it generates new problems. Specifically, it gives rise to four domains of questions to which the subsequent sections of this work are addressed: the first two within the domain of straightforward empirical science, and the latter two in the domain of critical reflection on the work of science and its relation to human interests. These questions are discussed further here.

SOCIAL FORCES IN THE LIFE COURSE: HOW DOES SOCIAL STRUCTURE ORGANIZE DEVELOPMENT AND AGE?

If the nature of development and aging is not structured and programmed by the internal growth processes of the human organism, what does structure it? How are we to understand the principles of their organization, and the fact that fairly common patterns of growth and aging can be discerned in most human populations? The macro-dynamics of social context that provide one set of answers to this question are examined in Chapters 4 through 6.

THE MATTER OF SOCIOSOMATICS: HOW DO SOCIAL FORCES IMPACT GROWTH AND AGE OF BODY AND MIND?

The structural parameters set by exterogestation, neoteny and world-construction provide only the first level of analysis of how the physical body's development and aging are affected by social dynamics. We are now learning the extent to which many aspects of experience over the life course shape the physical body on a daily basis, right down to matters such as neuron generation and gene expression. This matter was touched on in Chapter 2 and will be the primary subject of Chapter 7.

SCIENCE AS HUMAN ACTIVITY AND AS IDEOLOGY: HOW ARE UNDERSTANDINGS OF AGE CONSTRAINED BY SOCIAL, POLITICAL AND CULTURAL INTERESTS THAT SHAPE BOTH POPULAR AND SCIENTIFIC NARRATIVES?

Part of what must be recognized is that science itself is a human enterprise. Scientific activity, its disciplined care and rigor notwithstanding, is human activity. It reflects the particular assumptions and experiences of the scientist, which are organized by paradigmatic knowledge and by the economic and political forces that allocate resources to scientific endeavor. Paradigmatic knowledge is essential and valuable to organize the work of science, yet—as is well known and as we have already seen—a cost of paradigmatic knowledge is the restrictions it places on inquiry. That is why neither neoteny, exterogestation, nor any other terms referring to these principles of development are to be found in any textbooks on infancy, child development or human development. They are largely confined to specialized literatures in physical anthropology and evolutionary and developmental biology. How is it possible that such distinctive, foundational features of the species *homo sapiens* go entirely unremarked in the scientific accounts that purport to describe the nature of the species? I take up these problems in Chapters 8 and 9.

WHAT IS TO BE DONE? AGE AND SOCIOLOGICAL IMAGINATION

Dealing with these three sets of issues is essential, yet it does not answer the bigger question, the "so what" question, the notorious "Lenin" question, "What is to be done?" In the final chapters, I explore the implications of these arguments for future research, and also for how to think imaginatively about age and the life course in the social worlds of everyday life.

REFERENCES

Amery, C. F. 1892. "Instinct." *Science* 20(512): 300–2.

Archer, Margaret S. 2017. "Does Intensive Morphogenesis Foster Human Capacities or Liabilities?" Pp. 115–35 in *Morphogenesis and Human Flourishing*, edited by M. S. Archer. Cham, Switzerland: Springer.

Baars, Jan. 1991. "The Challenge of Critical Gerontology: The Problem of Social Constitution." *Journal of Aging Studies* 5(3): 219–43.

Banerjee, Debanjan, and Mayank Rai. 2020. "Social Isolation in Covid-19: The Impact of Loneliness." *International Journal of Social Psychiatry* 66(6): 525–27. doi: 10.1177/0020764020922269.

Beall, Cynthia M. 2000. "Oxygen Saturation Increases During Childhood and Decreases During Adulthood Among High Altitude Native Tibetans Residing at 3800-4200 m." *High Altitude Medicine and Biology* 1(1): 25-32.

Beall, Cynthia M. 2007. "Two Routes to Functional Adaptation: Tibetan and Andean High-Altitude Natives." *Proceedings of the National Academy of Sciences of the United States of America* 15(1): 8655–60.

Beall, Cynthia M. and Melvyn Goldstein, 1982. "Biological Function, Activity and Dependency Among Elderly Sherpa in the Nepal Himalayas." *Social Science and Medicine* 16(2): 135-140.

Berger, Peter L., and Hannsfried Kellner. 1964. "Marriage and the Construction of Reality: An Exercise in the Microsociology of Knowledge." *Diogenes* 12: 1–24.

Berger, Peter L., and Thomas Luckmann. 1967. *The Social Construction of Reality: A Systematic Treatise in the Sociology of Knowledge*. New York: Anchor.

Berlin, Isaiah. 1939. *Karl Marx*. Oxford, UK: Oxford University Press.

Blumer, Herbert. 1969. *Symbolic Interactionism: Perspective and Method*. Englewood Cliffs, NJ: Prentice Hall.

Bourdieu, Pierre. 2013 (1977). *Outline of a Theory of Practice*. Cambridge, UK: Cambridge University Press.

Bourdieu, Pierre. 1986. *Distinction: A Social Critique of the Judgement of Taste*. New York: Routledge.

Brandstädter, Joachim. 1998. "Action Theory in Developmental Psychology." Pp. 807–64 in *Handbook of Child Psychology: Theoretical Models of Human Development*. 5th edition, edited by W. Damon and R. M. Lerner. New York: Wiley.

Broughton, John M. 1987. *Critical Theories of Psychological Development*. New York: Springer Publishing Company.

Burawoy, Michael. 2019. *Symbolic Violence: Conversations with Bourdieu*. Chapel Hill, NC: Duke University Press.

Collins, Randall. 2004. *Interaction Ritual Chains*. Princeton, NJ: Princeton University Press.

Dannefer, Dale. 1999. "Freedom Isn't Free: Power, Alienation, and the Consequences of Action." Pp. 105–32 in *Action & Development: Origins and Functions of Intentional Self-Development*, edited by J. Brandstadter and R. Lerner. New York: Springer Publishing Company.

Dannefer, Dale. 2008. "The Waters We Swim: Everyday Social Processes, Macro Structural Realities, and Human Aging." Pp. 3–22 in *Social Structure and Aging: Continuing Challenges*, edited by K. Warner Schaie and Ronald P. Abeles. New York: Springer Publishing Company.

Dannefer, Dale, and Wenxuan Huang. 2017. "Precarity, Inequality, and the Problem of Agency in the Study of the Life Course." *Innovation in Aging* 1(3): igx027.

Dannefer, Dale, and Marion Perlmutter. 1990. "Development as a Multidimensional Process: Individual and Social Constituents." *Human Development* 33(2–3): 108–37.

Dawe, Alan. 1978. "Theories of Social Action." Pp. 362–417 in *A History of Sociological Analysis*, edited by T. Bottomore and R. Nisbet. New York: Basic Books.

Du Bois, W.E.B. 1994 (1903). *The Souls of Black Folk*. Mineola, NY: Dover Publications.

Elias, Norbert. 2000 (1939). *The Civilizing Process*. New York: Blackwell Publishing.

Erdmans, Mary P. 2004. *The Grasinski Girls: The Choices They Had and the Choices They Made*. Athens, OH: Ohio University Press.

Fernandez, David Lorgente. 2015. "Children's Everyday Learning by Assuming Responsibility for Others: Indigenous Practices as a Cultural Heritage Across Generations." Pp. 54–89 in *Advances in Child Development and Behavior*. Vol. 49, edited by M. Correa-Chávez, R. Mejía-Arauz, and B. Rogoff. New York: Elsevier.

Giddens, Anthony. 1984. *The Constitution of Society: Outline of the Theory of Structuration*. Berkeley, CA: University of California Press.

Giddens, Anthony. 1991. *Modernity and Self-Identity: Self and Society in the Late Modern Age*. Stanford, CA: Stanford University Press.

Gilbert, Scott F., and David Epel. 2008. *Ecological Developmental Biology: Integrating Epigenetics, Medicine and Evolution*. Sunderland, MA: Sinauer Associates.

Gluckman, Petter D., and Mark A. Hanson. 2005. *Mismatch: The Developmental Origins of Health and Disease*. New York: Oxford University Press.

Goldfarb, Ben. 2018. "Beavers Rebooted." *Science* 360(6393): 1058–1061. https://doi.org/10.1126/science.360.6393.1058.

Good, Kenneth R., and David Chanoff. 1991. *Into the Heart: One Man's Pursuit of Love and Knowledge among the Yanomama*. New York, NY: Simon & Schuster.

Holt-Lunstad, Julianne. 2020. "The Double Pandemic of Social Isolation and COVID-19: Cross-Sector Policy Must Address Both | Health Affairs Blog." *Health Affairs*. Retrieved November 15, 2020 (https://www.healthaffairs.org/do/10.1377/hblog20200609.53823/full).

Joas, Hans. 1996. *The Creativity of Action*. New York: Polity.

Marshall, Victor W. 2005. "Agency, Events, and Structure at the End of the Life Course." *Advances in Life Course Research* 10(1): 57–91.

Marshall, Victor W., and Philippa J. Clarke. 2010. "Agency and Social Structure in Aging and Life-Course Research." Pp. 294–305 in *The Sage Handbook of Social Gerontology*, edited by C. Phillipson and D. Dannefer. Thousand Oaks, CA: Sage.

Marx, Karl. 1978 (1932). "Economic and Philosophical Manuscripts of 1844." Pp. 66–125 in *The Marx-Engels Reader*. 2nd edition, edited by R. C. Tucker. New York: Norton.

Marx, Karl. 2015 (1867). *Capital a Critique of Political Economy Volume I Book One: The Process of Production of Capital*. Moscow, USSR: Progress Publishers.

Mcauley, Christopher A. 2019. *The Spirit vs. the Souls: Max Weber, W.E.B. DuBois and the Politics of Scholarship*. Notre Dame, IN: Notre Dame Press.

McLuhan, Marshall. 1966. "Symposium Discussion: Cited in Technology and World Trade: Proceedings of a Symposium." P. 29 in *National Bureau of Standards, U.S. Department of Trade*. Washington: U.S. Government Printing Office.

Meacham, John A. 1984. "The Social Basis of Intentional Action." *Human Development* 27(3–4): 119–24.

Mead, George H. 1934. *Mind, Self, and Society: From the Standpoint of a Social Behaviorist*. Chicago: University of Chicago Press.

Merrotsky, Peter. 2013. "A Note on Big-C and Little-c Creativity." *Creativity Research Journal* 25(4): 474–6. https://doi.org/10.1080/10400419.2013.843921.

Merton, Robert. 1968. *Social Theory and Social Structure*. New York: Free Press.

Mills, C. Wright. 1940. "Situated Actions and Vocabularies of Motive." *American Sociological Review* 5(6): 904–13.

Morss, John. 2017 (1990). *The Biologising of Childhood: Developmental Psychology and the Darwinian Myth*. London: Routledge.

Morss, John. 1995. *Growing Critical: Alternatives to Developmental Psychology*. London: Routledge.

Pallas, Aaron M., and Jennifer L. Jennings. 2009. "Cumulative Knowledge about Cumulative Advantage." *Swiss Journal of Sociology* 35(2): 211–29.

Parsons, Talcott. 1951. *The Social System*. New York: Free Press of Glencoe.

Pfefferbaum, Betty, and Carol S. North. 2020. "Mental Health and the Covid-19 Pandemic." *New England Journal of Medicine* 383(6): 510–12. doi: 10.1056/NEJMp2008017.

Richard, P. B. 1983. "Mechanisms and Adaptation in the Constructive Behaviour of the Beaver (Castor Fiber L.)." *Acta Zoologica Fennica* 174: 105–8.

Rogoff, Barbara. 2003. *The Cultural Nature of Human Development*. New York: Oxford University Press.

Rogoff, Barbara. 2011. *Developing Destinies: A Mayan Midwife and Town*. New York: Oxford University Press.

Rogoff, Barbara, Rebeca Mejia-Arauz, and Maricela Correa-Chavez. 2015. "A Cultural Paradigm: Learning by Observing and Pitching." Pp. 1–22 in *Advances in Child Development and Behavior*. Vol. 49, edited by M. Correa-Chávez, R. Mejía-Arauz, and B. Rogoff. New York: Elsevier.

Ruedemann, Rudolf, and W. J. Schoonmaker. 1938. "Beaver-Dams as Geologic Agents." *Science New Series* 88(2292): 523–5.

Russ, Sandra W., and Julia A. Fiorelli. 2010. "Developmental Approaches to Creativity." Pp. 233–49 in *The Cambridge Handbook of Creativity*, edited by J. C. Kaufman and R. J. Sternberg. Cambridge, UK: Cambridge University Press.

Shapin, Steven. 2010. *Never Pure: Historical Studies of Science as If It Was Produced by People with Bodies, Situated in Time, Space, Culture, and Society, and Struggling for Credibility and Authority.* Baltimore, MD: Johns Hopkins University Press.

Shutz, Alfred. 1971. *The Phenomenology of the Social World.* Evanston, IL: Northwestern University Press.

Simmel, George. 1950 (1908). *The Sociology of Georg Simmel* (K. Wolf, Trans.). New York: Free Press.

Staudinger, Usula. M. 1996. "Wisdom and the Social-Interactive Foundation of the Mind." Pp. 276–315 in *Interactive Minds: Life-Span Perspectives on the Social Foundation of Cognition*, edited by P. B. Baltes and U. M. Staudinger. New York: Cambridge University Press.

Stetsenko, Anna. 2004. "Introduction to Vygotsky's 'The Tool and Sign in Child Development.'" Pp. 499–510 in *Essential Vygotsky*, edited by R. Rieber and D. Robinson. New York: Kluwer Academic/Plenum.

Stetsenko, Anna. 2016. *The Transformative Mind: Expanding Vygotsky's Approach to Development and Education.* Cambridge, UK: Cambridge University Press.

Tedlock, Barbara. 1991. "From Participant Observation to the Observation of Participation: The Emergence of Narrative Ethnography." *Journal of Anthropological Research* 47(1): 69–94.

Vygotsky, Lev S. 1978. *Mind in Society: The Development of Higher Psychological Processes.* Cambridge, MA: Harvard University Press.

Wacquant, Loic. 2005. "Habitus." Pp. 317–21 In *International Encyclopedia of Economic Sociology*, edited by J. Beckert and M. Zafirovski. London: Routledge.

Weber, Max. 1964. *The Theory of Social and Economic Organization* (A. M. Henderson and T. Parsons, Trans.). New York: Free Press.

Wexler, Philip. 1996 (1983). *Critical Social Psychology.* London: Routledge.

Wilsson, Lars. 1971. "Observations and Experiments on the Ethology of the European Beaver." *Viltrevy* 8: 115–266.

Żurowski, Wirgiliusz. 1992. "Building Activity of Beavers." *Acta Theriologica* 37(4): 403–11.

CHAPTER 4
THE SOCIAL ORGANIZATION OF DEVELOPMENT AND AGE, I: HISTORICAL AND CULTURAL VARIATIONS

The paradigmatic view that continues to dominate both contemporary popular culture and the human sciences assumes that human development and aging are largely governed by a fixed and universal set of biologically driven, chronometric imperatives programmed into the human organism. In the foregoing chapters, I have shown that this view is demonstrably incorrect because in the human case, such "natural" imperatives are relatively few. We have seen that throughout the life course, humans are *hard-wired for flexibility* with regard to key characteristics and many aspects of developmental change (Rogoff 2003).

Thus, in contrast to the rigid stages of ontogenetic development and instinctually preprogrammed behaviors of many other species, human development and aging are malleable, flexible and contingent, characterized by the indeterminacy of *world-openness*. Human life trajectories are constituted through intentional, purposeful action rather than instinct-guided behavior and fixed ontogenetic stages. This indeterminacy raises the obvious question: If human development and aging are not structured and organized by internally regulated organismic imperatives, what does structure them? What accounts for their patterning? What other kinds of factors operate to produce the manifest orderliness of humans in terms of age and development?

Although it is important to recognize this question, the answer to it is actually quite straightforward. Development and age are in substantial part organized by the particularities of one's *experience* in everyday life activities, and such everyday experience virtually always occurs in a *particular social context, and it takes its practices, its rhythms and its meaning from that context*. This includes not only the entire structure of the social world with its meaning structures, rules and routines, but also its material aspects, involving matters such as nutrition, climatic and environmental conditions, as well as physical safety and exertion.

CONCEPTUALIZING AND ASSESSING SOCIAL CONTEXT

Social context is thus crucially important. But how do we grasp this elusive domain of reality, "social context"? Part of the problem with this term, perhaps especially in developmental and life-course studies, is that it often seems to reference some ill-defined and amorphous but mostly rather unimposing entity (Dannefer 1992) that is vaguely "out there". In actuality, social context is neither unimposing nor amorphous. It only seems that way because we are so deeply immersed in it, in everyday life, that its continuous impact remains largely overlooked and its effects unrecognized. Since, too often, there is an intellectual contentment with leaving the matter of context as a rather vaguely apprehended domain, both of these adjectives—"unimposing" and "amorphous"—warrant comment.

First, social context is anything but unimposing. It is ever-present, all-encompassing and provides the linguistic and cultural frames that organize consciousness and activity. Part of the issue, as noted earlier, is precisely that its constant pervasiveness makes it largely unnoticeable, and the onslaught of stimuli and constraints that it imposes are generally difficult to discern as a systemic set of forces. Everyone is immersed in social context, beginning in prenatal experience and extending through the life course. In many of its consequential manifestations, context is so intermixed in the continuous experience of human activity and human actors—even for trained social and behavioral scientists—that it goes unnoticed. Again, it is like McLuhan's fish, who lived its life without ever once noticing water.

Thus, as described earlier, context provides an ordering structure within which human action and human actors are habituated, so that it seems as taken-for-granted as the air we all breathe—as pervasive and integral to everyday experience and as "natural" as water is to the fish. It is the production site for the "world-constructing" processes described in Chapter 3. Its everyday taken-for-grantedness is central to how social systems are maintained, and for those whose lives are habitualized into relatively comfortable routines, its familiarity may often make it seem incidental. Yet what is accomplished through this continuous process entails nothing less than the reproduction of the social order and of virtually all human "knowledge", including knowledge of what is plausible, what is relevant and interesting to notice, and, significantly, the rules (including age-based rules) that specify acceptable parameters of behavior.

If any confirmation of the ubiquitous power of socially constructed taken-for-grantedness is needed, the reader is invited to perform his or her own experiment by violating an established social script or norm (e.g., of physical modesty or of civility and politeness, or just try standing or lying down on a table in a respectable restaurant). It was as a strategy for discovering and demonstrating the power of the unnoticed rules governing everyday social life that Harold Garfinkel developed ethnomethodology, an approach to social inquiry that deliberately disrupts the taken-for-grantedness of the everyday, in order to discover its boundaries and its obdurate character. In short, social context provides the dynamics that define what is socially possible, and that frame and constitute the lives and experience of individual human beings.

Second, although the term "social context" also references a complex domain of reality, it is hardly *amorphous*. Rather, it is *systemic* and in large part highly predictable, in patterns that extend intricately across multiple levels of social organization, from micro to macro. The dynamics through which it shapes experience operate at each of these levels, and involve interactions across levels.

As we consider the range of social forces that organize and impact the developmental patterns and experiences of aging, the most fundamental and universal forces are to be found at the micro-level. Indeed, when one looks across the historical and cultural ranges of known human social arrangements, many societies have lacked the kind of large-scale and depersonalized organization that are often associated with the term "macro", even though they will, of course, necessarily have some measure of overarching structure that defines and orders the lives of its members and its existence as a society.

Microsocial interaction is fundamental because the direct agentic action of human beings is present in virtually every human situation, in every society, throughout human history— even virtual ones and, albeit indirectly, those driven by algorithms. However, micro-level dynamics are also the most difficult to detect precisely because, as just recounted, they are so pervasively part of our experience, and they are also dynamically interactive. For this reason, I begin at the other extreme—at the "30,000-foot view" of the social landscape. From such a distance, one can see most clearly the stark differences in patterns of human development over the life course that are found in different social contexts, and we can begin to glimpse a sense of how diverse social practices lead to diversity in the experience of age and life-course development.

HISTORICAL VARIATIONS IN LIFE-COURSE PATTERNING

Examining age and life-course patterns in varying historical and cultural contexts makes clear both the short timespan of cultural memory and the ethnocentric impulses of local knowledge. It provides an informative window onto the context-dependency of patterns that are often assumed to be "natural", and hence again part of the "social stock of knowledge" (Berger and Luckmann 1967)—integral to what "everyone knows".

The negative perceptions of old age that were illustrated with ageist jokes and incidents at the beginning of Chapter 1 comprise an entrenched element of the contemporary stock of knowledge, despite the presence of contrary evidence and alternative counter-narratives that seek to present later life in upbeat terms (e.g., Castel 2018; Gallagher 2012; Rowe and Kahn 1997).

It remains a familiar staple of taken-for-granted contemporary knowledge that as one moves through the life course, living into older ages is mainly bad news—cognitive decline as well as physical decline form an implicit logical basis for social stigmatization, as does the latent feeling that elders impose an inordinate cost on society. Thus, the basis for gloom is multidimensional (see, e.g. Abramson 2015; Billig 1987; Callahan 1995; Carr 2019; Davenhill 2019; Elias 1985; Peterson 1999, 2005; Samuel 2017). Yet a view of the meaning and significance in other historical and cultural settings make clear that the present-day experience of aging is not so endemic to human nature as it is to the nature of contemporary social forms.

BEFORE INDUSTRIALIZATION: OLDER PEOPLE IN TRADITIONAL AND PREMODERN CONTEXTS

In reviewing the evidence from historically diverse settings, I must begin with the disclaimer that I am not a historian. As a sociologist, I make no claim to mastering the scope, intensity and complexity of historical scholarship. The following review of historical evidence risks overlooking key linkages or nuances that an adequately or fully informed historical approach would require. Nevertheless, there is now quite a long tradition of cross-disciplinary fertilization in life-course studies (e.g., Bengtson 2016; Bengtson and Achenbaum 1993; Hareven 2013 [1978]; Riley, Kahn, and Foner 1994) that has been mutually provocative and productive.

Thus, I begin with the caveat that the subject matter of "history" covers extraordinarily long periods of time lived through in as many different places as communities of human beings are found, and in each of those time and places, it covers all the complexity and diversity of social practices and human lives. Thus, even well-informed accounts of "how things were in the past" are certain to be incomplete, and to adumbrate some elements of past social arrangements while arguably neglecting others. Historical generalizations—even when limited to a specific time period and locale—thus mask considerable variability. Nevertheless, historical scholarship typically identifies discernible trends, markers, themes and patterns, even as it may identify exceptions or qualifying complexities to those general patterns. Given the purposes and limits of the current project, I must necessarily focus on the primary character of the contexts under discussion, at the same time recognizing that such a broad overview cannot do justice to the rich diversity of experience in every human context.

Yet one does not have to go far back in time, nor even to go too far geographically, to find social contexts within which the expected capabilities and roles of older people follow quite a different trajectory than that implied by the current narrative of marginalization, irrelevance and decline. As recently as 150 years ago, the activities and engagement of older people in North America and Europe looked very different than they do currently. Healthy older people were typically economically engaged, and notions such as "retirement" or "disengagement" were all but nonexistent. Elders were also often seen as sources of wisdom in matters such as health and virtuous living (Achenbaum 1978; Fischer 1978; Haber and Gratton 1994; Simmons 1945). For individuals who survived and remained relatively healthy, this apparently led to a very different experience of old age than the sense of disengagement and irrelevance that currently holds sway.

Although we have no systematic psychometric test results nor standardized life satisfaction scores for pre-20th-century elders, it is plausible to speculate that for many, the personal sense of social importance and efficacy was very different than that experienced by contemporary retirees and elders, who often express feelings of marginalization or exclusion (Mann 2001). Even the clothing and hairdressing (e.g., white-powdered wigs) fashions of the period were designed to make individuals look older and to flatter the features of older people (Fischer 1978). According to Dychtwald:

Men's clothing was cut in a way that emphasized the posture and build of the elderly; narrow and rounded shoulders, broad hips and waist, and coat backs designed to make the spine appear to be bent by the weight of many years.

As for women's fashions . . . dresses also stressed mature features. Heavy swirling skirts accentuated broad hips, and those who lacked the pear shape of advanced years were encouraged to add hoops and whalebone extenders. The popular empire-line dress, form-fitting until just under the breast, did not discriminate against a spreading torso.

(2000:9–10)

It is possible to overstate the case; the existence of social arrangements that privilege and flatter old age should clearly not be taken as evidence of a generalized "golden age" of old age in the West or elsewhere, as had been proposed by the now largely debunked modernization theory of aging (Cowgill and Holmes 1972) and related works (see Katz 1996 for a critical review). Even in traditional societies that claimed to venerate elderhood, old age was often not an easy time (Cole 1992:62–4; Demos 1978:264; Goldstein and Beall 1981; Hashimoto 1996; Parkin 2003).

Nor was respect for elders applied universally. In substantial part, the status of older persons derived from their control over economic resources. In preindustrial, agrarian contexts, those who controlled wealth and resources were typically in the senior generation, but it does not follow that all elders were affluent. Many who survived to old age lived in abject poverty, and others' lives were shortened by severe want.

How older people were treated clearly reflected such variation in resources. This could be seen, for example, in the differential treatment of older men even in public records, indexed by the use of the pejorative "old" to replace first names. As historian John Demos recounts:

The distinction was one of social rank, pure and simple. Thus the man listed as Simon Stone (age 72) was wealthy, a deacon of the Watertown church and frequently a town officer, whereas 'old Knapp' (age 74) was a sometime carpenter of little means.

(1978:S276–7; see also Quadagno 1986:131)

Thus, the idea that older people were accorded respect may be in substantial part an artifact of the confound of wealth and age, and one that eclipses the circumstances of the many less visible older people, often including widows and men who had little in the way of either status or resources (Cole 1992:51–5; Haber and Gratton 1994; Walker 1981). Moreover, even visibly affluent and "economically powerful" elders sometimes encountered financial precarity and anxiety—often around exchange arrangements involving old-age care and property inheritance (e.g., Hareven 1994).

Such complexities notwithstanding, there seems to be little question that two centuries ago, the kinds of opportunities and meanings that defined the lives of individuals who survived to old age and their positions in society were dramatically different from the present (see, e.g., Achenbaum 1978, 2010; Fischer 1978; Laslett and Wall 1972; Samuel 2017; Stearns 1976; Troyansky 2015).

How did the shift in the experience of old age occur? What factors led to a situation where "disengagement" has been scientifically advanced as a universal stage of human development, and where older people are normatively and in many societies legally excluded from key forms of economic and social participation? European and American historians who agree that a dramatic shift did indeed occur have debated vigorously both its timing and the kind of factors that accounted for it. At least three broad types of hypotheses have been proposed, which can be termed cultural, technological and demographic.

Some scholars, notably David Hackett Fischer (1978), emphasized the emergence of a *new set of philosophical ideas* adumbrating individual rights and providing the foundation for a culture of individual dignity and freedom, associated with the French and American revolutions, which were argued to undermine the traditional structures of gerontocratic power and influence. By contrast, Andrew Achenbaum (1978, 2010) has emphasized various aspects of *scientific and technological advance* associated with the industrial revolution and progress in science through the 19th century, putting the inflection point of change close to a century later.

Both Fischer and Achenbaum also noted the importance of changes resulting from the *demographic transition*, as have others (Laslett 1977; Laslett and Wall 1972; Uhlenberg 1974, 1978). In 1790, no more than 3% of the population was over 65, and octogenarians were extremely rare. No one could doubt their demonstrated "life success" in surviving the vicissitudes of seven or more decades of living, during a time when death was not correlated with old age but could be experienced at any age—a frequent theme of colonial sermons (Cole 1992:61–4). Thus, the very fact of survival alone may have gone a considerable distance in qualifying elders as possessing expertise in matters of wisdom and successful living and aging—an appraisal further reinforced if a socioeconomic gradient in mortality were operative.

Before the ascendancy of modern medical expertise early in the 20th century, it was the elders, not often ineffectual physicians, who were defined as the experts in matters of health and longevity (Achenbaum 1978:11–16). This may have been especially true for elder women, who had experience with childbirth and infant care at a time when "great prestige was accorded fertility and survival" (Cole 1992:53).

Figure 4.1 presents age pyramids for the US in 1850, 1950 and 2000, making clear the dramatic transformation occurring over the relatively brief span of 150 years with regard to the likelihood of survival into old age, and marking the demographic transition. The figure makes clear that both the absolute numbers and the proportion of surviving elders have grown dramatically. It is no longer such a big deal to be 75 or even 85. Indeed, in many societies, those over 85 currently represent the fastest growing age group.

A plausible case can be made that each of these factors—cultural, economic, scientific and demographic—contributed to the transformation in the circumstances and opportunities available to older people. In particular, it seems clear that numerous developments in science and technology made strong and independent contributions to the change. Of

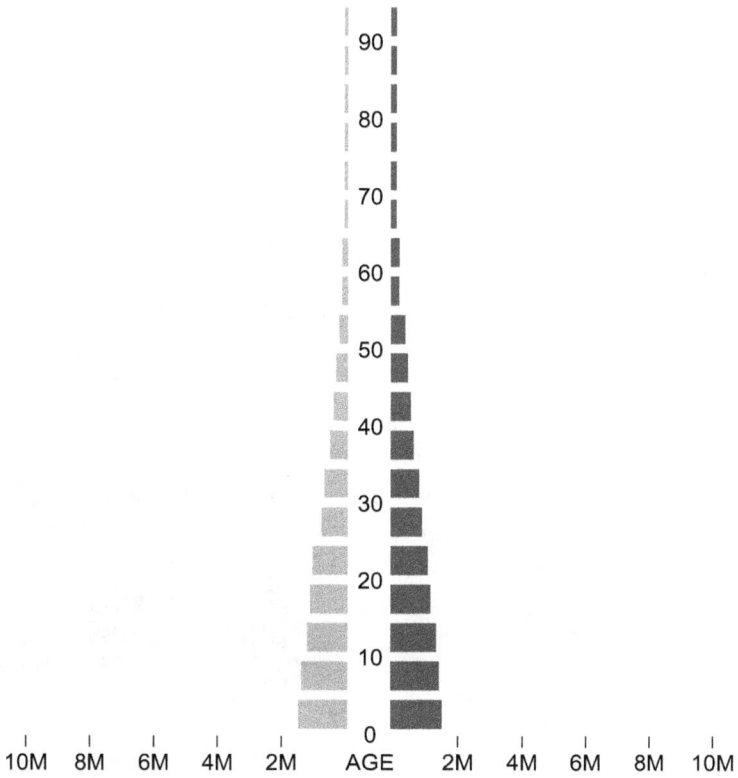

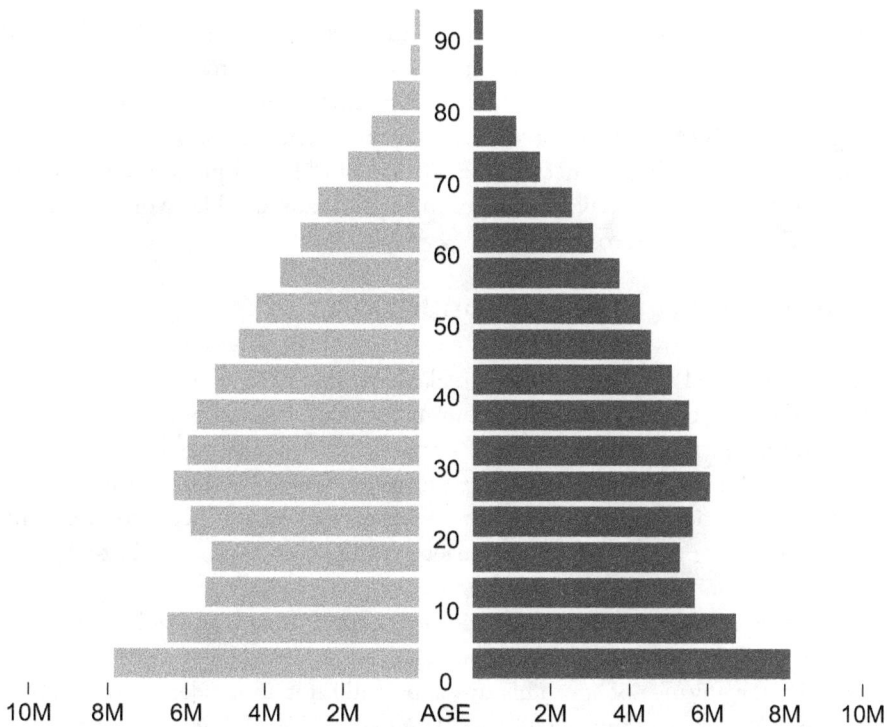

Figure 4.1 US age structure (top to bottom): 1850, 1950 and 2000

Source: U.S. Census & Minnesota Population Center 2020

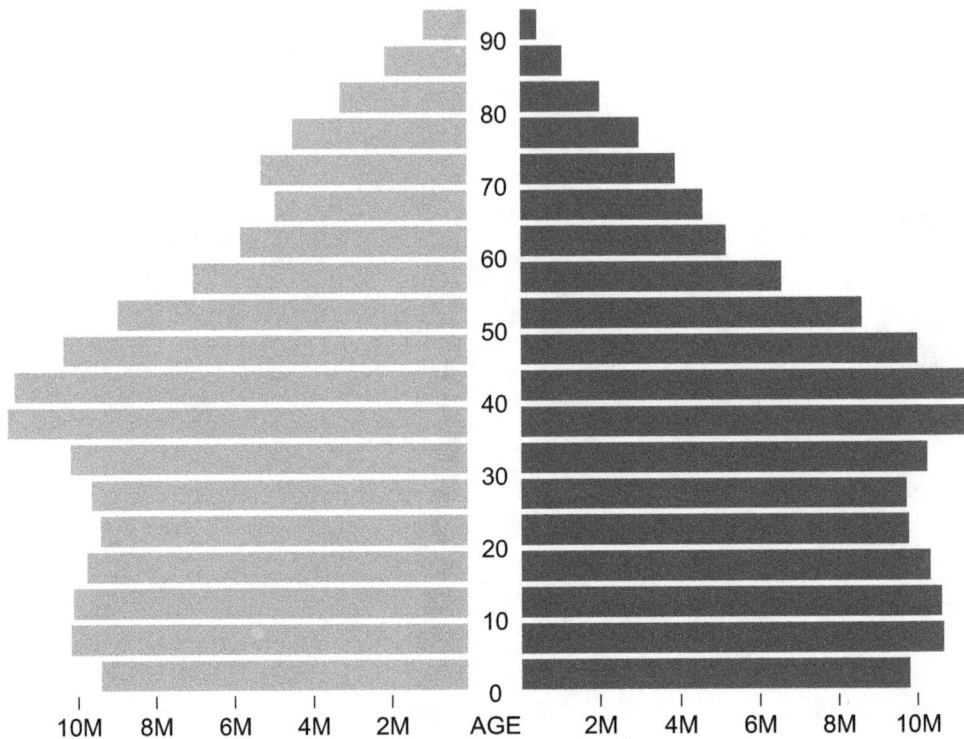

Figure 4.1 (Continued)

course, scientific progress in areas impacting nutrition, sanitation and medical advance also contributed importantly to long-term alteration of population demography—for example, in the control of infectious disease and in facilitating migration and mobility. But beyond the demographic transition, the advance of science and technology also had more direct effects on changing the circumstances of the relation of older people to the economy. Some of these effects had to do with changes in the situation of older workers that accompanied the industrial revolution.

AGE, CRAFT AND INDUSTRIAL PRODUCTION

Firsthand reports as well as archival records make clear that prior to industrialization, older people were often valued participants in economic production and other aspects of the lives of their communities. Achenbaum (1978:19) presents evidence that American society was then guided by a "prevailing notion that the old were seasoned veterans of productivity, whose advice and participation enhanced prospects for successfully accomplishing many tasks, justified ascribing to aged persons a variety of important societal tasks to perform".

A central dimension of the involvement and leadership of mature and older adults was located in the economic domain, where many skills were honed by years of experience, and hence with the advance of age. This was apparently not an incidental matter, but one central to economic productivity. The Lynds' landmark study of *Middletown*, its limitations notwithstanding (Lassiter 2004), is instructive in this regard. Consider the craft of glassblowing in the production of glass jars:

The furnace in which the glass was melted held eight to fourteen 'pots' of molten glass, each pot being the focus of the activities of a 'shop' or crew of two highly skilled glass blowers and three boy assistants. . . . Through a narrow, protected ring hole . . . (one boy assistant) collected a small gob of glass on a long iron blow-pipe from the blistering interior of the pot. Moving back to a tub six feet from the furnace, he quickly smoothed the ball of glass in a 'block' and passed it to one of the blowers. The latter swung to the rhythm of his work at a distance eight feet from the furnace, setting the pipe to his lips, swinging it up until the glowing ball on the other end was above the level of his lips, blowing, lowering the balloon of glass into jaws of a waiting mold shut with a foot treadle, blowing a third time until a thin bright 'blow-over' of molten glass oozed over the mouth of the mold, and he could twist the pipe free from the glass without hurting the part of the jar inside. It took as a rule three deep breaths to jar and he averaged about twenty-five seconds to a jar—something under 100 dozen quart jars a day. At his side on a stool by the molds sat a third worker, the taking-out boy, who took the red-hot jar from the mold and placed it on a tray for a fourth worker, who carried it several yards to the annealing oven. . . . It was hot steady work with only a couple of five-minute breaks from 7:00 to 10:00, when a fifteen-minute 'tempo' occurred, during which one of the boys might be sent across the street with a row of buckets strung on a long pole for beer; then at it from 10:15 to 12:00 with one or two more five minute breaks; lunch 12:00–1:00; work 1:00–3:00; another 15-minute tempo, then the last leg until 5:00. . . . On hot days in early summer the pauses might have to come every half hour. . . . It is important to note that the speed and rhythm of the work were set by the human organism, not by a machine. And with all the repetition of movement involved, the remark of an old glass-blower should be borne in mind, that 'you never learn all there is to know about glass-blowing, as there's always some new twist occurring to you'.

(Lynd and Lynd 1957 [1929]:40–1)

This account is instructive in multiple respects. First one may note the rigorous physical exertion demanded of all the workers involved in the glassblowing operations. This includes the journeyman glassblowers—the highly skilled craftsmen who were also the oldest workers in the setting. Second, if the "old glass-blower's" comment is to be believed, it offers evidence for fully engaged, lifelong learning and continued skill development on the part of older workers—"always some new twist"—suggesting that advancing age may have brought veteran glassblowers gains in efficiency. Third, no indication of any concept like "retirement" or "disengagement" in the lives of these workers or in anyone else in the Middletown of 130 years ago; neither term is to be found in the highly detailed, 540-page tome.

Finally, what is strikingly evident from this passage is the necessity of skilled craftspeople who were capable of keeping to a rigorous routine demanding precision and endurance for efficient production of serviceable goods. Since such skills take time to develop and become sharpened and refined with experience, and hence with age, the economic engagement of older glass-blowers was integral to the production process. Their accumulated knowledge was crucial for its success.

These conditions illustrate the position of many veteran and aging workers in economic activity generally and in society prior to the advance of industrialization (see Braverman

1998), and it applied even to former slaves, both men and women, who were skilled craftspersons (Haber and Gratton 1994:91–2). This is likely a major part of the reason that, as Achenbaum puts it, "[O]ur predecessors would have been surprised to learn that the elderly as a group would be described one day as roleless and unproductive persons who inevitably and wittingly disengage from active life" (1978:9). Indications are that except for being positively correlated with the skill and refinement that benefit from years of experience in practicing one's craft, age was largely irrelevant, both physically and socially. In colonial New England, even military conscription was no respecter of age, at least until the age of 70 (Demos 1978:S250).

As many readers will know, in writing *Middletown* the Lynds used 1890 as a baseline. The study extends over a 35-year time period that encompassed major changes in production techniques. The changes they report offer a major clue to the kinds of social dynamics that shape the relation of age and the accessibility of social resources and status. In contrast to the previously mentioned situation observed in 1890, here is what the Lynds have to say about glass-blowing in the mid-1920s:

> Today this entire process, save the last step of transporting to the packing room, occurs without the intervention of the human hand. The development of . . . bottle blowing machines shortly after 1900 eliminated all skill and labor and rendered a hand process that had come down largely unchanged from the early Egyptians as obsolete as the stone ax. Batteries of these Briareus machines revolve endlessly day and night, summer and winter, in this factory today. . . .
>
> In 1890, 1600 dozen quart jars could be turned out in a one-shift day . . . by twenty-one men and twenty-four boys. Today . . . a human crew of eight men turns out 6600 dozen quart jars in a one-shift day of the same length.
>
> (Lynd and Lynd 1957 [1929]:42)

As the Lynds made clear, "the cunning hand of the master craftsman" was rendered obsolete by machines that dictated specialized repetitive actions of the human worker, and thereby are more suited to less costly young workers who bring more raw strength and endurance to the physically demanding, albeit less skilled, work demanded by industrial machinery.

Similar transformations characterized other industries. Noting that "as late as 1885 there was apparently no (age) discrimination in the printing industry", historian William Graebner details how the introduction of the Linotype machine transformed the meaning and value of experience, craft and age for veteran printers in the decades that followed (1980:21ff), and similar changes occurred in many other occupations, including accounting (Cooper and Taylor 2000) and social work (Carey 2007). The adverse impact of technological change on the meaning and value of age was thus not limited to the industrial world per se but extended to its indirect effects elsewhere. It could also be seen in declines in traditional agriculture and attendant domestic crafts, which reduced the status of older women as well as men (Haber and Gratton 1994:100).

Such examples arguably reflect what has been an even longer term devaluation of age with the advance of new technologies (Braverman 1998; Burawoy 1982). This general trend apparently extends at least as far back as the introduction of the printing press which, according to Branco and Williamson (1982), prompted an erosion of the status of elders, as their value as oral historians was undermined by the production and distribution of printed accounts.

Industrial mechanization thus represents a moment in an historic process of technological development that has, as an incidental consequence, contributed to the undermining of the value and status of older workers. Especially when such change entails the rapid introduction of new technologies, their introduction also favors the young who can be more easily trained, rendering the skills of mature and aging workers more dated and obsolete.

When one considers the pace of more recent technological change and especially the digital revolution, it clearly continues to impact seasoned and established workers (e.g., Minda 1997). With the potentials of AI to replace even many cerebral forms of human labor, the undermining of skilled mental work now threatens to render obsolete the specialized abilities of experienced and valued workers in many enterprises in an expanding array of information-based occupations (e.g., Press 2019; Smith and Anderson 2014).

Paradoxically, mechanization and automation in manufacturing were, Graebner (1980:27) argues, hastened by worker, union and public pressures for both a shorter work week and expanded retirement, since reducing workers' time on the job increased employers' anxieties about productivity. I return later to the implications of 21st-century technological change and productivity growth for contemporary possibilities of life-course innovations and social-structural transformations.

YOUTH AND MODERNIZATION: STANDARDIZING THE EARLY LIFE COURSE

The impact of such developments on the organization of age and the life course, and in shaping the character of a defined stage of life, was not limited to old age. It similarly transformed the situation of youth. In the agrarian contexts that preceded industrialization, the value and significance of young people was also tied to labor. Beyond the demands and exigencies of work on the farm or other modes of economic productivity, few guidelines defined age-appropriate behavior for young people. Work eligibility and capabilities were defined largely by the needs and opportunities of productive enterprises, not by age (Field 2015). Given economic strains and limited opportunities within their families of origin, many young people left home and were on their own for long periods from ages as early as 10; others were hired out as apprentices; others stayed home as dependent offspring for decades. Historian Joseph Kett (1977, 1993) uses the term "semi-dependence" to describe the situation of youth at this time, which involved "not a gradual removal of restraints but . . . a jarring mixture of complete freedom and total subordination". Prior to 1840, "the immediate environment of young people was likely to be casual and unstructured rather than planned or regulated" (1977:29, 111). Moreover, until the mid-19th-century great heterogeneity applied to the population of children in school. At least in some areas, children as young as 2 or less were sent to school (Kaestle and Vinovskis 1978).

Thus, the lives of children and youth, or at least boys and young men, alternated dramatically between independence and dependence. Some boys became independent from parents before they were 16 (e.g., running away, joining the crews of sailing ships or the military). Or consider Harmen Meynderstz van den Bogaert, who at age 18 was already an apprenticed barber-surgeon when he arrived in New York from the Netherlands in about 1630, and at 22 was deployed to lead a crucial and successful diplomatic mission into previously unexplored Mohawk territory to revive trade in beaver pelts that had been disrupted by the French (Shorto 2005:110–11). In other regions, boys were often bound out before the age of 12, or contributed to the family economy by working in farms or mines (Schmidt 2015:160). Again, the definitions ascribed to them were dictated more by their roles and activities than by age, and sometimes with more than a touch of socioeconomic discrimination folded into the mix. In New England, those who left to attend school at 14 were called "young men", while others who stayed home and engaged in farm labor were termed "large boys" or "great boys" (Kett 1977:13–14), a term that might last well past the teenage years.

For young men with healthy and long-lived parents, a situation of enforced dependency extending across the years of adulthood (often while waiting to inherit the family farm) was a not uncommon risk. Girls and women of all ages also risked multiple forms of dependency and discrimination as they navigated a patriarchal world that legally defined them as perennially childlike, and ensured their structural powerlessness (Field 2014).

Given attention to these other axes of social organization, indications are that for the great majority of children, little attention was paid to age-calibrated roles or developmental imperatives or needs, or anything like general educational expectations (Field 2015). Instead, the circumstances of children and teenagers were dictated heavily by familial economic circumstances.

Similar conditions applied in Europe. According to John Gillis (1974), who studied changes in age relations in Europe since 1770:

> [t]he modern reader is inevitably struck not only by the extraordinary duration of the period defined as 'youth', but by the lack of clear distinctions between younger and older members of that age group. . . . Personal, social and economic tasks of development were concurrently rather than sequentially organized. . . .
>
> There was no universal schooling to postpone entry into the world of work, and because social mobility was more limited, occupation was less of a problem. Many a lad followed his father's plow from the age of 7 or 8 without thought to alternatives. . . . In the less tightly structured occupations, a boy or girl might move in or out of jobs, but here again there was no pattern that would mark a break between early and later youth. The sons of aristocracy entered the university at an average age of 15 in seventeenth century England, spending a variable amount of time there, many not even bothering to graduate. . . . In any case, education was taken by all strata in bits and pieces, constantly being interrupted by season and other important demands on the children's time.
>
> (1974:5–6)

As with the transformation in the experience of old age, the question again arises of how such dramatic change could occur. How can we account for the dramatic contrast between the present "reality-taken-for-granted" of universal, age-graded K-12 schooling and a time not so long ago when the teenage years were undefined, and were lived out under the varied opportunities and demands of local economic exigencies?

Again, some principal contours of the operant social forces are readily discernible. Large-scale population movements and steadily increasing urbanization meant that the activities of youth were not so easily channeled into orderly involvement of productive labor as they had been on the farm, and the regulation of their activities and conduct came increasingly to be seen as a significant problem of social control. In the US, the situation was made more challenging by the lack of an established cultural anchorage of young people, prompting added interest in education as a form of youth management: "political elites increasingly came to fear the power of uncontrolled masses of voters in a free polity", so that "calls for training republican citizens became almost an annual ritual" (Schmidt 2015:153). This situation was rendered more urgent, and more challenging, by westward migration. Thus, a complex web of interrelated economic, demographic and cultural factors worked in concert to press for a practical and publicly recognized need to manage a growing subpopulation of often detached and free-roving youth through their teenage years.

THE IDEOLOGY OF NURTURE AND THE INVENTION OF ADOLESCENCE: A THEORY FOR PRACTICE

While it comprised a daunting array of challenges, the problem of youth actually may have provided a solution, of sorts, for life-course "crises" of two other subpopulations disrupted by the expansion of commerce and then by industrialization and technological advance—women and the clergy. The ideology of the "domestic sphere" that emerged in the early 19th century found fertile ground in middle-class families when men took employment in commercial enterprises and the family was no longer the primary unit of economic production. In this circumstance, women no longer participated in economic activity as they had done when the family was integrally devoted to its farm, mill or other cottage industry. Historian Nancy Cott (1977) traces the appeal of the ideology of the domestic sphere that emerged from this complex web of changes, as work was removed from the home and, hence, women from its setting. In this context, a growing awareness of the challenges of youth, their need for nurture and the expansion of schooling simultaneously served adult women's needs by providing them with an outlet for voluntary activities directed to nurturing youth and their development. In addressing this set of needs, women found allies with clergy—another group whose traditional sources of power and influence were eroding, and who joined with women in advancing the education and nurturance as general needs of youth.

For women, such endeavors were pursued under structurally challenging circumstances. Field (2014) shows that 19th-century women themselves already confronted a denial of adult status and hence an imposed definition of childhood simply by virtue of gender; women lacked the right to vote and other legal rights, often including property legal rights apart from their husbands. The power imbalance and dependency of women likely increased still further as the site of economic production shifted from farm or other family enterprises to factories, since women's skills and work were typically essential as long as the family remained the primary unit of economic production. While this general pattern is not to discount the enduring contributions of many women whose energy, leadership and prophetic vision had an impact on the status of women and on the course of society, the overriding realities of women's lives continued to be framed by patriarchal ideologies and power structures (e.g., Lerner 1987).

The political and cultural impulses to address a sustained situation of uncontrolled and often migrant youth and the growing pressures to define and manage the teenage years found a viable intellectual rationale in G. Stanley Hall's ambitious work *Adolescence: Its Psychology and its Relations to Physiology, Anthropology, Sociology, Sex, Crime, Religion and Education*, published in 1907 (Kett 1977). The increasing focus on nurturance—reinforced from many directions, both instrumental and moral—had by the 1870s generated what Chudacoff terms a "nascent psychological imperative", to articulate needs of youth in developmental and psychosocial terms (Chudacoff 1989:40).

Hall's opus arguably provided a coherent response to these perceived societal needs. It offered a narrative account with prescriptions for policymakers and others in power who were confronted by urgent challenges in the management of a growing, economically insecure yet mobile, and sometimes unruly and vagrant youth population. *Adolescence* presented a theoretical narrative declaring that activities of teenagers need to be controlled and nurtured to entrain them for adult citizenship (Kett 1977; see also Schmidt 2015:153). Given the challenges confronting many local communities and by the society as a whole, the idea of an authoritative scientific treatise calling for the nurturance of youth in an orderly environment seemed highly plausible and was embraced by the child welfare experts and psychologists. It was a concept that reinforced ideas of childhood nurture that, as noted earlier, were being advanced by women and clergymen as well as educational leaders (Cott 1977; Kaestle and Vinovskis 1978:150–60).

These forces, Joseph Kett argues, interacted to produce the normative life stage now taken for granted as adolescence. Historians agree that nothing like a "developmental stage" of adolescence had been recognized before this time, but the concept rapidly caught hold after the publication of Hall's work.

Beyond defining an age-specific stage of development, adolescence also had the effect of heightening the extent to which the lives of young people had an age-graded order imposed upon them. Increased reliance on age as a basis for social sorting was already underway, resulting in part from two factors: 1) age-grading in schools was implemented as an economic measure, since female teachers—cheaper to hire than males—could manage younger students, but not physically maturing boys (Kaestle 1983:17; Kett 1977:123–4) and 2) the belief that small children would be contaminated by co-mingling with older ones.

Such historical analyses of age-specific subgroups begin to illuminate the diverse and often seemingly unordered character of the life course, including its opening decades— thereby making clear the widely varied range of sequences experienced by human beings moving through their lives under different social and cultural conditions. Such work also illustrates the sensitivity of lifestyles as well as life patterning to changes in culturally accepted "knowledge". For example, the strong emphasis on individual development offered by Hall's paradigm arguably supplied not only an ideology for age-graded schooling but also contributed to the ideological frame for the individuation from families of origin and rejection of tradition celebrated in the youth cultures of the 1920s, for both men and women (Fass 1977).

Such research makes clear the utility of theories that authoritatively defined "human nature" and "human development" as cultural and ideological narratives that served the purposes of social control, defining the age-specific needs of young people. Thus, from their beginnings, scholarly writings on development and age have had a political salience (see also Broughton 1987; Morss 2013; Schmidt 2015:149). This is a matter to which I return in Chapter 8.

In sum, across the life course, the expansion and increased scale of commerce, industry and science in the late 18th and 19th centuries began to organize individual lives in terms defined by the priorities of industry and large-scale organization, rather than local and familistic demands. As agrarian and cottage-industry labor gradually diminished, individual life stages—youth, old age, and gender-differentiated adulthood—became increasingly "recognized" as individually anchored characteristics in an individualizing society, a characteristic that could be leveraged by political and economic as well as cultural interests. New and more restrictive age-graded ideas and norms emerged, defining adolescence, woman's sphere, and then retirement in ways consistent with the overall organization of modern society.

The revolutionary changes in social arrangements brought by industrialization and modernization left no domain of experience and social life untouched. Their impact clearly extended to family life, but not always in expected ways. For example, despite the Waltonesque inclination to romanticize nostalgically premodern family life and living arrangements, the structural integrity of families in the US actually appeared to become stronger over the late 19th and 20th centuries.

Examining family patterns in birth cohorts from 1870 to 1954, Peter Uhlenberg's findings contradicted the frequently repeated late-20th-century admonitions of family disintegration. Uhlenberg found that more people were living in two-parent families in the most recent decades observed than at any time in the prior century (1978:94; see also Hareven 1994). Moreover, thanks primarily to mortality declines, the proportion of women who experienced a "normatively expected" life course of marrying, having children and remaining in the first marriage until at least age 50 increased, and the number of children who live in intact families until age 15 increased six-fold over that time.

Such findings square with the assertion that "what strikes most historians about the family in the past is less its strength than its fragility" (Kett 1977:4). Popular idealizations of the frontier family thus appear as mythical, depicting a way of life that never existed as anything approaching a modal empirical reality. While recent increases in single parenting and cohabitation may mark a reversal (Fasang and Raab 2014; Robette 2010), it is important to recognize that the prevalence of the "normal" life course sequence of intact family roles is a relatively recent—and perhaps transitory—phenomenon that emerged in parallel with increasingly "normative" and often age-graded patterns of life-course arrangement in the domains of education and work.

In sum, these historical accounts make it clear that, just as in the case of elders, the contours of the lives of children and teenagers and the issues they faced in the preindustrial past look nothing like the "universal" developmental stages or "tasks" declared by contemporary child development experts and professionals to be "natural" and necessary for successful development through childhood and adolescence (Kett 1993; Morss 2013; Rogoff 2003).

While we have scant systematic data on skill development or psychological constructs like self-esteem or identity, it is reasonable to hypothesize that the wide variations in circumstances and opportunities experienced by premodern youth would have enormous consequences for both the development of knowledge and skills, and for the development of identity and mental resilience.

THE CO-EMERGENCE OF AGE AWARENESS AND THE INSTITUTIONALIZATION OF THE LIFE COURSE

The massive changes recounted here affected not only the meanings of specific ages, but the very notion of age itself. In a carefully documented examination tracing changes in age representations in the US through the 19th and 20th centuries, historian Howard Chudacoff (1989) demonstrates that the very idea of "age"—the precision with which it is calibrated and the public attention to its significance—was itself equally transformed over this period.

What accounts for this historically rapid ascendance of "age awareness"? Clearly it is a development that can be explained neither as random nor as the direct outcome of anyone's conscious intentions. Rather the answer again lies in identifiable social forces.

Although much attention is paid by Chudacoff and others to the industrial revolution and its aftermath, it is important to recognize that in North America, age was mobilized even earlier for purposes of social control. This happened in multiple domains, for example, at the time of the Revolutionary War, as a legal mechanism used to hold young people in bondage. At that time, young African-Americans in "free" northern states could be held by former masters until age 28—an example of "northern emancipation acts offering 'the opportunity to engage in philanthropy at bargain prices', given masters' ability to continue exploiting their former slaves as laborers" (Sundue 2015:47–8, see also Fogel and Engerman 1974).

Such incidents illustrate James Schmidt's claim that the establishment of age consciousness, especially in relation to work, is "tied directly to questions of political economy" (2015:149). While such exploitative usages of age did not evaporate, the expanding 19th-century interest in education as a means of both social control and nurturance, and the invention of adolescence as its scientific legitimation, became the basis for an age consciousness of unprecedented breadth and precision.

In the putatively rational-bureaucratic "public sphere" domains, reliance on age as a major axis of social organization and calculation increased across the 20th century—in schooling (with age-graded classrooms; Chudacoff 1989:32–5; Kaestle 1983:17); in medicine, with the emergence of pediatrics, geriatrics and the increased reliance upon age as a "risk factor" for innumerable maladies (Starr 2017); in the workplace (with increasingly fine-grained "career steps" and credentials being devised as bureaucratic organizations expanded in size and complexity (Crozier 2010 [1963]; Whyte 2012); in science, including medicine, developmental psychology and beyond (Broughton 1987; Chudacoff 1989:39–47; Hermanowicz 2011; Morss 1990, 2013 [1996]) and in matters of law and policy (where age operates as an eligibility criterion and as a key dimension of demographic data). In this latter regard, it is interesting to note that the very word "statistics" had as an original definition "questions concerning matters of state" (Sinclair 1791; Hacking and Hacking 1990:16–25; see also Katz 1996, Ch. 2)

THE SOCIAL ORGANIZATION OF AGE AND THE INSTITUTIONALIZATION OF THE LIFE COURSE

As will be well known to some readers, Martin Kohli has shown that 1) the established reliance on age as a principle of social organization, combined with 2) the sequential structure typifying biographical experience, has led to the crystallization of the life course as a fundamental social institution in modern societies (Kohli 1986, 2007). As a social institution, the life course serves to organize individual lives into the broad tripartite division of school/work/retirement—sometimes called the "three boxes of life". Within each of the "boxes", finer gradations can often be found—with annual age-graded calibrations of K-12 schooling, career promotion regimes in many work organizations and professions, gerontological divisions of the "young-old" and "old-old" and more.

LIFE-COURSE INSTITUTIONALIZATION AND STANDARDIZATION

According to Kohli (2007), the key features of the general phenomenon of institutionalization of the life course are anchored in the logic of modernity. These features include a focus on an individual-level biographic progression or "life-time" (entailing *temporalization*), which is "keyed to chronological age" (*chronologization*; 2007:255). Kohli rightly notes that the primary impulses for sustaining this organization come from the world of work which organizes career sequences that form the basis of a sense of biographical progression ("normal work biography") and that, as such, they comprise a method of social control, and are thus systemically relevant to the structural integration and continuity of modern states.

Given the primacy of work experience and economic factors in organizing individual lives, Kohli's emphasis on worklife as a fulcrum of life-course organization offers a welcome corrective to the imbalanced attention paid to family issues in life-course studies—a further manifestation of the impact of the functional-organismic nexus outlined in Chapter 1.

Although anchored in work and education, institutionalization clearly extends to other domains, including retirement (e.g., Moen, Sweet, and Swisher 2005; Hudson 2010) and health issues across the life course (Clarke and Wheaton 2005). Even institutions of long-term care are set up with a logic of care provision that provides a generally unwanted "career progression" for nursing home residents, who often move from the relatively high-functioning "health-related" floor to "special" (secured dementia) care levels or to skilled nursing care (Dannefer, Stein, and Gelein 1998). I return later to the irrationality and human destructiveness of this arrangement.

One way of grasping how long-term forces of social change have reshaped human arrangements and with them patterns of aging can be seen in studies of trends of change in life-course transitions. Such analyses have been conducted by a number of demographers and historical scholars as well as sociologists. A focus on transition patterns refocuses the level of analysis from the individual to the cohort, providing a revealing window on the shift from a time when the experience of youth was less standardized and predictable to regimented, age-graded systems of contemporary schooling.

Trends toward the age-based homogenization of school experience are discernible as early as the mid-19th century. Studying educational policy and practice in Massachusetts, Kaestle and Vinovskis (1978:146–9) document a notable reduction in regional (urban-rural) differences across the state of Massachusetts between 1860 and 1880, and a corresponding shift toward a greater uniformity in schooling and the school experience.

This tendency toward standardization and homogenization of life-course patterns is well documented in the 20th century US. Defining the transition to adulthood as consisting of the three events of leaving school, entering the workforce and marrying, Dennis Hogan (1981) calculated the duration of this transition for a nationally representative sample of cohorts of males born between 1907 and 1952. Using the interquartile range as a measure, Hogan demonstrates a reduction in the duration of this transition of more than 50%, from about 18 to 8 years (see Figure 4.2).

The reduction in variability in the transition to adulthood resulted from several factors, notably the expansion of mass education, leading to a standardization, as well as a lengthening, of years of schooling across the population. Similar patterns of increasing homogenization have also been reported by several other analysts in the US (Hagestad 1988; Hagestad and Neugarten 1985; Modell 1991; Modell, Furstenberg, and Strong 1978; Winsborough 1979; Spanier and Glick 1980) and Europe (Brückner and Mayer 2005; Gillis 1974; Laslett 2004; Mayer and Müller 1986). The trend of an increasingly standardized transition to adulthood extending across much of the 20th century may be considered remarkable given the social upheaval of two major wars (Buchmann 1989; Kohli and Woodward 2004; Mayer and Schoepflin 1989). As a concomitant to modernization, similar trends have also been reported elsewhere, including in China (Kohli 2007:260; Leisering, Gong, and Hussain 2002).

What do these trends mean for individual aging and life-course patterns? For youth moving through the teenage years and entering adulthood, they clearly reflect a sustained

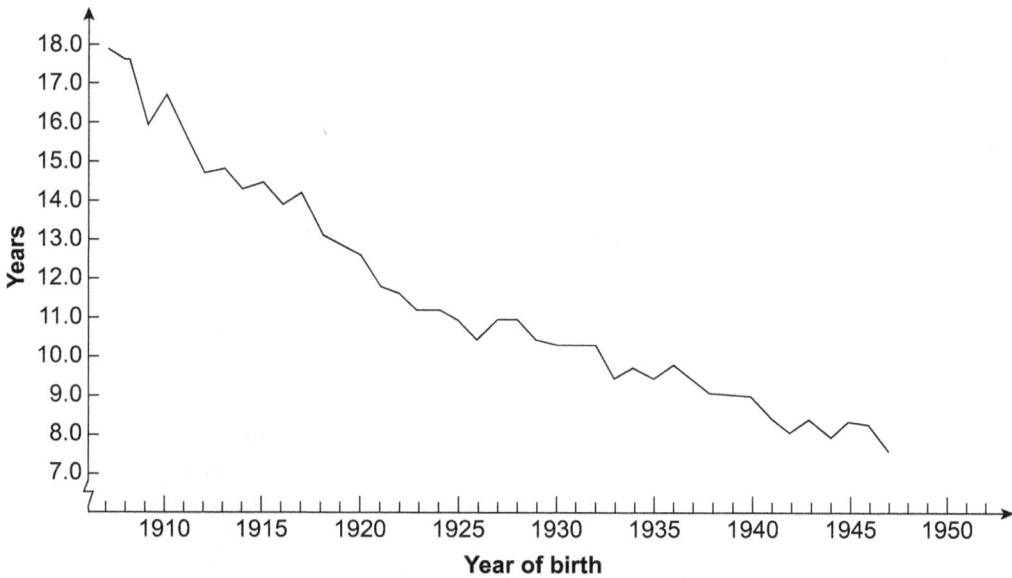

Figure 4.2 The duration of the transition to adulthood for single-year birth cohorts of American males born 1907–1952

Source: Hogan 1981

trend of growing age-graded standardization of experience over much of the 20th century, and often a deliberate reliance on age as a criterion for social participation. Age peers tend to go through the same socially imposed transitions and to deal with similar, often socially constituted issues together. Thus, annual cohort membership became increasingly relevant, both as an aspect of social organization and as an element of personal identity and self-reflexive comparison with others (Jaret, Reitzes, and Shapkina 2005; Rosenberg, Schooler, Schoenbach, and Rosenberg 1995; Stryker and Burke 2000). Age even becomes a factor *within* cohorts, as the annual age-grading of education has led to concerns about the pros and cons of being born early versus late in the year (Grenet 2010; Verachtert, De Fraine, Onghena, and Ghesquière 2010).

Of course, such standardization has not been limited to the early life course. With the expansion of national and private pension schemes and retirement policies in advanced industrial societies, pressures to retire had a broad impact on the life planning, identity and self-identity of individuals moving into their sixties.

Thus, in a relatively brief period of historical time, the transitions of youth and entry to adulthood on one hand and retirement on the other became relatively standardized, and this imposed homogenization came to be seen as "normal". In everyday life, it is a small step from an assumption of normality to an assumption of naturalness, and these transitions also became *naturalized* and taken-for-granted as a normal and often "normative" part of everyday life, abetted by developmental theories, whether of adolescence or disengagement.

The naturalization of the institutionalized life course (ILC) raises broader issues for sociological theory and analysis. Beyond the immediate question of the impact on the actual experience of individuals and the patterning of individual movement through the life course are questions of the political, economic and social sources of the policies and practices behind these social changes, and their ideological implications.

The institution of the life course can thus be regarded as a "social fact"—an emergent social phenomenon *sui generis* constituted by the crystallization of these trends toward age-grading and bureaucratization. It is particularly worth noting, however, that Kohli's analysis claims to offer more than a descriptive sketch the empirical contours of the ILC; he regards it as solving key problems of social control by providing a sense of stability and security to individual experience in modern society:

> The institutionalized life course has come to achieve social order by processing people through the social structure and articulating their actions, in other words, by providing the rules by which individuals unfold and conduct their lives. . . . Through these rules, the life course helps to solve some of the structural problems that arose with the transition from a household economy to an economy of free labor based (mostly) on formal employment contracts between workers and enterprises.
>
> These problems include the problem of rationalization, both of economic production and of individual lives; the problem of integration of the newly differentiated life domains and their corresponding careers (especially work and family); the problem of succession (in terms of regulating the flow of individuals and cohorts through the economy and society by providing clear criteria for replacing them); and the problem of social control under the conditions of an individualized life form.
>
> (Kohli 2007:256)

The ILC is thus claimed to provide continuity, order and some degree of meaning in the lives of modern citizens, via a coherent articulation of biographical progression and change with social structure that achieves predictability and security by standardizing "collective transitions" (Kohli 2007:56; see also Buchmann 1989; Field and Syrett 2015).

This view of the ILC can be criticized for reflecting a standard functionalist approach— an element in the "utopian reconstruction of civil society" (Burawoy 2016:381), and for uncritically embracing other problematic aspects of the functionalist narrative of modernity, including not only its neglect of power but also its studied avoidance of issues of meaning, death and finitude (see Baars 2017). However, in the context of the often-reductionist impulses of gerontology and the sociology of aging, Kohli's depiction makes the key contribution of properly locating individual "life stages" as socially constructed and historically specific phenomena, rather than ontogenetically driven by imperatives of individual development, thereby recognizing them as the product of social forces and clearly separating them from matters of individual organismic development. Whether one sees the ILC as a solution to problems of social and personal integration, or as imposing a rigid and oppressive structure that often squelches individuals' development (Bolles 1981), it constitutes a measurable empirical phenomenon, whose continued growth through much of the 20th century appears unmistakably clear. However, some contend that the same empirical metrics now point in a different direction.

LIFE-COURSE DEINSTITUTIONALIZATION?

Despite the continuing importance of the ILC, several scholars contend that the trend toward increasing homogeneity in the patterning of the life course has for the past several decades been in retrenchment. Beginning in the 1970s or 1980s, the timing of leaving home, entering the workforce and partnering all became more varied (Billari and Liefbroer 2010; Blossfeld, Klijzing, Mills and Kurz, 2005; Brückner and Mayer 2005; Buchmann 2011; Huang 2021; Mayer 2001; Schoon 2015; Schoon and Silbereisen 2009; Widmer and Ritschard 2009), which manifested in the "boomerang child" trend and other such phenomena. The timing of retirement (Alley and Crimmins 2007) has also become more varied, as has movement between work and educational experiences during adulthood (e.g., Elman and O'Rand 1998; Heinz 2003). Diversity in the timing and structuring of roles in family and personal life has also increased (Cherlin 2004; Huang 2021; Zimmerman and Konetzka 2018).

The reversal of the long-term trend toward life-course standardization brings into focus several longstanding questions surrounding the phenomenon of institutionalization. Does the "deinstitutionalizing" trend result from "individuation"—that is, a rather happy manifestation of personal autonomy and control that "transcends" the normative strictures of the ILC? Or, alternatively, does it result from increasing precarity deriving from the expansion of neoliberal policies and other forms of imposed risk (see, e.g., Bynner, Ferri, and Shepherd 1997; Dannefer, Lin, and Gonos 2021). Again, such alternative interpretations are bound up with broader evaluative questions—is life-course institutionalization desirable (providing order and structure to lives, as Kohli contends), or is it unduly oppressive (imposing a normative and in some cases legally rigid life-course sequence that restricts opportunity)?

A full resolution of these questions must lie beyond the scope of this discussion. However, available evidence clearly indicates that the force of the impulses toward destandardization can only be accounted for by the contemporaneous trends toward occupational precarity and economic inequality that have been an overriding story of advanced industrial societies over the last several decades (Case and Deaton 2020; Piketty 2015).

The evidence for this is more than correlational. Wenxuan Huang has demonstrated clearly that, with respect to the transition to adulthood, "destandardization" is not randomly distributed but is more likely to be found among the most economically insecure and socially vulnerable (Huang 2021). To claim that such individuals are "choosing" to have disordered lives would be even more dubious than the paradoxical claim made in earlier historical demography (e.g., Modell 1991) that the increasing conformity in the transition to adulthood in the mid-20th century resulted from an increase in personal control (see Dannefer 1984:112)! Instead, Huang's findings are likely a reflection of the subpopulation who confront growing economic and personal insecurity, arguably constituting a new "precariat class" (Barker and Christensen 1998; Gonos 1997; Horowitz, Parker, and Rohal 2015; Kalleberg 2013; Standing 2011, 2014). Thus, such evidence also raises a caution for those who would too easily treat deinstitutionalization as a unilateral signal of individual freedom (e.g., Arnett 2007; Settersten and Ray 2010) rather than as the decline of opportunity, as indexed by employers' increasing reliance on temporary workers and independent contractors (gig workers; see, e.g., Bieber and Moggia 2020; Carey

2007; Freeman and Gonos 2009; Gonos and Martino 2011; Hacker 2008). As a historical marker of the magnitude of change, consider the palpable shift in workers' concerns at GM's Lordstown, Ohio, plant which, in the 1970s, was the site of well-publicized worker complaints and protests over its high-speed assembly line (Zwerdling 1980). Such complaints have long since been supplanted by workers' angst and manifest vulnerability, as GM closed the plant in 2018 and sold it a year later (e.g., Colias 2019).

LIFE-COURSE INSTITUTIONALIZATION AND NOMIZATION

Thus, both the long-term emergence of the ILC and the more recent indications of its erosion can be accounted for by broader social forces and dynamics. These dynamics provide a specific example of a more general and comprehensive principle to guide understanding of the life course.

This is the principle that *life-course institutionalization as a generic process is a general tendency of social life*. The actual form of the life course, the degree of its age-based precision, the number and fixity of transitions and stages, etc. vary widely, as will be illustrated by the examples that follow. However, what underlies this variation is a basic human interest, implied in Kohli's interpretation of the significance of the life course, to find or construct order. This is, again, the common human process of *nomization* which, as discussed in Chapter 2, Peter Berger (1968:22) identifies as "the most important function of society".

Life-course institutionalization of whatever form extends nomizing impulses beyond the immediacy of present meanings and understanding to discern order in the biographical sequencing of experience. It is constituted through the direct result of human action and social processes, and the form it takes and the degree of its durability are regulated by the broader features of the social world in which actors are located.

ALTERNATIVE FORMS OF LIFE-COURSE INSTITUTIONALIZATION

Thus, entirely novel patterns of life-course institutions, deriving their specificity from community-based patterns of daily living rather than from state policies, can also be readily documented. Some such patterns are robust and enduring, although they have been little noticed by mainstream life-course scholarship. I will here discuss briefly three examples of such alternative forms of life-course institutionalization—first, life in a Mexican-American community, second, a deliberate attempt to create African-centered rites of passage across societies and third, the ILC patterns of disadvantaged youth who face systemic barriers to mainstream access, and rely on gang membership to organize their lives.

First, consider the work of Robert Courtney Smith (2006) whose 15-year "life-course ethnography" documents a quite standardized program of life-course sequences that entail a regular annual migration of a community of Mexican-American families between New York City and the small Mexican town from which the senior generation had migrated. These regularities and sequences, with their own internal complexities and intersections with the life-course development of members of different ages, were observed for more than a decade (Smith 2006; esp. Chapters 8 and 9).

Such a case illustrates how life-course standardization may be internally generated as an internal feature of local subcultures and may be entirely compelling for those immersed in them, even if they go unnoticed by others.

As a second example, consider the National Rites of Passage Institute (NROPI), which seeks to create and establish life-course rites of passage integral to personal maturation and social inclusion, and thus constitutes an intentional effort at life-course nomization. The mission of NROPI is to provide a framework and context for community-building via African-centered rites of passage. The African-centered rites of passage process used by NROPI provide training, education, socialization and promotes cultural awareness (https//nropi. org/about-us/, see also Hill 2013, 2018; Warfield-Coppock 1994). Founded by organizer and author Paul Hill Jr. as an outgrowth of similar earlier initiatives, NROPI now has an international reach with rites of passage community partners in Canada, West Indies, West Africa and Great Britain (Goggins and Shelton 2018; Turner 2018; Walker 2018).

NROPI's process is designed to provide a deliberate institutionalization of key life-course transitions as a form of social and cultural empowerment (Karlin 2009). It appears as a proactive effort to offer meaningful structure to organize the lives of young people in their preparation for adulthood and elders even while challenging mainstream values and the life course narratives. As described by noted scholar-practitioner Nsenga Warfield Coppock:

> The rites of passage can thus be considered a social and cultural "inoculation" process that facilitates healthy, African-centered development among African-American youth and protects them against the ravages of a racist and sexist, capitalist, and oppressive society. Most importantly, it prepares them physically, mentally, and spiritually. For active resistance and struggle against the seductive lure of the American Way.
>
> (1994:474)

NROPI thus sets forth a model of development that grounds the experience of young people within a larger community, anchored in an alternative, Afro-centric framework. It frames individual experiences as intrinsic to the life of the community, instead of viewing one's life experience as isolated or individualistic, and thereby is premised on a paradigm that offers a fundamental critique and alternative to the dominant, individualized narrative of the institutionalized life course. As we will see in Section III, its paradigm resonates with and may add to other critical responses to both popular and scientific understandings of the life course.

NROPI is perhaps unusual, in that it represents a deliberate effort to institutionalize a normative life course within an alternative cultural framework. More commonly, such challenges have generated their own "homegrown" standard and even normative life-course patterns that bear little resemblance to the mainstream "three boxes of life". Some readers will be familiar with notions of "step-grandparenthood" (Burton and Bengtson 1985), the "accelerated life course" (Burton 1990; Baker and Burton 2018) and adultification (e.g., Burton, Winn, Stevenson, and McKinney 2015; Epstein, Blake, and

González 2017), all pattens reflecting disadvantaged families' efforts to respond to daunting challenges.

In the US, this is true not only for young women who are navigating difficult circumstances but for young men as well. Indeed, even the severely truncated and precarious life-course expectations of youth who are urban street-gang members have developed their own alternative, homegrown institutionalized life course, a widely shared understanding of "gangster career development". Consider the following exchange between two young members from the Crips and Bloods gangs, Tiny Vamp and G-Roc, chatting with each other at a Los Angeles detention facility (adapted from Bing 1991:21; see also Dannefer 2003).

Tiny Vamp: You still a little homie, or what?

G-Roc: Li'l Homie. I ain't probably gonna reach the O.G. stage for a while yet. I got outta baby homie when I was like thirteen and a half. How 'bout you?

Tiny Vamp: I'm still a tiny. In my set you get a rep by straight killin'. I been on drive-bys and I been stabbed.

Sidewinder, another 15-year-old Crip detained for participating in a drive-by shooting, sees himself an O.G. (Original Gangster) in 5 or 10 years.

(Bing 1991:47, 50)

Here, then, is a structure of an *objective* (again, in the way that Durkheim [1897] describes "social facts") set of life stages defined by this delimited but institutionally stable social world: homeboys graduate from "baby homie" to "li'l homie" to "homeboy" status by getting "jumped in". Getting jumped in refers to an initiation ritual, a rite of passage, for which a kind of informal counseling is available from older gang members (Bing 1991:24).

It's like when I got jumped in—all my homeboys and my cousins told me 'You in now, man. . . . Either you be down for it or get out now.' Cause you KNOW you gonna have go to jail. You KNOW you might end up gettin' killed, gettin' stabbed, gettin' shot. You know all this. My homeboy, Lil' Lazy, just got killed, and he only sixteen.

If homeboys survive, they may graduate again to O.G. (Original Gangster) status in their twenties. Life-course stages beyond O.G., the mature stage of the twenties, are apparently less well defined. In a social world in which gang-related homicides are commonplace, a preoccupation with funerals, especially one's own funeral, is a frequent topic for teenage and pre-teenage gang members.

These terms are sufficiently institutionalized that they are shared across rival gangs, and formal names have given rise to an argot of abbreviations and slang or nicknames that are as taken-for-granted as are "frosh" or "preppie" in mainstream institutions. Homeboys are "homies" or "homes"; gangsters are O.G.s or T.G.s.

The phenomenon of an alternative "institutionalized life course" among gang members warrants consideration in this context because it demonstrates that whatever the timing and content of life-course "stages", those stages develop as part of the meaning structure of a social world. The mainstream institutionalized "three boxes of life" construct derives its dominance from the movement of developing human beings through time in a very specific social world, and the same can be said for the gangster life course.

To understand how institutionalization in general is constituted, it is instructive to consider the contours of gang culture. The social world of gang culture has its own heroes—not Martin Luther King or Malcolm X, but gang legends such as Raymond Washington or "Tookie" Williams (Alonso 1999:3)—both founding Crip leaders. In their collective memory the Watts rebellion may hold a significance analogous to that held for many American citizens by the Revolutionary War. Even the correction officers who deal with incarcerated gang members do not expect these young people to develop an appreciation of the "founders of the Republic". A skilled corrections officer who had himself logged brig time while serving in the U.S. Marines (for refusing to wear the required dress on July 4) commented: "American Independence Day wasn't important to me because my particular forefathers were still slaves. . . . I didn't, and don't, feel a freedom based on that event" (Bing 1991:11).

The case of the gangster life course offers another clear example of the more general point that the generic human processes of meaning-making and reality construction occur in specific social worlds and will take their character from that world. The exposition of the dominant cultural form of the institutionalized life course (Kohli 2007; Levy 1996; Mayer and Schoepflin 1989) remains a dominant social and biographical element of the modern state and late modernity. The gangster life course serves as both clarification and reminder that such a form—despite its taken-for-granted familiarity and dominance—is entirely contingent on the broader apparatus of the social world within which it is organized.

Anyone inclined to dismiss the social world of gang life as some peripheral aberration should be reminded that gangs emerged and began to operate as encompassing social worlds in American cities prior to the implementation of mass public K–12 education, often attracting immigrants marginalized and excluded from mainstream opportunities. The *gang career* as an organizing reality for members is probably as old as the mainstream institutionalized life course. Even on the west coast, gangs developed early in the 20th century. According to estimates, nearly 1.5 million Americans are currently members of more than 30,000 criminal gangs active in 800 North American cities. While predominantly male, estimates are that overall about 10% of gang members are female, and all-female gangs have existed for the past century (Chesney-Lind and Hagedorn 1999; National Gang Intelligence Center 2011, 2013).

However, there is yet a more timely and compelling reason to take seriously the phenomenon of such alternative life-course patterns, which concerns the pattern of their intersection with contemporary mainstream institutions. The notorious "school-to-prison pipeline" is much broader than the gang culture, and references an increasingly common and familiar experience of disadvantaged youth generally. As numerous analysts have pointed out, for many young people this has become a predictable and expected component of the life course (Black 2009; Black and Keyes 2021), and one that has grown dramatically in the US, along with mass incarceration (Alexander 2010) .

THE STATE AND THE INSTITUTIONALIZED LIFE COURSE: EXCLUSIONARY VARIANTS

Some scholars have argued that the school-to-prison pipeline and associated developments cannot be understood as merely unfortunate by-products of globalization or the challenges facing schools. In particular, Black and Wacquant have both argued that this trend results from expanding neoliberal efforts at *poverty governance* (see also, e.g., Schram, Fording, and Soss 2008). The expansion of neoliberal policy over the past several decades has accounted not only for the flattening of wage growth, reduction in welfare benefits and expansion of workfare but also the continuing expansion of mass incarceration. As Wacquant (2000:292) observes:

> The operant purpose of welfare has shifted from passive 'people processing' to active 'people changing' after 1988 and especially after the abolition of AFDC in 1996, while the prison has traveled in the other direction, from aiming to reform inmates (under the philosophy of rehabilitation, hegemonic from the 1920s to the mid-1970s) to merely warehousing them.

Given the emphasis placed upon the state as a more or less beneficent provider of life-course stability and benefit in the original analyses offered of the institutionalized life course (e.g., Kohli and Meyer 1986; Kohli 2007; Mayer and Schoepflin 1989), it is important to recognize at the same time a longstanding yet recently expanding "dark side" of state regulation of the life course. Just as the benefits of the ILC as portrayed by Kohli and others are not guaranteed to endure the advance of neoliberalism, neither are they universal (see, e.g., Dannefer et al. 2021). With the continuing strength of racism and other forms of prejudice and with the expansion of the neoliberal state and with it the precariat, it is entirely possible that regular life-course sequences endured by disadvantaged and vulnerable subpopulations—involving regular patterns cycling among schooling, workfare and prison time—may continue to expand.

If the sociology of age and the life course intends to describe and analyze the full range of socially significant, age-related sequencing of human experience and to consider the range of human possibilities, then such phenomena clearly require attention from life-course scholars.

LIFE-COURSE INSTITUTIONALIZATION AS GENERIC NOMIZATION

In the foregoing discussion, I have tried to make clear that the institutionalization of the life course is a generic social process that can occur as a by-product of other social forces and changes (as in the mainstream modern ILC), and can sometimes be supported by deliberate efforts at provisioning social support (as in the case of NROPI). The degree to which it develops the chronometrically precise mode of life-course regulation typical of late modernity will depend on the character of the social world within which it emerges, and its continued plausibility depends on the stability of that world.

When pressure for change develops, what seemed almost "cast in stone" suddenly begins to appear tentative and uncertain. As an example consider the pervasively taken-for-granted institution of retirement. As is now widely known, over recent decades the established parameters of retirement have come under increasing assault (Duvvury and Ni Leime, 2017; Ekerdt 1998, 2009; O'Rand and Farkas, 2002), with the collapse of pension funds, dire predictions about federal programs such as Social Security in the US (Peterson 1999), and the raising of the eligible minimum retirement age in many countries. Along with such pressures is evident a growing ideological narrative of the appeal of work for senior citizens, sometimes boldly sponsored by private corporate interests (Park 2013; Wright and Goodwin 2013). Whatever their sources, changes in retirement age or pension policy offer opportunities to examine their potential impact on the distribution of normative expectations regarding age and life stage.

By whatever means such institutional arrangements are altered, the cultural impetus to interpret the change and to redefine expectations around the newly emergent parameters imposed by the state or from elsewhere stand as examples, again, of the human impulse for nomization—for extending meaning-making to the provision of a sense of temporal and biographical as well as structural regularities and predictability.

LIFE-COURSE PATTERNS IN CROSS-CULTURAL PERSPECTIVE

While I have focused on changes within North American and European societies to illustrate the historical and cultural constitution of developmental and life-course variation, many readers will be aware that a voluminous body of evidence also exists regarding cross-cultural variations.

Turning from historical comparative evidence, variations of similar magnitude in patterns of development and aging are equally apparent, from childhood to later life, and continue to be observed despite cross-societal commonalities, such as the expansion of population aging (see, e.g., Kunkel, Brown, and Whittington 2014). Although considerable variation exists among modern and postindustrial societies, even sharper differences are often evident when comparing modern and indigenous societies. Children's development of skills and social position in such settings has long been a topic of scholarship in psychology and anthropology (e.g., Bronfenbrenner 1986; Kessen 1979; Rogoff 2003). Nevertheless, the depths to which the experience of childhood and the attendant opportunities varies according to the technological and other practices of culture have often been underappreciated.

For example, consider the appropriate age for knife or machete use. Although US middle-class adults typically do not entrust preschool children with sharp knives or red-hot objects (and in fact might risk being charged with child endangerment were they to do so), among the Efe of the Democratic Republic of Congo, infants routinely use machetes safely (Rogoff 2003:5), and among the Taita of Kenya, at about age 3, a child "reached the age of sense . . . judged by its ability to perform certain actions competently. For example, taking a brand from the hearth and carrying it to its father (for lighting his pipe)" (Harris 1978:56). At the other end of the activity spectrum, children under the age of 7 and even as young as age 3 are routinely tasked with multiple domestic chores, notably including the role of careperson for their younger siblings, in places as diverse as Oceania (Watson-Gegeo 1990) and the mountains of Guatemala (Rogoff, Sellers, Pirotta, Fox, and White 1975).

Cross-cultural work also makes clear a high degree of variability in adult experience, and in the significance and status of older people. Such variability has received extensive treatment in anthropology (e.g., Fry 2004; Simmons 1945, 1960; Sokolovsky 1990). In many indigenous societies, older people may be venerated so long as they are able to fulfil role expectations. Nevertheless, as in the case of traditional Western societies discussed earlier, it would be erroneous to romanticize the situation of elders. In many indigenous societies, when seniors are no longer able to perform their roles or take care of themselves, abandonment—"death-hastening" actions—or in some cases outright killing has occurred (Fry 2010; Glascock 1983). The attendant tensions have sometimes become the stuff of legend in such social worlds (Wallis 2004).

Cultural variability in the experience of aging is not limited to the matters of social status, values and roles; it can also produce differences in physiological aspects of aging. As an example, consider the familiar matter of blood pressure. Increasing blood pressure has often been assumed to be an unavoidable and universal concomitant of aging. However, evidence from multiple societies has shown over recent decades that blood pressure and its age trajectory vary systematically across societies (e.g., Stevenson, 1999; Waldron et al., 1982).

SUMMARY: SOCIAL FORCES AND THE ORGANIZATION OF THE LIFE COURSE

This chapter began by reviewing the "world-openness" and the range of potential developmental possibilities of the malleable human individual over the life course, and by posing the question of how, given that malleability, the observed orderliness of processes of human development is organized through both micro- and macro-dynamics of social life.

By examining how aging and development are experienced by both older people and youth in earlier historical periods in parts of Europe and the US as well as in other societies, we have been able to see that the character of age takes its form from the specific features of the social context within which an individual is located.

For individuals who mature, age and move through the life course in the preindustrial West or in indigenous settings, patterns of development and aging appear surprisingly different and less age-graded, compared to what moderns take for granted, revealing the cohort-centric and ethnocentric presumptions of supposedly universal "stages of development" (see, e.g., Dannefer 1984; Morss 1990). Yet such stage-graded assumptions remain culturally powerful, imposing normative expectations on contemporary youth and subtly but relentlessly discouraging or excluding elders from full social participation.

It thus becomes clear that the marginalization and withdrawal that often accompanies retirement and that is predicted by disengagement theory are revealed as social inventions found mainly in the modern West, just as is the case for the widely accepted belief that the teenage years are governed by a set of supposedly universal imperatives of "adolescent development".

In indigenous and premodern societies, growing older does not appear to reduce the societal need for the skills and productive engagement of older people, nor does it always carry the same kind of pervasive stigmatization that has been endemic to late modern societies. Despite the reality of growing risk of maladies with advancing age, individuals in indigenous cultures and traditional cultures often do not confront the same magnitude of social deprecation and exclusion based on age and may be integrated into the life of a community, even with significant limitations (Cohen 1998). Older individuals do not conform to anything like a universal stage of disengagement nor do children necessarily conform to Piagetian stages of child development (Buck-Morss 1975; Rogoff 2003:7, 38–42; Morss (2013 [1996]); Stetsenko 2012, 2016). While key aspects of social life are often organized around developmental progressions in such settings, relatively little reliance is placed on precisely calibrated age-grading (Foner and Kertzer 1978).

It is clearly evident that the observed variation can be accounted for neither by universal imperatives of individual development (since a variable cannot be explained by a constant) nor by individual "free choice" and decision-making. It is neither organismically determined nor is it volitional. Instead, what determines the parameters of individual aging and life-course patterns has a great deal to do with the imperatives of the social system in which the individual is living and constructing her life course.

Given the inherent malleability of the human organism and the shaping of human development over the life course, this chapter has offered a first installment in demonstrating the systemic interconnections between patterns of human development and broader social, technological and economic circumstances. By starting with the "30,000 foot view" afforded by a macro-level examination of historical and comparative contrasts, it becomes clear that the experiences of age and templates of the life course are defined by the context in which one ages, and are intricately and systemically linked to the dynamics of each particular setting. In sum, the dramatically different distribution of life patterns does not derive from characteristics *within* the individual, but from the opportunities, demands and expectations characterizing the *context in which lives are lived*, all of which are systemically linked and which *constitute* the observed patterns of development and age (Baars 1991).

Yet the analysis of different historical and societal contexts is only one level at which the experience of development and age require macro-level analysis. It is already clear from the material covered in this chapter that despite the dominant characteristics of specific historical and geographic settings, a great deal of within-age variability exists within each of those settings. Like the settings themselves, the variability within them is also, to a large extent, socially organized.

Thus, a second axis of macro-analysis, focused on the cohort-based differentiation among age peers *within* a given social context, is the subject of the next chapters. As we will see, such differentiation and stratification reveals a great deal about the social organization, the structure and possibilities of the life course, and also requires an accounting.

REFERENCES

2011 National Gang Threat Assessment: Emerging Trends. 2011. *National Gang Intelligence Center* (Report). FBI.gov.

2013 National Gang Threat Assessment: Emerging Trends. 2013. *National Gang Intelligence Center* (Report). FBI.gov.

Abramson, Corey M. 2015. *The End Game*. Cambridge, MA: Harvard University Press.

Achenbaum, W. Andrew. 1978. *Old Age in the New Land: The American Experience Since 1790*. Baltimore, MD: Johns Hopkins University Press.

Achenbaum, W. Andrew. 2010. "Past as Prologue: Toward a Global History of Ageing." Pp. 20–31 in *The Sage Handbook of Social Gerontology*, edited by D. Dannefer and C. Phillipson. London: Sage.

Alexander, Michelle. 2010. *The New Jim Crow: Mass Incarceration in an Age of Colorblindness*. New York: The New Press.

Alley, Dawn, and Eileen Crimmins. 2007. "The Demography of Aging and Work." Pp. 7–23 in *Aging and Work in the 21st Century*, edited by K. S. Shultz and G. A. Adams. New York: Psychology Press.

Alonso, Alejandro A. 1999. *Territoriality Among African-American Street Gangs in Los Angeles*. MS Thesis, University of Southern California, Los Angeles.

Arnett, Jeffery J. 2007. "Emerging Adulthood: What Is It and What Is It Good For?" *Child Development Perspectives* 1(2): 68–73. https://doi.org/10.1111/j.1750-8606.2007.00016.x.

Baars, Jan. 1991. "The Challenge of Critical Gerontology: The Problem of Social Constitution." *Journal of Aging Studies* 5(3): 219–43.

Baars, Jan. 2017. "Human Aging, Finite Lives and the Idealization of Clocks." *Biogerontology* 18: 285–92.

Baker, Regina S., and Linda M. Burton. 2018. "Between a Rock and a Hard Place: Socioeconomic (Im)mobility among Low-Income Mothers of Children with Disabilities." Pp. 57–72 in *Marginalized Mothers, Mothering from the Margins*, edited by T. Taylor and K. Bloch. Bingley, UK: Emerald Group Publishing.

Barker, Kathleen, and Kathleen Christensen, eds. 1998. *Contingent Work: American Employment Relations in Transition*. Ithaca, NY: Cornell University Press.

Bengtson, Vern L., ed. 2016. *Handbook of Aging Theory*. New York, NY: Springer Publishing Company.

Bengtson, Vern L., and W. Andrew Achenbaum. 1993. *The Changing Contract Across Generations*. Chicago: Aldine.

Berger, Peter L. 1968. *The Sacred Canopy: Elements of a Sociological Theory of Religion*. New York: Anchor.

Berger, Peter L., and Thomas Luckmann. 1967. *The Social Construction of Reality: A Systematic Treatise in the Sociology of Knowledge*. New York: Anchor.

Bieber, Friedemann, and Jakob Moggia. 2020. "Risk Shifts in the Gig Economy: The Normative Case for an Insurance Scheme against the Effects of Precarious Work." *Journal of Political Philosophy*: 1–24. doi: 10.1111/jopp.12233.

Billari, Francesco C., and Aart C. Liefbroer. 2010. "Towards a New Pattern of Transition to Adulthood?" *Advances in Life Course Research* 15(2–3): 59–75.

Billig, Nathan. 1987. *To Be Old and Sad: Understanding Depression in the Elderly*. Washington: Lexington Books.

Bing, Leon. 1991. *Do or Die: America's Most Notorious Gangs Speak for Themselves.* New York: Harper Collins.

Black, Timothy. 2009. *When a Heart Turns Solid Rock.* New York: Vintage.

Black, Timothy, and Sky Keyes. 2021. *It's a Set-Up: Fathering from the Social and Economic Margins.* New York: Oxford University Press.

Blossfeld, Hans-Peter, Eric Klijzing, Melinda Mills and Karin Kurz. 2005. *Globalization, Uncertainty and Youth in Society.* Abingdon, UK:Routledge.

Bolles, Richard N. 1981. *The Three Boxes of Life and How to Get Out of Them.* Berkeley, CA: Ten Speed Press.

Branco, Kenneth J., and John B. Williamson. 1982. "Stereotyping and the Life Cycle: Views of Aging and the Aged." *In the Eye of the Beholder: Contemporary Issues in Stereotyping* 4(7): 364.

Braverman, Harry. 1998. *Labor and Monopoly Capital: The Degradation of Work in the Twentieth Century.* New York: New York University Press.

Bronfenbrenner, Urie. 1986. "Ecology of the Family as a Context for Human Development: Research Perspectives." *Developmental Psychology* 22(6): 723–42.

Broughton, John M., ed. 1987. *Critical Theories of Psychological Development.* New York: Plenum Press.

Brückner, Hannah, and Karl Ulrich Mayer. 2005. "The De-Standardization of the Life Course: What It Might Mean? And If It Means Anything, Whether It Actually Took Place? In R. Macmillan (Ed.), *The Structure of the Life Course: Standardized? Individualized? Differentiated?" Advances in Life Course Research* 9: 27–54. Amsterdam: Elsevier. https://doi.org/10.1016/S1040-2608(04)09002-1.

Buchmann, Marlis C. 1989. *The Script of Life in Modern Society: Entry into Adulthood in a Changing World.* Chicago/London: University of Chicago Press.

Buchmann, Marlis C. 2011. "School-to-Work Transitions." Pp. 306–13 in *Encyclopedia of Adolescence*, edited by B. B. Brown and M. J. Prinstein. https://doi.org/10.1016/B978-0-12-373951-3.00085-5.

Buck-Morss, Susan. 1975. "Socio-Economic Bias in Piaget's Theory and Its Implications for Cross-Culture Studies." *Human Development* 18(1–2): 35–49.

Burawoy, Michael. 1982. *Manufacturing Consent: Changes in the Labor Process Under Monopoly Capitalism.* Chicago: University of Chicago Press.

Burawoy, Michael. 2016. "Sociology as a Vocation." *Contemporary Sociology* 45(4): 379–93.

Burton, Linda M. 1990. "Teenage Childbearing as an Alternative Life-Course Strategy in Multigeneration Black Families." *Human Nature* 1(2): 123–43.

Burton, Linda M., and V. L. Bengston. 1985. "Black Grandmothers: Issues of Timing and Continuity of Roles." Pp. 61–78 in *Grandparenthood*, edited by V. L. Bengston and J. F. Robertson. Beverly Hills, CA: Sage.

Burton, Linda M., Donna-Marie Winn, Howard Stevenson, and Marvin McKinney. 2015. "Childhood Adultification and the Paradox of Parenting: Perspectives on African American Boys in Economically Disadvantaged Families." Pp. 167–82 in *Family Problems: Stress, Risk, and Resilience*, edited by J. Arditti. New York: Wiley-Blackwell.

Bynner, John, Elsa Ferri, and Peter Shepherd. 1997. *Twenty-Something in the 1990s: Getting On, Getting By, Getting Nowhere.* Aldershot, UK: Ashcroft Publishing.

Callahan, Daniel. 1995. *Setting Limits: Medical Goals in an Aging Society with "A Response to My Critics"*. Washington: Georgetown University Press.

Carey, Malcolm. 2007. "White-Collar Proletariat? Braverman, the Deskilling/Upskilling of Social Work and the Paradoxical Life of the Agency Care Manager." *Journal of Social Work* 7(1): 93–114.

Carr, Deborah S. 2019. *Golden Years?: Social Inequality in Later Life*. New York: Russell Sage.

Case, Anne, and Angus Deaton. 2020. *Deaths of Despair and the Future of Capitalism*. Princeton, NJ: Princeton University Press.

Castel, Alan D. 2018. *Better with Age: The Psychology of Successful Aging*. London: Oxford University Press.

Cherlin, Andrew J. 2004. "The Deinstitutionalization of American Marriage." *Journal of Marriage and Family* 66(4): 848–61.

Chesney-Lind, Meda, and John M. Hagedorn, eds. 1999. *Female Gangs in America: Essays on Girls and Gender*. Chicago: Lakeview Press.

Chudacoff, Howard P. 1989 (1992). *How Old Are You? Age Consciousness in American Culture*. Princeton, NJ: Princeton University Press.

Clarke, Philippa, and Blair Wheaton. 2005. "Mapping Social Context on Mental Health Trajectories Through Adulthood." *Advances in Life Course Research* 9: 269–301. doi: 10.1016/S1040-2608(04)09010-0.

Cohen, Lawrence. 1998. *No Aging in India: Alzheimer's, the Bad Family, and Other Modern Things*. Berkeley: University of California Press.

Cole, Thomas R. 1992. *The Journey of Life: A Cultural History of Aging in America*. Cambridge: Cambridge University Press.

Colias, Mike. 2019. "GM Sells Lordstown Plant That Became Flashpoint for Trump, UAW." *Wall Street Journal* November 7. Retrieved from www.wsj.com/articles/gm-sells-lordstown-plant-that-became-flash-point-for-trump-uaw-11573160818

Cooper, Christine, and Phil Taylor. 2000. "From Taylorism to Ms. Taylor: The Transformation of the Accounting Craft." *Accounting, Organizations and Society* 25(6): 555–78.

Cott, Nancy. 1977. *Bonds of Womanhood: "Woman's Sphere" in New England, 1780–1835*. New Haven, CT: Yale University Press.

Cowgill, Donald O., and Lowell Don Holmes, eds. 1972. *Aging and Modernization*. New York: Appleton-Century-Crofts.

Crozier, Michel. 2010 (1963). *The Bureaucratic Phenomenon*. New Brunswick, NJ: Transaction Publishers.

Dannefer, Dale. 1984. "Adult Development and Social Theory: A Paradigmatic Reappraisal." *American Sociological Review* 49(1): 100–16.

Dannefer, Dale. 1992. "On The Conceptualization of Context in Developmental Discourse: Four Meanings of Context and Their Implications." Pp. 84–105 in *Life-Span Development and Behavior*. Vol. 11, edited by D. L. Featherman, R. M. Lerner, and M. Perlmutter. Hillsdale, NJ: Lawrence Erlbaum Associates, Inc.

Dannefer, Dale. 2003. "Whose Life Course Is It, Anyway? Diversity and 'Linked Lives' in Global Perspective." Pp. 259–68 in *Invitation to the Life Course: Toward New Understandings of Later Life*, edited by R. A. Settersten. Amityville, NY: Baywood.

Dannefer, Dale, Jielu Lin, and George Gonos. 2021. "Age-Differentiated vs. Age-Integrated: Neoliberal Policy and the Future of the Life Course." *Journal of Elder Policy* 1(2): 59–82.

Dannefer, Dale, Paul Stein, and Janet Gelein. 1998. "Microtemporal and Macrotemporal Linkages in Life Course Institutionalization: The Case of the Resident Career in Long

Term Care." Paper presented at the XIV World Congress of Sociology, Montreal (July).

Davenhill, Rachael, ed. 2019. *Looking into Later Life: A Psychoanalytic Approach to Depression and Dementia in Old Age (Tavistock Clinic Series)*. Abingdon, UK: Routledge.

Demos, John. 1978. "Old Age in Early New England." Pp. S248–87 in *Turning Points*, edited by J. Demos and S. S. Boocock. Chicago: University of Chicago Press.

Durkheim, Emile. 1951 (1897). *Suicide: A Study in Sociology* (English translation). London: Routledge.

Duvvury, Nata and Aine Ni Leime (2017) "Erosion of pension rights. Experiences of women in Ireland." *European Journal of Cultural and Political Sociology* 5(3): 266–294.

Dychtwald, Ken. 2000. *Age Power*. New York: TarcherPerigee.

Ekerdt, David J. 1998. "Entitlements, Generational Equity, and Public Opinion Manipulation in Kansas City." *The Gerontologist* 38(5): 525–36.

Ekerdt, David J. 2009. "Population Retirement Patterns." Pp. 471–91 in *International Handbook of Population Aging*, edited by P. Uhlenberg. New York, NY: Springer-Verlag.

Elias, Norbert. 1985. *The Loneliness of the Dying*. London: Basil Blackwell.

Elman, Cheryl, and Angela M. O'Rand. 1998. "Midlife Work Pathways and Educational Entry." *Research on Aging* 20(4): 475–505.

Epstein, Rebecca, Jamilia Blake, and Thalia González. 2017. "Girlhood Interrupted: The Erasure of Black Girls' Childhood." Available at SSRN 3000695.

Fasang, Anette E., and Marcel Raab. 2014. "Beyond Transmission: Intergenerational Patterns of Family Formation among Middle-Class American Families." *Demography* 51(5): 1703–28.

Fass, Paula S. 1977. *The Damned and the Beautiful: American Youth in the 1920s*. New York: Oxford University Press.

Field, Corinne T. 2014. *The Struggle for Equal Adulthood: Gender, Race and Age in the Fight for Citizenship in Antebellum America*. Chapel Hill, NC: University of North Carolina Press.

Field, Corinne T. 2015. "'If You Have the Right to Vote at 21 Years, Then I Have': Age and Equal Citizenship in the Nineteenth-Century United States." Pp. 69–85 in *Age in America: The Colonial Era to the Present*, edited by C. T. Field and N. L. Syrett. New York: New York University Press.

Field, Corinne T., and Nicholas L. Syrett, eds. 2015. *Age in America: The Colonial Era to the Present*. New York: New York University Press.

Fischer, David Hackett. 1978. *Growing Old in America: The Bland-Lee Lectures Delivered at Clark University*. Oxford: Oxford University Press.

Fogel, Robert William, and Stanley L. Engerman. 1974. "Philanthropy at Bargain Prices: Notes on the Economics of Gradual Emancipation." *The Journal of Legal Studies* 3(2): 377–401.

Foner, Anne, and David Kertzer. 1978. "Transitions Over the Life Course: Lessons from Age Set Societies." *American Journal of Sociology* 83(5): 1081–104.

Freeman, H., and George Gonos. 2009. "Taming the Employment Sharks: The Case for Regulating Profit-Driven Labor Market Intermediaries in High Mobility Labor Markets." *Employee Rights and Employment Policy Journal* 13(2): 285–360.

Fry, Christine L. 2004. "Kinship and Supportive Environments of Aging." Pp. 313–33 in *Annual Review of Gerontology and Geriatrics*, Vol. 23, edited by H. W. Wahl, R. J. Scheidt, and P. G. Windley. New York: Springer.

Fry, Christine L. 2010. "Social Anthropology and Aging." Pp. 48–60 in *The Sage Handbook of Social Gerontology*, edited by D. Dannefer and C. Phillipson. Thousand Oaks, CA: Sage.

Gallagher, David P. 2012. *Aging Successfully: How to Enjoy, Not Just Endure, the Second Half of Life*. Eugene, OR: Wipf and Stock Publishers.

Gillis, John. 1974. *Youth and History: Tradition and Change in European Age Relations 1770-Present*. New York: Academic.

Goggins, Lathardus H., and Terrence Shelton. 2018. "African Inspired Rites of Passage in Practice and for People of African Descent: Critical Lessons Learned and Cultivated by Practitioners . . . When There Is No Village." *Black Child Journal Journal* Fall: 95–106.

Glascock, Anthony P. 1983. "Death-Hastening Behavior: An Expansion of Eastwell's Thesis." *American Anthropologist* 85(2): 417–20.

Goldstein, Melvyn, and Cynthia M. Beall. 1981. "Modernization and Aging in the Third and Fourth World: Views from the Rural Hinterland in Nepal. *Human Organization* 40(1): 48–55.

Gonos, George. 1997. "The Contest Over 'Employer' Status in the Postwar United States: The Case of Temporary Help Firms." *Law & Society Review* 31(1): 81–110.

Gonos, George, and Carmen Martino. 2011. "Temp Agency Workers in New Jersey's Logistics Hub: The Case for a Union Hiring Hall." *Working USA: The Journal of Labor and Society* 14(4): 499–525.

Graebner, William. 1980. *A History of Retirement: The Meaning and Function of an American Institution, 1885–1978*. New Haven: Yale University Press.

Grenet, Julien. 2010. "La date de naissance influence-t-elle les trajectoires scolaires et professionnelles ?" *Revue économique* 61(3): 589. http://dx.doi.org/10.3917/reco.613.05.

Haber, Carole, and Brian Gratton. 1994. *Old Age and the Search for Security*. Bloomington: Indian a University press.

Hacker, Jacob S. 2008. *The Great Risk Shift: The New Economic Insecurity and the Decline of the American Dream*. New York: Oxford University Press.

Hacking, Ian, and Tim Hacking. 1990. *The Taming of Chance*. New York: Cambridge University Press.

Hagestad, Gunhild O. 1988. "Demographic Change and the Life Course: Some Emerging Trends in the Family Realm." *Family Relations* 37(4): 405–10.

Hagestad, Gunhild O., and Bernice L. Neugarten. 1985. "Age and the Life Course." Pp. 36–61 in *Handbook of Aging and the Social Sciences*, edited by E. Shanas and R. Binstock. 2nd edition. New York: Van Nostrand and Reinhold Company.

Hareven, Tamara K. 1994. "Aging and Generational Relations: A Historical and Life Course Perspective." *Annual Review of Sociology* 20: 437–61.

Hareven, Tamara K., ed. 2013 (1978). *Transitions: The Family and the Life Course in Historical Perspective*. New York: Academic.

Harris, Grace G. 1978. *Casting Out Anger: Religion Among the Taita of Kenya*. Cambridge, UK: Cambridge University Press.

Hashimoto, Akiko. 1996. *The Gift of Generations: Japanese and American Perspectives on Aging and the Social Contract*. Cambridge, UK: Cambridge University Press.

Heinz, Walter R. 2003. "From Work Trajectories to Negotiated Careers: The Contingent Life Course." Pp. 185–204 in *Handbook of the Life Course*, edited by J. T. Mortimer and M. J. Shanahan. New York: Kluwer Academic.

Hermanowicz, Joseph C. 2011. *The American Academic Profession: Transformation in Contemporary Higher Education*. Baltimore, MD: Johns Hopkins University Press.

Hill, Paul, Jr., ed. 2013. *Black Child Journal: Rites of Passage Foundations & Practices (Special Edition)*. Cleveland, OH: National Rites of Passage Institute.

Hill, Paul, Jr., ed. 2018. *Black Child Journal: International Rites of Passage (Special Edition)*. Cleveland, OH: National Rites of Passage Institute.

Hogan, Dennis. 1981. *Transitions and Social Change*. New York: Academic Press.

Horowitz, Juliana M., Kim Parker, and Molly Rohal. 2015. Parenting in America: Outlook, Worries, Aspirations are Strongly Linked to Financial Situation. Washington: Pew Research Center.

Huang, Wenxuan. 2021. *Individualized Choice or Expanded Inequality: A Cohort Comparison of Transition to Adulthood between Late Baby Boomers and Millennials*. Doctoral Dissertation, Case Western Reserve University, Cleveland, OH.

Hudson, Robert B., ed. 2010. *The New Politics of Old Age Policy*. Baltimore, MD: Johns Hopkins University Press.

Jaret, Charles, Donald C. Reitzes, and Nadezda Shapkina. 2005. "Reflected Appraisals and Self-Esteem." *Sociological Perspectives* 48(3): 403–19.

Kaestle, Carl F. 1983. *Pillars of the Republic: Common Schools and American Society, 1780–1860*. New York: Hill and Wang.

Kaestle, Carl F., and Vinovskis, Maris A. 1978. "From Fireside to Factory: School Entry and School Leaving in Nineteenth-Century Massachusetts." Pp. 135–85 in *Transitions: The Family and the Life Course in Historical Perspective*, edited by T. K. Hareven. Cambridge, MA: Academic Press.

Kalleberg, Arne L. 2013. "Globalization and Precarious Work." *Contemporary Sociology* 42(5): 700–6. https://doi.org/10.1177/0094306113499536.

Karlin, Michael. 2009. *Changing Narratives, Changing Destiny: Myth, Ritual and Afrocentric Identity Construction at the National Rites of Passage Institute*. M.A. Thesis, Georgia State University, Atlanta.

Katz, Stephen. 1996. *Disciplining Old Age: The Formation of Gerontological Knowledge*. Charlottesville, VA: University of Virginia Press.

Kessen, William. 1979. "The American Child and Other Cultural Inventions." *American Psychologist* 34(10): 815–20.

Kett, Joseph F. 1977. *Rites of Passage: Adolescence in America 1790 to the Present*. New York: Basic Books.

Kett, Joseph F. 1993. "Discovery and Invention in the History of Adolescence." *Journal of Adolescent Health* 14(8): 605–12.

Kohli, Martin. 1986. "The World We Forgot: A Historical Review of the Life Course." Pp. 271–303 in *Later Life: The Social Psychology of Aging*, edited by V. W. Marshall. Beverly Hills, CA: Sage.

Kohli, Martin. 2007. "The Institutionalization of the Life Course: Looking Back to Look Ahead." *Research in Human Development* 4(3–4): 253–71.

Kohli, Martin, and John W. Meyer. 1986. "Social Structure and Social Construction of Life Stages." *Human Development* 29(3): 145–9.

Kohli, Martin, and Alison Woodward, eds. 2004. *Inclusions and Exclusions in European Societies*. London: Routledge.

Kunkel, Suzanne R., J. Scott Brown, and Frank J. Whittington. 2014. *Global Aging: Comparative Perspectives on Aging and the Life Course*. New York, NY: Springer Publishing Company.

Laslett, Peter. 1977. *Family Life and Illicit Love in Earlier Generations*. Cambridge, UK: Cambridge University Press.

Laslett, Peter. 2004. *The World We Have Lost: Further Explored*. London: Routledge.

Laslett, Peter, and Richard Wall. 1972. *Household and Family in Past Times*. London: Cambridge University Press.

Lassiter, Luke E. 2004. *The Other Side of Middletown*. Chicago: University of Chicago Press.

Lawrence, Barbara. 1986. "An Organizational Theory of Age Effects." In *Research in the Sociology of Organizations*, edited by N. DiTomaso and S. Bacharach. Greenwich, CT: JAI Press.

Leisering, Lutz, Sen Gong, and Athar Hussain. 2002. *People's Republic of China: Old-Age Pensions for the Rural Areas: From Land Reform to Globalization*. Manila, Philippines: Asian Development Bank.

Lerner, Gerda. 1987. *The Creation of Patriarchy*. New York: Oxford University Press.

Levy, René. 1996. "Toward a Theory of Life Course Institutionalization." Pp. 83–108 in *Society and Biography. Interrelationships between Social Structure, Institutions and the Life Course*, edited by A. Weymann and W. Heinz. Weinheim, Germany: Deutscher Studien Verlag.

Lynd, Robert Staughton, and Helen Merrell Lynd. 1957 (1929). *Middletown; a Study in Contemporary American Culture*. New York: Harcourt, Brace, and Company.

Maddox, George. 1963. "Activity and Morale: A Longitudinal Study of Selected Elderly Subjects." *Social Forces* 42: 195–204.

Mann, Kirk. 2001. *Approaching Retirement: Social Divisions, Welfare and Exclusion*. Bristol, UK: Policy Press.

Mayer, Karl Ulrich. 2001. *The Paradox of Global Social Change and National Path Dependencies: Life Course Patterns in Advanced Societies*. https://doi.org/10.4324/9780203167366-12.

Mayer, Karl Ulrich, and Walter Müller. 1986. "The State and the Structure of the Life Course." Pp. 217–45 in *Human Development and the Life Course: Multidisciplinary Perspectives*. Hillsdale, NJ: Lawrence Erlbaum Publishers.

Mayer, Karl Ulrich, and Urs Schoepflin. 1989. "The State and the Life Course." *Annual Review of Sociology* 15(1): 187–209.

Minda, Gary. 1997. "Opportunistic Downsizing of Aging Workers: The 1990's Version of Age and Pension Discrimination in Employment." *Hastings Law Journal* 48(3): 511.

Modell, John. 1991. *Into One's Own: From Youth to Adulthood in the United States, 1920–1975*. Los Angeles: University of California Press.

Modell, John, Frank F. Furstenberg, Jr., and Douglas Strong. 1978. "The Timing of Marriage in the Transition to Adulthood: Continuity and Change, 1860–1975." *American Journal of Sociology* 84: S120–50.

Moen, Phyllis, Stephen Sweet, and Raymond Swisher. 2005. "Embedded Career Clocks: The Case of Retirement Planning." *Advances in Life Course Research* 9: 237–65. doi: 10.1016/S1040-2608(04)09009-4.

Morss, John R. 1990. *The Biologising of Childhood: Developmental Psychology and the Darwinian Myth*. London: Taylor & Francis.

Morss, John R. 2013 (1996). *Growing Critical: Alternatives to Developmental Psychology*. New York: Routledge.

O'Rand, Angela M. and Janice I. Farkas. 2002. "Couples' Retirement Timing in the United States in the 1990s: The Impact of Market and Family Role Demands on Joint Work Exits." *International Journal of Sociology* 32 (2): 11–29.

Park, Keun-Hee. 2013. "Welcome Message." *Encore Life, Encore Career*. International Conference presented by Samsung Life Insurance Company, in conjunction with the 20th IAGG World Congress of Gerontology and Geriatrics, Seoul, Korea (June).

Parkin, Tim G. 2003. *Old Age in the Roman World: A Cultural and Social History*. Baltimore, MD: Johns Hopkins University Press.

Peterson, Peter C. 2005. *Running on Empty*. New York: Picador.

Peterson, Peter G. 1999. *Grey Dawn*. New York: Random House.

Piketty, Thomas. 2015. "About Capital in the Twenty-First Century." *American Economic Review* 105(5): 48–53.

Press, Gil. 2019. "Is AI Going To Be a Jobs Killer? New Reports about the Future of Work." *Forbes*. July 15.

Quadagno, Jill. 1986. "The Transformation of Old-Age Security." Pp. 129–55 in *Old Age in a Bureaucratic Society*, edited by D. V. Tassel and P. Stearns. New York: Greenwood Press.

Riley, Matilda W., Robert L. Kahn, and Anne Foner. 1994. *Age and Structural Lag: The Mismatch Between People's Lives and Opportunities in Work, Family, and Leisure*. New York: John Wiley & Sons.

Robette, Nicolas. 2010. "The Diversity of Pathways to Adulthood in France: Evidence from a Holistic Approach." *Advances in Life Course Research* 15(2–3): 89–96.

Rogoff, Barbara. 2003. *The Cultural Nature of Human Development*. New York: Oxford University Press.

Rogoff, Barbara, Martha J. Sellers, Sergio Pirotta, Nathan A. Fox, and Sheldon H. White. 1975. "Age of Assignment of Roles and Responsibilities in Children: A Cross-Cultural Survey." *Human Development* 18(5): 353–69.

Rosenberg, Morris, Carmi Schooler, Carrie Schoenbach, and Florence Rosenberg. 1995. "Global Self-Esteem and Specific Self-Esteem: Different Concepts, Different Outcomes." *American Sociological Review* 60(1): 141–56.

Rowe, John W., and Robert L. Kahn. 1997. "Successful Aging." *The Gerontologist* 37(4): 433–40.

Samuel, Julia. 2017. *Grief Works: Stories of Life, Death and Surviving*. Berkeley CA: Penguin Books.

Schmidt, James. 2015. "Rendered More Useful: Child Labor and Age Consciousness in the Long Nineteenth Century." Pp. 148–65 in *Age in America: The Colonial Era to the Present*, edited by C. T. Field and N. L. Syrett. New York: New York University Press.

Schoon, Ingrid. 2015. "Gender and the Transition to Adulthood: A Diverse Pathways View." Pp. 1–15 in *Emerging Trends in the Social and Behavioral Sciences*. New York: Wiley Online Publishing https://doi.org/10.1002/9781118900772.etrds0138.

Schoon, Ingrid, and Silbereisen, R. K. 2009. *Transitions from School to Work: Globalization, Individualization, and Patterns of Diversity*. Cambridge, UK: Cambridge University Press. Retrieved from http://ebookcentral.proquest.com/lib/case/detail.action?docID=461103

Schram, Sanford, Richard C. Fording, and Joe Soss. 2008. "Neo-Liberal Poverty Governance: Race, Place and the Punitive Turn in US Welfare Policy." *Cambridge Journal of Regions, Economy and Society* 1(1): 17–36.

Settersten, Richard A., and Barbara Ray. 2010. *Not Quite Adults: Why 20-Somethings Are Choosing a Slower Path to Adulthood, and Why It Is Good for Everyone?* New York: Bantam Book Trades Paperback.

Shorto, Russell. 2005. *The Island at the Centre of the World*. London: Black Swan.

Simmons, Leo William. 1945. *The Role of the Aged in Primitive Society*. New Haven, CT: Yale University Press.

Simmons, Leo William. 1960. "Aging in Preindustrial Societies." In *Handbook of Social Gerontology: Societal Aspects of Aging*, edited by Clark Tibbitts. Chicago: University of Chicago Press.

Sinclair, Sir John. 1791. *First Statistical Account of Scotland*. 21 Volumes. London.

Smith, Aaron, and Janna Anderson. 2014. "Views from Those Who Expect AI and Robotics to Displace More Jobs Than They Create by 2025." Washington: *Pew Research Report on Internet and Technology*. Washington, DC: Pew Research.

Smith, Robert C. 2006. *Mexican New York: Transnational Lives of New Immigrants*. Berkeley, CA: University of California Press.

Sokolovsky, Jay. 1990. *The Cultural Context of Aging: Worldwide Perspectives*. New York: Bergin & Garvey.

Spanier, Graham, and Glick Paul. 1980. "The Life Cycle of American Families: An Expanded Analysis." *Journal of Divorce* 3 (Spring): 283–98.

Standing, Guy. 2011. *The Precariat: The New Dangerous Class*. London: Bloomsbury Academic.

Standing, Guy. 2014. *A Precariat Charter: From Denizens to Citizens*. London: Bloomsbury Academic.

Starr, Paul. 2017. *The Social Transformation of American Medicine*. Updated edition. New York: Basic Books.

Stearns, Peter N. 1976. *Old Age in European Society: The Case of France*. Teaneck, NJ: Holmes & Meier Publishers.

Stetsenko, Anna. 2012. "Personhood: An Activist Project of Historical Becoming through Collaborative Pursuits of Social Transformation." *New Ideas in Psychology* 30(1): 144–53.

Stetsenko, Anna. 2016. *The Transformative Mind: Expanding Vygotsky's Approach to Development and Education*. Cambridge, UK: Cambridge University Press.

Stevenson, David R. 1999. "Blood Pressure and Age in Cross-Cultural Perspective." *Human Biology* 71(4): 529-551.

Stryker, Sheldon, and Peter J. Burke. 2000. "The Past, Present, and Future of an Identity Theory." *Social Psychology Quarterly* 63(4): 284–97.

Sundue, Sharon B. 2015. "'Beyond the Time of White Children': African American Emancipation, Age, and Ascribed Neoteny in Early National Pennsylvania." Pp. 24–47 in *Age in America: The Colonial Era to the Present*, edited by N. L. Syrett and C. T. Field. New York: NYU Press.

Troyansky, David G. 2015. *Aging in World History (Themes in World History)*. Abingdon, UK: Routledge.

Turner, Tana. 2018. "The Rites of Passage For African Boys." "I Found My Tribe: An Evaluation of Woodgreen Community Services Rites of Passage Program." *Black Child Journal* Fall: 41–66.

Uhlenberg, Peter. 1974. "Cohort Variations in Family Life Cycle Experiences of U.S. Females." *Journal of Marriage and the Family* 36(2): 284–92.

Uhlenberg, Peter. 1978. "Changing Configurations of the Life Course." Pp. 65–98 in *Transitions: The Family and the Life Course in Historical Perspective*, edited by T. K. Hareven. New York: Academic Press.

Verachtert, Pieter, Bieke De Fraine, Patrick Onghena, and Pol Ghesquière. 2010. "Season of Birth and School Success in the Early Years of Primary Education." *Oxford Journal of Education* 36(3): 285–306. https://doi.org/10.1080/03054981003629896.

Wacquant, Loic. 2000. *Punishing the Poor*. Durham, NC: Duke University Publishing.

Waldron, Ingrid, Michele Nowotarski, Miriam Freimer, James P.Henry, Nancy Post and Charles Witten. 1982. "Cross-cultural variation in blood pressure: A quantitative analysis of the relationships of blood pressure to cultural characteristics, salt consumption and body weight." *Social Science & Medicine* 16(4): 419-430.

Walker, Alan. 1981. "Towards a Political Economy of Old Age." *Ageing & Society* 1(1): 73–94.

Walker, Robin. 2018. "The Rights of Passage for African Boys." *Black Child Journal* Journal Fall: 14–40.

Wallis, Velma. 2004. *Two Old Women: An Alaska Legend of Betrayal, Courage and Survival*. New York: Harper Perennial.

Warfield-Coppock, Nsenga. 1994. "The Rites of Passage: Extending Education into the African American Community." In *Too Much Schooling, Too Little Education: A Paradox of Black Life in White Societies*. Africa World Press. YR - 1994 UL - https://www.library.yorku.ca/find/Record/1209397 OP - 412 CN - LC2717.

Watson-Gegeo, Karen. 1990. "The Social Transfer of Cognitive Skills in Kawara'ae." *Quarterly Newsletter of the Laboratory for Comparative Human Cognition* 12: 86–90.

Whyte, John. 2012. *Is This Normal? The Essential Guide to Middle Age and Beyond* (Dean Ornish, Foreword). Allentown, PA: Rodale Books.

Widmer, Eric D., and Gilbert Ritschard. 2009. "The De-Standardization of the Life Course: Are Men and Women Equal?" *Advances in Life Course Research* 14(1–2): 28–39.

Winsborough, Hal. 1979. "Changes in the Transition to Adulthood." Pp. 137–152 in *Aging from Birth to Death: Interdisciplinary Perspective*, edited by M. W. Riley, Ronald P. Abeles, and Michael S. Teitelbaum. Boulder, CO: Westview Press.

Wright, Tom, and James Goodwin. 2013. "Extending Working Lives: Challenges and Solutions in the UK." *Encore Life, Encore Career*. International Conference presented by Samsung Life Insurance Company, in conjunction with the 20th IAGG World Congress of Gerontology and Geriatrics, Seoul, Korea (June).

Zimmerman, Okka, and Dirk Konetzka. 2018. "Social Disparities in Destandardization: Changing Family Life Course Patterns in Seven European Countries." *European Sociological Review* 34(1): 64–78. https://doi.org/10.1093/esr/jcx083.

Zwerdling, Daniel. 1980. *Workplace Democracy*. New York: Harper Colophon.

CHAPTER 5
THE SOCIAL ORGANIZATION OF DEVELOPMENT AND AGE, II: INTRACOHORT VARIABILITY AND CUMULATIVE DIS/ADVANTAGE

Research and scholarship in gerontology and related fields have focused heavily on age-based generalizations that often rely on measures of central tendency: "mean differences" between age groups on a given characteristic, "normative" differences between cohorts, patterns of age-related change over the life course, or contrasts between different historical periods or cultural settings, as was the focus of Chapter 4.

As a new area of study seeking to establish the importance of its subject matter, such a focus is understandable. It has been a useful first step in efforts to establish baseline information on age. It also made sense to many scholars interested in age, because of the widespread assumption that age constitutes a powerful explanatory variable, and a powerful predictor of other characteristics. As pioneering gerontologist James Birren puts it:

> Chronological age is one of the most useful single items of information about an individual if not the *most* useful. From this knowledge alone an amazingly large number of general statements or predictions can be made about his anatomy, physiology psychology and social behavior.
>
> (Birren 1959:8)

Following this general logic, researchers understandably relied, and continue to rely, on comparisons of age-based averages, or other such data, which provided information that helped answer questions of how people differ by age (Offer and Sabshin, 1984; Riley, Johnson and Foner, 1972; Roberts, Walton and Viechtbauer, 2006; Schnurr, Spiro, Vielhauer, Findler, and Hamblen, 2002).

At the same time, gerontologists and others interested in age and the life course have long emphasized the *diversity* of older people. Respected scholars have frequently asserted that older people may be the most heterogeneous of any age group (Bass, Kutza, and Torres-Gil 1990; Bornstein and Smircana 1982; Butler 1974; Daatland and Biggs 2006; Maddox 1987; Motel-Klingebiel 2006). This notion has been articulated by geriatricians (e.g., Rowe and Kahn 1997, 1987; Williams 1993), psychologists (e.g., Baltes 1983), economists (e.g., David and Menchik 1984; Wolff and Greenwood 1988) and sociologists (Maddox and Douglass 1974; Neugarten 1982; Riley 1983). It has from the beginning been a staple observation of the "successful aging" narrative (Rowe and Kahn 1987).

HOMOGENEITY, HETEROGENEITY AND THE DIVERSITY OF OLDER PEOPLE

The counterpoint to the idea of "normative aging" offered by the phenomenon of diversity is relevant to both commonsense and theoretical images of older people. At the broadest level, it has served to challenge stereotypes and negative images of aging (Maddox 1974; Neugarten 1982; Riley 1980; Rowe and Kahn 1997) and efforts at forced overgeneralization, such as the claims of a universally experienced stage of disengagement discussed earlier (Hochschild 1975; Maddox 1963). It is indeed ironic that old people are perhaps more typecast by age, and hence implicitly assumed to be more homogeneous, than people of any other age category except young children.

In addition, the diversity of older people has obvious implications for policy and practice, as a diverse population has a more differentiated set of resource and service-delivery needs (Butler 1974; Crystal 1982; Maddox 1987). Sometimes, a callout to diversity has been used in a celebratory way, to emphasize the uniqueness of each individual person and the integrity of individual personality (Butler 1974; Daatland and Biggs 2006; Friedan 1994; Hickey 1980; Westerhof and Bode 2006).

Initially, this "heterogeneity discourse" remained largely at the level of casual observation. It provoked almost no intellectual curiosity and fostered little empirical research (Bornstein and Smircana 1982; Nelson and Dannefer 1992; Stone, Lin, Dannefer, and Kelley-Moore 2017). If noted at all, it remained an incidental or anecdotal observation or casual note, perhaps a qualifier to the dominant quest to understand normal aging.

Yet even as throwaway line or offhand comment, it prompted questions: What actual evidence exists concerning the relationship of variability and age? Does within-cohort diversity increase with age, or does the diversity of older persons simply reflect the diversity of the population as a whole? Alternatively, some have asked whether increasing variability on some characteristics might simply reflect a decrease in within-person stability with age (Baltes 1979, 1983; Lin and Kelley-Moore 2017a, 2017b).

Still other possibilities presented themselves. For example, might greater diversity among older people simply reflect a *cohort effect*? That is, the observation of increases in heterogeneity with age relied on cross-sectional samples, the observation could reflect a "life-course fallacy" (as discussed in Chapter 1)—an artifact of cross-sectional impressions about lifelong processes of individual and cohort aging. This could occur, for example, if societal trends (e.g. in education) disproportionately affected younger cohorts, making them seem less different from one another than age peers who had grown up when schooling and early adulthood sequencing were less uniformly experienced throughout the population (Dannefer and Sell 1988). Of course, such an idea is more than hypothetical; it describes precisely the set of 20th-century trends of educational upgrading and life-course standardization and institutionalization that were discussed in Chapter 4 (Buchmann 1989; Hogan 1981; Kohli 1986, 2007).

On the other hand, if increasing heterogeneity is found to be a *life-course* trend, displaying age-related increases in longitudinal data, to what causal factors could such a pattern be attributed?

An important early exception to the field's incuriosity about the phenomenon of diversity was Maddox and Douglass's analysis (1974), demonstrating that variability increased with age on a number of characteristics. This was a theme to which George Maddox returned in his 1986 Kleemeier Award address at the annual meeting of the Gerontological Society of America. Soon thereafter, Maddox and coeditor Powell Lawton made diversity the theme of Volume 8 of the *Annual Review of Gerontology* ("Varieties of Aging"—Maddox and Lawton 1988). With the near-simultaneous publication of that volume and a number of other articles (Bengtson and Dannefer 1987; Dannefer and Sell 1988; Nelson and Dannefer 1992; Rowe and Kahn 1987), the literature devoted to the age-heterogeneity relation began to cumulate. It marked the beginning of the expanding problematization in gerontology of two influential concepts—successful aging (Rowe and Kahn 1987, 1997) and cumulative dis/advantage (Crystal and Shea 1990; Dannefer 1987, 1988).

INTRACOHORT TRAJECTORIES OF VARIABILITY AND INEQUALITY: THE LIFE-COURSE PATTERNING OF DIVERSITY

The increasing focus on heterogeneity and inequality over the life course drew attention to the need to examine trajectories of variability. It brought a recognition that—once the question of variability is posed—a number of alternative trajectory patterns were already implied by the research literature. Figure 5.1 presents five such alternative trajectories, adapted from Dannefer and Sell's (1988) earlier depiction (see also Dannefer 1988; Settersten 1999): 1) steady divergence, 2) "U-shaped", 3) trigger-event, 4) convergence and 5) constancy.

The first trajectory, "divergence", corresponds to the general empirical pattern of increasing variability with age that has been shown to characterize the life-course patterning of many physical, psychological and social characteristics (Bass et al. 1990; Maddox and Lawton 1988; Nelson and Dannefer 1992; Stone et al. 2017). The general notion of increasing variability and inequality with age figures prominently in the discussion that follows. The second, "U-shaped" trajectory, is inspired by the human capital perspective in economics, which from its beginnings proposed that those who enter the labor force early will earn more initially, but those who have delayed entry to obtain more education will, upon labor force entry, surpass and continue to diverge in earnings from those with less education (Becker 1975, Mincer 1974; see also Dannefer and Sell 1988).

Third, a "trigger-event" trajectory fits with multiple scenarios described in the gerontological literature. It reflects the longstanding concern of several gerontologists with old-age poverty. The emphasis in much of this literature has tended to focus on poverty as a

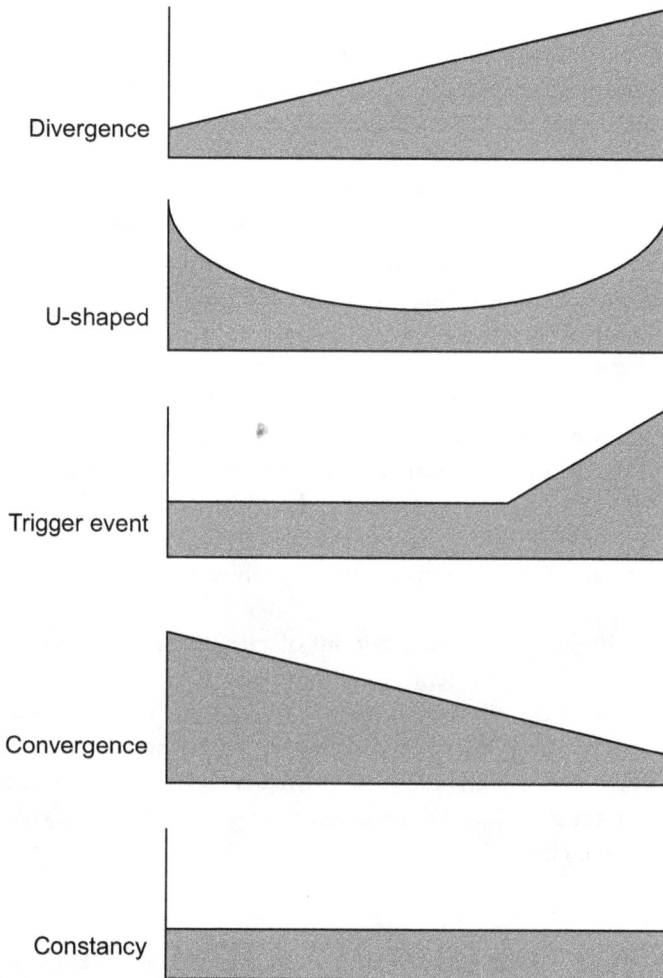

Figure 5.1 Alternative trajectories of variability
Source: Dannefer and Sell 1988

condition triggered by retirement, widowhood, or other adverse economic developments in later life, and represent an example of the "trigger-event" trajectory described previously. "The old grow poor," as Butler argued (1974:24), consistent with the emphasis of the political economy perspective (Estes 1979; Phillipson 1982; Walker 1981). As has been widely noted, this is especially true for women (Calasanti 2008; Calasanti and King 2018; Estes 1979, 2001; Hagestad 1985).

The trigger-event trajectory also fits a volitional interpretation of old-age diversity. For example, it has been proposed that the advent of retirement liberates cohort members from the role and lifestyle restrictions and habits of decades of work, allowing for "the real self" to bloom (Bass et al. 1990; Giervekd 2006; Hickey 1980; Turner 1976; Westerhof and Bode 2006). For example, as psychologist Tom Hickey contends, "Social roles may well be discontinuous, but people themselves are not" (1980:81; see also Hendricks and Hendricks 1977).

Some variant of a "convergence" trajectory pattern could be consistent with the well-known "age-as-leveler" hypothesis. Especially with regard to health-related characteristics in advanced old age, the "age-as-leveler" hypothesis predicts that the vicissitudes of aging will eventually overtake whatever advantages the healthier members of the cohort have enjoyed, leading to a tendency toward a cohort-wide homogenization of health status among surviving cohort members (e.g., Beckett 2000; Dupre 2007; Ferraro and Farmer 1996; Hoffman 2011). The first thing to note about the final trajectory depicted in Figure 5.1, "constancy", is that it is the trajectory that is implicitly assumed by longitudinal studies that do not include an examination of variability in their data analysis. It is unfortunate for the advancement of our understanding of life course and aging that this has long been, and remains, the dominant practice of gerontological researchers. Although the equivalence is not exact, "constancy" has sometimes been treated as a representation of the "status maintenance" hypothesis of depicting the intracohort trajectory of social status over the life course, since status maintenance refers to the relative stability of cohort members' relative positions in relation to each other (Henretta and Campbell 1976; O'Rand 2006). It should be noted, however, that relative stability of status does not necessarily imply stability in the amount of inequality among cohort members.

As greater attention began to be paid to notions of variability, it was recognized as posing a set of intriguing intellectual problems for gerontology. If variability in either form increases with age, why is this the case? Could it reflect some form of selection bias? To the extent that it is a genuine empirical phenomenon of increasing inequality among cohort members as they move through the life course, what is its source? What individual or social mechanisms account for it? What is the relation of observed trajectories of variability to social and demographic change?

INCREASING INEQUALITY WITH AGE: CUMULATIVE DIS/ADVANTAGE OVER THE LIFE COURSE

As the "heterogeneity narrative" developed, it rapidly became clear that a great deal of what was captured in analyses of diversity and variability was actually a reflection of socioeconomic inequality and its ramifications in health, family life and other domains. The concern with such issues led several researchers, myself included, to begin to explore the age-inequality relationship at the cohort level.

Such questions intersected with a longstanding concern of many gerontologists with old-age poverty and adversity, which had been an interest of some scholars since the early days of gerontology (Gordon 1960; Tibbitts 1960). After the social movements of the 1960s, it emerged as a major theme in a number of important works such as Butler's prize-winning *Why Survive? The Tragedy of Being Old in America* (1974), and in the work of social and policy analysts and in the development of the political economy of aging, both in the US (e.g., Binstock 1983a, 1983b; Crystal 1982; Estes 1979, 2001; Hagestad 1985; Quadagno 1984, 1996) and elsewhere (Myles 1989; Phillipson 1982; Phillipson and Walker 1986; Walker 1981, 1982, 1992). Although dramatic reductions in old-age poverty have been made in the US and other postindustrial societies over the past century, the tendency to merge discussions of inequality and poverty in gerontological thinking and writing has continued (see, e.g., Cann and Dean 2009; Scharf 2009; Vincent 1995).

Analyzing patterns of variability over the life course added a new dimension to the study of the age/inequality relationship by directing attention to its regular temporal and biographical patterning. From these earliest analyses onward, the dominant pattern that has been found for numerous important socioeconomic and health characteristics in the US and other societies has been a steady increase in inequality over the life course of a cohort, corresponding to the notion of *cumulative dis/advantage.*

To my knowledge, the first such finding was published in 1988, based on Current Population Survey data analyzed by Judy Treas (Dannefer and Sell 1988). This analysis traced trajectories of family income inequality for seven successive US ten-year birth cohorts spanning the years 1883 to 1952, and revealed a remarkably robust relationship between age and family income inequality across multiple cohorts. As can be seen in Figure 5.2, the only exception to the general trend of increasing inequality with age occurred for the 1923–32 "Good Times" cohort (Kelley-Moore and Huang 2017) whose members enjoyed the benefits of the GI Bill and post WWII prosperity, and who were in their late thirties and early forties during the 1960s.

Shortly after this analysis was published and entirely independently, Stephen Crystal and Dennis Shea (1990) published a cross-sectional analysis showing the same pattern, and Crystal and Waehrer (1996) followed up this cross-sectional effort with a longitudinal analysis of trajectories of income inequality in three cohorts over a 20-year period.

While longitudinal samples help avoid the problem of the life-course fallacy, they inevitably present other challenges, including the potentially vexing problem of selective mortality. In such studies it is always difficult to know the extent to which the observed trajectories reflect actual patterns of aging as opposed to the attrition of the sample over an extended period of time. Some argued that the likely effect of selective mortality would be to reduce rather than increase heterogeneity, since it would presumably remove the bottom tail of the distribution on many relevant characteristics.

To address this issue, Crystal and Waehrer conducted two separate analyses: One based on the entire available sample at each ten-year data point, and a second utilizing only those who had survived and were still in the sample at Wave 4. As is evident from Figures 5.3 and 5.4, the essential pattern remains the same. In both cases, intracohort inequality steadily increases with age.

This general pattern has also been reported in several other studies in the US (e.g. Easterlin, Macunovich, and Crimmins 1993) and in subsequent comparative work (Crystal and Shea 2002; O'Rand and Henretta 1999:200–5) including recent analyses of Canada (Beach 2016), Japan (Lise, Sudo, Suzuki, Yamada, and Yamada 2014), Korea (Hwang 2016) and Sweden (Mosquera et al. 2016).

As an indicator of inequality over the collective life course of a cohort, income is a limited and imperfect measure. Other studies have focused on consumer behavior as a preferred

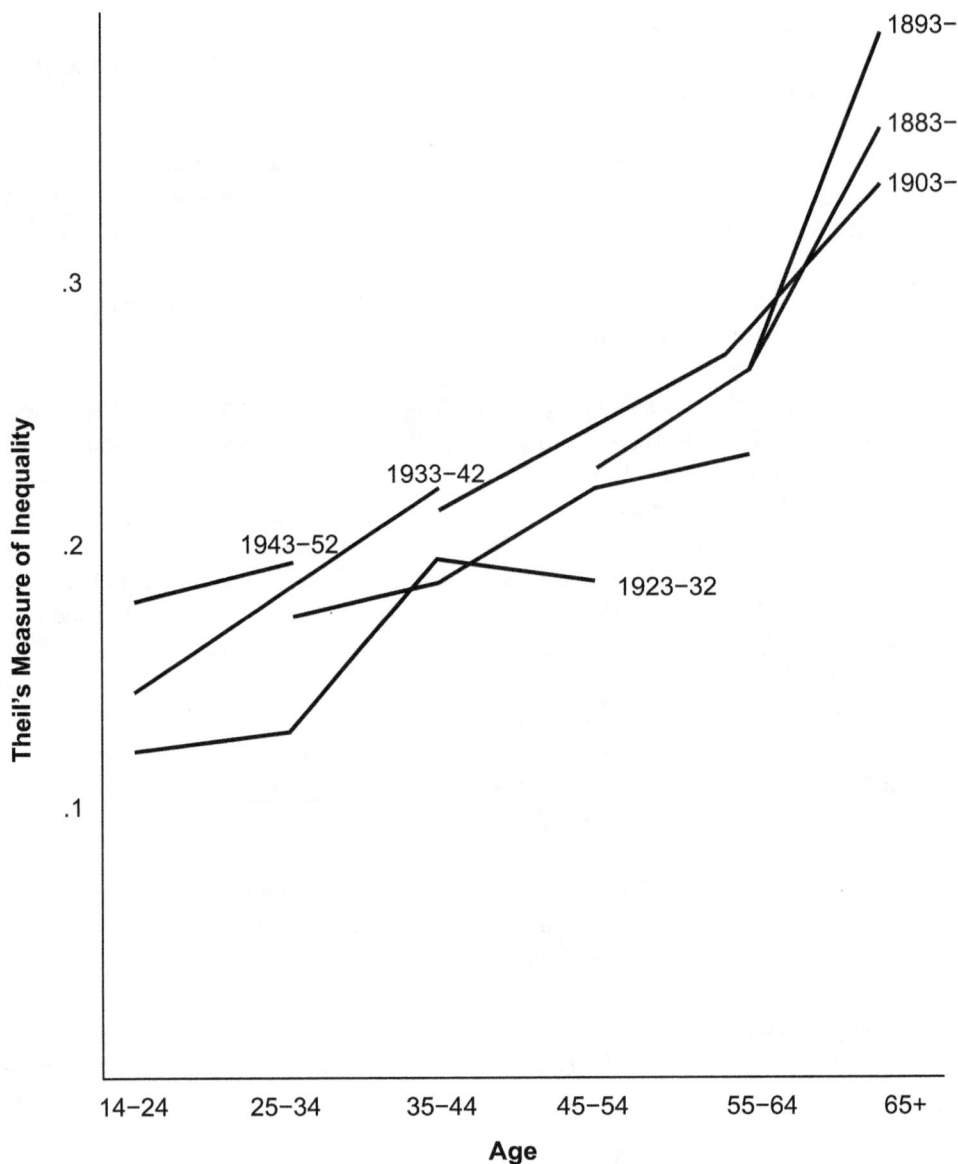

Figure 5.2 Inequality over the life course for seven cohorts

Source: Falletta and Dannefer 2014

indicator (e.g., Banks, Blundell, Levell, and Smith 2019; Shavitt, Jiang and Cho 2016) and still others have focused on household wealth. One cross-national analysis of trajectories of wealth inequality showed life-course increases in both the US and England, although the increase in the US was more pronounced (Kelley-Moore, Vanhoutte, Nazroo, Dannefer, and Lin 2014).

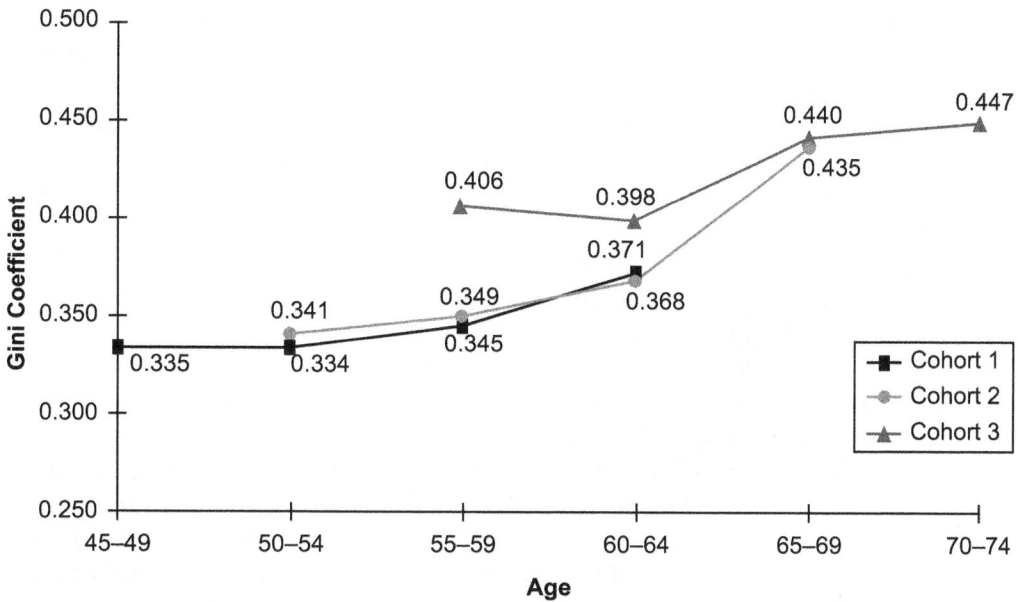

Figure 5.3 Gini coefficient by age, all respondents at each observation period
Source: Crystal and Waehrer 1996

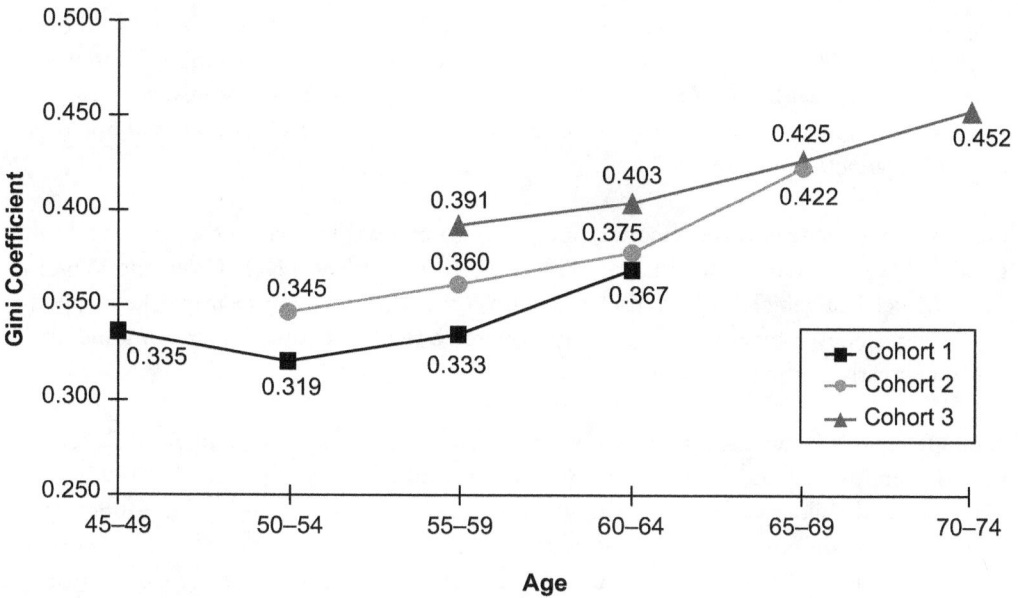

Figure 5.4 Gini coefficient by age, survivors only
Source: Crystal and Waehrer 1996

In the US, increasing attention is being paid to wealth inequality because of its association with the perpetuation of ethnic and race inequality generally. Although there are well-established race differences in income inequality, those differences are dwarfed by race differences in wealth and race-based wealth inequality. While Black workers earn on average about three quarters of the pay of White workers, Black wealth is less than 10% of White wealth (Kochbar and Fry 2014; Shapiro 2004, 2017).

But how much importance should be attached to income and wealth? Although not necessarily of intrinsic value, measures of material resources are considered important metrics because of their connection to other resources, and especially because of their connection to health. Many readers will be familiar with the concept of the *socioeconomic gradient*, a term which refers to the strong connection between resources and health that extends over much of the life course. Not surprisingly, intracohort inequalities in health, morbidity and mortality appear to follow a similar trajectory. Following the socioeconomic gradient, such increases in health inequality appear to be strongly related to social circumstances. While there is some evidence that such effects may be attenuated late in the life course (when selection effects have changed the composition of the surviving population of the cohort [e.g., Beckett 2000; Jackson, 1990; (Sieber et al., 2020' van der Linder et al., 2020)] the socioeconomic gradient nevertheless appears generally to remain robust across adulthood.

For example, in a longitudinal study of the relation between education level and physical functioning, Catherine Ross and Chia-Ling Wu found that trajectories of physical functioning diverged quite similarly in two different longitudinal studies, both based on national probability samples (see Figure 5.5). A similar pattern of increasing education-based divergence with age in a measure of mental health (specifically depressive symptoms) was also found in an analysis of data from using the National Longitudinal Study of Youth (NLSY) (Dannefer and Falletta 2005).

Nor are the tendencies for intracohort inequality to increase limited to the resource-health gradient. They have been demonstrated in quality of life (Blane, Higgs Hyde and Wiggins, 2004; Motel-Klingebiel 2006), and in numerous other domains. For example, key aspects of psychological development have also demonstrated a tendency toward increasing inequality, beginning early in the life course.

Such effects were dramatically shown by the psychologists Betty Hart and Todd Risley in their longitudinal, observational study of young children in family context (1995). They sampled children of professional, working-class and welfare parents and found that socioeconomic differences in vocabulary exposure and growth were amplified across time. Figures 5.6 and 5.7, drawn from their study, present trajectories of language experience and vocabulary growth in early childhood.

In addition to enlarging the scope of life domains and characteristics (extending to cognitive development) reflecting a pattern of increasing inequality with

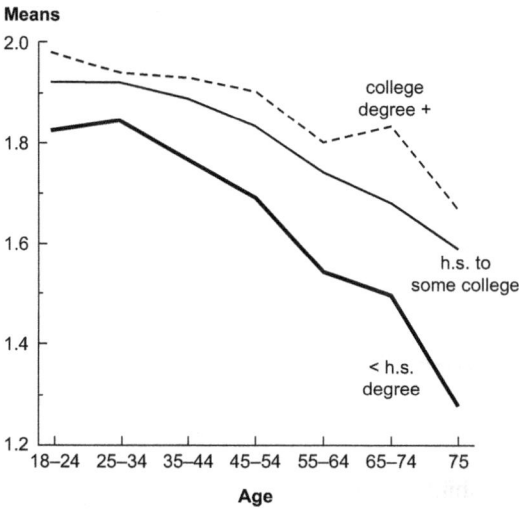

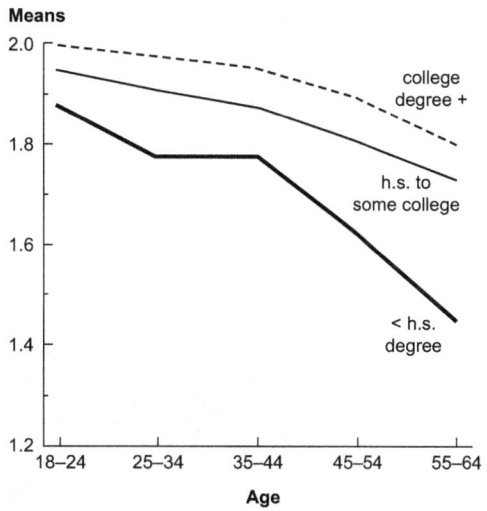

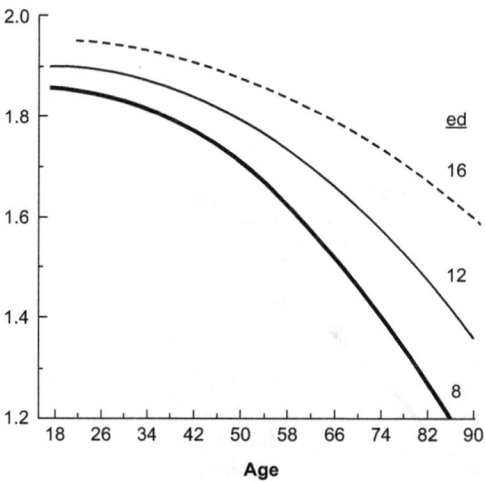

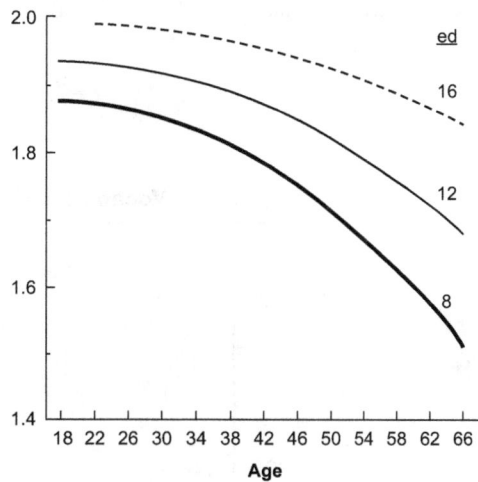

Figure 5.5 Age, physical functioning and education in two longitudinal samples

Source: Ross and Wu 1996

age, this study demonstrates that an intracohort divergence in skills and an increase in variability and inequality do not wait until the adult years or even for the commencement of schooling. They clearly begin very early in the life course. Evidence for such a pattern is not limited to small-scale studies. Using NLSY data, Farkas and Beron (2004) report a similar pattern of stratification along both socioeconomic and race lines in early childhood, although it appears to be attenuated by schooling.

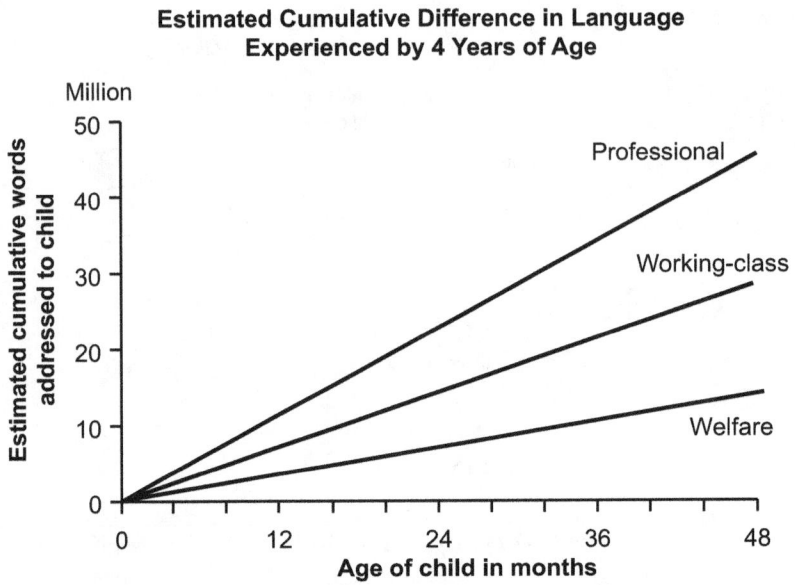

Figure 5.6 Estimated cumulative words addressed to child by social class, ages 1–4

Source: Hart and Risley 1995

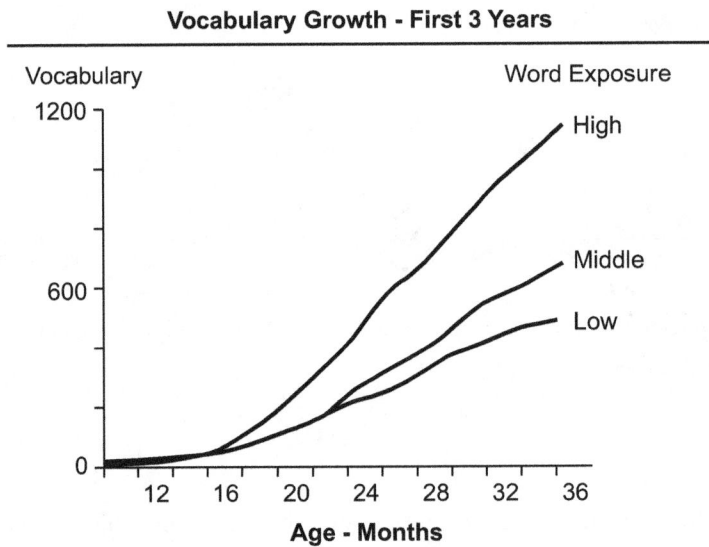

Figure 5.7 Vocabulary growth by social class, first three years by age

Source: Hart and Risley 1995

SUMMARY: THE ROBUSTNESS OF INCREASING INEQUALITY AS A LIFE-COURSE PATTERN AND UNDERLYING DYNAMICS

The array of findings just reviewed are impressive in their multidimensional breadth: they encompass a range of different types of outcome phenomena, different types of research and different segments of the life course to illustrate the remarkable consistency of the tendency for intracohort variability and inequality to increase with the passage of time, and hence with increasing age.

Taken together, these findings from multiple cohorts and multiple societies suggest that increasing inequality in resources and health and over the life course is, at least in many social contexts, a regular feature of cohort aging. This robust finding poses a challenge to characterizations of aging that are content to focus on measures of central tendency. It should prompt concern regarding the continuing predisposition of researchers to investigate age differences and age-related changes by focusing on central tendency rather than variability (Stone et al. 2017). The apparent robustness of the phenomenon of increasing variability with age brings into focus a number of emerging problems for life-course studies. First is this straightforward point: *if variability tends to increase regularly* with age as each successive cohort moves through its collective life course, *it is clearly misleading to characterize "age differences" within a population in terms of averages* or other central tendency characterizations. The standard practice in human development, gerontology and related fields of characterizing aging in such homogeneous terms generally misrepresents the empirical phenomena being studied, and hence must be rethought. Second, the tendency for variability and inequality to increase obviously raises questions of the *underlying processes* that are at work: if this is a tendency that cuts across multiple types of phenomena and segments of the life course, what are the factors that account for it? What "causes" it? Third is the observation that a great deal of what researchers have frequently called *"increasing heterogeneity" or "the diversity of older people" actually reflects age-related disparities and inequalities.*

Such questions open a new set of horizons for the exercise of sociological imagination, some of which have been pursued in investigations of the dynamics of cumulating advantage and disadvantage over the life course. Yet it has also become a primary site for the resurgence of the functional-organismic nexus, which can be seen in efforts to reframe such patterns in reductionistic, individualized terms and in the heuristic logic of containment—of containing the potential scope of sociological explanation.

To address this problem, it is necessary to consider systematically the concept that has been at the center discussions of this phenomenon in the sociological and gerontological literatures, *cumulative advantage and disadvantage.* Cumulative dis/advantage (CDA) has been viewed as a key concept for understanding patterns of increasing intracohort inequality over the life course since this discussion began in the mid–1980s. It has opened a new set of horizons for the exercise of sociological imagination, some of which have been pursued in investigations of the dynamics of cumulating advantage and disadvantage over the life course. Yet as just noted and as we will see in the next chapter, it has also become a primary site for resistance, in that it often seems to inspire a resurgence of the functional-organismic nexus.

REFERENCES

Baltes, Paul B. 1979. "Life-Span Developmental Psychology: Some Converging Observations on History and Theory." Pp. 256–79 in *Life-Span Development and Behavior*, Vol. 2, edited by P. B. Baltes and O. G. Brim, Jr. New York: Academic Press.

Baltes, Paul B. 1983. "Life-Span Developmental Psychology: Observations on History and Theory Revisited." Pp. 79–111 in *Developmental Psychology: Historical and Philosophical Perspectives*, edited by R. M. Lerner. Hillsdale, NJ: Erlbaum.

Banks, James, Richard Blundell, Peter Levell, and James P. Smith. 2019. "Life-Cycle Consumption Patterns at Older Ages in the US and the UK: Can Medical Expenditures Explain the Difference?" *American Economic Journal: Economic Policy* 11(3): 27–54.

Bass, Scott A., Elizabeth A. Kutza, and Fernando M. Torres-Gil. 1990. *Diversity in Aging: Challenges Facing Planners and Policymakers in the 1990s.* Glenview, IL: Scott, Foresman.

Beach, Charles M. 2016. "Changing Income Inequality: A Distributional Paradigm for Canada." *Canadian Journal of Economics/Revue Canadienne d'économique* 49(4): 1229–92.

Becker, Gary. 1975. *Human Capital: A Theoretical and Empirical Analysis with Special Reference to Education.* 2nd edition. New York: Columbia University Press.

Beckett, Megan. 2000. "Converging Health Inequalities in Later Life: An Artifact of Mortality Selection?" *Journal of Health and Social Behavior* 41(1): 106–19.

Bengtson, Vern L., and Dale Dannefer. 1987. "Families, Work, and Aging: Implications of Disordered Cohort Flow for the Twenty-First Century." Pp. 256–89 in *Health in Aging: Sociological Issues and Policy Directions*, edited by R. A. Ward and S. S. Tobin. New York: Springer Publishing Company.

Binstock, Robert H. 1983a. "The Aged as a Scapegoat." *The Gerontologist* 23(2): 136–43.

Binstock, Robert H. 1983b. "The Elderly in America: Their Economic Resources, Income Status and Costs." Pp. 19–33 in *Aging and Public Policy: The Politics of Growing Old in America*, edited by W. P. Browne and L. Olson. Westport, CT: Greenwood Press.

Birren, James E. 1959. "Principles of Research on Aging." Pp. 3–42 in *Handbook of Aging and the Individual: Psychological and Biological Aspects*, edited by J. E. Birren. Chicago: University of Chicago Press.

Blane, David, Paul Higgs, Martin Hyde and Richard D. Higgins. 2004. "Life Course Influences on Quality of Life in Early Old Age." *Social Science and Medicine* 58(11): 2171–9.

Bornstein, Robert, and Mark A. Smircana. 1982. "The Status of the Empirical Support of the Hypothesis of Increased Variability in Aging Populations." *The Gerontologist* 22(3): 258–60.

Buchmann, Marlis C. 1989. *The Script of Life in Modern Society: Entry into Adulthood in a Changing World.* Chicago/London: University of Chicago Press.

Butler, Robert N. 1974. *Why Survive? The Tragedy of Being Old in America*. New York: Harper & Row.

Calasanti, Toni. 2008. "Gender and Class Relations in the Struggle for Old-Age Security." *Journal of Aging, Humanities, and the Arts* 2(3–4): 238–50. https://doi.org/10.1080/19325610802471031.

Calasanti, Toni, and Neal King. 2018. "The Dynamic Nature of Gender and Aging Bodies." *Journal of Aging Studies* 45: 11–17.

Cann, Paul, and Malcolm Dean, eds. 2009. *Unequal Ageing: The Untold Story of Exclusion in Old Age*. Bristol, UK: Policy Press.

Crystal, Stephen. 1982. *America's Old Age Crisis: Public Policy and the Two Worlds of Aging*. New York: Basic Books.

Crystal, Stephen, and Dennis Shea. 1990. "Cumulative Advantage, Cumulative Disadvantage, and Inequality among Elderly People." *Gerontologist* 30(4): 437–43.

Crystal, Stephen, and Dennis Shea, eds. 2002. *Annual Review of Gerontology and Geriatrics, Volume 22, 2002: Economic Outcomes in Later Life: Public Policy, Health and Cumulative Advantage*. New York, NY: Springer Publishing Company.

Crystal, Stephen, and Keith Waehrer. 1996. "Later-Life Economic Inequality in Longitudinal Perspective." *The Journals of Gerontology Series B: Psychological Sciences and Social Sciences* 51(6): S307–18.

Daatland, Sven Olav, and Simon Biggs. 2006. *Aging and Diversity: Mulitple Pathways and Cultural Migrations*. Bristol, UK: Policy Press.

Dannefer, Dale. 1987. "Aging as Intracohort Differentiation: Accentuation, the Matthew Effect and the Life Course." *Sociological Forum* 2(2): 211–36 (Spring).

Dannefer, Dale. 1988. "Differential Gerontology and the Stratified Life Course: Conceptual and Methodological Issues." Chapter 1 in *Annual Review of Gerontology & Geriatrics*, Vol. 8, edited by M. Powell Lawton and George Maddox. New York, NY: Springer Publishing.

Dannefer, Dale, and Lynn Falletta. 2005. "Cumulative Advantage/Disadvantage and Health: Data from the National Longitudinal Survey of Youth." Presented paper, Annual Meeting of the Gerontological Society of America, Orlando, FL (November).

Dannefer, Dale, and R. R. Sell. 1988. "Age Structure, the Life Course and 'Aged Heterogeneity': Prospects for Theory and Research." *Comprehensive Gerontology Section B, Behavioural, Social, and Applied Sciences* 2(1): 1–10.

David, Martin, and Paul L. Menchik. 1984. "Nonearned Income, Income Instability and Inequality: A Life-Cycle Interpretation." Pp. 53–73 in *The Collection and Analysis of Economic and Consumer Behavior Data: In Memory of Robert Ferber*, edited by S. Sudman and M. Spaeth. Chicago: University of Illinois Press.

Dupre, Matthew. 2007. "Educational Differences in Age-Related Patterns of Disease: Reconsidering the Cumulative Disadvantage and Age-as-leveler Hypotheses." *Journal of Health and Social Behavior* 48(1): 1–15.

Easterlin, Richard A., Diane J. Macunovich, and Eileen M. Crimmins. 1993. "Economic Status of the Young and Old in the Working Age Population, 1964 and 1987." Pp. 67–86 in *The Changing Contract Across Generations*, edited by V. L. Bengtson and W. A. Achenbaum. New York, NY: Aldine De Gruytor.

Estes, Carroll L. 1979. *The Aging Enterprise*. San Francisco, CA: Jossey-Bass.

Estes, Carroll L. 2001. *Social Policy and Aging: A Critical Perspective*. New York: SAGE Publications.

Falletta, Lynn, and Dale Dannefer. 2014. "The Life Course and the Social Organization of Age." Pp. 607–25 in *Handbook of the Social Psychology of Inequality*, edited by J. Macleod, E. J. Lawler, and M. Schwalbe. New York: Springer Publishing Company.

Farkas, George, and Kurt Beron. 2004. "The Detailed Age Trajectory of Oral Vocabulary Knowledge: Differences by Class and Race." *Social Science Research* 33(3): 464–97.

Ferraro, Kenneth F., and Melissa M. Farmer. 1996. "Double Jeopardy, Aging as Leveler, or Persistent Health Inequality? A Longitudinal Analysis of White and Black Americans." *The Journals of Gerontology: Series B* 51B(6): S319–28.

Friedan, Betty. 1994. *The Fountain of Age*. New York: Simon & Schuster.

Gierveld, Jenny De Jong. 2006. "Societal Trends and Life Course Events Affecting Diversity in Later Life." Pp. 175–88 in *Aging and Diversity: Mulitple Pathways and Cultural Migrations*, edited by S. O. Daatland and S. Biggs. Bristol, UK: Policy Press.

Gordon, F. 1960. "Aging and Income Security." Pp. 208–60 in *Handbook of Social Gerontology: Societal Aspects of Aging*, edited by C. Tibbitts. Chicago: University of Chicago Press.

Hagestad, Gunhild O. 1985. "Older Women in Intergenerational Relations." Pp. 137–51 in *The Physical and Mental Health of Aged Women*, edited by M. R. Haug. New York: Springer Publishing Company.

Hart, Betty, and Todd R. Risley. 1995. *The Social World of Children Learning to Talk*. Baltimore, MD: P. H. Brookes Publisher.

Hendricks, John, and C. Davis Hendricks. 1977. *Aging in Mass Society: Myths and Realities*. Cambridge, MA: Winthrop.

Henretta, John C., and Richard T. Campbell. 1976. "Status Attainment and Status Maintenance: A Study of Stratification in Old Age." *American Sociological Review* 41(6): 981–92.

Hickey, Tom. 1980. *Health and Aging*. Monterey, CA: Brooks/Cole.

Hochschild, Arlie. R. 1975. "Disengagement Theory: A Critique and Proposal." *American Sociological Review* 40(5): 553–69.

Hoffman, Rasmus. 2011. "Illness, Not Age, Is the Leveler of Social Mortality Differences in Old Age." *Journals of Gerontology Social Sciences* 66(5): 374–9.

Hogan, Dennis. 1981. *Transitions and Social Change*. New York: Academic Press.

Hwang, Sun-Jae. 2016. "Public Pensions as the Great Equalizer? Decomposition of Old-Age Income Inequality in South Korea, 1998–2010." *Journal of Aging & Social Policy* 28(2): 81–97.

Kelley-Moore, Jessica, Bram Vanhoutte, James Nazroo, Dale Dannefer, and Jielu Lin. 2014. "Education Differences in Health Inequality for US and England: Is Cumulative Dis/Advantage Country-Centric?" Paper presented at the annual meeting of the Gerontological Society of America. Washington, DC.

Kelley-Moore, Jessica, and Wenxuan Huang. 2017. "The 'Good Times' Cohort in Late Life: Black-White Differences in Pathways to Functional Limitations." *Research on Aging* 39(4): 526–48. https://doi.org/10.1177/0164027516655582.

Kochbar, Rakesh, and Richard Fry. 2014. "Wealth Inequality Has Widened along Racial, Ethnic Lines Since End of Great Recession." *FactTank: News in the Numbers*. Washington, DC: Pew Research Center December 14. Retrieved from www.pewresearch.org/fact-tank/2014/12/12/racial-wealth-gaps-great-recession/

Kohli, Martin. 1986. "The World We Forgot: A Historical Review of the Life Course." Pp. 271–303 in *Later Life: The Social Psychology of Aging*, edited by V. W. Marshall. Beverly Hills, CA: Sage.

Kohli, Martin. 2007. "The Institutionalization of the Life Course: Looking Back to Look Ahead." *Research in Human Development* 4(3–4): 253–71.

Lin, Jielu, and Jessica Kelley-Moore. 2017a. "From Noise to Signal: The Age and Social Patterning of Intra-Individual Variability in Late-Life Health." *The Journals of Gerontology, Series B: Psychological Sciences and Social Sciences* 72(1): 168–79.

Lin, Jielu, and Jessica Kelley-Moore. 2017b. "Intraindividual Variability in Late-Life Functional Limitations Among White, Black, and Hispanic Older Adults: Implications for the Weathering Hypothesis." *Research on Aging* 39(4): 549–57.

Lise, Jeremy, Nao Sudo, Michio Suzuki, Ken Yamada, and Tomoaki Yamada. 2014. "Wage, Income and Consumption Inequality in Japan, 1981–2008: From Boom to Lost Decades." *Review of Economic Dynamics* 17(4): 582–612.

Maddox, George. 1963. "Activity and Morale: A Longitudinal Study of Selected Elderly Subjects." *Social Forces* 42: 195–204.

Maddox, Gorge L. 1987. "Aging Differently." *The Gerontologist* 27(5): 557–64.

Maddox, Gorge L., and Elizabeth B. Douglass. 1974. "Aging and Individual Differences: A Longitudinal Analysis of Social, Psychological and Physiological Indicators." *Journal of Gerontology* 29(5): 555–63.

Maddox, Gorge. L., and M. Powell Lawton. 1988. *Annual Review of Gerontology and Geriatrics 8: Varieties of Aging*. New York: Springer Publishing Company.

Mincer, Jacob. 1974. *Schooling, Experience and Earnings*. New York: National Bureau of Economic Research.

Mosquera, Paola A., Miguel San Sebastian, Anna-Karin Waenerlund, Anneli Ivarsson, Lars Weinehall, and Per E. Gustafsson. 2016. "Income-Related Inequalities in Cardiovascular Disease from Mid-Life to Old Age in a Northern Swedish Cohort: A Decomposition Analysis." *Social Science & Medicine* 149: 135–44.

Motel-Klingebiel, Andreas. 2006. "Quality of Life and Social Inequality in Old Age." Pp. 190–205 in *Ageing and Diversity: Multiple Pathways and Cultural Migrations*, edited by S. O. Daatland and S. Biggs. Bristol, UK: The Policy Press.

Myles, John. 1989. *Old Age in the Welfare State*. Lawrence, KS: University Press of Kansas.

Nelson, E. Anne, and Dale Dannefer. 1992. "Aged Heterogeneity: Fact or Fiction? The Fate of Diversity in Gerontological Research." *The Gerontologist* 32(1): 17–23.

Neugarten, Bernice L. 1982. *Age or Need: Public Policies and Older People*. Beverly Hills, CA: Sage.

Offer, Daniel and Melvin Sabshin. 1984. *Normalilty and the Life Cycle: A Critical Integration*. New York: Basic Books.

O'Rand, Angela M. 2006. "Stratification and the Life Course: Life Course Capital, Life Course Risks, and Social Inequality." Pp. 145–62 in *Handbook of Aging and the Social Sciences*, edited by R. H. Binstock and L. K. George. New York: Elsevier.

O'Rand, Angela M., and John C. Henretta. 1999. *Age and Inequality: Diverse Pathways through Later Life*. Boulder, CO: Westview Press.

Phillipson, Christopher. 1982. *Capitalism and the Construction of Old Age*. London: Macmillan.

Phillipson, Christopher and Alan Walker. 1986. *Ageing and Social Policy: A Critical Assessment*. London: Gower.

Quadagno, Jill. 1984. "Welfare Capitalism and the Social Security Act of 1935." *American Sociological Review* 49(5): 632–47.

Quadagno, Jill. 1996. "Social Security and the Myth of the Entitlement Crisis." *The Gerontologist* 36(3): 391–9.

Riley, Matilda W. 1980. "Age and Aging: From Theory Generation to Theory Testing." Pp. 339–48 in *Sociological Research: Vol. 1: A Case Approach*, edited by H. B. Blalock, Jr. New York: Harcourt Brace Jovanovich.

Riley, Matilda W. 1983. "A Mosaic of Knowledge." Pp. 1–3 in *Aging in Society: Selected Reviews of Recent Research*, edited by M. W. Riley, B. B. Hess, and K. Bond. Hillsdale, NJ: Erlbaum.

Roberts, Brent W., Kate E Walton andWolfgang Viechtbauer. 2006. "Patterns of mean-level change in personality traits across the life course: a meta-analysis of longitudinal studies." *Psychological Bulletin 132*(1): 1-25. doi: 10.1037/0033-2909.132.1.1.

Ross, Catherine, and Chia-Ling Wu. 1996. "Education, Age, and the Cumulative Advantage in Health." *Journal of Health and Social Behavior* 37(1): 104–20.

Rowe, John W., and Robert Kahn. 1987. "Human Aging: Usual and Successful." *Science* 237 (4811): 143–9.

Rowe, John W., and Robert L. Kahn. 1997. *Successful Aging*. New York: Dell Publishing.

Scharf, Thomas. 2009. "Too Tight to Mention: Unequal Income in Older Age." Pp. 25–52 in *Unequal Ageing: The Untold Story of Exclusion in Old Age*, edited by P. Cann and M. Dean. Bristol, UK: Policy Press.

Schnurr, Paula P., Avron Spiro III, Melanie J. Vielhauer, Marianne N. Findler, and Jessica L. Hamblen. 2002. "Trauma in the Lives of Older Men: Findings From the Normative Aging Study." *Journal of Clinical Geropsychology* 8(3): 175–87.

Settersten, Richard A. 1999. *Lives in Time and Place: The Problems and Promises of Developmental Science (Society and Aging Series)*. Amityville, NY: Baywood Publishing Company.

Shapiro, Thomas M. 2004. *The Hidden Cost of Being African American: How Wealth Perpetuates Inequality*. New York: Oxford University Press.

Shapiro, Thomas M. 2017. *Toxic Inequality: How America's Wealth Gap Destroys Mobility, Deepens the Racial Divide, and Threatens Our Future*. New York: Basic Books.

Shavitt, Sharon, Duo Jiang, and Hyewon Cho. 2016. "Stratification and Segmentation: Social Class in Consumer Behavior." *Journal of Consumer Psychology* 26(4): 583–93. https://doi.org/10.1016/j.jcps.2016.08.00.

Sieber, Stefan, Boris Cheval, Dan Orsholits, Bernadette W. A. van der Linden, Idris Guessous, Rainer Gabriel, Matthias Kliegel, Martina von Arx, Michelle Kelly-Irving, Marja Aartsen, Matthieu P. Boisgontier, Dalphine Courvoisier, Claudine Burton-Jeangros and Stephane Cullati. 2020. "Do Welfare Regimes Moderate Cumulataive Dis/advantages Over the Life Course? Cross-National Evidence from Longitudinal Share Data." *Journal of Gerontology Social Sciences* 75(6): 1312–25.

Stone, Mary E., Jielu Lin, Dale Dannefer, and Jessica A. Kelley-Moore. 2017. "The Continued Eclipse of Heterogeneity in Gerontological Research." *Journals of Gerontology: Psychological Sciences and Social Sciences* 72(1): 162–7.

Tibbitts, Clark, ed. 1960. *Handbook of Social Gerontology: Societal Aspects of Aging*. Chicago: University of Chicago Press.

Turner, Ralph. 1976. "The Real Self: From Institution to Impulse." *American Journal of Sociology* 81(5): 989–1016.

van der Linden, Wilhelmina Bernadette, Antonio, Boris Cheval, Stefan Sieber, Dan Orsholits, Idris Guessous, Silvia Stringhini, Rainer Gabriel, Marja Aartsen, David Blane, Delphine Courvoisier, Claudine Burton-Jeangros, Matthias Kliegel and

Stephane Cullati. 2020. "Life Course Socioeconomic Conditions and Frailty at Older Ages." *Journal of Gerontology Social Sciences* 75(6): 1348-58.

Vincent, John. 1995. *Inequality and Old Age*. London: Routledge.

Walker, Alan. 1981. "Towards a Political Economy of Old Age." *Ageing & Society* 1(1): 73–94.

Walker, Alan. 1982. "Dependency and Old Age." *Social Policy & Administration* 16(2): 115–35.

Walker, Alan. 1992. "The Persistence of Poverty under Welfare States and the Prospects for Its Abolition." *International Journal of Health Services* 22(1): 1–17.

Westerhof, Gerben J., and Christina Bode. 2006. "The Personal Meaning of Individuality and Relatedness: Gender Differences in Middle and Late Adulthood." Pp. 29–44 in *Ageing and Diversity: Multiple Pathways and Cultural Migrations*, edited by S. O. Daatland and S. Biggs. Bristol, UK: Policy Press.

Williams, T. Franklin. 1993. "Aging Versus Disease." Pp. 21–5 in *The Biology of Aging*, edited by R. L. Sprott, H. R. Warner, and T. F. Williams. New York: Springer Publishing Company.

Wolff, Edward, and Daphne Greenwood. 1988. "Relative Wealth Holdings of Children and the Elderly in the United States." Pp. 123–48 in *The Vulnerable*, edited by J. Palmer, T. Smeeding, and B. Torrey. Washington: Urban Institute Press.

CHAPTER 6
CUMULATIVE DIS/ADVANTAGE AS A COHORT PHENOMENON: LEVELS, PROCESSES AND PARADIGMATIC ALTERNATIVES

DEFINING CUMULATIVE DIS/ADVANTAGE

Cumulative dis/advantage (CDA) has a long history in folk sayings like "the rich get richer, the poor poorer", and "nothing succeeds like success". Such notions transcend history and culture; they can be found in contemporary non-Western societies as diverse as China and Uganda, where it is said that the "the fat ones grow fatter, the lean leaner" (Trentaz 2012:26). Often, the notion is applied to specific domains, as when it is declared that "best sellers . . . sell the best" (Alter 2020) and when experts warn of "a virtuous circle or 'flywheel' effect" of competitive advantage in the application of AI that can effectively lead to a monopoly of power (Bass 2018:5). Of course, Robert Merton's famous albeit dubious term, the "Matthew Effect", derives from an account of words spoken 2,000 years ago.

Beyond its "face validity", the phenomenon of CDA is rooted in a set of generative social dynamics that often go unrecognized. Regularly observed *patterns* of increasing inequality like those reported in the previous chapter can be more readily observed than can the *underlying processes* that produce such patterns.

Cumulative dis/advantage can be defined as "the systemic tendency for inter-individual divergence in a given characteristic (e.g., money, health or status) with the passage of time" (Dannefer 2003:S327). DiPrete and Eirich describe CDA as "a general mechanism across any temporal process . . . in which a favorable relative position becomes a resource that produces relative further gains" (2006:271)—and, it might be added, an unfavorable position becomes a liability likely to contribute to further losses.

These definitions contain two irreducible aspects of a sociological treatment of CDA, one processual and one structural. First, the term *systemic tendency* signals that the origins of CDA *inhere in the operation of social systems*. Grounded in social processes, its genesis is not in individual differences or volition, nor in chance. It is *irreducibly social*, deriving from identifiable mechanisms and processes that are embedded in everyday social life across system levels, from micro-interaction to more encompassing levels of social organization (Dannefer 1987, 2003; Elias and Feagin 2016:6; Pallas and Jennings 2009).

The second, structural aspect is contained in DiPrete and Eirich's defining emphasis on the *actor's social position as itself a resource*. A "mechanism . . . in which a favorable relative position becomes a resource" recognizes that one's structural position itself constitutes a socially generative force that can operate independently of individual characteristics. As reported in a recent study of funded academic research, "funding is an asset for later funding", net of issues of quality (Bol, de Vaan, and van de Rijt 2018). Again, this similarly implies that unfavorable positions increase the risk of further loss.

Combining the essential elements of these two definitions—one processual and one structural—I propose as a refined definition the following:

> the systemic tendency for inter-individual divergence in a given characteristic (e.g., money, health or status) with the passage of time, in which the relative value of one's social position itself operates as a factor (resource or liability) in producing relative further gains or losses.

Although such a definition refers to CDA as a general social phenomenon that operates in many circumstances and situations, it also implies specific links to the life course. Because such mechanisms bear upon people's lives, they are *temporally* as well as *structurally* systemic: to say that an actor's location in a social system influences her position at a subsequent point in time implies a systemic interdependence in the life-course sequencing of positions. Contingencies based on role access or occupancy (e.g., educational ability grouping, selection processes into college or occupation) comprise a fundamental component of CDA.

A qualification: this is not to say that individual differences are irrelevant to the phenomenon of unequal life-course outcomes. I will return to approaches that focus on individual differences later. However, it is important to distinguish possible individual sources of difference from a purely *sociological* account of CDA. A sociological account focuses on those processes that are inherently social, and that hence render the matter of individual differences as a causal force to be definitionally irrelevant. As O'Rand observes, "cumulative advantage theory provides the social allocation logic of life course inequality that is not intrinsic to individualistic self-selection theory" (2003:15). To grasp the significance of this point, it may be helpful to consider a counterfactual world populated by clones. Even in such a world with no preexisting individual differences, social processes would on their own generate such differences (Dannefer 1987, 2008; Schwalbe 2008; Sorensen 1986).

A second qualification is also needed: the presence of inherent systemic dynamics that produce tendencies toward CDA does not preclude the possibility that exogenous forces—factors external to the system—may also influence CDA (in either direction). For example, external demand for a nation's products may increase national prosperity, which could reduce societal inequality while correspondingly attenuating intracohort trajectories of inequality. Changes in tax, pension or other policies may either ameliorate or exacerbate inequality overall, or especially in age groups targeted by the policy (as in the case of pension policies). While such externally injected stimuli events may impact intracohort trajectories of inequality (Falletta and Dannefer 2014; Crystal, Shea, and Reyes 2016; Turek, Perek-Bialas, and Stypinska 2015), they have no effect whatever on the underlying systemic processes that continuously operate to reproduce a stratified society and amplify individual differences in, for example, labor markets, marriage markets, schools and informal everyday interaction—all of which will continue, regardless of such events, linking the "durable inequality" (Tilly 1998) that is reproduced in every day social life to the life course.

Indeed, such external factors are sometimes *intentionally interjected* into social systems in efforts to disrupt or in some cases strengthen such dynamics. This can occur at every system level. At the micro-level, it happens, for example, when a family therapist seeks to help a family break a destructive cycle of scapegoating one sibling (Fingerman and Berman 2000; McGoldrick, Giordano, and Garcia-Preto 2005).

At the macro-level, state-level transfer-payment plans may help offset lifelong effects of adversity. Alternatively, in some cases such plans may be set up deliberately to reproduce existing structures of inequality. And, in a testament to the complexity of social phenomena at every level, both strategies can be part of the same initiative. As a well-known example, the US Social Security program was centrally important in reducing old-age poverty. Yet its original rules (from the 1930s) were deliberately formulated to exclude Black citizens (Dannefer, Gilbert, and Han 2020; Poole 2006), thereby reinforcing already-present arrangements that strengthened race-based CDA. It is important to recognize that for Black citizens, this was a policy intervention that cut both ways—providing unprecedented assistance to some Black citizens while also deliberately excluding large segments from receiving full benefits in order to appease segregationist Southern legislators (Katznelson 2005).

Whether the intention and the effects are positive or negative, the general point to be recognized is that in each case, an external influence disrupts or shifts the vectors of ongoing system dynamics. Whether or not such interventions succeed in altering outcomes, they have zero effect on the underlying systemic tendencies that generate CDA (e.g., in labeling, altercasting, typification and other common features of interpersonal interaction in everyday life).

Such examples offer further illustration of the more general point noted in Chapter 1: Social change is irrelevant to the basic social processes that govern and regulate the social organization of age. Like world-construction and the other social processes discussed in earlier chapters, *the inequality-generating tendencies that produce CDA comprise obdurate features of social-system dynamics and social life.* These processes are not subject to change but are a standard part of the operation of society. In this sense, they are inherent, law-like features of social life (Falletta and Dannefer 2014; Rigney 2010; Tilly 1998).

Again, the relentlessness of these processes does not mean that the effects of CDA cannot be ameliorated or even reversed. Human actors may devise progressive tax policies to counter tendencies toward capital accumulation, or develop teacher-training programs to deconstruct labeling processes that create invidious classroom distinctions. Such efforts do not eliminate the basic interactional tendency to typify others and assign labels, which is a fundamental element in general human processes of reality-construction (Berger and Luckmann 1967). Such processes will still be operative. Analogously, humans have devised ways to transcend gravity's effects with aircraft and space travel technologies but that does not negate the irrepressible force of gravity. Generally speaking, science does not seek to discover lawful relationships in order to become resigned to their inevitability but as a first step in seeking to understand how to control and live with them, including finding ways to regulate their humanly destructive aspects.

In sum, an essential bedrock principle is the *systemic* character of the genesis of CDA, manifest in continuously operative social processes, and beginning with the world-constructing processes of everyday interaction described in Chapter 3. As a general principle, the foundation of CDA in social-system processes has been, at best, unevenly appreciated in studies of age and the life course. One indication of this unevenness can be seen precisely in the fate of the word, "systemic". For example, when the previous definition "systemic tendency for interindividual divergence" is quoted, it is frequently misquoted or miscopied as "*systematic*". Although similar-sounding, the definitions of these two words differ profoundly. "Systemic" indicates forces and mechanisms that inhere in the ongoing dynamics of social interaction, and are thus irreducible and endogenous to everyday social life. Since "systematic" means simply "orderly" or "methodical", this misquotation obscures and dilutes the original meaning, losing the key point that CDA is generated from within the ubiquitous dynamics of everyday social life.

THEORETICAL PRESUPPOSITIONS: COMPETING SYSTEMIC PARADIGMS

Robert Merton's well-known writings about CDA (as the Matthew Effect) focus heavily on its linkages to science (1968, 1988; see also Zuckerman 1977). However, more than two decades before Merton published his first paper on the Matthew Effect in 1968, Gunnar Myrdal was writing about the phenomenon of systemically generated inequality with a more rigorous and critical theoretical lens. Myrdal first articulated "the principle of cumulative and circular causation" in his work on the US race problem (1944, 1957). It is curious that although Merton was clearly aware of this work and cites it on other points, he does not acknowledge this foundational aspect of Myrdal's contributions in his own discussions of the Matthew Effect.

Myrdal's formulation is of more than historical interest; it remains a particularly lucid and explicit statement of the elemental social dynamics that are responsible for cumulative advantage and disadvantage as generic and irrepressible social processes (see DiTomaso 2013:2). He presented his principle of "cumulative causation" in more explicit and delineated social-system terms than did Merton, and he also formulated it as an explicit critique of the functionalist paradigm. Myrdal's view thus directly contrasts with Merton's inclination to regard CDA as a functional process—increasing communication efficiency and facilitating "separation of wheat from chaff" in scientific work while maintaining overall system stability, even if disadvantaging some individuals (Merton 1968, 1988; Dannefer 2003:S29).

In Myrdal's analysis, the concept of cumulation represents a corrective to the functionalist "equilibrium" view, which assumes that social systems respond to any disturbance by returning to a state of static normality. His argument thus offers an early critique of this tenet of mainstream structural-functionalism:

> What is wrong with the stable equilibrium assumption . . . is the very idea that a social
> process follows a direction . . . toward a position which . . . can be described as a state
> of equilibrium between forces. Behind this idea is another assumption, namely, that a
> change will regularly call forth a reaction in the system in the form of changes which . . .
> go in the contrary direction to the first change.
>
> (1957:13)

Instead, Myrdal observes, human social systems tend to *amplify* difference, thereby
producing inequality through ongoing processes of interaction:

> On the contrary . . . there is no such tendency toward automatic self-stabilization in
> the social system. In the normal case such a change does not call forth countervailing
> changes but instead, supporting changes, which move the system in the same
> direction as the first change but much further. Because of such circular causation,
> a social process tends to become cumulative and often to gather speed at an
> accelerating rate.
>
> (1957:13)

This insight anticipates the application of general systems theory to sociology, which
recognized that *equilibrium* is an inappropriate concept to apply to any living system or
social system, since it implies a dissipation of energy and organization (as in physical
systems—e.g., balls colliding on a billiard table or planetary-solar systems; Buckley 1967).
By contrast, biological organisms operate through *homeostatic* mechanisms (Cannon 1939;
Gleick 2008) which entail the regulation and maintenance of energy, not the dissipation
implied by equilibrium. Such mechanisms, despite their dynamic quality, imply a systemic
rigidity allowing for only a narrow band of flexibility (e.g., the regulation of body
temperature), beyond which the organism cannot survive.

In contrast to such biological systems, social systems are founded on symbolic information
flows and inherently flexible relational forms that are inherently underdetermined,
dynamic and *morphogenetic* (Archer 2000, 2017; Buckley 1967). Symbolic information
(whether specialized knowledge, or simply a privileged position/role in an organization)
comprises a resource which becomes a basis of differential power and stratification that is
self-amplifying, tending to produce increasing divergence and inequality among system
members. The same can be said for the control of relational forms. As noted earlier, the
human potential for imagination and novelty is irrepressible, and the externalization of
novel ideas into action ensures the continual possibility of humanly generated change. Such
changes very often entail an amplification of emergent differences ("deviation amplification"
in systems terminology), often based on resource differentials among the relevant actors.
Noted organizational systems theorist Magoroh Maruyama (1963) regarded the deviation-
amplification processes inherent in human social systems as a "second cybernetics".

The systems framework thus recognizes social life as consisting of an energy-infused
set of processes that inherently generate emergent social characteristics in the course
of social interaction, and that cannot be reduced to individual characteristics or the
sum of individual actions. It is worth noting that this framework shares fully with the
Durkheimian organismic model the key recognition that social reality consists of "more

than the sum of its parts"—an emergent reality *sui generis* in its own right. Thus, it comprises a system of obdurate causal forces that are self-sustaining and that cannot be reduced to the individual level. On this specific and fundamental point there is full agreement with Parsons' functionalism and the broader Durkheimian tradition.

However, a critically and empirically grounded systems approach parts ways with the functional-organismic tradition in its recognition that the high-energy dynamics of social systems do not inherently tend only to stability and return to normality; rather, the inherent tendencies to generate difference and inequality as well as novelty and innovation are integral to its operation. Thus, emergent social phenomena that entail conflict and tension (e.g., election hacking, digisexuality, tolerance for surveillance) are no less the products of such systems than are basic mechanisms of interaction and social reproduction (e.g., Archer 2017; Collins 2005).

As elements of the ongoing dynamics of social life, CDA-generating processes operate at micro-, meso- and macro-levels of social context, at each level creating distinction, division and stratification among age peers as they move through the life course (Bourdieu 1984; Dannefer 1992, 2003; Pallas and Jennings 2009). It is in this sense that it has been said that aging is something that happens not just *within*, but also *between*, people (Dannefer 1987; Rosenbaum 1978).

The notion of a system-based set of dynamics of accumulation as described here is, of course, also consistent with Marxian ideas of capital accumulation (Luxemburg 1951; Marx 2015 [1867]; O'Connor 1986), which accord the general notion of accumulation a greater significance by making it central to social contradiction and pressure for change. In the Marxian framework, it is recognized that owners accumulate profits at the expense of labor, creating a greater and greater gulf of inequality. While there is ongoing cumulative advantage for capitalists, this framework anticipates ongoing cumulative disadvantage for workers.

It is important to be clear that the fact that inequality-generating CDA processes are rooted in irrepressible patterns of micro-interaction does not neutralize the fact that they create contradictions and thus may be a force for social change. While exploring such tensions would move us well beyond the present discussion, it should be noted that this obdurate tendency of cumulative processes comprises one source of pressure for systemic change.

CDA MECHANISMS ACROSS SYSTEM LEVELS

To provide some context for a consideration of recent research on CDA, I consider how CDA-generating processes operate across levels of analysis.

CDA AND MICRO-LEVEL PROCESSES

Much of the attention to the phenomenon of CDA literature has been focused on data and evidence at the population or macro- and meso-levels of social-system organization. However, as we have seen in earlier chapters, the most basic and pervasive social processes operate "closer to the ground", at the micro-level (Collins 2005; Dannefer 2008; Pallas and Jennings 2009). Moreover, as Macmillan notes (2018), the actual mechanisms that account for observed outcomes can be most clearly and directly observed in descriptive and narrative data that are anchored in the micro-level of experiences. The analysis of CDA is no exception to this. The microdynamics of world-construction and micro-interaction comprise the *most fundamental level* at which CDA processes operate (Dannefer 2009). Perhaps because of the large amount of attention given to studies of CDA in terms of population-level "macro" patterns, this foundational importance of microdynamics for a proper apprehension of CDA has received limited attention, and often appears to have not been recognized in some discussions of CDA (Beard and Williamson 2016; Ferraro and Shippee 2009).

In the sociology of age, the implications of micro-dynamics were first discussed in Vern Bengtson's application to aging of labeling theory in the *cycle of induced incompetence* in his underappreciated early monograph, *The Social Psychology of Aging* (1973).

As the reader can see, this diagram (Figure 6.1) begins with a structural reality—vulnerability deriving from ageism and loss, a vulnerability that positions individuals to be seen as inadequate or incompetent, and then traces its consequences in everyday life. Self-doubts as to one's continuing competence may well be an appraisal that others in one's network are predisposed to accept, creating a powerful context for the internalization of such notions by the vulnerable person herself. Self-definitions of incompetence may, in turn, lead to a lack of confidence or effort in exercising longstanding strengths and skills, leading to

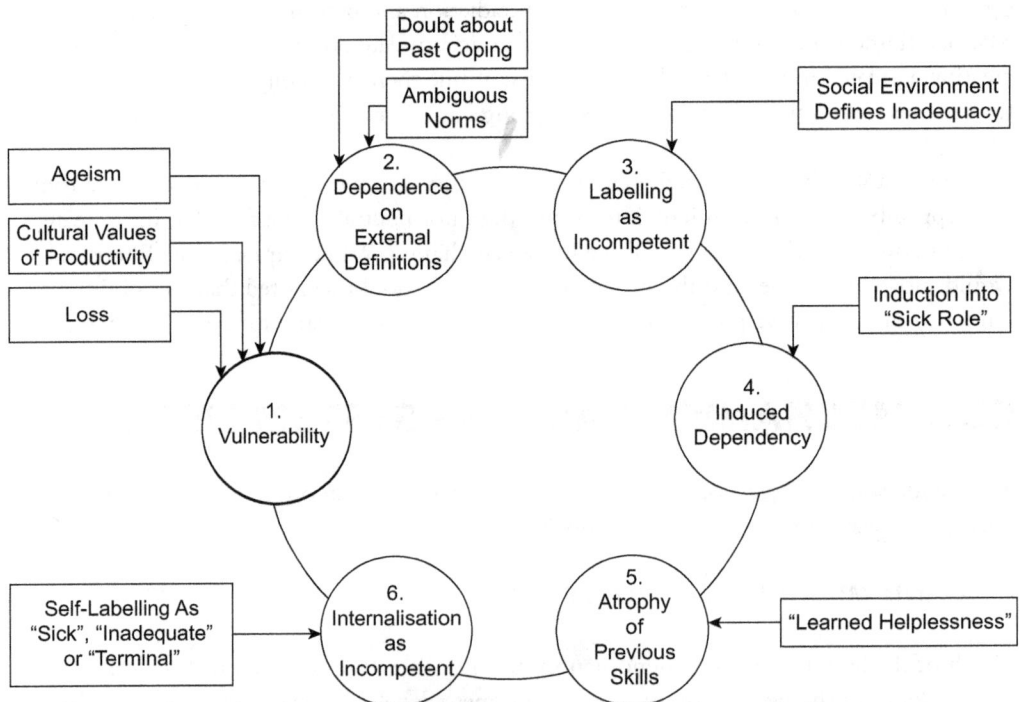

Figure 6.1 The cycle of induced incompetence

Source: Bengtson 1973; Kuypers and Bengtson 1984; see also Dannefer 2008; Falletta and Dannefer 2014

atrophy and perhaps to observable empirical evidence of incompetence, leaving the actor in question ever more vulnerable, unless something is done to challenge and disrupt this destructive cycle.

Again, it should be noted that such a cycle does not represent some occasionally operant or rarely observed social phenomenon. Such dynamics are integral to the reality-constructing processes described in Chapter 3. They are relentless and pervasive—constantly occurring in every single day of most every human life, and are thus bound up with the daily processes through which each human actor makes sense of herself and her relation to her social world. It is also important to recognize that the dynamics underlying Bengtson's cycle do not have to be negative; we can just as well trace positive spirals of interaction in which social affirmation leads to increased confidence, increased performance and increased social capital (Dannefer and Siders 2013). Everyday life experience is replete with examples of both.

Such dynamics have also been extensively demonstrated and elaborated in the work of Jay Gubrium and associates, who document how such processes contribute to organizational narratives that regulate individual access to developmental opportunities as individuals move through age-graded institutions. For example, conversations among teachers reinforce the "fact" that Child A is "hopeless" while Child B has "fantastic potential" (Holstein and Gubrium 2000; see also Dannefer 1999; Rist 2000). Similarly, in work settings, some employees come to be defined as "water-walkers", others as "dead wood" (Kanter 2008); in long-term care and medical settings, some residents and patients are triaged while others deemed worthy of investment (Gubrium and Buckholdt 1977; see also Chapter 9). While none of this is to deny the pervasive reality of individual differences, it indicates the extent to which such differences are shaped, strengthened or even constituted by processes such as labeling and altercasting, combined with organizational dynamics that guarantee stratification.

These generative tendencies of interpersonal interaction have been demonstrated in numerous social-psychological studies, as have their micro-structural aspects. As one telling example, consider a set of classical experiments on the effects of Indian caste membership on cognitive performance, which found that students' performance on a maze-solving problem was directly related to knowledge of their own and others' caste membership (Hoff and Pandey 2003, 2005). With membership unknown, no caste difference in student performance was found; when it was revealed, performance levels directly mirrored caste. The authors thus demonstrate that consequential metrics attached to the person are socially constructed and sustained, and existing patterns of stratification are taken into one's consciousness through interaction at the micro-level, in everyday life. Here, a student reproduces his/her externally applied label through performance on subsequent examinations. Such cases illustrate the continuous operation of social processes in face-to-face interaction and its role in the reproduction of institutionalized power arrangements that produce diverging trajectories over the life course. These also underscore how "position becomes a resource leading to further gains" at the micro-level.

While in this example the relevant power differential is deeply institutionalized in cultural definitions and expectations, in other cases—such as peer interaction on a school playground—power differentials may be informal and relatively transitory but nevertheless consequential.

In sum, studying CDA at the micro-level provides a window into its foundations in the most universal and elemental forms of social interaction, and hence its irreducibly social roots. A focus on the micro-level social processes that underlie CDA should not be confused, as is sometimes done, with discussions that treat *individual* characteristics (like resilience, planful competence or sense of control) as an aspect of micro-level explanations (e.g., Schafer, Shippee and Ferraro 2009) nor with individuals' accounts of the impact of macro-level realities (Wildman, 2020). However, the internalization of social reality within individual consciousness—akin to what Bourdieu's *habitus*—is integral to the microdynamics involved.

A sociological account of CDA thus begins with a recognition that making typifications and distinctions, which are fundamental and ubiquitous elements of the processes of world-construction and the constitution for the social world as described earlier, inherently involves the potential for "othering" (Berger and Luckmann 1967; Bourdieu 1984). Othering can rapidly create "imbalanced flows of resources", to use Michael Schwalbe's term (2008:26), and such interaction virtually guarantees the production of increasing inequality.

While schooling and other experiences of childhood have often been the focus of research demonstrating the inequality-generating tendencies of micro-interaction, such processes can readily be observed in other settings as well, including those at the other end of the life course. It is hardly news that the traditional nursing home operates on a medical/industrial model of warehousing residents and managing their medical conditions, placing them in a position of powerlessness and passivity. When residents are severely impaired, the daunting physical challenges that confront family and caregivers may mean that the operative social dynamics may be even more obscured than usual. As will be shown in Chapter 8, however, they are still operative.

Despite their fundamental importance, micro-level processes do not operate in a vacuum. As in the cases described previously, micro-interaction is virtually always organized by the overarching cultural, linguistic and social-structural forms that frame the sociocultural settings within which micro-interaction operates. And while strategies of individual-level navigation of perilous structures may work for some individuals in minimizing risks of disadvantage, it is clearly not the level at which interventions to ameliorate the effects of CDA will generally be effective (Macmillan 2018). To address such concerns, it is important to look to the meso- and macro-levels of social organization.

CDA AND MESO-LEVEL PROCESSES

Meso-level processes are the locus of one of CDA's long-recognized primary emphases—the allocation of persons to roles (Dannefer 1987, 2003; O'Rand 2003; Reskin 2002), a socially regulated event that typically occurs at multiple points in the life course. Empirically, this allocation process is illustrated by the matching of individuals to organizational roles and their movement through role sequences—whether within schools or schools systems (e.g., Pallas, 2002; Shavit and Blossfeld, 1993), with school grades and tracks (Lucas 1999), occupational positions in corporate, military or other organizational settings (Cole and Cole 1973; Hermanowicz 2011; Kanter 2008; Wilmoth, London, and Parker 2010) or stratified care levels in nursing homes, hospitals and other medical settings (Reskin and McBrier 2000; Rigney 2010).

In many cases, the design of organizations reinforces tendencies toward increasing intracohort stratification and inequality over the life course. A prototypical case of such an effect is the pyramidal shape of work organizations, and the inherent tension between a successively smaller number of positions as one advances to higher ranks on one hand and culturally idealized "career ladders" and norms of upward mobility on the other, as depicted in Figure 6.2 (see, e.g., Kanter 2008 [1977]; Moen and Roehling 2005). *Tournament mobility* (Rosenbaum 1978) describes the intersection of individuals with organizational structures, whereby an organizational imperative is the diminishing number of roles at each succeeding level of advance, virtually guaranteeing increasing inequality among age peers over time—not as a function of any individual characteristic but of organizational structures and processes (Dannefer 2003; Li and Walder 2001; Reskin 2000; Rosenbaum 1989; Sorensen 1986).

Although it is an important and pervasive example of how organizational structures themselves serve to generate inequality, the pyramidal structure of organizations frames only one type of inequality-generating dynamic at the meso-level.

Rosenbaum first articulated the concept of tournament mobility in his early study of students' track mobility in high school, which showed that—contrary to the meritocratic and "equal opportunity" ideologies—virtually all movement between tracks was downward movement, with broadly adverse consequences for students (Lucas 1999; Rosenbaum 1978).

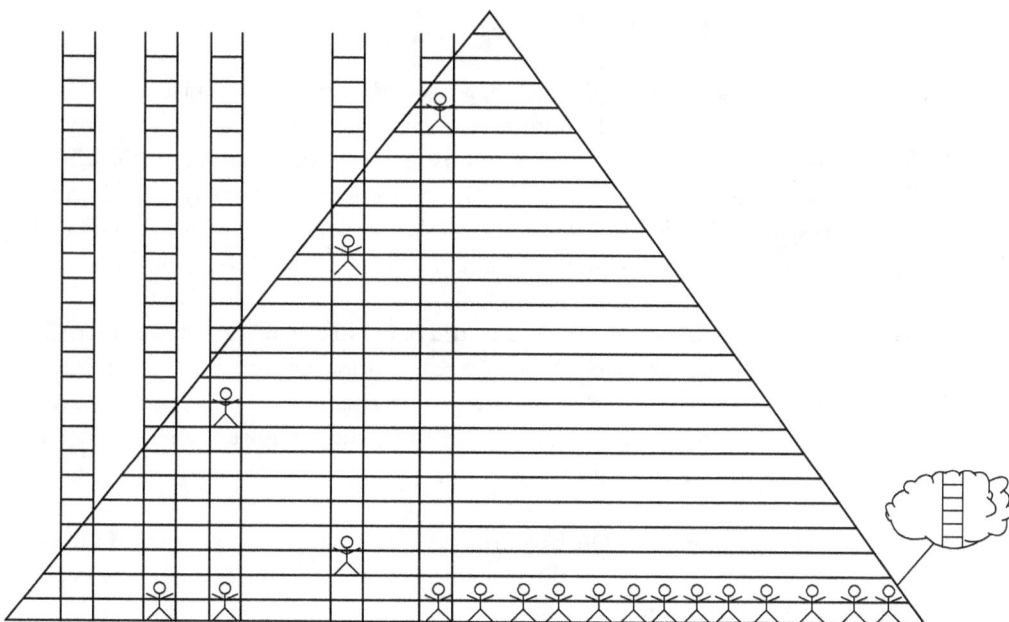

Figure 6.2 Ladders and pyramids: Career aspirations meet organizational realities

The discussion of meso-level structures would also be incomplete without considering how other age-correlated organizational contexts, including nursing homes and other long-term care settings, are structured by the "imbalanced flows of power" (Schwalbe 2008) that render the key actors in the situations—the residents—powerless and structurally passive, as will be discussed in Chapter 8.

CDA AND MACRO-LEVEL PROCESSES

Researchers who examine population-level patterns of life-course trajectories have emphasized the explanatory benefit of comparative data across societies or cohorts (e.g., Crystal et al. 2016; Dannefer 1987; Hoffman 2008). At the societal level, *intercohort* variation in trajectories of *intracohort* inequalities reflects, in part, the operation of large-scale social regulation of economic and policy factors within a society. Intercohort differences within societies also may reflect variation in policy, as illustrated by the impact of the GI Bill (Falletta and Dannefer 2014), long-term educational expansion (e.g., Masters, Hummer, and Powers 2012), regressive changes in tax and social policy (Quadagno 2010; Quadagno and Street 2005; Walker 2018; Walker and Naegele 2009) and other issues related to retirement (Ekerdt 2009; Phillipson 2013a, 2013b; Phillipson, Vickerstaff, and Lain 2016). In a recent analysis of US trends in economic resource inequality, Crystal et al. (2016) report findings illustrating how the slope of trajectories of inequality across cohorts responds to changing economic circumstances, suggesting that the recent increase in inequality in the US has hit those in midlife harder than older people. If this trend were to continue, with midlife inequality rates continuing to approach rates experienced in later life, it could have the effect of *reducing* the life-course increases from mid- to later life in intracohort inequality, since for these cohorts inequality is already high in midlife.

Such macro-comparisons can serve to indicate the degree to which financial, health or other inequalities vary by societal conditions and might be ameliorated or exacerbated by policy decisions or other large-scale influences.

At the macro-level, the role of discriminatory practices along the lines of race, gender or other bases of differentiation can also sometimes be observed with particular clarity (e.g., Calasanti 2010; Hagestad 1985; Minkler and Estes 1991). For example, in the US historically decisive and popular policies such as Social Security disadvantaged women (Foster 2001; Hagestad 1985; Gilbert 2017), and was deliberately designed to exclude and disadvantage African-Americans (Dannefer et al. 2020; Katznelson 2005; Poole 2006).

Macro-level examples of CDA are not limited to the policy domain. As noted earlier, some of the most important analyses of cumulative dis/advantage processes concerned the overall reward system of science, well illustrated by Zuckerman's (1977) important work on Nobel laureates. It is also worth noting that some of the earliest empirical analyses of CDA concerned the matter of citation counts (Price 1965).

In sum, sociological discussions of CDA have from the beginning been predicated on an understanding of the social world as a reality *sui generis*, and of the phenomenon of age-related CDA as generated directly from systemic processes endogenous to that world—most fundamentally at the micro-level and then extending to higher levels of social organization. Although its *consequences* are most directly evident in disparities between individuals as they move through the life course, its sources reside elsewhere, in the social organization of access and obligation, and related systemic dynamics.

CDA, SOCIAL PROCESSES AND LIFE-COURSE PRINCIPLES

From the foregoing depiction, two key principles central to a sociological understanding of CDA can be distilled: 1) *endogenous system dynamics* (ESD) and 2) *life-course reflexivity*, or contingency (LCR; Dannefer and Lin 2013; Erickson and Macmillan 2018). By placing social dynamics at the foundation of CDA, these principles take us beyond the assumptions of the functional-organismic nexus, which tend to naturalize age-related social arrangements as accommodations to "normal aging", with little interrogation of social processes and their independent contributions to shaping individual lives. Neither of these principles have been evenly applied in work on CDA and the life course. Thus, they warrant focused attention.

THE PRINCIPLE OF ENDOGENOUS SYSTEM DYNAMICS

ESD recognizes that CDA outcomes reflect *systemic social processes*. They are the product of tendencies inherent in the everyday operation of social systems generally, endogenous to any social world and context. Social-system dynamics have their own distinctive effects on the distribution of resources as on other aspects of societal operation. Such processes constitute a constellation of forces that impacts each individual yet is not reducible to the individual level.

These dynamics pose daunting conceptual and analytical challenges. Nevertheless, the effects of social reality on the life course can only be adequately apprehended if its continuous and irreducible systemic aspects are made visible and recognized, since it is through those effects that social forces contribute to the production of individual outcomes.

THE PRINCIPLE OF LIFE-COURSE REFLEXIVITY

Discussions that focus on age and cumulative dis/advantage have from their beginnings derived from an interest in demonstrating the workings of social processes over the collective life course of the cohort. This emphasis entails a focus on disparities and inequalities among cohort members, *within* the cohort—not just between age groups or cohorts. As noted earlier, analyses of age-based inequalities have often entailed mean comparisons *between* age groups or cohorts, thereby obscuring intracohort inequality. Nevertheless, intercohort comparisons do offer one important advantage for those seeking to understand the causal dynamics that underlie the phenomenon of increasing inequality with age, which is that they make clear that the magnitude of intracohort variability often observed (see, e.g., Huang and Hauser 1998; Neisser 1998; Preston 1998) cannot be accounted for by individual differences. That is to say, when cohorts differ significantly from each other in the patterning of any characteristic or its variability, such differences must reflect social and historical effects. They can seldom if ever be reduced to the level of individual differences.

The same cannot be said, or at least not quite so simply, for intracohort variation. While intracohort variation points to the effects of social stratification and exclusion on life-course outcomes, it also opens the possibility of individual-level explanations premised on the existence of individual differences. When I submitted my first paper discussing the relevance of the Matthew Effect (Merton's term for cumulative dis/ advantage) for publication, a reviewer rightly pointed out that the phenomenon of increasing inequality over the life course might plausibly be accounted for by psychosocial *accentuation*—a process introduced by psychologists to argue that differences in individuals, whether ascribed to inborn "temperament" or early experiences, become amplified or "accentuated" over time, and a by-product of such individually driven divergence would be, precisely, increasing variability and inequality with age (e.g., Elder 1969; Elder, Shanahan, and Jennings 2015; Rudolph and Troop-Gordon 2010).

In psychology as well as life-course sociology, accentuation and related concepts have long been used to reference the impact of early-life characteristics on later outcomes. Accentuation is premised on the notion that "[e]arly experience differentially marks individuals in ways that shape their understanding of the world, their development of skills, and their opportunities (which) . . . shape later life course outcomes (and) become magnified over time" (Dannefer 2003:S332). An example is provided by John Clausen's vigorous claim that "planful competence"—a putatively stable orientation developed early in the life course—had strong predictive effects on outcomes throughout the life course. Similarly, in the criminology literature, Terrie Moffitt argues that the interaction of "personal traits and environmental reactions" in early life course can produce a "life-course persistent offender" (2006).

The recent expansion of work on the long-term effects of childhood adversity makes clear the strong contemporary interest in such approaches. Of course, attention to the profound consequences of childhood experience for later development of health and quality of life is to be welcomed, and no one should deny the crucial importance of essential resources for healthy prenatal, infant and child development. It is a salutary change in emphasis from the characterization of age and development in normative terms.

Nevertheless, a restricted focus on childhood can be both scientifically and practically counterproductive if it leads researchers, policymakers and practitioners to emphasize childhood effects at the expense of overlooking or discounting the possibilities for amelioration and effective interventions to intercept difficult circumstances coming later in the life course. Too often it has been assumed, sometimes in the face of contrary evidence (e.g., Heckman 2013), that only childhood interventions matter—effectively writing off not only elders but midlife adults and postpubertal youth.

In response to such concerns, the principle of LCR asserts the importance of considering social-contextual effects throughout the life course (as opposed to only during early life) and raises the question of the extent to which research is designed and findings are analyzed to include consideration of the effects of social forces in adulthood as well as childhood. Of course, childhood has comprised a central and fruitful explanatory fulcrum for later-life outcomes since the beginning of life-course studies. And again, an emphasis on childhood effects remains warranted, and especially so in times of increased childhood adversity. Yet a recognition of the importance of childhood should not be confused with a need to consider carefully the causal dynamics at work over the life course. More specifically, it should not be taken as a warrant to ignore the more complex—but possibly no less impactful—factors and social forces that characterize lives across the adult years. Treating childhood events as the singular explanatory fulcrum for subsequent life-course effects risks the danger of *Time-One Encapsulation* (Dannefer and Kelley-Moore 2009)—that is to say, little or no consideration is given to the possible causal role of social conditions later in the life course (Dannefer and Kelley-Moore 2009; Hagestad and Dannefer 2001). This risk relates to the long-running debate in epidemiological discourse, recounted by Kuh and Ben-Shlomo (2004:20–7), between childhood-based ("life-course") and midlife ("adult-lifestyle") approaches to explanation.

These concerns pertain directly to the contemporary tension between "latency" and "pathways" approaches in life-course studies. Over the past two decades, extensive attention has been accorded to the concepts of latency and critical period as explanatory models. Consistent with the general notion of accentuation, latency "emphasizes the prospect that psychosocial and socioeconomic conditions very early in life will have strong impact later . . . *independent of intervening experience*" (Keating and Hertzman 1999:7). Thus, it "underscores the potentially critical impacts of early experiences on facets of adult life" (Goldman 2001:132; see also Bartley, Power, and Blane 1994; Carr 2003:155ff; Kuh and Ben-Shlomo 2004:8–10). Although latency effects are not necessarily limited to childhood (e.g., consequences of adult chemotherapy may show up years later), it has been applied in efforts to understand a range of early-life effects, including work in the traditions of "fetal origins of adult disease" (Barker 1990; Gluckman and Hanson 2005).

The *pathways* model is often framed as a competing hypothesis to the latency approach. Pathways "emphasizes the cumulative effect of life events and the reinforcing effect of differing psychosocial and socioeconomic circumstances throughout the life cycle" (Keating and Hertzman 1999:8; see also Singer, Ryff, Carr, and Magee 1998). As implied by the notion of a "differential reinforcing effect", the pathways model acknowledges the likelihood of sociogenically produced increases in divergence and inequality, continuing through the life course. Youth well situated in the primary economy may find a set of positively reinforcing events, while those who experience precarity and social exclusion may confront a negative dynamic. Such dynamics cross multiple system levels:

> The hypothesis underlying the pathways model is that, over time, the physiological aspects of less than optimal neurophysiological development, chronic stress and its physiological impacts, a sense of powerlessness and alienation, and "social support" network . . . similarly marginalized, will create a vicious cycle with short-term implications for education, criminality . . . and with long-term implications for the quality of working life, social support, chronic disease in midlife and degenerative conditions in late life.
>
> (Keating and Hertzman 1999:8)

This necessarily involves multiple levels of interdependent forces (ranging e.g., from micro-level labeling to macro-level denial of access to resources) that operate continuously in daily life and that, among their other effects, reinforce divergent trajectories of differently situated actors over a sustained period of time. Inevitably, such interacting forces influence many domains simultaneously, and negative experiences in one domain typically impact others, as illustrated in qualitative studies of how precarious housing affects family health, children's schooling, physical safety and job prospects (Black 2009; Desmond 2017; Burton and Whitfield 2006). Implicit in the pathways model is the assumption that interventions or other events that break the "pathway" or the cumulating spiral of events, whether negative or positive, may have the potential to change the direction of one's midlife trajectory.

It should be clear that the alternative mechanisms of CDA that are advanced by different positions in the latency-pathways discussion entail not just a matter of abstract theoretical argument but can have immediate practical implications. As Keating and Hertzman note, "intervention and prevention strategies that are aimed at core developmental processes and . . . at important transition points in development have enhanced prospects for success". Thus, well-designed midlife interventions "may permit redirection of problematic pathways" in adulthood as well as childhood (1999:8).

CDA PRINCIPLES AND LIFE-COURSE RESEARCH

Let us consider briefly how these two principles intersect with recent strands of research. Although mutually synergistic, they represent analytically distinct dimensions, and thus can be used to form a simple 2x2 property space within which various approaches can be located (Figure 6.3). Even though some relevant studies cannot be unambiguously contained within any one cell, this schema locates various efforts at conceptualizing and studying CDA in relation to each other, and examines their tendency to privilege certain types of explanations over others (e.g., early life versus midlife).

The criterion for the principle of ESD is whether (or not) a research project recognizes the potential for interactive, sociogenic processes to generate patterns of CDA, apart from individual differences. For LCR, it is whether the causal impact of conditions occurring throughout the life course is considered versus limiting explanatory consideration to early-life factors.

Attention to the long-term importance of childhood effects is carried forward in several currently popular ideas, including the claim of epigenetically fixed "predictive adaptive responses" involving metabolic parameters set in infancy and postulated to last a lifetime (Gluckman and Hanson 2005) and the "long arm of childhood." Regarding the latter, Hayward and Gorman's foundational article makes clear the impact on health of childhood effects may be mediated through adult occupational characteristics and socioeconomic achievement (2004:101). Nevertheless, the long-arm narrative has developed with a very strong emphasis on childhood, and the role of post-childhood circumstances has received relatively little attention and has sometimes been curiously understated. Despite an oft-manifest preferential interest in childhood, such work may also include an examination of the competing pathways approach. This is the case for some research examining "long-arm" effects. Several researchers have documented how childhood effects are mediated through adult circumstances (e.g., Cunha and Heckman 2007; see also Dannefer, Kelley-Moore, and Huang 2016; Laub and Sampson 2003).

At the same time, some researchers in this tradition have documented how childhood effects are mediated through adult circumstances (e.g., Haas and Rohlfsen 2010; Kelley and Huang 2017; Pudrovska and Anikputa 2014).

Other conceptual frameworks are also concerned with the continuing impact of socioenvironmental factors through adulthood. Prominent examples include weathering

ENDOGENOUS SYSTEM DYNAMICS

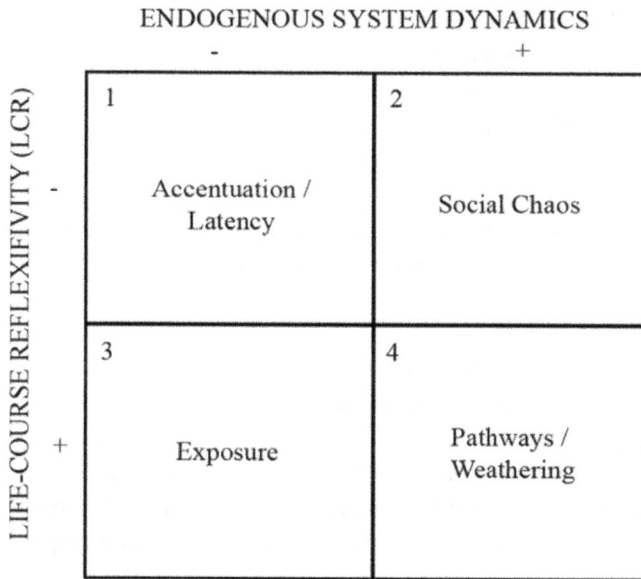

Figure 6.3 Cross-classifying the principles of life-course reflexivity (LCR) and endogenous system dynamics (ESD).

(Burton and Whitfield 2006; Geronimus 1992) and the epidemiological master concept of exposure (e.g., Ferraro and Morton 2018), both of which are intrinsically concerned with the role of post-youth causal factors in accounting for life-course outcomes.

Research documenting the importance of temporally proximate effects on later-life outcomes is an objective of many observational studies and related theorizing demonstrating the impact of daily experience in later life (e.g., Abramson 2015; Gubrium 1975). Again, Bengtson's "cycle of induced incompetence", which offers a schematic of labeling processes applicable to nursing home and related settings, has parallels in other domains of adulthood ranging from work and military careers to criminal recidivism (e.g., Kanter 2008 [1977]; Laub and Sampson 2003; London and Wilmoth 2006; Sampson and Laub 1997; Rosenbaum 1989).

I now turn to a consideration of the second dimension—of how these various approaches just reviewed handle the matter of ESD, which will simultaneously enable classification of various approaches into the cells of the 2x2 property space.

CELL 1. NEITHER LCR NOR ESD

Accentuation, which locates explanatory factors in the early life course and treats individual characteristics as relatively fixed and then amplified over time, clearly fits Cell 1. While experience may contribute to this amplification, it is not claimed to generate the characteristics in question, and social factors are generally brought in as static descriptors rather than as systemic elements. It is interesting that John Clausen does acknowledge one adult predictor which is more powerful than youthful planful competence, and that stronger predictor is planful competence when one is in one's thirties. In such analyses, the outcome of cumulative dis/advantage is seen as simply the aggregate result of stable individual differences working themselves out over the life course. The power of social forces is seen as nonexistent, at least beyond the original formation of the personality complex of planful competence.

CELL 2. LCR NO, ESD YES

Cell 2 is the most challenging to populate. After all, focusing on social-system dynamics inherently invites attention to open-ended and continuous cycles of influence that have no clear terminus in the life course, and it is difficult to identify very many latency-based approaches that incorporate a social-system framework.

Nevertheless, it is logically possible to contend that systemic social processes are important but only count early in the life course. Indeed, some research is particularly well suited to tracing such early-life systemic effects. For example, some studies provide evidence for latency effects that occur when there is a form of *extremely adverse social change*—when an existing social system is essentially destroyed or has its dynamics changed so that they result in significant social change, disruption or oppression, with negative impacts on development.

One example is provided by the well-known Dutch Hongerwinter studies (e.g., Schulz 2010), which documented the harmful consequences for life and health for individuals and unborn offspring who survive under imposed conditions of oppression and extreme deprivation resulting from social disruption and an oppressive and humanly unresponsive social order. The resultant nutritional deprivation "marked" these cohorts metabolically for life. A second example along the same lines, based on difficult prenatal and infant conditions and based on the work of Gluckman and Hanson (2005), will be discussed in the next chapter.

CELL 3. LCR YES, ESD NO

This cell contains approaches that examine LCR with little attention to ESD. This appears to be the case for the concept of *exposure*. Exposure has long been a central concern of epidemiology. It has been linked to the idea of cumulation in gerontology (Ferraro and Morton 2018), and in epidemiology proper, the interest in the notion of cumulative exposure is strong (Geronimus et al. 2015). The concept of an "exposome"—a complete environmental history that encompasses "all life-course environmental exposures (including lifestyle factors), from the prenatal period onwards" has also been proposed (Wild 2005:1848). Such concepts assume the potential relevance of experiences across the life course, and thus clearly accord with the LCR principle. However, such work has generally been unconcerned with understanding social-system dynamics and the attendant causal mechanisms that generate conditions of exposure.

Instead, exposure generally focuses on association between risk factors and outcomes. It assumes a unidirectional flow of influences, with little consideration of the systemic processes or mechanisms underlying the observed associations. The general image of a repeated, unidirectional effect applies equally to wind and rain eroding soil as it does to the assault of phosphate drinks on bone strength, or repeated encounters with racial stereotyping on stress.

Without question, exposure provides an important first window, offering key information as to where needed explanations are to be sought. Yet it has remained largely focused on identifying and characterizing dimensions of the risk factor itself (e.g., duration, intensity). Questions of how risk factors and other causal agents interact in the world as well as the character of the underlying mechanisms have remained largely beyond its scope. It generally posits individuals as largely passive—"sitting-duck" targets that simply absorb the repeated assaults of exposure.

These limitations have received some acknowledgment within the study of exposure itself. For example, in their critique of cumulative exposure, De Vocht, Burstyn and Sanguanchaiyakrit (2015) recommend that epidemiological researchers pay more attention to the complex interaction patterns of the factors involved—noting that the general practice of model fitting the exposure metric offers little information about mechanisms of disease. If potentially innovative notions such as the proposed exposome or an "exposure science" (Ferraro and Morton 2018) become developed, exposure may come to resemble more closely social-system analysis.

CELL 4. LCR YES, ESD YES

As anticipated in the earlier discussion, the general concept behind the *pathways* model acknowledges both LCR and ESD. Its definition assumes both short- and long-term life-course processes, and clearly allows for a systemic conception of the underlying dynamics.

It is noteworthy that one category of studies that demonstrates the operation of social-system processes and their impact on life-course outcomes are those focused at the micro-level. Detailing how this plays out in real time is a research task that plays to the strength of ethnographic and other descriptive approaches. However, such studies generally observe only immediately occurring effects, and thus tend to be "micro" with regard to temporality as well as the processes under study. Hence, they frequently cannot assess long-term impacts of micro-interactions.

Nevertheless, it is often possible to see the fateful long-term consequences of micro-interactional dynamics—for example, when teachers form impressions based on interactions with students that influence their recommendations about student placement within the stratified opportunity structures of schools—placements with long-term consequences for student opportunities (Holstein and Gubrium 2000; Rist 2000; Raudenbush 1984).

Turning to long-term longitudinal studies, Laub and Sampson describe pathways interactions in their study documenting the interplay of marriage and employment in turning around the lives of returning citizens (2003:131–44). Their analysis indicates that the long-term effects of early-life criminal involvement is contingent on subsequent life-course events occurring in adulthood.

The concept of *weathering* (Geronimus 1992, 1996) also attempts to deal with the systemic complexity of lives intersecting with social processes as they move through time. Focusing on African-Americans, Geronimus hypothesized "that the health status of women may begin to deteriorate . . . in young adulthood as a response to perpetual social and environmental insult or prolonged active coping with stressful circumstances" (1996:590). Primary among these circumstances is the systemic daily experience of racism ("prolonged, effortful, active coping with social injustice may, itself, exact a physical price" [1992:210]), and its interactions with other factors. Here, as elsewhere, recent work is exploring how

CDA processes intersect with epigenetics. In expanding research on weathering, Geronimus et al.'s (2015) work on telomere length demonstrates the connections of the body to larger social processes, and also the power of interacting macro-level forces, including the collapse of manufacturing, downward mobility of blue-collar workers, urban decline and race relations resulting from neoliberal policies and associated factors. Such findings cannot be accounted for by childhood effects, and thus clearly suggest the importance of social forces across adulthood.

A special set of relevant societal mechanisms linking early life to midlife concerns social selection effects. This work is important because the multilevel social forces that shape subsequent opportunities rarely have a "one-off" effect, and rarely influence subsequent opportunities only within a single domain (c.f., Haas and Rohlfson 2010; Kelley-Moore and Huang 2016; Pudrovska and Anikputa 2014). For example, the SES of the family of origin contributes not only to selectivity in educational attainment and quality but also to mate selection, health practices, communication styles, and emotional and instrumental support over the life course.

Thus the field can benefit from a more dynamic conceptual and subsequent analytic framing of social selection. With such relationships specified, researchers could begin more fully to ask and answer: Are persons "locked in" to a resilient mindset early in life, or are they influenced by a lifetime of interactions with relevant others who help to interpret and frame life events in "real time"?

It should be noted that the invocation of pathways language does not, by itself, automatically ensure the term will be used in ways that encompass the systemic element in its definition. When "pathways" is equated with "chains of risk" or "cascades" (Kuh and Ben-Shlomo 2004) or described as "setting in motion" events in a particular direction in someone's life (e.g., Hayward and Gorman 2004), it may introduce an intellectual deflection of the actual operation of social-system processes. For example, when "chain of risk" is used to describe "a sequence of linked exposures that lead to impaired function and increased disease risk because one bad experience or exposure leads to another and so on" (Kuh and Ben-Shlomo 2004:10) the actual mechanisms involved remain unaddressed, and we are sometimes left with a sense of resignation and inevitability that permit mystification and naturalization of the forces that produce and reinforce dis/advantage.

An adequate understanding of the operation of pathways will require specification of how multileveled systems of advantage and disadvantage—for example, White privilege at the cultural level, educational and occupational stratification at the organizational level and stereotype threat (Steele 2011) at the micro-level—interact to produce such outcomes.

Such dynamics are often potent; they are systemic and are essential to an understanding of the effects of CDA and related phenomena (e.g., the socioeconomic gradient, or childhood's "long arm"). While no single empirical study can examine every contingency in a complex web of systemic relations, the task of science requires a dedicated effort to understand that complexity rather than simply declaring it to be an example of how one bad thing leads to another, or as "set in motion". But more than avoiding complexity, inattention to such dynamics also allows naturalization—a return of such problems to the natural order, somehow outside the scope of the possibility of change. It precludes asking questions like, "Can the impact of factors that connect 'one bad thing to another' be changed"? "Under what structural arrangements might such CDA-generating tendencies be disrupted or ameliorated"?

Naturalizing as inevitable such dynamics without attempting to consider the extent to which they may entail systemic interactions that exist well beyond the level of individual action and capability is a scientific avoidance tactic that is encouraged by the logic of the functional-organismic nexus, which demands little curiosity about the actual social processes. It allows to remain invisible the issues that most crucially warrant attention. The questions raised by the age-inequality relationship and CDA processes compel us to move beyond such reductionistic and normalizing assumptions, yet it is clear that pressures remain to return to what is for many the comfort of traditional thought patterns.

THE FUTURE OF CDA

Contemplating the continuing explanatory potentials of CDA in the context of these current emphases in the research literature, two broad concerns appear immediately prominent: one regarding the conceptualization and analysis of empirical questions, and one that considers the broader human, political and social implications of CDA for life-course studies, for science and for society. The first concern is to remain focused on the initial premise of CDA, which recognizes the two key principles set forth previously—that CDA not only has its origins in irrepressible and systemic social processes that tend to generate dis/advantage but also that these dynamics operate throughout the life course, not only in infancy and childhood. This is arguably the case whether or not "age becomes a leveler" in later life (e.g., Sieber et al., 2020; van der Linden et al., 2020). An adequate understanding of the operation of pathways will require specification of how multileveled systems of advantage and disadvantage interact to produce such outcomes. It will require confronting head-on the complexity involved in measuring and tracking the interconnections of such forces and processes because they are too powerful to ignore. For example, it is becoming increasingly clear that CDA must attend to the impact of racism in shaping trajectories of inequality (Dannefer et al. 2020) throughout the life course, and to the foundational intersection of race and class, as being explored in work on racial capitalism (Burden-Stelly 2020; Cox 1970).

Second is the concern, practical as well as theoretical, with the broader political and human significance of CDA. This deals with the implications of CDA for human action. As noted earlier, to observe that CDA entail law-like social processes is not to say that its adverse effects are inevitable, and from the beginning, the study of CDA has been expected to have implications for social policy and also for organizational practices, both of which can be deliberately designed to reverse the destructive tendencies of systemic CDA processes (Crystal and Shea 1990; Dannefer 1987; Myrdal 1944) as will be illustrated in the final chapter.

In an effort to complement this macro-emphasis, others have argued for individual-level strategies, often in the form of "planful-competence" or "resilience-based" approaches, almost implying a series of "how-to" steps to navigating the minefields of the life course (Ferraro and Shippee 2009; Schafer et al. 2009). Professional social scientists—including gerontologists—are among those who regularly employ such strategies in navigating our own lives. Yet it must be pointed out that such an approach does not comprise a complement to policy-based strategies for ameliorating the tendency for advantage to accumulate, but rather a way of undermining such efforts by continuing to reproduce and legitimate the conditions that generate accumulative processes.

At a societal level, for example, one major way this occurs is through family-based wealth accumulation, and its role in the intergenerational preservation of patterns of inequality (Kohli 2004; Triventi, Skopek, Kulik, Buchholz, and Blossfeld, 2020). This constitutes a key set of mechanisms through which racial inequality is perpetuated. Reeves (2017) demonstrates how, despite often embracing progressive ideologies, educated parents aggressively plan for and defend educational advantages for their own offspring, thereby transmitting CDA intergenerationally and contributing to the reproduction of existing race and class divisions (Oliver and Shapiro 2006; Shapiro 2004, 2017).

Whether one's ideal is Machiavelli or Martin Luther King, modern citizens faithfully contribute to these patterns, since protecting one's offspring's interests is almost universally regarded as a key aspect of effective and good parenting. Yet the result is to reinforce and protect the interlocking array of structures and practices that reinforce and protect existing patterns of stratified advantage, and exclude others from them.

This circumstance poses challenges that are not only theoretical but also political and existential. Although the path out of this conundrum is not entirely clear, a diverse array of strategies have been proposed. One set of constructive suggestions is offered by some developments in other areas of social science research. A broad array of social and behavioral scientists working in multiple traditions have begun to study and develop concepts of *collective* agency, mobilized on behalf not of individuals but of communities (Stetsenko 2008) and *community* resilience (e.g., White 2017).

Others are more focused, taking on delimited manifestations of CDA. For example, a number of potential models have been advanced to deal with the race-wealth gap described in Chapter 5, including baby bonds (Hamilton and Darity 2010) and modes of reparation based on precedents used in other cases in the US and elsewhere (Darity and Mullen 2020). The individual and collective life-course implications of such proposals are obviously enormous.

In sum, the effects of CDA clearly visit unmerited advantage and/or disadvantage upon individuals' lives, yet the sources of CDA inhere, in large measure, irreducibly in social-system dynamics. Why, then, should those concerned with CDA as a collective (cohort-based) life-course process not seek to address its origins through deliberate resistance by way of collective or collaborative public action rather than being preoccupied solely with individual-level strategies and interests?

Such initiatives need not replace the need for attention to policies and initiatives that provide directly for individual needs nor should it prevent individuals from ongoing idiocratic efforts to maximize their own familistic rewards and "opportunity hoarding" (Reeves 2017; see also Tilly 1998). Yet I can see no warrant for ignoring concerns with social action and social justice as domains worthy of exploration as an analytically rigorous and social-structurally grounded approach to address the multilevel challenges of confronting the systemic character of cumulative dis/advantage. Such explorations are being undertaken in other substantive areas of sociology, psychology and related fields, and they address issues of major concern to developmental and life-course scholars and to sociology more generally. I return to these issues in Chapters 9 and 10.

NOTE

An earlier version of the material presented in Chapter 6 was published as "Systemic and Reflexive: Foundations of Cumulative Dis/Advantage and Life Course Processes", *Journal of Gerontology Social Sciences 75*, 6 (July 2020), pp. 1249–1263.

REFERENCES

Abramson, Corey M. 2015. *The End Game: How Inequality Shapes Our Final Years*. Cambridge, MA: Harvard University Press.

Alter, Alexandra. 2020. "Best Sellers Sell the Best." *New York Times, Sunday Business Section* September 20, pp. 1, 8–9.

Archer, Margaret S. 2000. *Being Human: The Problem of Agency*. Cambridge, UK: Cambridge University Press.

Archer, Margaret S. 2017. "Does Intensive Morphogenesis Foster Human Capacities or Liabilities?" Pp. 115–35 in *Morphogenesis and Human Flourishing*, edited by M. S. Archer. Cham, Switzerland: Springer.

Barker, David. 1990. "The Fetal and Infant Origins of Adult Disease." *The British Medical Journal* (Clinical Research Ed.) 301(6761): 1111.

Bartley, M., C. Power, D. Blane, G. Davey Smith, and M. Shipley. 1994. "Birth Weight and Later Socioeconomic Disadvantage: Evidence from the 1958 British Cohort Study." *British Medical Journal* 309(6967): 1475–8. https://doi.org/10.1136/bmj.309.6967.1475.

Bass, Alexandra Suich. 2018. "GrAIt Expectations: AI in Business." Special Report, *The Economist* March 31. Retrieved from www.economist.com/special-report/2018/03/28/non-tech-businesses-are-beginning-to-use-artificial-intelligence-at-scale?fsrc=scn%2Ffb%2Fte%2Fbl%2Fed%2Fnontechbusinessesarebeginningtouseartificialintelligenceatscalegraitexpectations

Beard, Renee L., and John B. Williamson. 2016. "Frames Matter: Aging Policies and Social Disparities." *Public Policy and Aging Report* 26: 48–52. doi: 10.1093/ppar/prw002

Bengtson, Vern. 1973. *The Social Psychology of Aging*. Indianapolis, IN: Bobbs-Merrill.

Berger, Peter L., and Thomas Luckmann. 1967. *The Social Construction of Reality: A Systematic Treatise in the Sociology of Knowledge*. New York: Anchor.

Black, Timothy. 2009. *When a Heart Turns Rock Solid*. New York: Pantheon Books.

Bol, Thijs, Mathijs de Vaan, and Arnout van de Rijt. 2018. "The Matthew Effect in Science Funding." *Proceedings of the National Academy of Sciences* 115(19): 4887–90.

Bourdieu, Pierre. 1984. *Distinction: A Social Critique of the Judgement of Taste*. New York: Routledge.

Bourdieu, Pierre, and Jean-Claude Passeron. 1990. *Reproduction in Education, Society and Culture*. 2nd edition. Thousand Oaks, CA: Sage.

Buckley, Walter F. 1967. *Sociology and Modern Systems Theory*. Englewood Cliffs, NJ: Prentice-Hall.

Burden-Stelly, Charisse. 2020. "Modern U.S. Racial Capitalism: Some Theoretical Insights." *Monthly Review* 72(3): 8–20.

Burton, Linda, and Keith E. Whitfield. 2006. "Health, Aging and America's Poor: Ethnographic Insights on Family Co-Morbidity and Cumulative Disadvantage." Pp. 215–30 in *Aging, Globalization and Inequality*, edited by J. Baars, D. Dannefer, C. Phillipson, and A. Walker. Amityville, NY: Baywood.

Calasanti, Toni. 2010. "Gender and Ageing in the Context of Globalization." Pp. 137–49 in *The Sage Handbook of Social Gerontology*, edited by D. Dannefer and C. Phillipson. London: Sage Publications.

Cannon, Walter B. 1939. *The Wisdom of the Body*. 2nd edition. New York: Norton & Company.

Carr, Deborah. 2003. "Socioeconomic Background and Midlife Health in the United States." Pp. 155–76 in *Annual Review of Gerontology and Geriatrics, Volume 22: Focus on Economic Outcomes in Later Life*, edited by S. Crystal and D. Shea. New York, NY: Springer Publishing Company.

Cole, Jonathan R., and Stephen Cole. 1973. *Social Stratification in Science*. Chicago: University of Chicago Press.

Collins, Randall. 2005. *Interaction Ritual Chains*. Princeton, NJ: Princeton University Press.

Cox, Oliver Cromwell. 1970 (1948). *Caste, Class, & Race: A Study in Social Dynamics*. New York: Modern Reader Paperbacks.

Crystal, Stephen, and Dennis Shea. 1990. "Cumulative Advantage, Cumulative Disadvantage, and Inequality among Elderly People." *Gerontologist* 304(4): 437–43.

Crystal, Stephen, Dennis G. Shea, and Adriana M. Reyes. 2016. "Cumulative Advantage, Cumulative Disadvantage, and Evolving Patterns of Late-Life Inequality." *The Gerontologist* 57(5): 910–20. https://doi.org/10.1093/geront/gnw056

Cunha, Flavio, and James Heckman. 2007. "The Technology of Skill Formation." *American Economic Review* 97(2): 31–47.

Dannefer, Dale. 1987. "Aging as Intracohort Differentiation: Accentuation, the Matthew Effect, and the Life Course." *Sociological Forum* 2(2): 211–36.

Dannefer, Dale. 1992. "On the Conceptualization of Context in Developmental Discourse: Four Meanings of Context and Their Implications." Pp. 84–105 in *Life-Span Development and Behavior*. Vol. 11, edited by D. L. Featherman, R. M. Lerner, and M. Perlmutter. Hillsdale, NJ: Lawrence Erlbaum Associates, Inc.

Dannefer, Dale. 1999. "Neoteny, Naturalization and Other Constituents of Human Development." Pp. 67–93 Chapter 3 in *The Self and Society of Aging Processes*, edited by Carol D. Ryff and Victor W. Marshall. New York: Springer.

Dannefer, Dale. 2003. "Cumulative Advantage/Disadvantage and the Life Course: Cross-Fertilizing Age and Social Science Theory." *Journals of Gerontology Social Sciences* 58B: S327–37.

Dannefer, Dale. 2008. "The Waters We Swim: Everyday Social Processes, Macro Structural Realities and Human Aging." Pp. 3–22 in *Social Structures and Aging Individuals: Continuing Challenges*, edited by K. Warner Schaie and Ronald P. Abeles. New York: Springer Publishing Company.

Dannefer, Dale, Marissa Gilbert, and Chengming Han. 2020. "With the Wind at Their Backs: Racism and the Amplification of Cumulative Dis/Advantage." Pp. 105–26 in *Annual Review of Gerontology and Geriatrics*, edited by J. Kelley and R. J. Thorpe. New York: Springer Publishing Company.

Dannefer, Dale, and Jessica Kelley-Moore. 2009. "Theorizing the Life Course: New Twists in the Path." Pp. 389–412 in *Handbook of Theories of Aging*, edited by M. Silverstein, V. L. Bengtson, M. Putnam, N. M. Putney, and D. Gans. New York: Springer Publishing Company.

Dannefer, Dale, Jessica Kelley-Moore, and Wenxuan Huang. 2016. "Opening the Social: Sociological Imagination in Life Course Studies." Pp. 87–110 in *Handbook of the Life Course*, edited by J. Mortimer, M. J. Shanahan, and M. K. Johnson. New York: Springer Publishing Company.

Dannefer, Dale, and Jielu Lin. 2013. "Commentary: Contingent Aging Naturalisation and Some Rays of Intellectual Hope." Pp. 181–96 in *Ageing, Meaning and Social Structure: Connecting Critical and Humanistic Gerontology*, edited by Jan Baars and Joseph Dohmen. Bristol, UK: Policy Press.

Dannefer, Dale, and Rebecca A. Siders. 2013. "Social Change, Social Structure, and the Cycle of Induced Solidarity." Pp. 284–92 in *Kinship and Cohort in an Aging Society: From Generation to Generation*, edited by Merril Silverstein and Roseann Giarrusso. Baltimore, MD: Johns Hopkins University Press.

Darity, William, Jr., and A. Kirsten Mullen. 2020. *Resurrecting the Promise of 40 Acres: The Imperative of Reparations for Black Americans*. New York: Roosevelt Institute.

Desmond, Mathew. 2017. *Evicted: Poverty and Profit in the American City*. New York: Broadway Books.

De Vocht, Frank, Igor Burstyn, and Nuthchyawach Sanguanchaiyakrit. 2015. "Rethinking Cumulative Exposure in Epidemiology, Again." *Journal of Exposure Science & Environmental Epidemiology* 25: 467–73. doi: 10.1038/jes.2014.58.

DiPrete, Thomas A., and Gregory M. Eirich. 2006. "Cumulative Advantage as a Mechanism for Inequality: A Review of Theoretical and Empirical Developments." *Annual Review of Sociology* 32: 271–97.

DiTomaso, Nancy. 2013. *The American Non-Dilemma: Racial Inequality without Racism*. New York: Russell Sage Foundation.

Ekerdt, D. J. 2009. "Population Retirement Patterns." Pp. 471–91 in *International Handbook of Population Aging*, edited by P. Uhlenberg. New York: Springer-Verlag.

Elder, Glen H. 1969. "Appearance and Education in Marriage Mobility." *American Sociological Review* 34(4): 519–33.

Elder, Glen H., Michael J. Shanahan, and Julia A. Jennings. 2015. "Human Development in Time and Place." Pp. 6–54 in *Handbook of Child Psychology and Developmental Science*. Vol. 4, edited by R. M. Lerner. New York: Wiley.

Elias, Sean, and Joe R. Feagin. 2016. *Racial Theories in Social Science: A Systemic Racism Critique*. New York: Routledge Taylor & Francis Group.

Erickson, Gina, and Ross Macmillan. 2018. "Disability and the Transition to Adulthood: A Life Course Contingency Perspective." *Longitudinal and Life Course Studies* 9(2): 188–21.

Falletta, Lynn, and Dale Dannefer. 2014. "The Life Course and the Social Organization of Age." Pp. 607–25 in *Handbook of the Social Psychology of Inequality*, edited by J. Macleod, E. J. Lawler, and M. Schwalbe. New York, NY: Springer Publishing Company.

Ferraro, Kenneth F., and Patricia M. Morton. 2018. "What Do We Mean by Accumulation? Advancing Conceptual Precision for a Core Idea in Gerontology." *The Journals of Gerontology, Series B: Psychological Sciences and Social Sciences* 73(2): 269–78. doi: 10.1093/geronb/ gbv09.

Ferraro, Kenneth, and Tetyana P. Shippee. 2009. "Aging and Cumulative Inequality: How Does Inequality Get Under the Skin?" *The Gerontologist* 49(3): 333–43. doi: 10.1093/ geront/gnp034.

Fingerman, Karen L., and Eric Bermann. 2000. "Applications of Family Systems Theory to the Study of Adulthood." *International Journal of Aging and Human Development* 51(1): 5–29.

Foster, Laura Ann. 2001. "Social Security and African American Families: Unmasking Race and Gender Discrimination." *UCLA Women's Law Journal* 12(1): 55–86.

Geronimus, Arline T. 1992. "The Weathering Hypothesis and the Health of African-American Women and Infants: Evidence and Speculations." *Ethnicity & Disease* 2(3): 207–21.

Geronimus, Arline T. 1996. "Black/White Differences in the Relationship of Maternal Age to Birthweight: A Population-Based Test of the Weathering Hypothesis." *Social Science & Medicine* 42(4): 589–97.

Geronimus, Arline T., Jay A Pearson, Erin Linnenbringer, Amy J Schulz, Angela G Reyes, Elissa S Epel, Jue Lin, and Elizabeth H Blackburn. 2015. "Race-Ethnicity, Poverty, Urban Stressors, and Telomere Length in a Detroit Community-Based Sample." *Journal of Health and Social Behavior* 56(2): 199–224. doi: 10.1177/002214651558210.

Gilbert, Neil, ed. 2017. *Gender and Social Security Reform: What's Fair for Women?* New York: Routledge.

Gleick, James. 2008. *Chaos: Making a New Science.* New York: Penguin.

Gluckman, Peter, and Mark Hanson. 2005. *Mismatch: Why Our World No Longer Fits Our Bodies.* New York: Oxford University Press.

Goldman, Nick. 2001. "Social Inequalities and Health: Disentangling the Underlying Mechanisms." Pp. 118–39 in *Health and Aging: Strengthening the Dialogue Between Epidemiology and Demography*, edited by M. Weinstein, A. J. Hermalin, and M. A. Stoto. New York: New York Academy of Sciences.

Gubrium, Jaber F. 1975. *Living and Dying at Murray Manor.* New York: St. Martins Press.

Gubrium, Jaber F., and David R. Buckholdt. 1977. *Toward Maturity.* San Francisco: Jossey-Bass.

Haas, Steve, and Leah Rohlfsen. 2010. "Life Course Determinants of Racial and Ethnic Disparities in Functional Health Trajectories." *Social Science & Medicine* 70(2): 240–50. doi: 10.1016/j. Socscimed.2009.10.00.

Hagestad, Gunhild O. 1985. "Older Women in Intergenerational Relations." Pp. 137–51 in *The Physical and Mental Health of Aged Women*, edited by M. R. Haug. New York: Springer Publishing Company.

Hagestad, Gunhild O., and Dale Dannefer. 2001. "Concepts and Theories of Aging." Pp. 3–21 in *Handbook of Aging and the Social Sciences.* 5th edition, edited by R. H. Binstock and L. K. George. San Diego: Academic Press.

Hamilton, Darrick, and W. Darity, Jr. 2010. "Can 'Baby Bonds' Eliminate the Racial Wealth Gap in Putative Post-Racial America?" *The Review of Black Political Economy* 37(3–4): 207–16.

Hayward, Mark D., and Bridget K. Gorman. 2004. "The Long Arm of Childhood: The Influence of Early-Life Social Conditions on Men's Mortality." *Demography* 41(1): 87–107. https://doi.org/10.1353/dem.2004.0005.

Heckman, James J. 2013. "Lifelines for Poor Children." *New York Times Opinionator.* Retrieved October 5, 2020 (https://opinionator.blogs.nytimes.com/2013/09/14/lifelines-for-poor-children/)

Hermanowicz, Joseph C. 2011. *The American Academic Profession: Transformation in Contemporary Higher Education.* Baltimore, MD: Johns Hopkins University Press.

Hoff, Karla, and Priyanka Pandey. 2003. "Belief Systems and Durable Inequalities: An Experimental Investigation of Indian Caste." *Word Bank Policy Research Working Paper 3351.* doi: 10.1596/1813-9450-3351.

Hoff, Karla, and Priyanka Pandey. 2005. "Opportunity Is Not Everything: How Belief Systems and Mistrust Shape Responses to Economic Incentives." *Economics of Transition* 13: 445–72.

Hoffmann, Rasmus. 2008. *Socioeconomic Differences in Old Age Mortality*. Vol. 25. Dordrecht, Netherland: Springer Science & Business Media.

Holstein, James A., and Jaber F. Gubrium. 2000. *The Self We Live By: Narrative Identity in a Postmodern World*. New York: Oxford University Press.

Huang, Min-Hsiung, and Robert Hauser. 1998. "Trends in Black-White Test Score Differentials: II. The WORDSUM Vocabulary Test." Pp. 303–32 in *The Rising Curve: Long-Term Gains in IQ and Related Measures*, edited by Ulrich Neisser. Washington: American Psychological Association.

Jackson, Jazqueline Johnson. 1990. Minorities and Aging. Belmont, CA: Wadsworth.

Kanter, Rosabeth M. 2008 (1977). *Men and Women of the Corporation*. 4th edition. New York: Basic Books.

Katznelson, Ira. 2005. *When Affirmative Action Was White: An Untold History of Racial Inequality in Twentieth-Century America*. New York: WW Norton & Company.

Keating, Daniel P., and Clyde Hertzman. 1999. *Developmental Health and the Wealth of Nations*. New York: Guilford Press.

Kelley-Moore, Jessica, and Wenxuan Huang. 2016. "The 'Good Times' Cohort in Later-Life: Black-White Differences in Pathways to Functional Limitations." *Research on Aging* 39(4): 526–48. https://doi.org/10.1177/0164027516655582.

Kohli, Martin. 2004. "Intergenerational Transfers and Inheritance: A Comparative View." Pp. 266–89 in *Annual Review of Gerontology and Geriatrics*. Vol. 24, edited by M. Silverstein. New York, NY: Springer Publishing Company.

Kuh, Diana, and Yoav Ben-Shlomo. 2004. *A Life-Course Approach to Chronic Disease Epidemiology*. Oxford: Oxford University Press.

Kuypers, Joseph A., and Vern L. Bengtson. 1984. "Perspectives on the Older Family." Pp. 2–20 in *Independent Aging: Family and Social Systems Perspectives*, edited by William H. Quinn and George A. Houston. Rockville, MD: Aspen Systems.

Laub, John H., and Robert J. Sampson. 2003. *Shared Beginnings, Divergent Lives: Delinquent Boys to Age 70*. Cambridge, MA: Harvard University Press.

Li, Bobai, and Andrew G. Walder. 2001. "Career Advancement as Party Patronage: Sponsored Mobility into the Chinese Administrative Elite, 1949–1996." *American Journal of Sociology* 106: 1371–1408.

London, Andrew, and Janet Wilmoth. 2006. "Military Service and (Dis)continuity in the Life Course: Evidence on Disadvantage and Mortality from the HRS and AHEAD." *Research on Aging* 28(1): 135–59.

Lucas, Samuel. 1999. *Tracking Inequality: Stratification and Mobility in American High Schools*. New York: Teachers College Press.

Luxemburg, Rosa. 1951 (1913). *The Accumulation of Capital* (Agnes Schwarzchild, Trans.). London: Routledge & Kegan Paul.

Macmillan, Ross. 2018. "Causality in Life Course Research: Do We Do Enough, or Should We Even Care? Keynote Address." Annual meeting of the Society for Longitudinal and Life Course Studies, Milan, Italy (July).

Maruyama, Magoroh. 1963. "The Second Cybernetics: Deviation-Amplifying Mutual Causal Processes." *American Scientist* 51(1): 164–79.

Marx, Karl. 2015 (1867). *Capital a Critique of Political Economy Volume I Book One: The Process of Production of Capital*. Moscow, USSR: Progress Publishers.

Masters, Ryan K., Robert A. Hummer, and Daniel A. Powers. 2012. "Educational Differences in U.S. Adult Mortality: A Cohort Perspective." *American Sociological Review* 77(4): 548–72. doi: 10.1177/00031224124510.

McGoldrick, Monica, Joseph Giordano, and Nydia Garcia-Preto. 2005. *Ethnicity and Family Therapy*. New York: Guilford Press.

Merton, Robert K. 1968. "The Matthew Effect in Science: The Reward and Communication System of Science." *Science* 199: 55–63.

Merton, Robert K. 1988. "The Matthew Effect in Science, II: Cumulative Advantage and the Symbolism of Intellectual Property." *Isis* 79(4): 606–23. doi: 10.1086/354848.

Minkler, Meredith, and Carroll Estes, eds. 1991. *Critical Perspectives on Ageing: The Political and Moral Economy of Growing Old*. Amityville, NY: Baywood Publishing Company.

Moen, Phyllis, and Patricia Roehling. 2005. *The Career Mystique: Cracks in the American Dream*. Lanham, MD: Rowman & Littlefield.

Moffitt, Terrie E. 2006. "A Review of Research on the Taxonomy of Life-Course Persistent versus Adolescence-Limited Antisocial Behavior." Pp. 277–311 in *Taking Stock: The Status of Criminological Theory*, edited by F. T. Cullen, J. P. Wright, and K. R. Blevins. New Brunswick, NJ: Transaction Publishers.

Myrdal, Gunnar. 1944. *An American Dilemma: The Negro Problem and Modern Democracy*. New York/London: Harper and Brothers.

Myrdal, Gunnar. 1957. *Rich Lands and Poor: The Road to the World Property*. New York: Harper and Brothers.

Neisser, Ulrich. 1998. *The Rising Curve: Long-Term Gains in IQ and Related Measures*. Washington: American Psychological Association. https://doi.org/10.1037/10270-000.

O'Connor, James. 1986. *Capital Accumulation*. Oxford: Basil Blackwell.

Oliver, Melvin, and Thomas M. Shapiro. 2006. *Black Wealth, White Wealth: A New Perspective on Racial Inequality*. New York: Routledge.

O'Rand, Angela M. 2003. "Cumulative Advantage Theory in Aging Research." Pp. 14–30 in *Annual Review of Gerontology and Geriatrics*, edited by S. Crystal and D. Shea. New York, NY: Springer Publishing Company.

Pallas, Aaron M. 2002. "Educational participation across the life course: Do the rich get richer?" Pp. 327–54 in Timothy Owens and Richard Settersten, Jr. (Eds.), *New Frontiers in Socialization: Advances in Life Course Research*, Vol. 7. Oxford, UK: Elsevier Science.

Pallas, Aaron M., and Jennifer L. Jennings. 2009. "Cumulative Knowledge about Cumulative Advantage." *Swiss Journal of Sociology* 35(2): 211–29.

Phillipson, Christopher. 2013a. *Ageing*. Cambridge: John Wiley & Sons Ltd.

Phillipson, Christopher. 2013b. "Reconstructing Work and Retirement: Labour Market and Policy Issues." Pp. 445–60 in *The Sage Handbook of Aging, Work and Society*. 1st edition. London: Sage.

Phillipson, Christopher, Sarah Vickerstaff, and David Lain. 2016. "Achieving Fuller Working Lives: Labour Market and Policy Issues in the United Kingdom." *Australian Journal of Social Issues* 51(2): 187–203.

Poole, Mary. 2006. *The Segregated Origins of Social Security: African Americans and the Welfare State*. Chapel Hill: University of North Carolina Press.

Preston, Samuel H. 1998. "Differential Fertility by IQ and the IQ Distribution of a Population." Pp. 377–87 in *The Rising Curve: Long-Term Gains in IQ and Related Measures*, edited by U. Neisser. Washington: American Psychological Association.

Price, Derek J. de Solla. 1965. "Networks of Scientific Papers." *Science* 149: 510–5.

Pudrovska, Tetyana, and Benedicta Anikputa. 2014. "Early-Life Socioeconomic Status and Mortality in Later Life: An Integration of Four Lifecourse Mechanisms." *The Journals of Gerontology, Series B: Psychological Sciences and Social Sciences* 69: 451–60. doi: 10.1093/geronb/gbt12.

Quadagno, Jill B. 2010. "Institutions, Interests and Ideology: An Agenda for the Sociology of Health Care Reform." *Journal of Health and Social Behavior* 51(2): 125–36.

Quadagno, Jill B., and Debra Street. 2005. "Ideology and Public Policy: Antistatism in American Welfare State Development." *Journal of Policy History* 17(1): 57–75.

Raudenbush, Stephen W. 1984. "Magnitude of Teacher Expectancy Effects on Pupil IQ as a Function of the Credibility of Expectancy Induction: A Synthesis of Findings from 18 Experiments." *Journal of Educational Psychology* 76(1): 85–97. https://doi. org/10.1037/0022-0663.76.1.85.

Reeves, Richard V. 2017. *Dream Hoarders: How the American Upper Middle Class Is Leaving Everyone Else in the Dust, Why That Is a Problem, and What to Do about It.* Washington, DC: Brookings Institution Press.

Reskin, Barbara F. 2000. "The Proximate Causes of Employment Discrimination." *Contemporary Sociology* 29(2): 319–28.

Reskin, Barbara F. 2002. "Imagining Work Without Exclusionary Barriers." *Yale Journal of Law & Feminism* 14(2): 313–31.

Reskin, Barbara F., and Debra Branch McBrier. 2000. "Why Not Ascription? Organizations' Employment of Male and Female Managers." *American Sociological Review* 65(2): 210–33.

Rigney, Daniel. 2010. *The Matthew Effect: How Advantage Begets Further Advantage.* New York: Columbia University Press.

Rist, Ray C. 2000. "Student Social Class and Teacher Expectations: The Self-Fulfilling Prophecy in Ghetto Education." *Harvard Educational Review* 70(3): 257–301.

Rosenbaum, James. 1978. "The Structure of Opportunity in School." *Social Forces* 57(1): 236–56.

Rosenbaum, James. 1989. "Organizational Career Systems and Employee Misperceptions." Pp. 329–53 in *Handbook of Career Theory*, edited by M. Arthur, D. T. Hall, and B. Lawrence. New York: Cambridge University Press.

Rudolph, Karen D., and Wendy Troop-Gordon. 2010. "Personal-Accentuation and Contextual-Amplification Models of Pubertal Timing: Predicting Youth Depression." *Developmental Psychology* 22(2): 433–51. doi: 10.1017/S0954579410000167.

Sampson. Robert J., and John H. Laub. 1997. "A Life-Course Theory of Cumulative Dis/ Advantage." Pp. 1–29 in *Advances in Criminological Theory, Vol 7: Developmental Theories of Crime and Delinquency*, edited by T. Thornberry. Piscataway, NJ: Transaction Publishers.

Schafer, Markus H., Tetyana P. Shippee, and Kenneth F. Ferraro. 2009. "When Does Disadvantage Not Accumulate? Toward a Sociological Conceptualization of Resilience." *Swiss Journal of Sociology* 35(2): 231–51.

Schulz, Laura C. 2010. "The Dutch Hunger Winter and the Developmental Origins of Health and Disease." *Proceedings of the National Academy of Sciences of the United States* 107(39): 16757–8. https://doi.org/10.1073/pnas.1012911107.

Schwalbe, Michael. 2008. *Rigging the Game: How Inequality Is Reproduced in Everyday Life.* New York: Oxford University Press.

Shapiro, Thomas M. 2004. *The Hidden Cost of Being African American: How Wealth Perpetuates Inequality.* New York: Oxford University Press.

Shapiro, Thomas M. 2017. *Toxic Inequality: How America's Wealth Gap Destroys Mobility, Deepens the Racial Divide, and Threatens Our Future.* New York: Basic Books.

Shavit, Yossi and Hans-Peter Blossfeld. 1993. *Persistent Inequality: Changing Educational Stratification in Thirteen Countries.* Boulder, CO: Westview Press.

Sieber, Stefan, Boris Cheval, Dan Orsholits, Bernadette W. A. van der Linden, Idris Guessous, Rainer Gabriel, Matthias Kliegel, Martina von Arx, Michelle Kelly-Irving,

Marja Aartsen, Matthieu P. Boisgontier, Dalphine Courvoisier, Claudine Burton-Jeangros and Stephane Cullati. 2020. "Do Welfare Regimes Moderate Cumulataive Dis/advantages Over the Life Course? Cross-National Evidence from Longitudinal Share Data." *Journal of Gerontology Social Sciences* 75(6): 1312–25.

Singer, Burton, Carol D. Ryff, Deborah Carr, and William J. Magee. 1998. "Linking Life Histories and Mental Health: A Person-Centered Strategy." *Sociological Methodology* 28(1): 1–51.

Sorensen, Aage. 1986. "Social Structure and Mechanisms of Life-Course Processes." Pp. 177–97 in *Human Development and the Life Course: Multidisciplinary Perspectives*, edited by A. B. Sorensen, F. Weinert, and L. Sherrod. New York: Psychology Press.

Steele, Claude. 2011. *Whistling Vivaldi: How Stereotypes Affect Us and What We Can Do.* New York: W.W. Norton & Company.

Stetsenko, Anna. 2008. "From Relational Ontology to Transformative Activist Stance: Expanding Vygotsky's (CHAT) Project." *Cultural Studies of Science Education* 3: 465–48.

Tilly, Charles. 1998. *Durable Inequality.* Berkeley, CA: University of California Press.

Trentaz, Cassie. 2012. *Theology in the Age of Global AIDS & HIV: Complicity and Possibility.* New York: Palgrave Macmillan.

Triventi, Moris, Jan Skopek, Nevena Kulik, Sandra Buchholz, and Hans-Peter Blossfeld. 2020. "Advantage 'Finds Its Way': How Privileged Families Exploit Opportunities in Different Systems of Secondary Education." *Sociology* 54(2): 237–57. https://doi.org/10.1177/0038038519874984.

Turek, Konrad, Jolanta Perek-Bialas, and Justyna Stypinska. 2015. "Socioeconomic Status in Aging Poland: A Question of Cumulative Advantages and Disadvantages." Pp. 85–105 in *Population Ageing from a Lifecourse Perspective*, edited by Kathrin Komp and Stina Johannson. Bristol, UK: Policy Press.

van der Linden, Wilhelmina Bernadette, Antonio, Boris Cheval, Stefan Sieber, Dan Orsholits, Idris Guessous, Silvia Stringhini, Rainer Gabriel, Marja Aartsen, David Blane, Delphine Courvoisier, Claudine Burton-Jeangros, Matthias Kliegel and Stephane Cullati. 2020. "Life Course Socioeconomic Conditions and Frailty at Older Ages." *Journal of Gerontology Social Sciences* 75(6): 1348–58.

Walker, Alan. 2018. "Why the UK Needs a Social Policy on Ageing." *Journal of Social Policy* 47(2): 253–73.

Walker, Alan, and Gerhard Naegele, eds. 2009. *Social Policy in Ageing Societies: Britain and Germany Compared.* London: Palgrave MacMillan.

White, Monica M. 2017. "Collective Agency and Community Resilience: A Theoretical Framework." *Journal of Agriculture, Food Systems, and Community Development* 7(4): 17–21. doi: 10.5304/ jafscd.2017.074.014.

Wild, Christopher P. 2005. "Complementing the Genome with an 'Exposome': The Outstanding Challenge of Environmental Exposure Measurement in Molecular Epidemiology." *Cancer Epidemiology, Biomarkers & Prevention* 14: 1847–50. doi: 10.1158/10559965.EPI-05-0456.

Wildman, Josephine M. 2020. "'It's Luck What Sort of Family You're Born Into': Cumulative Dis/Advantage Generative Systmic Processes Across the Life Course of a Baby Boom Cohort." *Journal of Gerontology Social Sciences* 75(6): 1302–11.

Wilmoth, Janet, Andrew London, and Wendy Parker. 2010. "Military Service and Men's Health Trajectories in Later Life." *Journal of Gerontology: Social Sciences* 56(6): 744–55.

Zuckerman, Harriet. 1977. *Scientific Elite: Nobel Laureates in the United States.* New York: Free Press.

CHAPTER 7
SOCIOSOMATICS AND THE LIFE COURSE: THE SOCIAL ORGANIZATION OF HUMAN PHYSIOLOGY AND GENE REGULATION

With Kathryn Douthit

INTRODUCTION

In the last several chapters, the essential role of social context in organizing experience and regulating the patterning of the life course has been examined. In Chapter 4, life-course differences across societies and historical time were considered. In Chapters 5 and 6, we reviewed how social processes operate at "ground-level", to impact aging and the patterning of the life course within a given social setting. This evidence makes clear that, as a field, we are still early in the process of grasping the extent to which age and aging are organized by social forces and social processes.

Equipped with this understanding of how social processes organize experience and the allocation of opportunities and resources across the life course, it is now time to return to a more detailed consideration of how these social dynamics impact physical and mental health and capabilities as individuals age. It is important to consider questions of how, and with what effect, the social organization of age becomes embodied—how it "gets under the skin" (Ferraro and Shippee 2009)—and how it impacts the nature and experience of physical growth and aging.

As a foundation for this exploration, it is important to begin by remembering the principles outlined in Chapter 2. As was established then, the structuring of human body and mind are "socialized"—or, more precisely, are shaped by the structures of the social world—to a much greater extent than is generally acknowledged, even by those of us working in the social and behavioral sciences. The human actor is not merely "influenced" but is *constituted* through these processes of social structuration (Baars 1991). This social structuration of the human actor is rendered both possible and necessary by the universal human characteristic of being "hard-wired for flexibility", in Rogoff's (2003) phrase—a flexibility that is reflected in the distinctly "world-open" morphological and developmental features of the human organism, including exterogestation and the extraordinary malleability of physical, affective and cognitive development in human childhood, and in adulthood, the sustained, lifelong flexibility captured by the concept of neoteny.

SOCIAL PROCESSES, AGE AND HEALTH

Beyond the directly observable and structural features of individual development associated with these fundamental anthropological characteristics, it has become increasingly clear that the social also has a pervasive impact on individual health across the life course. Indeed, many aspects of everyday physiological functioning have also been shown to be highly sensitive to environmental conditions and to change rapidly in response to environmental inputs. These effects, which generally have gone entirely unnoticed until documented in relatively recent research discoveries, can be seen in many domains of physiological research. To illustrate, we briefly review three such domains: 1) psychoneuroimmunology, 2) gut microbiome dynamics and 3) neurogeneration.

PSYCHONEUROIMMUNOLOGY

Psychoneuroimmunology examines how socially influenced psychological properties like mood and stress affect a range of immunological and endocrinological states (Kiecolt-Glaser, McGuire, Robles, and Glaser 2002).

Such processes often have clear links to age-related change. For example, chronic stress can lead to immunological changes that, over time, accelerate disabling processes in late life. One such change is where production of Interleukin-6 (IL-6), one of the most widely studied among an array of immune-regulating substances known as cytokines, can become dysregulated in response to enduring negative emotions triggered by environmental factors. This dysregulation results in adverse inflammatory processes implicated in various destructive disease processes including cardiovascular disease, dementia, arthritis, fibromyalgia and depression (Douthit and Russotti 2017; Kiecolt-Glaser et al. 2003; Marketon and Glaser 2008). The effects of such environmental factors on the everyday biochemistry of the organism are imprinted at the molecular level, and over time may reflect the cumulative traces of experiences across the life course.

THE SOCIAL ORGANIZATION OF THE GUT MICROBIOME

As a second instance, several lines of epidemiological work have demonstrated even more direct health consequences of environmental effects. Research on the nutritional effects on intestinal health has demonstrated the dramatic impact of gut microbiome health on susceptibility to diseases such as obesity and diabetes (see Kelley and Thorpe 2021) and also suggests that mental health status varies with microbiota composition (Järbrink-Sehgal and Andreasson 2020). Although the influence of diet and other cultural factors in regulating the gut microbiota has been recognized for some time, this work enables a much more specific understanding of the mechanisms at work, particularly in relation to nutritional and other contextual inputs over the life course ranging from ongoing psychosocial stress to environmental pollutants to the character of social relations (Dowd and Renson 2018; Prescott and Logan 2017; Valdes, Walter, Segal, and Spector 2018). Overall, "a significant source of variation in older adults' gut microbiome is their immediate social environment" (Kelley and Thorpe 2021). Further, the potential for rapid change in the gut microbiome across the life course has clear positive implications for the value of interventions in adulthood and the importance of attention to deleterious social-structural arrangements (Herd, Palloni, Rey, and Dowd 2018a; Herd et al. 2018b).

Such discoveries are, of course, relevant to the "latency-pathways" debate reviewed in Chapter 6, since they make clear the impact across the life course of everyday experience and context on health. To understand health and formulate useful health strategies, it is clearly important to consider the ongoing circumstances and conditions of the adult life course, in addition to early childhood.

BIOCHEMICAL DETERRENTS TO CELLULAR AGING AND BRAIN-BASED NEUROGENESIS IN ADULTHOOD

A further consequential set of discoveries of direct relevance to age concern the regulation and regeneration of key features of the body itself, including the case of telomeres and telomerase, and instances of neurogenesis—the development of new nerve cells. We briefly discuss each of these here.

TELOMERES AND TELOMERASE

Telomeres, which can be found as cap-like configurations at the ends of chromosomes, consist of complex, dynamic molecular structures in which a repeated base-pair sequence (TTAGGG) is surrounded by a protective protein called shelterin. In addition to its protective role, shelterin—along with the enzyme telomerase—also has a central role in regulating the length of the telomere (Blackburn, Epel, and Lin 2015). Functionally, the telomere is in place to protect the ends of chromosomes from DNA damage that occurs in the presence of repair mechanisms that have the potential to cause fusion of the end of one chromosome to the end of a chromosome in close proximity. Following each cell division, the telomere shortens; however, the action of the enzyme complex, telomerase, normally functions to restore some of the telomere length. Once the telomere shortens to below a critical length, the cell is no longer able to divide and goes into a state of senescence and cell death, which triggers an inflammatory response (Blackburn et al. 2015; Epel and Prather 2018). The length of the telomere reflects the maximum number of cell divisions that a cell can still achieve before becoming senescent and dying. As some readers will know, the number of remaining divisions is called the "Hayflick limit" (Shay and Wright 2000). As cells reach their Hayflick limit, the organism becomes more susceptible to diseases common to the aging process such as heart disease, diabetes, osteoporosis, arthritis and cancer (Ridout et al. 2018). It is now recognized that a myriad of socially promulgated stressors (e.g., child maltreatment, air pollution, smoking, food deserts) are associated with telomere shortening, which is in turn associated with diseases of aging, decline in mental health and premature mortality (Blackburn et al. 2015; Epel and Prather 2018).

ADULT NEUROGENESIS

The phenomenon of adult neurogenesis, particularly in the human brain, has received considerable attention over the past 20 years. Evidence for neurogenesis has challenged the long-held belief that in adulthood, neural regeneration—that is, neurogenesis—ceases. "The common wisdom was that after childhood the brain changed only when it began the long process of decline; that when brain cells failed to develop properly, or were injured, or died, they could not be replaced" (Doidge 2007:xvii–xviii).

Some of the most promising research in adult neurogenesis has focused on the hippocampus, a brain structure associated with memory and learning (Lucassen et al. 2020), and known to atrophy in the progression of Alzheimer's dementia (Anand and Dhikav 2012). One well-established line of research documenting hippocampal growth, described in some detail in Chapter 2, can be found in Eleanor Maguire and colleagues' work studying individuals as they prepared for the examination to become London taxi drivers, requiring memorization of the map of London (Maguire et al. 2000; Woollett and Maguire 2011; see also Aimone et al. 2014; Deng, Aimone, and Gage 2010; Kuzumaki et al. 2011; Muotri, Zhao, Marchetto, and Gage 2009). The central findings of this work appear solidly established, despite predictable but to date ineffectual efforts at critique (Lucassen et al. 2020).

SOCIAL PROCESSES AND G-E INTERACTION

As discoveries of the responsiveness of physiological function to context have continued to be made, it has become clear that the effects of the social go deeper still, as they are deeply embedded in the molecular biology of the organism, in some cases with implications for human development and aging (see, e.g., Bearman 2008; Gilbert and Epel 2015; Gluckman and Hanson 2005; Shostak and Freese 2011). Indeed, some of the most surprising and consequential developments have exemplified how the effects of context reach deeply into the genome itself and work to change both the qualitative and quantitative expressions of genes. The many instances of this have become the subject of a broad and growing array of research on gene-environment (G-E) interaction.

The literature on G-E interaction continues to expand rapidly as new techniques for genetic measurement and analysis are regularly introduced (Kudryashova, Burka, Kulaga, Vorobyeva, and Kennedy 2020) and high-throughput technology generates genomic data at a speed and efficiency heretofore unachievable (Feil and Fraga 2012). Particularly in the social sciences, the increase in G-E empirical research is attributable to the expanding availability of genomic data, as more genetic measures have been added to large-scale studies, including the Health and Retirement Study (HRS) and National Longitudinal Study of Adolescent Health (Add Health). Similar integrations of genomic data are being developed in other large-scale panel studies in the US and internationally, including, for example, English Longitudinal Study of Aging (ELSA) and China Health and Retirement Longitudinal Study (CHARLS).

Empirical research on G-E interaction has been focused—understandably—on the opportunities for data analysis provided by the explosion of accessible genomic data for studying G-E interactions in major longitudinal studies. These efforts have for the most part been framed by the established paradigm of inquiry commonly known as the Central Dogma of Biology. As is widely understood, the Central Dogma, based on the work credited to Crick and Watson (Watson and Crick 1953; see also Crick 1958, 1970), postulated that phenotypic outcomes are the product of a unidirectional, biochemical sequence. This sequence begins with the genetic code embedded in DNA, is transcribed into messenger RNA, and then translated into protein through a mechanism involving transfer RNA and ribosomes. It envisions a unidirectional process beginning with a DNA code and passing the code to RNA intermediaries, which then leads to construction of a protein sequence specified by the original DNA code.

The introduction of the Central Dogma remains one of the most commonly recognized scientific revolutions of the 20th century, and its widespread acceptance rested on an unquestioned assumption of these unidirectional translation/transcription processes leading to observable gene effects. The Watson–Crick formulation (1953) was rapidly and near-universally accepted as true (hence its description as "Central Dogma"), and provided a paradigm that framed the narrative of genetic effects in the ensuing decades, not only in the natural sciences but in other fields of scholarship as well as popular culture.

Despite the influence and the hegemony of the Central Dogma, subsequent advances have made clear that it is greatly oversimplified, especially in its assertion of unidirectionality and, most importantly, in its failure to recognize the conditionality and regulation of gene expression. The discovery of gene regulation, in fact, came on the heels of the initial ascendency of the Central Dogma with the trailblazing work of Jacob and Monod (1961), who demonstrated an elaborate regulatory mechanism for lactose metabolism in E. coli known as the, Lac operon (see also Jacob 2011). Further, the early research on the Lac operon revealed that the expression of genes is not constant, but rather that genes must be "turned on" in order for their information to be expressed. In what can be considered, in many ways, a nascent moment in the history of G–E research, Jacob and Monod also established that gene expression can be controlled by conditions in the extracellular environment. It is noteworthy that, despite the profound importance of this early work on environmental gene regulation, it would be decades before the pace and volume of scientific developments in this new field of genetic inquiry would begin to parallel more conventional Central Dogma research.

The relevance of this line of research in gene regulation to the sociological imagination became clear when work published by Barker (1986) demonstrated that an array of noncommunicable diseases, with direct effects on late-life health and longevity, can be induced by environmental exposure to conditions of poverty during fetal development. This work was a precursor to the field of Developmental Origins of Health and Disease (later discussed in detail), which demonstrates clearly that many of the key factors regulating gene expression are environmental—thereby awarding to social forces an unprecedented and largely unanticipated explanatory role in gene-level outcomes (Gluckman, Hanson, and Spencer 2005) . In short, it is now understood that much of the gene regulation that occurs at the cellular level occurs in response to contextual factors—within and beyond the organism itself.

Epigenetics is perhaps the term most prominently associated with this discovery. Epigenetics is defined as a group of processes responsible for altering gene expression without imposing changes in the nucleotide sequence of DNA, that is, the genetic code carried in the cells of the organism. Some widely known processes included under the heading of epigenetics include DNA methylation and histone modification. However, an added array of well-documented processes including micro-RNA production, retrotransposition ("jumping genes"), mitochondrial DNA, copy number variations and aneuploidy are also known to promote alteration of gene expression (e.g., Armstrong et al. 2014; Bird 2007; Feil and Fraga 2012; Li and Biggin 2015; McClintock 1950; Pennisi 2015; Seifert, Schofield, Barton, and Hay 2015; Wei et al. 2016; Whitelaw and Martin 2001). Of particular relevance for social and behavioral scientists are ongoing sets of discoveries in gene biology making clear that environmental factors continuously participate in gene regulation. Such discoveries have spawned a new and rapidly growing subfield in biology, *ecological developmental biology* (e.g., Gilbert and Epel 2015; Gilbert, Bosch, and Ledón-Rettig 2015; Naviaux 2019).

Driven by this growing body of gene-regulation literature, the study of G-E interactions has entered what some scholars are calling a "postgenomic" (Plomin, DeFries, Craig, and McGuffin 2002; Senier, Brown, Shostak, and Hanna 2017; Shostak and Moinester 2015) or "neogenomic" (Charney 2012) period that reflects growing emphases on "phenotypic plasticity" (Fusco and Minelli 2010:547–56), and "polyphenism", a concept that is of central importance in the rapid expansion of ecological developmental ("eco-devo") biology (Gilbert and Epel 2015), and reflected at cellular and genetic levels (e.g., Naviaux 2019, 2020). These discoveries have made clear that many domains of gene expression regulation are, to a substantial extent, socially organized. Therefore, any full accounting of when and under what conditions these environmentally integrated domains of genes are expressed, will necessarily have to take into account social conditions. Thus, they create a new frontier or unexplored explanatory terrain for sociological explanation.

THE SOCIAL ORGANIZATION OF GENE REGULATION

In the service of this burgeoning postgenomic/neogenomic research enterprise, scholars outside the social sciences have taken steps to create a comprehensive accounting of environmental and social factors that impact genetic outcomes (Naviaux 2019, 2020), an accounting that we term the *social organization of gene regulation* (SOGR). Analogous to the efforts driving genomics, which provided a detailed understanding of the human genome, epigenome and transcriptome (Kudryashova, Burka, Kulaga, Vorobyeva, and Kennedy 2020), a comprehensive elucidation of the human "envirome" or "exposome" aims to produce an equally detailed accounting of all manner of environmental impact on gene expression (Wild 2005). A central feature of any envirome or exposome is to identify comprehensively the range of features of lived experience able to reach to the functioning genome at the molecular level to impose their influence on gene expression (Landecker and Panofsky 2013:333–57), thereby identifying the ways in which social and cultural forces exert influence on biochemical processes.

The relevance to social science of this postgenomic/neogenomic lens is reflected in collaborative efforts between biologists and social and behavioral scientists, and has fueled development of the field of s*ocial genomics* (Cole 2009; see also Shanahan 2013). This field is dedicated to understanding how social context and experiences within a given context regulate the mechanisms that constitute gene expression.

As more is learned about the sensitivity of gene expression to everyday circumstances and experiences, it is clear that an adequate understanding of both a) human health and aging in general, and b) the mechanisms via which social forces impact the organism both require that careful attention be paid to how gene expression and related processes are organized and regulated by social processes. Readers may be familiar with the well-publicized work of Steven Cole and associates (2007), in which high degrees of loneliness were found to be associated with the expression of 209 genes in circulating leukocytes. Cole and his colleagues also found that high levels of loneliness are associated with an over-expression of pro-inflammatory genes and an under-expression of genes associated with anti-inflammatory processes.

Social genomics thus focuses on mechanisms that involve environmentally imposed changes in the molecular expression of the gene itself. It entails a range of research initiatives seeking to understand the mechanisms by which the social world gets not only "under the skin", but reaches all the way down to the molecular mechanisms driving gene expression.

As described previously, epigenetic mechanisms are among the most widely studied modalities of gene expression regulation and have been implicated in developmental mechanisms related to a range of consequential characteristics including neuroplasticity, appetite, cardiovascular health, and diseases such as dementia and various cancers. In light of its central importance in the study of gene expression regulation, particularly as it pertains to social forces, we turn to a more detailed description of epigenetics.

THE ROLE OF EPIGENETICS IN HEALTH AND DISEASE

The epigenetic mechanisms mediating genetic expression operate in the form of extra-DNA molecules that facilitate interaction between gene products and environmental forces. Epigenetic mechanisms, which act largely through physical contact with genes or proteins associated with structural support of genes called histones, can take several forms including the most widely studied of these mechanisms, DNA methylation, histone acetylation and histone methylation (Feinberg 2007). Processes associated with epigenetics impact various levels of phenotype production including: inhibiting or promoting DNA transcription, qualitatively altering the transcription process, altering the translation process and modifying post-translational protein (Bonasio, Tu, and Reinberg 2010; Douthit 2006; Jablonka and Raz 2009). To illustrate such processes, we briefly present three examples of epigenetic action with profound life course consequences: 1) the Barker hypothesis, 2) child maltreatment, and 3) smoking.

FETAL PROGRAMMING AND THE BARKER HYPOTHESIS

As noted in Chapter 6, the Barker hypothesis contends that fetal circumstances have a major impact on life-course health, extending though adulthood into later life. The Barker hypothesis is one example of a phenomenon known as "fetal programming", which refers to a set of processes whereby social and environmental factors such as nutrition, chemical exposure and aspects of maternal physiology (e.g., blood pressure) epigenetically alter physiological regulatory processes in the fetus. Some of the resultant alterations are hypothesized to persist throughout the life course, often with significant health-related consequences (Adair 2008; Bush et al. 2018; Cunliffe 2016; Gluckman and Hanson 2005; Lussier, Weinberg, and Kobor 2017; Nathanielsz 2000).

Recent iterations have linked the social factor of fetal nutrition to adult cardiovascular disease and the current epidemics of juvenile obesity and diabetes (Austin 2011; Bush et al. 2018; Davis and Carpenter 2009; Martin 2008). The Barker hypothesis proposes that these problems may be driven by a combination of fetal/infant malnourishment (which programs gene expression for caloric scarcity) with a subsequent energy-dense and high-fat diet in adolescence and adulthood (Gluckman and Hanson 2005; Zanetti et al. 2018). Thus, the experience of infant malnourishment prompts epigenetic triggers that set metabolic and hormonal parameters for a low-calorie diet, leaving such individuals physiologically ill-equipped to deal with high-calorie foods.

The effects of fetal programming on adult health are currently being explored in relation to numerous other health problems, including Alzheimer's dementia and various cancers (Gabory, Attig, and Junien 2011; Gluckman, Hanson, Cooper, and Thornburg 2008; McMullen et al. 2012; Roseboom, de Rooij, and Painter 2006; Skogen and Øverland 2012).

Cohort-level evidence in support of the Barker hypothesis has been found in the study of individuals whose prenatal development coincided with the Dutch Hongerwinter. As described in Chapter 6, the Dutch Hongerwinter was a period of German-imposed famine in the western portion of the Netherlands from 1944 to 1945. Researchers demonstrated that six decades after prenatal exposure to famine, the gene locus for insulin-like growth factor II (IGF2) was consistently hypomethylated in individuals with prenatal exposure relative to same-sex unexposed siblings (Heijmans et al. 2008).

Since IGF2 plays a central role in growth and development, the lowered binding of methyl groups to regions that control its expression resulted in a slowed growth of the fetus. This suggests that epigenetic hypomethylation, prompted by famine, serves as a rapid-response adaptation that conserves scarce energy-generating food sources (Heijmans et al. 2008). The life-course consequences of this are evident in that sixty years later, members of this population had an abnormal lipid profile, higher prevalence of coronary disease and altered coagulation function (Roseboom et al. 2006).

While the Dutch Hongerwinter case illustrates the impact of prenatal adversity, other types of regulation of genetic expression may be triggered at any age. It is well known, for example, that factors related to social circumstances (e.g., diet or exposure to stress-inducing environments), can alter gene expression across the life course (Gluckman and Hanson 2005; Mathews and Janusek 2011).

CHILD ADVERSITY
Numerous other epigenetic responses occurring in childhood also have consequences that reverberate across the life course (Bath, Schilit, and Lee 2013). A wide range of debilitating physiological and psychiatric conditions in adulthood have been associated with adverse child experiences (ACEs), including an impaired neuroendocrine stress response, obesity, depression, anxiety, suicidality, attention-deficit hyperactivity disorder (ADHD), learning disabilities and schizophrenia (Gluckman and Hanson 2005; Jiang, Postovit, Cattaneo,

Binder, and Aitchison 2019; McClelland, Korosi, Cope, Ivy, and Baram 2011; McGowan and Szyf 2010; Mill and Petronis 2008; Nestler 2014; Szyf 2011; Uddin et al. 2010). Such processes have obvious implications for the latency-pathways debate discussed in Chapter 6.

The preponderance of ACE-related epigenetic modifications associated with emotional, cognitive and behavioral impairments are mediated by DNA methylation and histone modification. One hypothesized outcome of ACE-related epigenetic action of particular relevance to the life course involves decreased synthesis of brain-derived *neurotropic* factor (BDNF; Radtke et al. 2015).

BNDF is a member of a family of substances called neurotrophins, which are key substances in development and lifelong maintenance of the central nervous system. Again, related to the "latency-pathways" debate discussed in Chapter 6, the extent to which childhood experience may be mediated by adult experience is in such cases unclear. In addition to its role in early development, for example, it is now well understood that BDNF plays a role across the life course in neuron maintenance and neuroplasticity support (Scharfman, Kramár, Luine, and Srivastava 2013).

MATERNAL SMOKING

As a third example, consider the effects of maternal smoking. Abundant evidence shows distinct methylation patterns resulting from in utero exposure to both maternal and secondhand smoke (Ambatipudi et al. 2016; Knopik, Maccani, Francazio, and McGeary 2012). While a connection between specific epigenetic changes and phenotype is drawn primarily through mediational analysis (Rogers 2019), a plethora of epigenetic outcomes of cigarette smoke are highly suspect in both metabolic and behavioral outcomes of prenatal exposure (Ambatipudi et al. 2016). Metabolically, a particularly strong case has been made that features from cigarette smoke exposure in utero mimic some of the epigenetically driven outcomes of maternal malnutrition (see Dutch Hongerwinter discussed earlier). In particular, features associated with metabolic syndrome—for example, obesity, hypertension, insulin resistance—to varying degrees, are associated with prenatal smoke exposure (Rogers 2019).

A sizable amount of literature also points to an association between neonatal exposure to nicotine and symptoms of attention-deficit hyperactivity disorder (ADHD) (Tiesler and Heinrich 2014; Tran and Miyake 2017). In addition, numerous studies looking at the normal functions of the particular genes targeted by nicotine-related epigenetic markers have underscored the likelihood that the enduring cognitive and behavioral aspects of ADHD have a causal relationship with epigenetically modified gene expression (Tran and Miyake 2017).

Such discoveries suggest the need for a basic reassessment of the established understandings of ADHD and related maladies, and clearly point to the relevance of environmental forces and the need for sociological imagination. One needs to only consider the influential role played by psychiatry and psychology in framing ADHD as being a familial disorder passed intergenerationally through candidate gene inheritance (Faraone and Doyle 2001) to see the practical implications of such a narrow conceptualization of the disorder (Douthit and Marquis 2006; Douthit and Sullivan 2014). This constrained view of ADHD has resulted in intervention strategies heavily dependent on pharmaceutical solutions to what are fundamentally socially driven phenomenon involving often unwitting maternal health practices (Cohen 2006).

The previous examples illustrate the wide proliferation of work demonstrating how environmental factors regulate gene expression. Many other equally compelling cases exist, including neuroendocrine and immunological responses to chronic stress in adulthood (Glaser and Kiecolt-Glaser 2005) and exposure to environmental toxins, often connected to social circumstances (Collotta, Bertazzi, and Bollati 2013).

THE SOCIAL ORGANIZATION OF GENE REGULATION AND SOCIOLOGICAL IMAGINATION

It should be clear from these few limited examples that the discovery of the social organization of genetic regulation compels a new level of attention to the explanatory power of social forces. Obviously, this does not mean that DNA no longer matters. In many instances the kinds of regulation described earlier entail interaction with specific genotypes—indicating that the way these complex processes interact in the real world is even more complex than assumed. And, in the case of non-Mendelian point mutations and their associated diseases, DNA of course remains a "single-locus" determinant.

All such ancillary considerations notwithstanding, it is clear that social genomics introduces a game-changing new paradigmatic framework for understanding the role of genes in phenotypic development and characteristics over the life course, and the power of social forces in regulating that role. Unlike anything coming before, it compels researchers to recognize that that the general significance of genes cannot be understood without systematic attention to environmental factors.

One obvious question before us, then, is how this information is being activated by social scientists interested in G-E interactions.

G-E INTERACTION, THE DOMINANT PARADIGM AND THE HEURISTIC OF CONTAINMENT

It is perhaps telling to consider that the need to attend carefully to the power of social and environmental forces in influencing gene expression was initially articulated primarily by biologists, not social scientists (Cole 2009; Cole et al. 2007, 2011; Gluckman et al. 2008; Gluckman and Hanson 2005), and is being vigorously pursued by biologists in research on multiple species (e.g., Cullis 2017; Cullis and Cullis 2019; Gilbert and Epel 2008). For related reasons, researchers working in behavioral genetics have been among those who have changed course and begun trying to integrate environmental factors into their thinking and research (Panofsky 2014:186–9).

THE SOCIAL CONTROL APPROACH: NEUTRALIZING THE SOCIAL

Given the manifest interest from some in biology in increasing our understanding of social and environmental effects on gene expression, it is ironic that much of the sociological research on G–E interactions continues to emphasize the traditional, unidirectional logic of biology's Central Dogma. As Liu and Guo assert (2016:2–3):

> In the social sciences, it is commonly assumed that . . . differences across individuals are attributed to social cultural and environmental influences. This assumption has been challenged by rapid development in molecular genetics. In recent decades, considerable effort and resources have been devoted to discovering genetic causes . . . (and establishing) associations between thousands of genetic loci and human diseases as well as other traits.

It is clear that the overarching commitment of such work, premised on the assumption of fixed genome effects, is targeted not to understanding the *social organization of genetic expression* or regulation but rather to the *genetic organization of social expression*—for the use of genes to more precisely predict individual characteristics, actions (behaviors) and social outcomes—that is, the ways in which genes create, among other things, phenotypic characteristics and behavioral predispositions. It is a particular form of biologization that has been perhaps stronger in the social and behavioral sciences than in the practice of medicine (Rose 2001).

In sociological research on G–E interactions, this general approach underlies the well-known "social control" perspective (see, e.g., Shanahan and Hofer 2005), which proceeds from the logic that strong forms of social control suppress genetically driven predispositions. Thus, when normative, legal or other forms of "social control" are reduced, such predispositions are less likely to be squelched and more likely to be observed in human action and conduct ("behavior"). It is an approach which "removes or adjusts influences of social exposures resulted from genetic propensities (e.g., alcoholics cluster due to their shared genetic propensities for drinking). This strategy is based on the idea that genotypes are fixed, but social exposures might be alterable" (Liu and Guo 2016:143–4).

Perhaps paradoxically, the logic of social control can encourage a disinterest in social dynamics, beyond their utility in revealing the modulation of genetic effects. From this perspective, social forces can be considered "noise"—an obstruction in the way of getting to the explanation of interest—as explained in Boardman and associates' study of genetic propensities to smoke:

> [C]hanges in social norms regarding smoking can affect the relevance of genetic influences by minimizing or maximizing 'noise' that has the potential to overwhelm and hide the influences. On one hand, genetic associations are most clearly observable in benign environments that lack social factors encouraging genetically influenced addictive behaviors. When social noise is minimized, it allows for 'biology to shine through' (Raine 2002:14).
>
> (Boardman, Blalock, and Pampel 2010)

Guided by similar paradigmatic logic, behavioral geneticists sometimes contend that genes will have their maximum impact when variation due to environmental influences approaches zero (e.g., Turkheimer 2000). While such a claim makes sense in term of abstract logic, it is abundantly clear no environment "lacks social factors" and that "zero environmental influence" is not possible in the real world. As was made clear in earlier chapters, human beings are in large part constituted and sustained in concert and continuous interaction with environmental influence.

Yet if one continues to accept the traditional dogma, the logic of these arguments is clear and appealing. And it can indeed be acknowledged that this general approach has been a source of fruitful work within as well as beyond social science. It has spawned ingenious study designs and provocative findings (see, e.g., Boardman et al. 2013; Guo, Roettger, and Cai 2008; Guo and Stearns 2002) and has contributed some useful discoveries such as genetic predispositions to Alzheimer's disease (Singleton and Hardy 2016) and a breast cancer susceptibility gene, BRCA2 (Wooster et al. 1995). In both cases, knowledge of propensity can be an antecedent to prophylactic measures that have the potential to avert serious disease (Barnard et al. 2014; Evans, Howell, and Howell 2019).

When a study can claim significant findings on apparent effects of genes and find its way to publication without going to the trouble of dealing with the complexity that social genomics introduces, researchers may understandably find little incentive to attend to more complex interactions, despite their ultimate importance for understanding the actual causal connections involved, and despite what they may reveal about the power of social forces. Such work seeks to increase predictive efficacy of behavioral outcomes by incorporating genetic information, and the hope is that the continued expanse of available data will enhance prediction:

> As more and more different types of genomic data and more and more measures within a type of genomic data are discovered and utilized, predictability of the human genome for human outcomes will increase. Improved predictability can enrich and deepen our understanding of social science models.
>
> (Liu and Guo 2016:15)

We can readily agree, in principle, that in many cases it may be revealing to measure the effect of genes in this straightforward way, and that studies that report an apparent "genetic effect on social expression" may be capturing something real. This notion often becomes strikingly clear when the interactive character of such effects becomes clarified, as happens with personalized medicine and with the growing recognition of differential genetic sensitivity in relation to particular socioenvironmental characteristics (Belsky 2013). However, even in such cases, it would be premature to assume that such associations mean that the social is irrelevant, because such correlations and predictions do little to specify the mechanisms involved, and to clarify the extent to which such mechanisms may be social.

THE GENETIC ORGANIZATION OF SOCIAL EXPRESSION, OR THE SOCIAL ORGANIZATION OF GENETIC DIFFERENCES?

When one turns attention to the question of exactly what it is about a putatively hard-wired genetic characteristic that produces its environmental effect, the social again often becomes relevant, because the effects of some relatively fixed genetic characteristics (e.g., height, hair and skin color, physical attractiveness) have a culturally ascribed value that will impact socially regulated access to resources and opportunities:

> [I]f red-haired children were discriminated against in school and if, as a result of that discrimination, performed worse on cognitive tests, one might conclude in a study that genes associated with red hair had caused low performance. It would in a sense be correct, but not because the genes were a direct cause of IQ. . . . The genes caused hair color, the hair color 'caused' the discrimination, and the discrimination, not the genes, was the culprit.
>
> (Marmot 2004:44)

What Michael Marmot is describing here is something that operates perennially and pervasively. In the US and other societies, skin color is not unrelated to adversity and attendant health and social challenges. However, the actual cause of those factors has nothing to do with skin color; instead it involves human history and culture. The growth of awareness of systemic racism makes the pervasive power of such processes increasingly clear, and it can be ignored only at our serious peril.

Yet this general point applies much more broadly, and to even much more nuanced forms of discrimination based on appearance. This has not been entirely overlooked by those operating within the traditional assumptions of the Central Dogma:

> [P]revious research has made it clear that identical twin pairs are more likely than dizygotic twins to have the same friends, classmates, spend more time with one another, and dress the same.
>
> (Cronk et al. 2002; Boardman, Domingue, and Daw 2015:3)

Although this is an important acknowledgment, it is unclear that its implications have been accorded the attention they warrant. Even if it were true that—for some purposes—the paradigmatic assumptions of the Central Dogma might continue to be relevant or acceptable, it does not follow that correlations or predictions between genes and conduct, or genes and aptitudes, would represent biochemical causal processes within the organism rather than the social allocation of opportunities. Social allocation processes regulate differential access to social resources—distributing it to some and withholding it from others on the basis of social constructs such as race and gender, which are built on gene-controlled biological features but go far beyond them in organizing social inclusion, exclusion and opportunity. Because of this, the potential for uncontrolled and unmeasured social "noise" remains daunting, and it is clear that the forces involved cannot be understood without paying attention to their social organization. Thus, for this work as much as for epigenetics, sociological imagination is not just an "optional accessory" to the enterprise of explanation of processes that involve genes; it is essential to any effort to develop a full understanding of the relevant processes.

CONCLUDING OBSERVATIONS

Since the introduction of the Central Dogma more than half a century ago, the social and behavioral sciences have generally joined with other disciplines and the lay public in assuming the genes can stand as the default explanation to account for an expanding range of phenotypic characteristics. In the years leading up to the mapping of the genome in 2004, scientists and others highly anticipated a new era of precision and power in the expansion of genetic explanation. By and large, those expectations were met with a surprising lack of success.

Instead, over the past two decades, work demonstrating the importance of socioenvironmental factors on health—and with significant implications for processes of aging—has continued to mount, and has been given a new order of importance by the discovery of social effects on gene regulation and expression, manifest in discussions of epigenetics and related processes. This work has generated rapidly expanding subfields, such as social genomics and ecological developmental biology, and attendant developments in the biological sciences that were devoted to exploring and understanding the explanatory importance of environmental factors, and prominently include the power of social forces, which is necessary to apprehend if a full understanding of genetic effects and phenotypic outcomes is to be achieved. These developments have created not just an *opening*, but a *demand* and a *necessity* for sociological imagination.

In this chapter, we have shown that despite this necessity and the attendant new opportunities for sociological explanation, social and behavioral sciences have thus far been reluctant to embrace the challenge, and in some respects have actively resisted its implications—arguably comprising another instance of containment and of the alignment of inquiry with the functional-organismic nexus. The spectre of seeing social scientists resisting such opportunities to mobilize their sociological imaginations in the service of advancing science at the very same time that some biologists appear very interested in such openings is surprising and perplexing. It raises a number of compelling questions about the assumptions and interests that drive social science inquiry. These questions have no quick and easy answers, but they cannot be ignored. They are the subjects of the next two chapters.

REFERENCES

Adair, Linda S. 2008. "Child and Adolescent Obesity: Epidemiology and Developmental Perspectives." *Physiology & Behavior* 94(1): 8–16.

Aimone, James B., Yan Li, Star W. Lee, Gregory D. Clemenson, Wei Deng, and Fred H. Gage. 2014. "Regulation and Function of Adult Neurogenesis: From Genes to Cognition." *Physiological Reviews* 94(4): 991–1026. doi: 10.1152/physrev.00004.2014.

Ambatipudi, Srikant, Cyrille Cuenin, Hector Hernandez-Vargas, Akram Ghantous, Florence Le Calvez-Kelm, Rudolf Kaaks, Myrto Barrdahl, Heiner Boeing, Krasimira

Aleksandrova, Antonia Trichopoulou, Pagona Lagiou, Androniki Naska, Domenico Palli, Vittorio Krogh, Silvia Polidoro, Rosario Tumino, Salvatore Panico, Bas Bueno-de-Mesquita, Petra HM Peeters, José Ramón Quirós, Carmen Navarro, Eva Ardanaz, Miren Dorronsoro, Tim Key, Paolo Vineis, Neil Murphy, Elio Riboli, Isabelle Romieu, and Zdenko Herceg. 2016. "Tobacco Smoking-Associated Genome-Wide DNA Methylation Changes in the EPIC Study." *Epigenomics* 8(5): 599–618. doi: 10.2217/epi-2016-0001.

Anand, Kuljeet Singh, and Vikas Dhikav. 2012. "Hippocampus in Health and Disease: An Overview." *Annals of Indian Academy of Neurology* 15(4): 239–46. doi: 10.4103/0972-2327.104323.

Armstrong, David W. J., M. Yat Tse, Philip G. Wong, Nicole M. Ventura, Jalna A. Meens, Amer M. Johri, Murray F. Matangi, and Stephen C. Pang. 2014. "Gestational Hypertension and the Developmental Origins of Cardiac Hypertrophy and Diastolic Dysfunction." *Molecular and Cellular Biochemistry* 391(1–2): 201–9. doi: 10.1007/s11010-014-2003-9.

Austin, S. Bryn. 2011. "The Blind Spot in the Drive for Childhood Obesity Prevention: Bringing Eating Disorders Prevention into Focus as a Public Health Priority." *American Journal of Public Health* 101(6): e1–4. doi: 10.2105/AJPH.2011.300182.

Baars, Jan. 1991. "The Challenge of Critical Gerontology: The Problem of Social Constitution." *Journal of Aging Studies* 5(3): 219–43. doi: 10.1016/0890-4065(91)90008-G.

Barker, David, and C. Osmond. 1986. "Infant Mortality, Childhood Nutrition, and Ischaemic Heart Disease in England and Wales." *The Lancet* 327(8489): 1077–81.

Barnard, Neal D., Ashley I. Bush, Antonia Ceccarelli, James Cooper, Celeste A. de Jager, Kirk I. Erickson, Gary Fraser, Shelli Kesler, Susan M. Levin, Brendan Lucey, Martha Clare Morris, and Rosanna Squitti. 2014. "Dietary and Lifestyle Guidelines for the Prevention of Alzheimer's Disease." *Neurobiology of Aging* 35 (suppl 2): S74–8. doi: 10.1016/j.neurobiolaging.2014.03.033.

Bath, K. G., A. Schilit, and F. S. Lee. 2013. "Stress Effects on BDNF Expression: Effects of Age, Sex, and Form of Stress." *Neuroscience* 239: 149–56.

Bearman, Peter. 2008. "Introduction: Exploring Genetics and Social Structure." *American Journal of Sociology* 114(S1):c-x. doi: 1086/596596.

Belsky, Jay. 2013. "Differential Susceptibility to Environmental Influences." *International Journal of Child Care and Education Policy* 7(2): 15–31. doi: 10.1007/2288-6729-7-2-15.

Bird, Adrian. 2007. "Perceptions of Epigenetics." *Nature* 447(7143): 396–8. doi: 10.1038/nature05913.

Blackburn, Elizabeth H., Elissa S. Epel, and Jue Lin. 2015. "Human Telomere Biology: A Contributory and Interactive Factor in Aging, Disease Risks, and Protection." *Science* (New York, NY) 350(6265): 1193–8. doi: 10.1126/science.aab3389.

Boardman, Jason D., Casey L. Blalock, and Fred C. Pampel. 2010. "Trends in the Genetic Influences on Smoking." *Journal of Health and Social Behavior* 51(1): 108–23.

Boardman, Jason D., Jonathan Daw, and Jeremy Freese. 2013. "Defining the Environment in Gene-Environment Research: Lessons from Social Epidemiology." *American Journal of Public Health* 103(suppl 1): S64–72. doi: 10.2105/AJPH.2013.301355.

Boardman, Jason D., Benjamin W. Domingue, and Jonathan Daw. 2015. "What Can Genes Tell Us about the Relationship between Education and Health?" *Social Science & Medicine* 127: 171–80. doi: 10.1016/j.socscimed.2014.08.001.

Bonasio, Roberto, Shengjiang Tu, and Danny Reinberg. 2010. "Molecular Signals of Epigenetic States." *Science* 330(6004): 612–16. doi: 10.1126/science.1191078.

Bush, Nicole R., Rachel D. Edgar, Mina Park, Julia L. MacIsaac, Lisa M. McEwen, Nancy E. Adler, Marilyn J. Essex, Michael S. Kobor, and W. Thomas Boyce. 2018. "The Biological Embedding of Early-Life Socioeconomic Status and Family Adversity in Children's Genome-Wide DNA Methylation." *Epigenomics* 10(11): 1445. doi: 10.2217/epi-2018-0042.

Charney, Evan. 2012. "Behavior Genetics and Postgenomics." *The Behavioral and Brain Sciences* 35(5): 331–58. doi: 10.1017/S0140525X11002226.

Cohen, David. 2006. "Critiques of the 'ADHD' Enterprise." Pp. 12–33 in *Critical New Perspectives on ADHD*, edited by G. Lloyd, J. Stead, and D. Cohen. London/New York: Routledge.

Cole, Steven W. 2009. "Social Regulation of Human Gene Expression." *Current Directions in Psychological Science* 18(3): 132–7. doi: 10.1111/j.1467-8721.2009.01623.x.

Cole, Steven W., Jesusa M. G. Arevalo, Kavya Manu, Eva H. Telzer, Lisa Kiang, Julienne E. Bower, Michael R. Irwin, and Andrew J. Fuligni. 2011. "Antagonistic Pleiotropy at the Human IL6 Promoter Confers Genetic Resilience to the Pro-Inflammatory Effects of Adverse Social Conditions in Adolescence." *Developmental Psychology* 47(4): 1173–80. doi: 10.1037/a0023871.

Cole, Steve W., Louise C. Hawkley, Jesusa M. Arevalo, Caroline Y. Sung, Robert M. Rose, and John T. Cacioppo. 2007. "Social Regulation of Gene Expression in Human Leukocytes." *Genome Biology* 8(9): R189. doi: 10.1186/gb-2007-8-9-r189.

Collotta, M., P. A. Bertazzi, and V. Bollati. 2013. "Epigenetics and Pesticides." *Toxicology* 307: 35–41. doi: 10.1016/j.tox.2013.01.017.

Crick, Francis H. 1958. "On Protein Synthesis." *Symposia of the Society for Experimental Biology* 12: 138–63.

Crick, Francis. 1970. "Central Dogma of Molecular Biology." *Nature* 227(5258): 561–3.

Cronk, Nikole J., Wendy S. Slutske, Pamela A. F. Madden, Katheleen K. Bucholz, Wendy Reich, and Andrew C. Heath. 2002. "Emotional and Behavioral Problems among Female Twins: An Evaluation of the Equal Environments Assumption." *Journal of the American Academy of Child & Adolescent Psychiatry* 41(7): 829–37. doi: 10.1097/00004583-200207000-00016.

Cullis, Christopher A. 2017. "Mechanisms of Induced Inheritable Genome Variation in Flax." Pp. 77–90 in *Somatic Genome Variation in Animals, Plants and Microorganisms*. 1st edition, edited by Xiu-Qing Li. Hoboken, NJ: Wiley-Blackwell.

Cullis, Christopher A., and Margaret Cullis. 2019. "Flax Genome 'Edits' in Response to the Growth Environment." Pp. 196–214 in *Plant Genetics and Genomics: Crops and Models 23: Genetics and Genomics of Linum*, edited by C. A. Cullis. Chaim, Switzerland: Springer.

Cunliffe, Vincent T. 2016. "The Epigenetic Impacts of Social Stress: How Does Social Adversity Become Biologically Embedded?" *Epigenomics* 8(12): 1653–69.

Davis, Brennan, and Christopher Carpenter. 2009. "Proximity of Fast-Food Restaurants to Schools and Adolescent Obesity." *American Journal of Public Health* 99(3): 505. doi: 10.2105/AJPH.2008.137638.

Deng, Wei, James B. Aimone, and Fred H. Gage. 2010. "New Neurons and New Memories: How Does Adult Hippocampal Neurogenesis Affect Learning and Memory?" *Nature Reviews Neuroscience* 11(5): 339–50. doi: 10.1038/nrn2822.

Doidge, Norman. 2007. *The Brain That Changes Itself: Stories of Personal Triumph from the Frontiers of Brain Science.* New York: Penguin.

Douthit, Kathryn Z. 2006. "The Convergence of Counseling and Psychiatric Genetics: An Essential Role for Counselors." *Journal of Counseling and Development* 84(1): 16–28.

Douthit, Kathryn, and Andre Marquis. 2006. "Empiricism in Psychiatry's Post-Psychoanalytic Era: Contemplating DSM's 'Atheoretical' Nosology." *Constructivism in the Human Science* 11(1): 32–59.

Douthit, Kathryn, and Justin Russotti. 2017. "The Biology of Marginality: A Neurophysiological Exploration of the Social and Cultural Foundations of Psychological Health." Pp. 45–60 in *Neurocounseling: A Brain-Based Approach to Clinical Case Conceptualization, Assessment, and Intervention*, edited by T. Field, L. Jones, and L. Russell-Chapin. Alexandria, VA: American Counseling Association.

Douthit, Kathryn, and Tamara Sullivan. 2014. "Attention-Deficit/Hyperactivity Disorder." Pp. 564–671 in *Understanding Psychopathology: An Integral Exploration*, edited by R. E. Ingersoll and A. Marquis. Boston, MA: Pearson.

Dowd, Jennifer Beam, and Audrey Renson. 2018. "'Under the Skin' and into the Gut: Social Epidemiology of the Microbiome." *Current Epidemiology Reports* 5(4): 432–41. doi: 10.1007/s40471-018-0167-7.

Epel, Elissa S., and Aric A. Prather. 2018. "Stress, Telomeres, and Psychopathology: Toward a Deeper Understanding of a Triad of Early Aging." *Annual Review of Clinical Psychology* 14(3): 71–97. doi: 10.1146/annurev-clinpsy-032816-045054.

Evans, D. Gareth, Sacha J. Howell, and Anthony Howell. 2019. "Should Unaffected Female BRCA2 Pathogenic Variant Carriers Be Told There Is Little or No Advantage from Risk Reducing Mastectomy?" *Familial Cancer* 18(4): 377–9. doi: 10.1007/s10689-019-00142-8.

Faraone, Stephen V., and Alysa E. Doyle. 2001. "The Nature and Heritability of Attention-Deficit/Hyperactivity Disorder." *Child and Adolescent Psychiatric Clinics of North America* 10(2): 299–316. doi: 10.1016/S1056-4993(18)30059-2.

Feil, Robert, and Mario F. Fraga. 2012. "Epigenetics and the Environment: Emerging Patterns and Implications." *Nature Reviews Genetics* 13: 97–109.

Feinberg, Andrew P. 2007. "Phenotypic Plasticity and the Epigenetics of Human Disease." *Nature* 447: 433–40. doi: 10.1038/nature05919.

Ferraro, Kenneth F., and Tetyana Pylypiv Shippee. 2009. "Aging and Cumulative Inequality: How Does Inequality Get Under the Skin?" *The Gerontologist* 49(3): 333–43. doi: 10.1093/geront/gnp034.

Fusco, Giuseppe, and Alessandro Minelli. 2010. "Phenotypic Plasticity in Development and Evolution: Facts and Concepts." *Philosophical Transactions of the Royal Society B: Biological Sciences* 365(1540): 547–56.

Gabory, Anne, Linda Attig, and Claudine Junien. 2011. "Developmental Programming and Epigenetics." *The American Journal of Clinical Nutrition* 94(suppl 6): 1943S–52S. doi: 10.3945/ajcn.110.000927.

Gilbert, Scott F., Thomas C. G. Bosch, and Cristina Ledón-Rettig. 2015. "Eco-Evo-Devo: Developmental Symbiosis and Developmental Plasticity as Evolutionary Agents." *Nature Reviews Genetics* 16(10): 611–22. doi: 10.1038/nrg3982.

Gilbert, Scott F., and David Epel. 2015. *Ecological Developmental Biology: The Environmental Regulation of Development, Health, and Evolution*. 2nd edition. Sunderland, MA: Sinauer Associates.

Glaser, Ronald, and Janice K. Kiecolt-Glaser. 2005. "Stress-Induced Immune Dysfunction: Implications for Health." *Nature Reviews Immunology* 5(3): 243–51. doi: 10.1038/nri1571.

Gluckman, Peter, and Mark Hanson. 2005. *Developmental Origins of Health and Disease*. Cambridge: Cambridge University Press.

Gluckman, Peter D., Mark A. Hanson, Cyrus Cooper, and Kent L. Thornburg. 2008. "Effect of in Utero and Early-Life Conditions on Adult Health and Disease." *New England Journal of Medicine* 359(1): 61–73.

Gluckman, Peter D., Mark A. Hanson, and Hamish G. Spencer. 2005. "Predictive Adaptive Responses and Human Evolution." *Trends in Ecology & Evolution* 20(10): 527–33. doi: 10.1016/j.tree.2005.08.001.

Guo, Guang, Michael E. Roettger, and Tianji Cai. 2008. "The Integration of Genetic Propensities into Social-Control Models of Delinquency and Violence among Male Youths." *American Sociological Review* 73(4): 543–68. doi: 10.1177/000312240807300402.

Guo, Guang, and Elizabeth Stearns. 2002. "The Social Influences on the Realization of Genetic Potential for Intellectual Development." *Social Forces* 80(3): 881–910.

Heijmans, Bastiaan T., Elmar W. Tobi, Aryeh D. Stein, Hein Putter, Gerard J. Blauw, Ezra S. Susser, P. Eline Slagboom, and L. H. Lumey. 2008. "Persistent Epigenetic Differences Associated with Prenatal Exposure to Famine in Humans." *Proceedings of the National Academy of Sciences of the United States of America* 105(44): 17046. doi: 10.1073/pnas.0806560105.

Herd, Pamela, Alberto Palloni, Federico Rey, and Jennifer B. Dowd. 2018a. "Social and Population Health Science Approaches to Understand the Human Microbiome." *Nature Human Behavior* 2: 808–15.

Herd, Pamela, Nora Cate Schaeffer, Kerryann DiLoreto, Karen Jacques, John Stevenson, Federico Rey, and Carol Roan. 2018b. "The Influence of Social Conditions across the Life Course on the Human Gut Microbiota: A Pilot Project with the Wisconsin Longitudinal Study." *The Journals of Gerontology: Series B* 73(1): 124–33. doi: 10.1093/geronb/gbx029.

Jablonka, Eva, and Gal Raz. 2009. "Transgenerational Epigenetic Inheritance: Prevalence, Mechanisms, and Implications for the Study of Heredity and Evolution." *The Quarterly Review of Biology* 84(2): 131–76.

Jacob, François. 2011. "The Birth of the Operon." *Science* 332(6031): 767. doi: 10.1126/science.1207943.

Jacob, François, and Jacques Monod. 1961. "Genetic Regulatory Mechanisms in the Synthesis of Proteins." *Journal of Molecular Biology* 3(3): 318–56.

Järbrink-Sehgal, Ellionore, and Anna Andreasson. 2020. "The Gut Microbiota and Mental Health in Adults." *Current Opinion in Neurobiology* 62: 102–14. doi: 10.1016/j.conb.2020.01.016.

Jiang, Shui, Lynne Postovit, Annamaria Cattaneo, Elisabeth B. Binder, and Katherine J. Aitchison. 2019. "Epigenetic Modifications in Stress Response Genes Associated with Childhood Trauma." *Frontiers in Psychiatry* 10: 808.

Kelley, Jessica, and Roland J. Thorpe, Jr. 2021. "The Interplay of Age, Period, and Cohort: Nutrition and Metabolic Diseases in Later Life." Pp. 162–77 in *Handbook of Aging and Social Sciences*. 9th edition, edited by Kenneth Ferraro and Deborah Carr. New York: Elsevier.

Kiecolt-Glaser, Janice K., Lynanne McGuire, Theodore Robles, and Ronald Glaser. 2002. "Psychoneuroimmunology: Psychological Influences on Immune Function and Health." *Journal of Consulting and Clinical Psychology* 70(3): 537–47. doi: 10.1037/0022-006x.70.3.537.

Kiecolt-Glaser, Janice K., Kristopher J. Preacher, Robert C. MacCallum, Cathie Atkinson, William B. Malarkey, and Ronald Glaser. 2003. "Chronic Stress and Age-Related Increases in the Proinflammatory Cytokine IL-6." *Proceedings of the National Academy of Sciences of the United States of America* 100(15): 9090–5. doi: 10.1073/pnas.1531903100.

Knopik, Valerie S., Matthew A. Maccani, Sarah Francazio, and John E. McGeary. 2012. "The Epigenetics of Maternal Cigarette Smoking during Pregnancy and Effects on Child Development." *Development and Psychopathology* 24(4): 1377. doi: 10.1017/S0954579412000776.

Kudryashova, Ksenia S., Ksenia Burka, Anton Y. Kulaga, Nataliya S. Vorobyeva, and Brian K. Kennedy. 2020. "Aging Biomarkers: From Functional Tests to Multi-Omics Approaches." *Proteomics* 20(5–6): 1900408. https://doi.org/10.1002/pmic.201900408.

Kuzumaki, Naoko, Daigo Ikegami, Rie Tamura, Nana Hareyama, Satoshi Imai, Michiko Narita, Kazuhiro Torigoe, Keiichi Niikura, Hideyuki Takeshima, Takayuki Ando, Katsuhide Igarashi, Jun Kanno, Toshikazu Ushijima, Tsutomu Suzuki, and Minoru Narita. 2011. "Hippocampal Epigenetic Modification at the Brain-Derived Neurotrophic Factor Gene Induced by an Enriched Environment." *Hippocampus* 21(2): 127–32. doi: 10.1002/hipo.20775.

Lahey, Benjamin B., Paul J. Rathouz, Steve S. Lee, Andrea Chronis-Tuscano, William E. Pelham, Irwin D. Waldman, and Edwin H. Cook. 2011. "Interactions between Early Parenting and a Polymorphism of the Child's Dopamine Transporter Gene in Predicting Future Child Conduct Disorder Symptoms." *Journal of Abnormal Psychology* 120(1): 33–45.

Landecker, Hannah, and Aaron Panofsky. 2013. "From Social Structure to Gene Regulation, and Back: A Critical Introduction to Environmental Epigenetics for Sociology." *Annual Review of Sociology* 39(1): 333–57. doi: 10.1146/annurev-soc-071312-145707.

Li, Jingyi Jessica, and Mark D. Biggin. 2015. "Statistics Requantitates the Central Dogma." *Science* 347(6226): 1066–7. doi: 10.1126/science.aaa8332.

Liu, Hexuan, and Guang Guo. 2016. "Opportunities and Challenges of Big Data for the Social Sciences: The Case of Genomic Data." *Social Science Research* 59: 13–22. doi: 10.1016/j.ssresearch.2016.04.016.

Lucassen, Paul J., Nicolas Toni, Gerd Kempermann, Jonas Frisen, Fred H. Gage, and Dick F. Swaab. 2020. "Limits to Human Neurogenesis: Really?" *Molecular Psychiatry* 25(10): 2207–9. doi: 10.1038/s41380-018-0337-5

Lussier, Alexandre A., Joanne Weinberg, and Michael S. Kobor. 2017. "Epigenetics Studies of Fetal Alcohol Spectrum Disorder: Where Are We Now?" *Epigenomics* 9(3): 291–311.

Maguire, Eleanor A., David G. Gadian, Ingrid S. Johnsrude, Catriona D. Good, John Ashburner, Richard S. J. Frackowiak, and Christopher D. Firth. 2000. "Navigation-Related Structural Change in the Hippocampi of Taxi Drivers." *Proceedings of the National Academy of Sciences* 97(8): 4398–403.

Marketon, Jeanette I., and Ronald Glaser. 2008. "Stress Hormones and Immune Function." *Cellular Immunology* 252(1–2): 16–26. doi: 10.1016/j.cellimm.2007.09.006.

Marmot, Michael. 2004. *The Status Syndrome*. New York: Henry Holt Publishing.

Martin, Molly A. 2008. "The Intergenerational Correlation in Weight: How Genetic Resemblance Reveals the Social Role of Families." *American Journal of Sociology* 114(suppl): S67.

Mathews, Herbert L., and Linda W. Janusek. 2011. "Epigenetics and Psychoneuroimmunology: Mechanisms and Models." *Brain, Behavior, and Immunity* 25(1): 25–39.

McClelland, Shawn, Aniko Korosi, Jessica Cope, Autumn Ivy, and Tallie Z. Baram. 2011. "Emerging Roles of Epigenetic Mechanisms in the Enduring Effects of Neonatal Stress and Experience on Learning and Memory." *Neurobiology of Learning and Memory* 96(1): 79–88.

McClintock, Barbara. 1950. "The Origin and Behavior of Mutable Loci in Maize." *Proceedings of the National Academy of Sciences* 36(6): 344–55. doi: 10.1073/pnas.36.6.344.

McGowan, Patrick O., and Moshe Szyf. 2010. "The Epigenetics of Social Adversity in Early Life: Implications for Mental Health Outcomes." *Neurobiology of Disease* 39(1): 66–72.

McMullen, S., S. C. Langley-Evans, L. Gambling, C. Lang, A. Swali, and H. J. McArdle. 2012. "A Common Cause for a Common Phenotype: The Gatekeeper Hypothesis in Fetal Programming." *Medical Hypotheses* 78(1): 88–94.

Mill, Jonathan, and Arturas Petronis. 2008. "Pre-and Peri-Natal Environmental Risks for Attention-Deficit Hyperactivity Disorder (ADHD): The Potential Role of Epigenetic Processes in Mediating Susceptibility." *Journal of Child Psychology and Psychiatry* 49(10): 1020–30.

Review of Biological Pathways." *Brain Behavior* 3(3): 302–26.

Muotri, Alysson R., Chunmei Zhao, Maria C. Marchetto, and Fred H. Gage. 2009. "Environmental Influence on L1 Retrotransposons in the Adult Hippocampus." *Hippocampus* 19(10): 1002–7.

Nathanielsz, Peter W. 2000. "Fetal Programming: How the Quality of Fetal Life Alters Biology for a Lifetime." *Neoreviews* 1(7): e126–31.

Naviaux, Robert K. 2019. "Incomplete Healing as a Cause of Aging: The Role of Mitochondria and the Cell Danger Response." *Biology* 8(2). doi: 10.3390/biology8020027.

Naviaux, Robert K. 2020. "Perspective: Cell Danger Response Biology: The New Science That Connects Environmental Health with Mitochondria and the Rising Tide of Chronic Illness." *Mitochondrion* 51: 40–5.

Nestler, Eric J. 2014. "Epigenetic Mechanisms of Depression." *JAMA Psychiatry* 71(4): 454–6.

Panofsky, Aaron. 2014. *Misbehaving Science: Controversy and the Development of Behavior Genetics*. Chicago: University of Chicago Press.

Park, Aesoon, Kenneth J. Sher, Alexandre A. Todorov, and Andrew C. 2011. "Interaction between the DRD4 VNTR Polymorphism and Proximal and Distal Environments in

Alcohol Dependence during Emerging and Young Adulthood." *Journal of Abnormal Psychology* 120(3): 585–95.

Pennisi, Elizabeth. 2015. "New Database Links Regulatory DNA to Its Target Genes." *Science* 348(6235): 618.

Plomin, Robert, John C. Defries, Ian W. Craig, and Peter McGuffin, eds. 2002. *Behavioral Genetics in the Postgenomic Era*. 1st edition. Washington, DC: American Psychological Association.

Prescott, Susan L., and Alan C. Logan. 2017. "Down to Earth: Planetary Health and Biophilosophy in the Symbiocene Epoch." *Challenges* 8(2): 19. doi: 10.3390/challe8020019.

Radtke, K. M., M. Schauer, H. M. Gunter, M. Ruf-Leuschner, J. Sill, A. Meyer, and T. Elbert. 2015. "Epigenetic Modifications of the Glucocorticoid Receptor Gene Are Associated with the Vulnerability to Psychopathology in Childhood Maltreatment." *Translational Psychiatry* 5(5): e571. doi: 10.1038/tp.2015.63.

Raine, Adrian. 2002. "Biosocial Studies of Antisocial and Violent Behavior in Children and Adults: A Review." *Journal of Abnormal Child Psychology* 30(4): 311–26. doi: 10.1023/A:1015754122318.

Ridout, Kathryn K., Mateus Levandowski, Samuel J. Ridout, Lindsay Gantz, Kelly Goonan, Daniella Palermo, Lawrence H. Price, and Audrey R. Tyrka. 2018. "Early Life Adversity and Telomere Length: A Meta-Analysis." *Molecular Psychiatry* 23: 858–71.

Rogers, John M. 2019. "Smoking and Pregnancy: Epigenetics and Developmental Origins of the Metabolic Syndrome." *Birth Defects Research* 111(17): 1259–69. https://doi.org/10.1002/bdr2.1550.

Rogoff, Barbara. 2003. *The Cultural Nature of Human Development*. New York: Oxford University Press.

Rose, Nikolas. 2001. "The Politics of Life Itself." *Theory, Culture & Society* 18(6): 1–30. doi: 10.1177/02632760122052020.

Roseboom, Tessa, Susanne de Rooij, and Rebecca Painter. 2006. "The Dutch Famine and Its Long-Term Consequences for Adult Health." *Early Human Development* 82(8): 485–91. doi: 10.1016/j.earlhumdev.2006.07.001.

Scharfman, H. E., E. A. Kramár, V. Luine, and D. P. Srivastava. 2013. "Introduction to 'Steroid Hormone Actions in the CNS: The Role of Brain-Derived Neurotrophic Factor (BDNF).'" *Neuroscience* 239: 1. doi: 10.1016/j.neuroscience.2012.10.022.

Seifert, Anne, Pietà Schofield, Geoffrey J. Barton, and Ronald T. Hay. 2015. "Proteotoxic Stress Reprograms the Chromatin Landscape of SUMO Modification." *Science Signaling* 8(384): rs7. doi: 10.1126/scisignal.aaa2213.

Senier, Laura, Phil Brown, Sara Shostak, and Bridget Hanna. 2017. "The Socio-Exposome: Advancing Environmental Health Science in a Postgenomic Era." *Environmental Sociology* 3(2): 107–21.

Shanahan, Michael J. 2013. "Social Genomics and the Life Course: Opportunities and Challenges for Multilevel Population Research." Pp. 255–76 in *New Directions in the Sociology of Aging*, edited by L. J. Waite and T. J. Plewes. Washington, DC: National Academies Press.

Shanahan, Michael J., and Scott M. Hofer. 2005. "Social Context in Gene-Environment Interactions: Retrospect and Prospect." *The Journals of Gerontology: Series B* 60(Special Issue 1): 65–76. doi: 10.1093/geronb/60.Special_Issue_1.65.

Shay, Jerry W., and Woodring E. Wright. 2000. "Hayflick, His Limit, and Cellular Ageing." *Nature Reviews Molecular Cell Biology* 1: 72–6.

Shostak, Sara, and Margot Moinester. 2015. "The Missing Piece of the Puzzle? Measuring the Environment in the Postgenomic Moment." in *Postgenomics: Perspectives on Biology after the Genome*, edited by Sarah Richardson and Hallam Stevens. Durham, NC: Duke University Press.

Singleton, Andrew, and John Hardy. 2016. "The Evolution of Genetics: Alzheimer's and Parkinson's Diseases." *Neuron* 90(6): 1154–63. doi: 10.1016/j.neuron.2016.05.040.

Skogen, Jens Christoffer, and Simon Øverland. 2012. "The Fetal Origins of Adult Disease: A Narrative Review of the Epidemiological Literature." *JRSM Short Reports* 3(8): 1–7.

Szyf, Moshe. 2011. "The Early Life Social Environment and DNA Methylation: DNA Methylation Mediating the Long-Term Impact of Social Environments Early in Life." *Epigenetics* 6(8): 971–8.

Tiesler, Carla M. T., and Joachim Heinrich. 2014. "Prenatal Nicotine Exposure and Child Behavioural Problems." *European Child & Adolescent Psychiatry* 23(10): 913–29. doi: 10.1007/s00787-014-0615-y.

Tran, Nguyen Quoc Vuong, and Kunio Miyake. 2017. "Neurodevelopmental Disorders and Environmental Toxicants: Epigenetics as an Underlying Mechanism." *International Journal of Genomics* 2017: e7526592.

Turkheimer, Eric. 2000. "Three Laws of Behavior Genetics and What They Mean." *Current Directions in Psychological Science* 9(5): 160–4.

Uddin, Monica, Allison E. Aiello, Derek E. Wildman, Karestan C. Koenen, Graham Pawelec, Regina de Los Santos, Emily Goldmann, and Sandro Galea. 2010. "Epigenetic and Immune Function Profiles Associated with Posttraumatic Stress Disorder." *Proceedings of the National Academy of Sciences* 107(20): 9470–5.

Valdes, Ana M., Jens Walter, Eran Segal, and Tim D. Spector. 2018. "Role of the Gut Microbiota in Nutrition and Health." *BMJ* 361: k2179. doi: 10.1136/bmj.k2179.

Watson, J. D., and F. H. C. Crick. 1953. "Molecular Structure of Nucleic Acids: A Structure for Deoxyribose Nucleic Acid." *Nature* 171(4356): 737–8. doi: 10.1038/171737a0.

Wei, Pei-Chi, Amelia N. Chang, Jennifer Kao, Zhou Du, Robin M. Meyers, Frederick W. Alt, and Bjoern Schwer. 2016. "Long Neural Genes Harbor Recurrent DNA Break Clusters in Neural Stem/Progenitor Cells." *Cell* 164(4): 644–55. doi: 10.1016/j.cell.2015.12.039.

Whitelaw, Emma, and David I. Martin. 2001. "Retrotransposons as Epigenetic Mediators of Phenotypic Variation in Mammals." *Nature Genetics* 27(4): 361–5.

Wild, Christopher Paul. 2005. "Complementing the Genome with an "Exposome": The Outstanding Challenge of Environmental Exposure Measurement in Molecular Epidemiology." *Cancer Epidemioly Biomarkers & Prevention* 14: 1847–50.

Woollett, Katherine, and Eleanor A. Maguire. 2011. "Acquiring 'the Knowledge' of London's Layout Drives Structural Brain Changes." *Current Biology* 21(24–2): 2109–14. doi: 10.1016/j.cub.2011.11.018.

Wooster, R., G. Bignell, J. Lancaster, S. Swift, S. Seal, J. Mangion, N. Collins, S. Gregory, C. Gumbs, and G. Micklem. 1995. "Identification of the Breast Cancer Susceptibility Gene BRCA2." *Nature* 378(6559): 789–92. doi: 10.1038/378789a0.

Zanetti, Daniela, Emmi Tikkanen, Stefan Gustafsson, James R. Priest, Stephen Burgess, and Erik Ingelsson. 2018. "Birthweight, Type 2 Diabetes Mellitus, and Cardiovascular Disease: Addressing the Barker Hypothesis with Mendelian Randomization." *Circulation: Genomic and Precision Medicine* 11(6): e002054.

CHAPTER 8
SITUATING KNOWLEDGE PRODUCTION: THE SOCIOLOGY OF SCIENTIFIC WORK IN STUDYING AGE AND THE LIFE COURSE

DISCOVERY AND RESISTANCE: A RECURRENT THEME

A recurring theme in the preceding chapters has been the introduction into the study of human aging of new evidence and empirical discoveries pointing to the central importance of social forces in shaping individual characteristics over the life course, followed in each case by a surprising resistance from mainstream life course and gerontological scholars. Here we review this briefly.

First, as shown in Chapter 1, the discovery of *cohort analysis* did not dethrone the idea of "normal aging" as it might have been expected to do. Rather than acknowledging the radical implications of cohort analysis, researchers responded by devising a tactic to contain the intellectual difficulty it posed by simply regarding each cohort as having its own approximation to a standard pattern and by constructing synthetic cohorts deemed to be normal, perhaps like independent samples forming a statistical sampling distribution. Thus, "normal aging" and the functional-organismic nexus survived the logical challenges posed by cohort analysis.

Another challenge presented as a growing attention to the phenomenon of *increasing heterogeneity* as an inherent feature of cohorts and cohort aging. The discovery that heterogeneity among age peers tends to expand with age might have been expected to shift thinking in the sociology of age beyond "normal aging". If heterogeneity tends to increase as a regular feature of cohort aging, it is obviously misleading to treat it as a normative phenomenon across the life course. The heterogeneity and diversity of aging seemed also to be a way to make clear that aging is *shaped by social experience and the dynamics of everyday life*, rather than organismic imperatives.

Once again, however, the functional-organismic logic provided its own framing of the phenomenon of heterogeneity by mobilizing arguments that required little or no sociological analysis. This was done by attempting to account for increasing variability in one of two ways—either in terms of a) individual choice-making and "agency" or b) "individual differences"—the accentuated maturation of increasingly unique individual personalities. As an example of the former, it was speculated that the demands of the workplace suppressed the uniqueness of personalities, and that after retirement their individuality was allowed to come to expression, resulting in greater diversity in later life.

This idea has been present from the beginning of discussions of variability (e.g., Hickey 1980:80–1), and iterations of it continued to resurface and to be applied to other segments of the life course, as in recent efforts to reframe the growing disorder in the transition to adulthood as a matter of individual choice (see Arnett 2014; Settersten and Ray 2010) rather than largely reflecting the growing precarity of young people in contemporary postindustrial societies (Huang 2019, 2021; Phillipson 2015; Standing 2011, 2014). Whether youth or retirement, the common idea is that when people are free to do what they want, they will make diverse choices and not conform to normative expectations and patterns.

When it was then documented (as recounted in Chapter 6) that a great deal of heterogeneity reflects not volitional matters but *inequality in health, resources and social processes of cumulative dis/advantage,* the heuristic logic of containment again resisted a sociological approach to explanation, by proposing that increasing inequality might be viewed as a matter of the life-course *accentuation of individual differences* rather than *inequality-generating social processes* operating over the life course (e.g., Clausen 1993; Martynova and Oschevskiy 2013; see also Dannefer 2003). Again, as with simple observations of diversity and inequality among age peers, resource and status differences reflecting a lifetime accumulation of advantage and disadvantage were reduced to the individual level, and were claimed to be anchored in personality differences, specifically in the extent to which individuals are "planfully competent" (Clausen 1993, see Chapter 6). While it might be allowed that, to some extent, these differences were the product of early-life experience, the question of the impact of post-childhood circumstances was ignored.

This argument—that diversity and inequality are accounted for by individual differences—has been recently answered on the macro-level, by cross-national and historical research demonstrating that cohort trajectories of inequality and patterns of CDA vary systematically with economic and policy differences within and across societies, indicating that growth in inequality cannot be reduced to individual differences (Crystal, Shea and Reyes, 2016; Sieber et al., 2020). Resistance to such evidence demonstrating the importance of social forces may well be manifested in a more nuanced argument within the recent debates between epidemiology and health sociology, comparing the so-called latency and pathways approaches. As reviewed in Chapter 6, both approaches recognize the importance of social forces; however, they differ in their sense of timing and life-course relevance. While the pathways perspective seeks to identify consequential influences occurring throughout the life course, the latency perspective focuses primarily on the effects of social forces as they occur in childhood. Thus, it tends to restrict its examination of the effects of the social to a delimited segment of time (early childhood), after which the social can be ignored. This is an example of Time 1 Encapsulation (Dannefer and Kelley-Moore 2009), which largely neglects the investigation of the degree to which social forces may operate across adulthood. Similarly, in the discipline of psychology, several strands of research attempt to explain individual differences by anchoring them in organismically based temperament or stable characteristics formed in childhood (e.g., Caspi and Moffitt 1993; Moffitt and Caspi 2001), thus discounting the significance of social forces.

This organismically grounded strategy to account for growing inequality was earlier fueled by speculations (e.g., Belsky, Steinberg, and Draper 1991; Belsky, Steinberg, Houts, and Halpern-Felsher 2010; Caspi and Moffit 1993; Moffitt 1993), then more recently (with the advent of genome sequencing and DNA-based genetic markers) by claims that specific genães and gene-driven forms of G-E interactions may account for differences in individual conduct, as discussed in the preceding chapter (see also Freese 2018).

Ironically, at the same time as such efforts were being advanced, advances in epigenetics and other mechanisms of gene regulation were making a very different point increasingly plain—that socioenvironmental influences upon individual health, development and aging are greater than even sociologists had imagined, and control the expression of genes in consequential ways. Yet, as shown in Chapter 7, social science research has been slow to embrace these discoveries and their potentially radical implications for sociological imagination.

A parallel form of resistant thought is focused on notions of agency and choice, and is found in psychology and, to some extent, in sociology. Despite some rigorous and thoughtful treatments (e.g., Marshall 2005; Marshall and Clarke 2010; Sewell 1992), agency is one of the most hastily applied, overused and ill-conceived notions in the behavioral and social sciences. As described in Chapter 3, the use of agency frequently disregards the role of social forces in shaping the individual foundation that creates intent within consciousness. Especially when applied to life-course issues, such as retirees being compelled to return to work or the "boomerang child" phenomenon and other struggles in the transition to adulthood, it is frequently used in an effort to look for some "silver lining" or "bright side" in grim or personally difficult circumstances (see, e.g., Dannefer 1999; Dannefer and Huang 2017; Wexler 1977).

Moreover, though conventional assertions of agency often seem to carry an implicit tendency to celebrate individual autonomy and efficacy, they actually sell short the power of individual action by failing to recognize its essential role in the constitution of social relations and social systems.

As reviewed in Chapter 3, agency is not just about the individual; it is also about the construction of social worlds. The denial of agency as the central social-constitutive force is yet another way those of us who are social and behavioral scientists, like the human actors we seek to understand, remain alienated from an understanding of our own actions and of the dynamics of social life. For the externalization of conscious intentions in action literally embodies the power to make and remake social worlds and is multiplied *sui generis* in collective action. One important meaning of alienation is the failure to recognize the products of one's own labor and productive activity for what they are—the result of one's actions in the world.

In sum, time after time, fresh discoveries and fresh evidence compelling recognition of the power of social forces has been met—and this is true even for social scientists—with a reductionist reframing that seeks to return causal efficacy to the individual level. This recurrent dynamic raises again the question, where is the sociological imagination?

When one considers this remarkably studied resistance of life-course and aging research to explore and embrace the implications of fresh evidence indicating the need for a sociologically grounded framework, one question that necessarily arises, very simply, is *why*. Why, in the face of a continued and steady onslaught of empirical evidence deriving from successive new scientific discoveries from multiple disciplines, all pointing in the same direction, does the functional-organismic nexus maintain its resilience? Why, in the face of an expanding body of indicators that point to a greater-than-anticipated role for social forces in the structuring of human development and the life course, do social scientists continue to revert to traditional, individualized approaches instead of pursuing such fresh clues for sociological imagination?

Clearly, the answer cannot be found in scientific discovery and reasoning alone since, as just reviewed, such reductionist claims contradict the science at every point. Empirical evidence and rational logic both make clear that social and environmental forces play a significant explanatory role in the processes of human development and aging. Given that the succession of discoveries (cohort analysis, intracohort variability, cumulative dis/advantage, gene regulation) all point to an expanded role for the explanatory power of social forces, what accounts for their neglect? From whence comes this irrepressible inclination of researchers, including sociologists, to avoid the consideration and integration of the aligned forces of empirical evidence and sociological explanation?

To answer this question, it is necessary to take a step or two (perhaps in a complete account, a series of steps) outside of the constricted logic of the "purely scientific" discourse of established research protocols and entrenched paradigms. This entails a critical, reflexive and self-reflexive turn to consider carefully factors beyond the evidence itself. What else—within the minds of researchers or the logic and organization of science—may be blocking the advance of understanding? What accounts for the continued resistance to recognizing the importance of social forces and its patterned preclusion by fresh iterations of individualized reductionism?

SCIENCE AS A SOCIAL ENTERPRISE

> Let the data speak for themselves, they say. The problem . . . is, of course, that data never do speak for themselves.
>
> —Evelyn Fox Keller

Scientific activity is a form of human activity, and as such, it is not conducted in a cultural and existential vacuum but by human actors located in a particular setting and at a particular historical moment, and is subject to the same kinds of reality-constructing processes and sequences and interpersonal and institutional power dynamics that pervade social life generally and that are discussed throughout this book. Interpersonal and sociohistorical locations give the entire scientific enterprise, as well as the lives of individual scientists working within it, a distinctive and—in relation to the phenomena it intends to illuminate—a somewhat particularistic setting at the point of knowledge production. As science historian Steven Shapin (2010) aptly depicts it in the subtitle of his book *Never Pure*, scientific knowledge is always and necessarily "Produced by People with Bodies, Situated in Time, Space, Culture and Society, and Struggling for Credibility and Authority".

Consequently, this is not just a matter of issues like confirmation bias, though that problem itself is so intractable that computers can apparently be taught to handle data more impartially than can human researchers (Obermeyer, Powers, Vogeli, and Mullainathan 2019). The problem goes much deeper—to the foundational worldviews and assumptions of the culture within which scientists operate; down to the bedrock of that most fundamental institution of any society: language.

Language is the primary carrier of culture, and the words scientists rely upon are embedded within sociohistorically specific cultural settings. Thus, it is not simply the discovery of the phenomenon that exists in nature but the *naming* of it (Keller 1985:17) in terms comprehensible to the social world within which the namer is located that defines its significance. The enterprise of science is a subculture or, more precisely, a system of subcultures that emerge from and are dialectically related to the interests and narratives of the wider society. It is ironic that science, which seeks to discern the *general* in the particular, always and necessarily conducts its search from the *particular* vantage point of the individual scientist with a specific sociohistorical location and a unique life history.

If the subject matter of social science is human activity, these considerations describe the compelling need to make scientific activity itself an object of study. Because scientific activity is indeed human activity, the process of inquiry always will be profoundly incomplete if attention to the ways in which the "search for truth" is directed by the perspective of the inquirer is not an integral part of the process. Such analysis is a primary task of the sociology of knowledge, the sociology of science and the sociology of scientific knowledge, all of which seek to understand the relationship of what passes for knowledge within the structure of society (see, e.g., Bloor 1991; Latour 2012; Latour and Woolgar 1985; Knorr-Cetina and Mulkay 1983; Shapin 2010).

The idea of science as detached, sanitized and objective is still a powerful ideal among many scientists, as it is in popular thought. John Broughton's observations on developmental psychology's optimistic self-definition are especially close to the present argument, and apply equally to other fields, including social gerontology and life-course studies:

> [A]n academic subdiscipline . . . that objectively observes and measures age-related changes contributed by human individuals . . . (and that) functions autonomously as it advances in specialized knowledge . . . independent of political motive or aim. As a science, it can serve no political purpose but rather possesses a privileged immunity from the machinations to which social institutions are subject. Its business is confined to the registering of the realities of human development. . . . It takes no liberties with language, but analyzes its data and discloses its findings by means of standard linguistic usage.
>
> (1987:2)

Although Broughton's critique was published three decades ago, it articulates a general premise of conventional approaches to research in the social and behavioral sciences. It is a premise that remains largely uninterrogated, although leading scientists across disciplines often acknowledge the mythology contained in the notion that that scientific work generally proceeds in some insulated and pure vacuum of objective discovery (see, e.g., Shapin 2010:32–3). As the production of scientific work remains a form of human activity, it will itself require scrutiny as an integral element in the scientific quest to understand fully the phenomena under study. The myth of scientific knowledge as emanating from domains of sanitized objectivity continues to undergird the dominant narrative, and remains central to its legitimation.

In actuality, scientific disciplines are themselves social institutions, each with unique social organization, histories and power structures, as well as their own paradigms of knowledge; they recruit and shape members who will contribute to their reproduction. This is as true of social science as of other fields. Indeed, a self-reflexive interrogation by every scientific researcher of how one's own particular perspectives, perceptions, interests, reward matrices and other constraints may inform one's naming and explaining of nature, would be a healthy and positive sign of dedication to science because those biographical and institutional forces—typically unexamined or even denied—contribute nontrivially to accounting for variation in defining and framing problems, and in the collecting, reporting and interpretation of data.

Thus, a complete exercise of sociological imagination cannot stop without interrogating the role of social forces in the production of scientific work. If scientific "knowledge" is constrained by the socially supported and self-reproducing particularisms of a given enterprise of "normal science" or unexamined paradigmatic commitments, then the true character of the subject matter cannot be fully grasped until that limitation is understood (Bourdieu 1984).

HUMAN FACTORS IN SCIENCE

The history of science, sociological studies of scientific knowledge and related fields have contributed much to understanding the extent to which the formulation of scientific problems and the interpretation given to findings are shaped by entire classes of extraneous factors that surround any process of inquiry (see, e.g., Bloor 1991; Shapin 2010:28). Of these, I discuss three in particular: childhood experience, professional training and the broader social and cultural context in which scientific activity is located.

CHILDHOOD EXPERIENCE

Scientists are no more immune than anyone else from the formative effects of one's own biography—those powerfully constitutive experiences of the early life course that are constitutive of her habitus. These include the basic internalization in childhood of a social world in which "relative patterns are experienced as absolute" (Berger and Berger 1979). Generally, this process is quite effective and positions young scientists to approach their work without confronting or introducing questions that challenge basic paradigmatic assumptions of either science or the modern societies in which they operate. It should be noted, however, that in some cases, early experience is precisely what prompts a challenge to the "absolute" assumptions of the dominant narrative. Thus, the desire of a young scholar, Freud, to come to terms with his own marginal identity as the son of a Jewish family from a remote town navigating the urbane world of Vienna has been hypothesized to be decisive for the later development of the structure of his theory (Cuddihy 1974; for other examples see Bourdieu 2007; Shapin 2010).

PROFESSIONAL TRAINING

A second broad class of factors has to do with professional training. The setting of the terms of discourse that guide scientific work are obviously crucial, and they are all the more effective for being nearly invisible, as is often the case. They become taken for granted and regarded as part of "normal science"—natural and given components of the objective language of scientific discourse. The impact of language on scientific work is not only important, it is also difficult to discern. The reflective scientist can much more readily discern how his or her childhood experiences or the current politics of the discipline shapes the direction of his or her work than can he or she discern the blinders of a dominant paradigm of scientific thought within which he or she is immersed. If one has been effectively trained in a discipline, the questions one can ask are constrained by its language. The difference between the situation of the young child who is learning to navigate her household and neighborhood on the one hand, and on the other, the graduate student learning a way of doing science, is one of degree, not kind. Each is participating in a process of social reproduction from a position of minimum power and knowledge.

It is the task of language of any paradigm of normal science to convey the particular understanding of reality delivered by that paradigm. So if a scientist working within a paradigm "takes no liberties with language," the same cannot be said of the paradigm itself. The strength of every scientific paradigm derives precisely from its ability to organize and "discipline" the subject matter, which inevitably requires the mobilization of language to articulate the paradigm's principles, accentuating some features and interpretations of reality and implicitly excluding others. In practice this entails taking great liberties with language. Indeed, to be effective, paradigms probably need to exercise a healthy amount of "linguistic domination" (Bourdieu 2001 [1998]:37; see also Burawoy 2019:116).

Thus, although embracing the foundational concepts is necessary for the viability of any paradigm and hence for the advance of scientific knowledge, it also entails risks and costs in terms of aspects of reality that go unnoticed. This dilemma has clearly been fateful in the study of development, age and the life course.

Factors related to professional training also include the interpersonal and political dynamics of everyday interaction. As one well-known social science example, it has been argued that the desire of a graduate student in anthropology (Margaret Mead) to please her luminary mentor (Franz Boas) influenced significantly the conclusions of her work (Freeman 1983; see also Zuckerman 1995). Still another set of forces to be analyzed are the immediate conditions under which scientific activity within a discipline occurs. These include the technical constraints of empirical research, which perennially pose a challenge to knowledge. Given the multileveled and rapidly interacting forces involved in gene regulation discussed in the last chapter, for example, constraints of measurement and analysis pose a key set of challenges to contemporary research on social genomics, in particular (e.g., Shanahan 2013).

The social reality of professional training also includes internal political dynamics—the realities of the power structure of a discipline, reflecting the paradigm under which "normal science" is conducted (Kuhn 1962; Miller 1991); the mechanisms through which dominant paradigms are maintained and would-be competitors are neutralized; and also the realities of interpersonal relations of everyday life in the lab, which can have decisive effects on the direction of scientific knowledge (Bloor 1991; Koestler 1971; Latour and Woolgar 1985; Rose and Rose 2012). Such analyses provide useful case examples for an analysis of the interaction of scientists in terms of, for example, symbolic interaction and group dynamics. However, a complete sociology-of-knowledge analysis must also attend to the external forces that condition scientific activity. These include, of course, such factors as the exigencies of funding agencies (Falletta 2011; Wheeler 1980) and the efforts of a discipline to react to threats of encroachment or attack from other disciplines or broader scientific, political or cultural developments (Noble 1984; Panofsky 2014).

THE BROADER SOCIAL AND CULTURAL CONTEXT

Finally, a third and even more fundamental set of constraints derives from the particular characteristics and interests of the dominant forces in the society and culture in which research activity is located and of which the scientific enterprise is an extension. This has economic, political and cultural dimensions, and given the relation between science and society as already outlined, it inevitably has ideological dimensions because of its legitimating functions. A familiar example of economic dimensions includes the profit potentials of newly introduced drugs—creating pressure for drug approvals (e.g., Angell 2004; Healy 2004; Rose and Rose 2012; Whitaker and Cosgrove 2015) or even for the "discovery" and naming of "new" diseases (e.g., George and Whitehouse 2010; Whitehouse and Moody 2006).

Such pressures are not unrelated to the decision-making processes involved in defining areas of federal or foundation research support (Falletta 2011; Panofsky 2014). The pervasive power of culture, which frames the broader cultural and linguistic context within which scientific discourse is immersed, is well illustrated by Evelyn Fox Keller's (1985) provocative analysis of the effects of the gendered nature of language on the general structure of scientific thought patterns.

Anything like a full account of the extra-scientific factors that may be at play in general, and in the specific case under consideration here, must remain well beyond the scope of this inquiry. For present purposes, I will seek, as a preliminary step, to begin to illuminate the kinds of extra-scientific factors that bear upon scientific discourses in age and development by focusing on two selected examples: 1) the power of paradigmatic language within the enterprise of science and 2) the relation of politics and science, including the ideological relevance of science to state and corporate interests. This entails scrutiny of how scientific work is positioned within the broader societal structures of political, economic and cultural power—such as educational, medical and clinical establishments—of corporations as employers, and of big pharma. These considerations compel a consideration of the ideological relevance of science, and the degree to which scientific questions, hypotheses and research directions are linked to private interests.

In the next section, I take up the first of these problems, the structuring of inquiry by paradigmatic language. In Chapter 9, I take up the second, the ideological utility of science.

ECLIPSE OF SOCIOLOGICAL IMAGINATION BY PARADIGMATIC LANGUAGE: TWO PROBLEMATIC CONCEPTS

The role of language in shaping and directing inquiry can be well illustrated by considering an issue featured earlier, the issue of the relation of aging to within-cohort heterogeneity and inequality. As discussed in Chapter 5, the phenomenon of the diversity of older people has long been acknowledged by gerontologists but was considered mostly an incidental curiosity before it began to be recognized as a research problem in the mid-1980s.

Among the reasons for this longstanding neglect must be included the linguistic framing supplied by the conceptual frameworks comprising the functional-organismic nexus. Specifically, I will here seek to demonstrate how the neglect of heterogeneity and variability was facilitated by the restrictions on inquiry imposed by two familiar and fundamental terms in the behavioral and social sciences: "development" in psychology and "socialization" in sociology (Dannefer 1988).

Both of these concepts—*development* and *socialization*—represent efforts to come to terms with important sets of phenomena and, given their pervasive and generally presumptive use, both warrant critical attention and unpacking. Such interrogation occurs infrequently and when it does happen, it generally remains superficial. Recall for example the discussion in Chapter 1, of how life-span development called for a revision of organismic models of psychological development to the extent of taking into account cohort differences, but not much further.

In their conventional, everyday usage, these two concepts seem unremarkable and taken-for-granted. They remain influential paradigms of organismically based psychology and sociological functionalism, respectively. Although they are typically assumed to be neutrally descriptive and unproblematic terms in their theoretical significance, in their respect of paradigms, they are anything but neutral and descriptive concepts. They are carriers of a definite way of viewing the world.

DEVELOPMENT

Despite some very important critical and progressive approaches to age-related change from infancy to old age in the discipline of psychology (Broughton 1987; Holzkamp 1992; Rogoff 2003; Stetsenko 2017, 2019), the organismic anchorage of both nomothetic and idiographic notions of "normal" developmental change and individual differences remains powerful (see, e.g., Morss 2017 [1990]) and has continued to be invigorated by a sustained interest in "temperament" or other stable individual characteristics (Caspi and Moffitt 1993, Moffitt 2006; Shiner and Caspi 2012) and by much of the ongoing research on G-E interactions, including research by sociologists, as touched upon in Chapter 7.

For researchers across traditions, the term "development" connotes the organismic paradigm of human development and aging. As reviewed earlier, this paradigm (exemplified in universalizing stage theories) posits internally guided, universal sequences of individual development and aging that accord little role to social and contextual factors in shaping development.

The empirical and logical untenability of theories that rely on this paradigm was demonstrated in Chapter 1. In addition to a false universalism that endeavors to force every variant into its rigid depictions of human development and resigns to a state of "abnormality" or "deviance" those who do not conform, this paradigm has the further problem of obscuring and ignoring human intention and intentional action (or "agency")—treating human activity as incidental or perhaps as a dependent variable in the outworking of some unseen ontogenetic imperative.

However, it must be noted that both 1) the universality that the organismic paradigm accords to age-related sequences of development and 2) the passivity and unimportance that this paradigm accords to human action, together give little reason for pause to researchers and scholars who have lived their entire lives immersed in a highly individualistic and yet conformistic culture—a culture in which individuals are declared to be "free" and "equal" at the same time their development is assumed to be shaped both by internally driven, age-governed processes and by putatively stable temperamental/ personality differences. Added to this is the "progress narrative" embedded in developmental logic which, it has been suggested, may contribute to the field's lack of self-awareness and its function as a carrier of false consciousness (Jacoby 1997). As Broughton observes:

> Developmentalists may lag behind . . . in the emergence of self-awareness precisely on account of a certain utopian optimism latent in the very notion of development (which) . . . may be one of the measures to which modern culture resorts in order to anaesthetize itself to the painful rending of personal and social fabrics.
>
> (1987:6)

Thus, the notion of development as generally applied provides a template for inquiry that is situated, biographically and culturally, well within the comfort zone of conventional patterns of thought. It asks questions and interprets data within that familiar and "safe" intellectual space, thereby defusing and obscuring the radical implications of a hard look at the contingency of developmental patterns and the reasons for their contingency. The intuitive appeal of orderly and easy-to-describe universal stages understood in familiar cultural terms and their affinity with popular cultural and politically legitimating notions of individual characteristics—accountability, accomplishment, resilience, personal culpability—all add to its seductive attractiveness. Its propositions are exactly aligned with the expectations and imagery of Western and perhaps especially North American individualism. It thus resonates with notions such as Margaret Thatcher's assertion that "there is no such thing as society", and offers the empirical project of science no space to interrogate such assertions. Thus, it is a perspective that is content to mystify and leave unexplored the connection between individual human action and the constitution of social relations and social-system action.

SOCIALIZATION

Like the term "development", *socialization* describes something real and indispensable to an adequate description of human aging: the shaping by social forces of an individual's consciousness and movement through the life course. And also like development, the concept of socialization has taken on connotations that go well beyond the bare essence of this process of internalization.

SOCIALIZATION AND STRUCTURAL-FUNCTIONALISM

In contrast to the notion of development as an ontogenetic, organismically based process, the concept of socialization—a key element in functionalism—would of course never tolerate the assumption that "there is no such thing as society". The reality of society is seen as central in functionalism, going back to Durkheim's principle of society as a reality *sui generis*. What the functionalist perspective does instead, however, is to assume that society is not only very important but also very *good*, and that the process of socialization is a beneficial necessity to integrate the raw energy of human actors—especially fledgling human actors (young children)—into the social system's productive apparatus.

Thus, socialization is viewed as an organic process integral to the beneficence of the overall social order (Wexler 1996). Bengtson and Black (1973:212) describe a dominant emphasis in socialization research as the study of "the processes that lead to a uniform cultural product"; it is also typically emphasized that the function of socialization is to shape individuals into "proficient members of society" (Little 2012). This general perspective implicitly, and often explicitly, assumes that social order is itself a unitary entity, with requirements for which individuals are prepared and fitted by socialization. These requirements are seen as altogether legitimate, normal and integral to an organic social order. Few in the current context would want to be as explicit as was Chicago sociologist Frank Freeman a century ago when he wrote, "it is the business of the school to help the child acquire such an attitude toward the inequalities of life, whether in accomplishment or reward, that he may adjust himself to its conditions with the least possible friction" (1924:170, quoted in Lewontin 1975). Nevertheless, this statement simply makes more explicit and graphic the implication of the more recent pronouncements just cited.

Socialization is thus seen as a process of social homogenization and legitimation, and one that is sustained over the life course. In discussing adult socialization, Brim (1968:184) writes: "the socialization experience of childhood is not enough to meet the demands of the later years. Adults must change and be socialized into new roles". Through socialization, individuals thus become responsible members, participants and contributors. It is a concept that conveys a sense of cooperation and consensus among age peers of unity of purpose, and almost of teamwork, rendering the divisions and differences existing among them to a secondary and infrequently examined, level of analysis.

In this general view, stratification and age-graded tensions within a cohort or age group are given little attention. A central emphasis is on what Parsons (1972; Parsons and Platt 1973) called "inclusiveness"—bringing about an integrated, consensual and smoothly operating social order—a goal articulated with no detailed analysis of the extent to which such a goal is unrealized, the reasons for associated societal failures and their persistence, or any detailed concern either with the robustness of *exclusionary* social practices or with specific mechanisms or strategies that might move toward ameliorating the problem.

Thus, normativity again emerges as a central narrative, framing individual action as in harmonious synchrony with public interests. There is no distinction or divide between public and private. If the reader has doubts about the particular cast this narrative gives to inquiry, it may be helpful to consider C. Wright Mills' famous emphasis on the centrality of the contradiction between "public issues" and "private troubles". Such a distinction would never arise, and cannot be comprehended, within the standard socialization paradigm. This normativity is of a different sort than the statistical normativity relied upon by psychometric and developmental logic. It is a normativity based on an assumption of an integrated and smoothly functioning social system within which most all individuals "contribute" and of the "needs" of which their actions are conformed. This view renders status differences between individuals tertiary, so long as they occupy the requisite roles in the division of labor for the operation of the social order.

Although "socialization" entails normativity of a different sort than "development", it thus shares a similar premise of developmental normativity. It is founded on an image of individuals who are seen as passively conforming to life stages (with the actual social-constitutive contributions of their everyday activities unnoticed) and as undifferentiated within age or cohort categories. This affinity is reflected in the work of sociologists in a wide range of practices that presuppose a normative developmental arc from birth through older adulthood, ranging from the construction of "age-normalized" synthetic cohorts to the uncritical acceptance and adoption, for example, adult development and disengagement theories, as discussed in Chapter 2.

This traditional view of socialization has received extensive criticism from those working from other perspectives, and numerous revisions have been proposed (see, e.g., Dannefer 1988, 1989; Höppner 2017; Morss 2017 [1990]; Wexler 1996). Nevertheless, it remains largely unchallenged as an implicit part of the sociology of aging and gerontological narratives, and it also is unwittingly shared by what has perhaps been the main alternative theoretical perspective in the sociology of aging, the symbolic interaction (SI) approach. Given the interest in SI among numerous gerontological researchers and related methodological developments (such as "grounded theory" methodologies), the relation of the concept of socialization to the SI perspective warrants some discussion.

SOCIALIZATION AND THE SYMBOLIC INTERACTION PERSPECTIVE

Despite its important limitations, Parsons' (1951) functionalist framework comprised an elegant and comprehensive approach that included and treated in detail the kinds of micro-level processes analyzed by symbolic interactionists (see also Joas 1996:7–10; Toby 1972). However, Parsons' micro-interactionist insights received relatively little emphasis in his subsequent work, allowing the tradition of symbolic interactionism, rooted in the work of George Herbert Mead, to claim these insights and to position itself in opposition to the mainstream functionalist enterprise and attendant methods (Blumer 1969). Thus, the elaboration of the micro processes of socialization by symbolic interactionists has typically been advanced by researchers who claim not to share the value-consensus and implicit passive-individual emphases of the paradigmatic functionalist version of socialization.

Based on a research tradition of careful empirical studies of micro-interaction, symbolic interactionism has contributed to discovering the details of processes of social internalization, and in particular to the recognition of their bidirectionality and potentially conflictual character—involving dynamics including labeling, stigmatization and "negotiated" identities and realities. Especially as regards the latter, the supposed *socializee* is recognized as not just a passive recipient but as a co-socializer in the course of social interaction (Bengtson and Black 1973; Denzin 1977; Nelissen, Kuczynski, Coenen, and Van den Bulck 2019).

Despite the critique offered to functionalism by such a view, however, the symbolic interaction framework has its own limitations. As has frequently been noted, it lacks a conception of macro-social structure and processes within which to frame and locate the analysis of micro-interaction. As a result, functionalism's consensus-theory version of social structure is rejected, not to be replaced by a more realistic and stratified view of structure, but rather as part of an overall rejection of a macro-structural conception of any sort. Since reality is a process of negotiation and social reality is fluid and dynamic, as the argument goes, an unduly objectified conception of social structure may risk the reification of something that does not exist. Thus, the rejection of a value-consensus view of social structure tends to lead to a denial of social structure altogether.

Although it appears to oppose traditional macro-approaches, symbolic interaction thus offers no alternative view of structure, thereby allowing the implicit and uncritical premises of structural-functionalism to stand by default. Here, it somewhat parallels within sociology what the life-span perspective attempted to do in developmental psychology—resist ontogenetic rigidity with notions like "bi-directional influence" and "individuals as producers of their own development" (Lerner and Busch-Rossnagel 1981). In both cases, rigid theories are rejected and a recognition of humans as intentional actors is proposed. Yet both views are incomplete in that they ignore and eclipse the imbalance in power—the *agentic asymmetry*—between social context and human actor, between structure and action (Dannefer 1999).

In the absence of an alternative conception of social structure, such formulations permit the major elements of the functional-organismic nexus to continue its reign unchecked, all the more effective for being unrecognized. The macro-level questions of structure and process—treated with a vague and unwarrantedly optimistic progressivism in functionalism, are typically not asked at all in symbolic interaction. In reality, of course, such macro-level processes clearly have a great deal to do with setting the agenda and the parameters of micro-interaction, especially in complex modern societies that operate with relatively high levels of central coordination.

Whether age-grading and tracking in education or policies like age-based mandatory retirement, age is imposed as a principle of mass social organization that shapes actors' perceptions, interpretations and actions in fundamental ways. Yet by its very logic, the symbolic interaction perspective does not acknowledge the constitutive role of such factors in social life, nor does it recognize the sources of shared perceptions beyond the immediacy of the situation of micro-interaction, or the extent of generality of shared perceptions, as essential matters of inquiry. The extent to which larger structures set the terms of the expression of creativity and voluntarism is simply not seen as part of the problem, nor is the extent to which entire populations are differentiated internally. If macro-structures are not recognized as existing, of course they cannot be recognized as differentiated in ways that systemically impact individuals as they age. Even in small-scale societies, institutionalized power dynamics create structures that shape the parameters of micro-interaction (Bahuchet 1990; Goffman 1974; Gonos 1977; Oberg 1955). Thus, micro-interactional views of socialization that lack a sense of structure perpetuate the twin emphases of 1) an undifferentiated voluntarism in individual action and 2) an undifferentiated macro-social reality.

None of this is to detract from the important contributions of the symbolic interaction perspective to understanding the dynamics of socialization. SI has stimulated and inspired, directly or indirectly, much valuable research on micro-interaction relevant to understanding aging and development. Yet despite its seemingly fresh emphasis on the immediacy of interaction, negotiated realities and the accompanying methodological practices, its lack of any framework for analyzing the larger social forces that frame micro-interaction means that work within this tradition aligns with functionalism, by default, in its lack of recognition of structural power differentials and the larger social forces shaping the phenomenon of human aging. When viewed from the vantage point of the dynamics of the larger social order, symbolic-interaction-based versions of socialization thus tend to perpetuate implicitly a sense of normativity and the broader assumptions of the functional-organismic nexus.

Similar to functionalism, symbolic interaction has had no problem embracing the dominant cultural narrative of the recent and contemporary West, with its presupposition of increasing individual freedom, control and agency. This is well illustrated in Ralph Turner's (1976) celebrated essay, "The Real Self: From Institution to Impulse" which received the Charles Horton Cooley Award from the Society for the Study of Symbolic Interaction when it was published. Turner proposed that the shift from traditional to modern society entailed a shift from being controlled by social institutions and rules to being self-directed and guided by one's own "impulses". The optimism of such a view is attractive and it continues to resonate with the expanding social-psychological literature on young adulthood (e.g., Arnett 2014; Settersten and Ray 2010). However, such arguments fail to interrogate the sources of "impulse". As Philip Wexler made clear (1977), the so-called impulses themselves are structured by the forces of mass society and mass culture, such as advertising (Ewen 1977, 1988) and the general role of mass media (Butsch 2007). This trend arguably has accelerated, as the promise of a free and democratizing internet utopia has given way to the politicized manipulations of internet trolls, increasingly monopolistic control of information access, and surveillance capitalism (Faroohar 2019; Foer 2017; Zuboff 2015, 2020).

As reviewed in Chapter 4, the increasing age-graded social regimentation that accompanied the 20th-century expansion of the institutions of mass society (education, retirement, formalized career ladders) continued to shape both individual selves and the resources for self-production in decisive ways. Indeed, social conformity in early life course reached unprecedented heights at the same time Turner was writing (Modell, Furstenberg, and Hershberg 1976). So much for impulses!

This paradox points to the problem of symbolic interaction's complicity in reductionism. "Impulse" reflects the emphasis of this approach upon personal expression. It is thus symptomatic of the logic of the theory which, without a concern for structural processes, tends to imply that individuals are differentiated mainly by their personal uniqueness expressed in interpretation and action, through which social reality is interactively created. Therefore, heterogeneity is of marginal importance since it is seen as simply a product of human spontaneity and diversity rather than structured social processes. It may be a cause for wonderment, but it is difficult to study systematically because the focus of analysis remains at the micro-level, and eschews the notion of structure, even of micro-level structures (Gonos 1977). When the empirical pattern of age-graded behavior is seen as impulsive and is also increasingly standardized, conformist and homogeneous as has been the case (at least through the 20th century), what could that imply about the forces that direct human action and conduct? Obviously, a major logical deduction would be that these forces, when given "freedom", follow some individual-level (read ontogenetic) template—thus unwittingly giving aid and comfort to the advocates of rigidly ontogenetic stage theories of development.

SOCIALIZATION, FUNCTIONALISM AND INTERACTIONISM

In sum, whether from functionalist or interactionist perspectives, socialization is typically conceived either implicitly or explicitly as a cooperative enterprise accompanied by images of teamwork, unity of purpose and consensus, and even *Gemeinschaft* (Wexler 1996:135). It is important to keep in mind that this imposed image of societal uniformity is not required by the essential, underlying processes of learning and internalization of language and the ways of habitus that are often referenced by the term socialization. Instead, these *Gemeinschaftlich* connotations derive from the concept's specific identification with the functionalist paradigm which links socialization to sustaining "pattern maintenance" (in Parsons' terms) of a beneficent and well-functioning macro-system. Within this framework, the complementary concepts of norm and role share the same dual characteristic of 1) referencing empirically real phenomena, yet 2) adding the prepackaged images of both society and person that are distorted by an imposed assumption of homogeneity and consensus, and a lack of recognition of differentiation and stratification, except on such traditional and naturalized axes as age and sex—which means a near-complete lack of acknowledgment of systemically generated inequality of matters of conflict, power and change—except as temporary matters that, in the functionalism's upbeat version of a society constantly getting happier and healthier, will hopefully soon be resolved.

Since these considerations do not affect the general principle underlying the term socialization, the social shaping of the individual, what is needed, then, is a reconceptualization of this process that systematically acknowledges that this social shaping process occurs not only in a structured fashion but in a structurally differentiating fashion.

That is why some have proposed that the processes of development and aging be decomposed into the empirically accessible, underlying dynamics, including *habituation* and *human generativity* (Dannefer 1989, 1999; Kastenbaum 1981; see also Broughton 1987). Here, the term *generativity* refers to the reality of an agentic, imaginative, reality-constructing sense that recognizes that generative impulses and potentials are present in all intentional human activity (Dannefer and Perlmutter 1990).

Similarly, to depict the processes of social internalization in a way that is faithful to the empirical realities of development and aging, it may be useful to think, at least provisionally, in terms of *social reproduction* (Bourdieu 1986; Bourdieu and Passeron 1990; Dannefer 1988, 2008; Willis 1978).

Whatever its own limitations as a concept, social reproduction replaces the mythical notions of normative consensus with a recognition that essential processes of internalization referenced by the term socialization are actually deployed within stratified structures of opportunity—reproducing social inequality, exclusion and precarity along multiple axes of stratification. Reproduction theory's own "functional analysis", which might be called functionalism in a minor key, has been rightly criticized for its lack of emancipatory imagination. Nevertheless, compared with the narrative of socialization, it certainly represents a move of science, in Herbert Blumer's (1969:29, 48) words, toward "respecting the nature of the empirical world".

SUMMARY

This chapter began with a review of the remarkable pattern of resistance, even by social scientists themselves, to a succession of fresh empirical discoveries pointing to the importance of social forces in shaping life-course patterns. I then turned to the question of the sources of such resistance. Since it can be accounted for neither by scientific evidence nor by rational thought, I have suggested that it must be sought and located outside the requirements of science itself, in the broader biographical and social milieus within which science is conducted, which has economic, political and cultural dimensions.

As a means of illustrating such factors, I reviewed some of the forces inevitably impinging on the life of any scientist, including the cultural entanglements of scientific language and training. In particular, I reviewed how the logic of the dominant paradigms of organismically anchored developmental theory and sociological structural-functionalism have governed the conceptual definitions of the key terms *development and socialization*. This restrictive logic has resulted in a limitation in the scope of inquiry and a suppression of the sociological imagination that distorts empirical reality and obscures the open horizon of human possibility and in maintaining the functional-organismic nexus.

However, even granting such human particularities, normal science does not and cannot operate independently of broader social forces. When we contemplate the question of why the science of development and aging has been so content to remain within an unimaginative and reductionist logic in comparison to many other fields of both psychology and sociology, a key part of the answer may require not only attention to how the questions and findings resonate with the larger culture but also how they relate to efforts to gain resources and support to the field of study, whether in the domain of research funding, professional credentialing or by some other means. These considerations inevitably raise questions of ideology and legitimation as key issues, which are the topics of the following chapter.

REFERENCES

Angell, Marcia. 2004. *The Truth about the Drug Companies: How They Deceive Us and What to Do about It*. New York: Random House.

Arnett, Jeffrey. 2014. *Emerging Adulthood: The Winding Road from the Late Teens through the Twenties*. New York: Oxford University Press.

Bahuchet, Serge. 1990. *Food and Nutrition in the African Rain Forest*. Lanham, MD: Bernan Press.

Belsky, Jay, Laurence Steinberg, and Patricia Draper. 1991. "Childhood Experience, Interpersonal Development, and Reproductive Strategy: An Evolutionary Theory of Socialization." *Child Development* 62(4): 647–70. doi: 10.2307/1131166.

Belsky, Jay, Laurence Steinberg, Renate M. Houts and Bonnie L. Halpern-Felsher. 2010. "The Development of Reproductive Strategy in Females: Early Maternal Harshness > Earlier Menarche > Increased Sexual Risk Taking." *Developmental Psychology* 46(1): 120–28.

Bengtson, Vern L., and Dean Black. 1973. "Intergenerational Relations and Continuities in Socialization." Pp. 207–34 in *Life-Span Developmental Psychology Personality and Socialization*, edited by P. Baltes and K. W. Schaie. New York: Academic Press.

Berger, Peter L., and Brigitte Berger. 1979. *Sociology*. New York: Basic Books.

Bloor, David. 1991. *Knowledge and Social Imaginary*. Chicago: University of Chicago Press.

Blumer, Herbert. 1969. *Symbolic Interactionism: Perspective and Method*. Englewood Cliffs, NJ: Prentice Hall.

Bourdieu, Pierre. 1984. *Homo Academicus*. Stanford: Stanford University Press.

Bourdieu, Pierre. 1986. *Distinction: A Social Critique of the Judgement of Taste*. New York: Routledge.

Bourdieu, Pierre. 2001 (1998). *Masculine Domination*. Stanford, CA: Stanford University Press.

Bourdieu, Pierre. 2007. *Sketch for a Self-Analysis*. Cambridge, UK: Polity.

Bourdieu, Pierre, and Claude Passeron. 1990. *Reproduction in Education, Society and Culture*. 2nd edition. Thousand Oaks, CA: Sage.

Brim, Orville G. 1968. "Adult Socialization." Pp. 182–226 in *Socialization and Society*, edited by J. Clausen. Boston: Little Brown.

Broughton, John M. 1987. "An Introduction to Critical Developmental Psychology." Pp. 1–30 in *Critical Theories of Psychological Development, Path in Psychology*, edited by J. M. Broughton. New York: Springer.

Burawoy, Michael. 2019. *Symbolic Violence*. Durham, NC: Duke University Press Books.

Butsch, R., ed. 2007. *Media and Public Spheres*. London: Palgrave Macmillan.

Caspi, Avshalom, and Terrie E. Moffitt. 1993. "When Do Individual Differences Matter? A Paradoxical Theory of Personality Coherence." *Psychological Inquiry* 4(4): 247–71.

Clausen, John A. 1993. *American Lives: Looking Back at the Children of the Great Depression*. New York: Free Press.

Crystal, Stephen, Dennis G. Shea, and Adriana M. Reyes. 2016. "Cumulative Advantage, Cumulative Disadvantage, and Evolving Patterns of Late-Life Inequality." *The Gerontologist* 57(5): 910–20. https://doi.org/10.1093/geront/gnw056.

Cuddihy, John M. 1974. *The Ordeal of Civility: Freud, Marx, Levi-Strauss, and the Jewish Struggle with Modernity*. Boston: Beacon Press.

Dannefer, Dale. 1988. "What's in a Name? An Account of the Neglect of Variability in the Study of Aging." Pp. 356–84 in *Emergent Theories of Aging*, edited by J. E. Birren and V. L. Bengtson. New York: Springer Publishing Company.

Dannefer, Dale. 1989. "Human Action and Its Place in Theories of Aging." *Journal of Aging Studies* 3(1): 1–20.

Dannefer, Dale. 1999. "Freedom Isn't Free: Power, Alienation, and the Consequences of Action." Pp. 105–31 in *Action & Development: Origins and Functions of Intentional Self-Development*, edited by J. Brandstadter and R. Lerner. New York Springer Publishing Company.

Dannefer, Dale. 2003. "Cumulative Advantage/Disadvantage and the Life Course: Cross-Fertilizing Age and Social Science Theory." *The Journals of Gerontology: Series B* 58(6): S327–37. doi: 10.1093/geronb/58.6.S327.

Dannefer, Dale. 2008. "The Waters We Swim: Everyday Social Processes, Macro Structural Realities, and Human Aging." Pp. 3–22 in *Social Structure and Aging: Continuing Challenges*, edited by K. W. Schaie and R. P. Abeles. New York: Springer Publishing Company.

Dannefer, Dale, and Wenxuan Huang. 2017. "Precarity, Inequality, and the Problem of Agency in the Study of the Life Course." *Innovation in Aging* 1(3). doi: 10.1093/geroni/igx027.

Dannefer, Dale, and Jessica Kelley-Moore. 2009. "Theorizing the Life Course: New Twists in the Path." Pp. 389–412 in *Handbook of Theories of Aging*, edited by M. Silverstein, V. L. Bengtson, M. Putnam, N. M. Putney, and D. Gans. New York: Springer Publishing Company.

Dannefer, Dale, and Marion Perlmutter. 1990. "Development as a Multidimensional Process: Individual and Social Constituents." *Human Development* 33(2–3): 108–37.

Denzin, Norman K. 1977. *Childhood Socialization*. San Francisco, CA: Jossey Bass Inc. Publishers.

Ewen, Stuart. 1977. *Captains of Consciousness Advertising and the Social Roots of the Consumer Culture*. New York: Basic Books.

Ewen, Stuart. 1988. *All Consuming Images: The Politics of Style in Contemporary Culture*. New York: Basic Books.

Falletta, Lynn. 2011. *'It's Not Just Pure Science': Federal Funding of Children's Mental Health Research through the Request for Applications (RFA) Process*. Unpublished Doctoral Dissertation, Case Western Reserve University, Cleveland, OH.

Faroohar, Rana. 2019. *Don't Be Evil: How Big Tech Betrayed Its Founding Principles and All of Us*. New York: Penguin Currency.

Foer, Franklin. 2017. *World without Mind: The Existential Threat of Big Tech*. New York: Penguin.

Freeman, Derek. 1983. *Margaret Mead and Samoa: The Making and Unmaking of an Anthropological Myth*. Cambridge, MA: Harvard University Press.

Freeman, Frank. 1924. "Sorting the Students." *Educational Review* 68: 169–74.

Freese, Jeremy. 2018. "The Arrival of Social Science Genomics." *Contemporary Sociology* 47(5): 524–36. doi: 10.1177/0094306118792214a.

George, Daniel R., and Peter J. Whitehouse. 2010. "Intergenerational Volunteering and Quality of Life for Persons with Mild-to-Moderate Dementia: Results from a 5-Month Intervention Study in the United States." *Journal of American Geriatrics Society* 58(4): 796–7.

Goffman, Erving. 1974. *Frame Analysis: An Essay on the Organization of Experience.* Cambridge, MA: Harvard University Press.

Gonos, George. 1977. "'Situation' versus 'Frame': The 'Interactionist' and the 'Structuralist' Analysis of Everyday Life." *American Sociological Review* 42(6): 854–67.

Healy, David. 2004. "Shaping the Intimate: Influences on the Experience of Everyday Nerves." *Social Studies of Science* 34(2): 219–45. doi: 10.1177/0306312704042620.

Hickey, Tom. 1980. *Health and Aging.* Monterey, CA: Brooks/Cole.

Holzkamp, Klaus. 1992. "On Doing Psychology Critically." *Theory and Psychology* 2(2): 193–204.

Höppner, Grit. 2017. "Rethinking Socialization Research through the Lens of New Materialism." *Frontiers in Sociology* (2): 13.

Huang, Wenxuan. 2019. *Agency as Ideology: Precarity and Disembedness in the 21st Century Life Course.* Paper presented at the Annual Meeting of the Gerontological Society of America, Boston (November).

Jacoby, Russell. 1997 (1975). *Social Amnesia: A Critique of Contemporary Psychology.* New Brunswick, NJ: Transaction Press.

Joas, Hans. 1996. *The Creativity of Action.* Chicago: University of Chicago Press.

Kastenbaum, Robert. 1981. "Habituation as a Model of Human Aging." *Aging and Human Development* 12(3): 159–70.

Keller, Evelyn F. 1985. *Reflections on Gender and Science.* New Haven, CT: Yale University Press.

Knorr-Cetina, Karin D., and Michael Mulkay. 1983. "Introduction: Emerging Principles in Social Studies of Science." Pp. 1–17 in *Science Observed: Perspectives on the Social Studies of Science,* edited by K. D. Knorr-Cetina and M. Mulkay. London: Sage.

Koestler, Arthur. 1971. *The Case of the Midlife Toad.* London: Hutchinson.

Kuhn, Thomas S. 1962. *The Structure of Scientific Revolutions.* Chicago: University of Chicago Press.

Latour, Bruno. 2012. *We Have Never Been Modern* (Catherine Porte, Trans.). Cambridge, MA: Harvard University Press.

Latour, Bruno, and Steve Woolgar. 1985. *Laboratory Life: The Construction of Scientific Facts,* 2nd edition. Princeton, NJ: Princeton University Press.

Lerner, Richard, and Nancy Busch-Rossnagel. 1981. *Individuals as Producers of Their Own Development: A Life-Span Perspective.* New York: Academic Press.

Lewontin, Richard C. 1975. "Genetic Aspects of Intelligence." *Annual Review of Genetics* 9: 387–405.

Little, William. 2012. *Introduction to Sociology.* Houston, TX: Openstax College.

Marshall, Victor W. 2005. "Agency, Events and Structure at the End of the Life Course." *Advances in Life Course Research* 10: 57–91.

Marshall, Victor W., and Philippa J. Clarke. 2010. "Agency and Social Structure in Aging and Life-Course Research." Pp. 294–305 in *The Sage Handbook of Social Gerontology,* edited by D. Dannefer and C. Phillipson. Thousand Oaks, CA: Sage.

Martynova, I. Rina, and D. S. Oschevskiy. 2013. "Coping Strategies in Adolescents with Accentuation of Character, Prone to Aggression." *Psychological Science and Education* 3: 191–201. https://doaj.org/article/9f9fe649ad5c49f6afa2d401e5494e90

Miller, Alice. 1991. *The Untouched Key: Tracing Childhood Trauma in Creativity and Destructiveness*. New York: Anchor Books.

Modell, John, Frank F. Furstenberg, Jr., and Theodore Hershberg. 1976. "Social Change and Transitions to Adulthood in Historical Perspective." *Journal of Family History* 1(1): 7–32.

Moffitt, Terrie E. 1993. "Adolescence-Limited and Life-Course-Persistent Antisocial Behavior: A Developmental Taxonomy." *Psychological Review* 100(4): 674.

Moffitt, Terrie E. 2006. "Life-Course-Persistent versus Adolescence-Limited Antisocial Behavior." Pp. 570–98 in *Developmental Psychology*. 2nd edition, edited by D. Cicchetti and D. Cohen. New York: Wiley.

Moffitt, Terrie E., and Avshalom Caspi. 2001. "Childhood Predictors Differentiate Life-Course Persistent and Adolescence-Limited Antisocial Pathways among Males and Females." *Development and Psychopathology* 13(2): 355–75. doi: 10.1017/s0954579401002097.

Morss, John R. 2017 (1990). *The Biologising of Childhood: Developmental Psychology and the Darwinian Myth*. Abingdon, UK: Routledge Publishing.

Nelissen, S., L. Kuczynski, L. Coenen, and J. Van den Bulck. 2019. "Bidirectional Socialization: An Actor-Partner Interdependence Model of Internet Self-Efficacy and Digital Media Influence between Parents and Children." *Communication Research* 46(8): 1145–70. doi: 10.1177/0093650219852857.

Noble, David. 1984. *Forces of Production: A Social History of Industrial Automation*. New Brunswick, NJ: Transaction Publishers.

Oberg, Kalervo. 1955. "Types of Social Structure among the Lowland Tribes of South and Central America." *American Anthropologist* 57(3): 472–87.

Obermeyer, Z., B. Powers, C. Vogeli, and S. Mullainathan. 2019. "Algorithmic Bias in Health Care: A Path Forward." Health Affairs Blog. Retrieved from www.healthaffairs.org/do/10.1377/ hblog20191031.373615/full/

Panofsky, Aaron. 2014. *Misbehaving Science: Controversy and the Development of Behavior Genetics*. Chicago: University of Chicago Press.

Parsons, Talcott. 1951. *The Social System*. London: New York: Free Press.

Parsons, Talcott. 1972. *The System of Modern Societies*. Englewood Cliffs, NJ: Prentice-Hall.

Parsons, Talcott, and Gerald M. Platt. 1973. *The American University*. Cambridge, MA: Harvard University Press.

Phillipson, Chris. 2015. "Placing Ethnicity at the Center of Studies of Later Life: Theoretical Perspectives and Empirical Challenges." *Ageing & Society* 35(5): 917–34.

Rogoff, Barbara. 2003. *The Cultural Nature of Human Development*. New York: Oxford University Press.

Rose, Hilary and Steven Rose. 2012. *Genes, Cells and Brains: The Promethean Promises of the New Biology*. New York: Verso Books.

Settersten, Richard A., and Babara Ray. 2010. *Not Quite Adults: Why 20-Somethings Are Choosing a Slower Path to Adulthood, and Why It Is Good for Everyone*, New York: Bantam Books Trades Paperback.

Sewell, William H. 1992. "A Theory of Structure: Duality, Agency and Transformation." *American Journal of Sociology* 98(1): 1–29.

Shanahan, Michael J. 2013. "Social Genomics and the Life Course: Opportunities and Challenges for Multilevel Population Research." Pp. 255–76 in *New Directions in the*

Sociology of Aging, edited by L. J. Waite and T. J. Plewes. Washington: National Academies Press.

Shapin, Steve. 2010. *Never Pure: Historical Studies of Science as If It Was Produced by People with Bodies, Situated in Time, Space, Culture, and Society, and Struggling for Credibility and Authority*. Baltimore, MD: Johns Hopkins University Press.

Shiner, Rebecca L., and Avshalom Caspi. 2012. "Temperament and the Development of Personality Traits, Adaptations, and Narratives." Pp. 497–516 in *Handbook of Temperament*, edited by M. Zentner and R. L. Shiner. New York: Guilford Press.

Sieber, Stefan, Boris Cheval, Dan Orsholits, Bernadette W. A. van der Linden, Idris Guessous, Rainer Gabriel, Matthias Kliegel, Martina von Arx, Michelle Kelly-Irving, Marja Aartsen, Matthieu P. Boisgontier, Dalphine Courvoisier, Claudine Burton-Jeangros and Stephane Cullati. 2020. "Do Welfare Regimes Moderate Cumulataive Dis/advantages Over the Life Course? Cross-National Evidence from Longitudinal Share Data." *Journal of Gerontology Social Sciences* 75(6): 1312–25.

Standing, Guy. 2011. *The Precariat: The New Dangerous Class*. London: Bloomsbury Academic.

Standing, Guy. 2014. *A Precariat Charter: From Denizens to Citizens*. London: Bloomsbury Academic.

Stetsenko, Anna. 2017. *The Transformative Mind: Expanding Vygotsky's Approach to Development and Education*. Cambridge, UK: Cambridge University Press.

Stetsenko, Anna. 2019. "Cultural-Historical Activity Theory Meets Developmental Systems Perspective: Transformative Activist Stance and Natureculture." Pp. 249–62 in *Cultural-Historical Approaches to Studying Learning and Development: Societal, Institutional and Personal Perspectives, Perspectives in Cultural-Historical Research*, edited by A. Edwards, M. Fleer, and L. Bøttcher. Singapore: Springer.

Toby, Jackson. 1972. "A Review Symposium of Talcott Parsons: The System of Modern Societies." *Contemporary Sociology* 1(5): 387–401.

Turner, Ralph H. 1976. "The Real Self: From Institution to Impulse." *American Journal of Sociology* 81(5): 178–85.

Wexler, Philip. 1977. "Comment on Ralph Turner's 'The Real Self: From Institution to Impulse'." *American Journal of Sociology* 83(1): 989–1016.

Wexler, Philip. 1996 (1983). *Critical Social Psychology*. New York: Peter Lang.

Wheeler, Stanton. 1980. "Selecting and Monitoring Foundation Projects." *Grants Magazine* 3: 88–98.

Whitaker, R., and L. Cosgrove. 2015. *Psychiatry under the Influence: Institutional Corruption, Social Injury, and Prescriptions for Reform*. New York: Palgrave Macmillan.

Whitehouse, Peter J., and Harry R. Moody. 2006. "Mild Cognitive Impairment: A 'Hardening of the Categories'?" *Dementia* 5(1): 11–25. doi: 10.1177/1471301206059752.

Willis, Paul E. 1978. *Learning to Labour : How Working Class Kids Get Working Class Jobs*. London: Routledge.

Zuboff, Shoshana. 2015. "Big Other: Surveillance Capitalism and the Prospects of an Information Civilization." *Journal of Information Technology* 30(1): 75–89. https://doi.org/10.1057/jit.2015.5.

Zuboff, Shoshana. 2020. *The Age of Surveillance Capitalism: The Fight for a Human Future at the New Frontier of Power*. New York: Public Affairs.

Zuckerman, Harriet. 1995. *Scientific Elite Nobel Laureates in the United States (Foundations of Higher Education)*. New Brunswick, NJ: Transaction Publishers.

CHAPTER 9
BRINGING IDEOLOGY BACK IN—SCIENCE AS A MECHANISM OF NATURALIZATION

This chapter extends the discussion of science as human activity to the consideration of its potential usages on behalf of economic, political and other interests, giving it an ideological salience. Scientific disciplines are institutions. Established fields of study are institutions and in the contemporary research world, they exist in relation to and rely on resources provided by other entities—universities, donors, corporate interests, media, funding agencies and other governmental institutions—often constrained by political actors and influential decision-makers.

Beginning in the 1970s, the analysis of ideological aspects of scientific activity emerged as a provocative and promising line of social science research. The analysis of "science as ideology" represented a major strand of work associated with the application of critical approaches to the subject matter of the human sciences (Baars, Dannefer, Phillipson, and Walker 2006:1–9; Broughton 1987; Lewontin 1977; Morss 1996).

IDEOLOGY AND POLITICAL ECONOMY

Analysis of ideology was from the beginning a foundational component of the Frankfurt School tradition (Horkheimer and Adorno 1947; Jay 1996; Wexler 1996) of critical social thought. Beginning from the premise that the power of the state cannot automatically be trusted to prioritize human interests and promote human emancipation, the Frankfurt School recognized that ideology and legitimation—the framing and highlighting of claims and ideas in ways favorable to those in power—are fundamental components of political authority and control, and work most effectively when they appear to be taking human interests into account.

This emphasis on ideology critique complements critical scholarship framed by the more structurally oriented political economy perspective (Baran and Sweezy 1966; Myles and Quadagno 1991; Phillipson 1982; Walker 1980, 1981). Applied to aging and the life course, political economy has focused on issues arising from socioeconomic inequalities between age groups and the exacerbation of economic adversity by efforts to advance the interests of private capital and the role of policy in addressing such issues (Estes 1991, 2001; Kail, Quadagno, and Keene 2009; Phillipson and Walker 1986). More recently, it has also come to include the strong emergent interest in within-cohort inequality as reflected in the foregoing discussions of cumulative dis/advantage (see also Crystal and Shea 2002; Crystal 2018; Dannefer 1987, 2003, 2020) which can, in a sense, be seen as the instantiation of perennial tendencies of capital accumulation within the life of each successive cohort.

In critical gerontology, as in other fields, the last several decades have seen a rapid growth of interest and concerns associated with the political economy tradition—especially those relating to social inequalities and attendant societal challenges (Baars et al. 2006; Phillipson 2013; Walker and Foster 2014). This growth of interest has continued as inequality itself has increased dramatically, especially since the expansion of neoliberal policies over the last several decades (Case and Deaton 2020; Crystal, Shea, and Reyes 2017; Dannefer, Lin, and Gonos 2021; Meyer 2010; Piketty and Saez 2003).

In contrast to the *political economy* strand of critical scholarship, the *ideology critique* strand focuses explicitly on the symbolic domain—on ideas, cultural "knowledge" and their relation to ongoing social conditions, including economically and politically powerful interests. "Ideology" is another one of those overused, misused and inconsistently used words, and one that has been given multiple definitions. For present purposes, ideology can be defined as an idea or set of interrelated ideas which help to legitimate a dominant interest, political agenda or perspective (see Couture, Cristy, and DuHaime 2010). This definition is squarely and appropriately in the tradition of Marx and Engels (1978 [1932]:172), who write:

> The ideas of the ruling class are in every epoch the ruling ideas. . . . The ruling ideas are nothing more than the ideal expression of the dominant material relationships, the dominant material relationships grasped as ideas.

In gerontology as in other fields, attention to ideology has not seen the same explosive growth of interest over recent decades as has the study of political economy. This may be due, in part, to the infatuation with postmodernism which unfortunately diverted intellectual attention and energy from rigorous critical and scientific analysis (see, e.g., Baars et al. 2006, Chapter 1; Beck 1992; Gilleard and Higgs 2014; Higgs 2013). A discussion of these and related debates lies beyond the scope of this project. It would, however, be a grave error to suppose that issues of ideology no longer warrant attention. Indeed, many practical gerontological developments of the past two decades in areas ranging from pension policy to drug prescriptions to the definition of care needs cannot be understood without engaging in a vigorous and self-reflexive process of ideology critique.

In exposing the particularities of scientific work, the analysis of ideology goes well beyond the matters explored in Chapter 8, such as the scientist's biography and training and the power of the habituated paradigmatic frameworks of normal science to reproduce themselves. Even though such factors are indeed important, the effects of the social world upon science are not limited simply to matters of biographical happenstance and paradigm reproduction. Beyond such factors, it must also be recognized that virtually all scientific work is conducted in institutions (universities, research institutes) that are themselves embedded in upon larger structures and centers of social power, and are dependent upon that power. Such powers, which include governmental, corporate, professional, and educational institutions and interests, comprise the apparatus of the modern state. Since legitimacy is an abiding challenge for institutions that exercise power and control over sizable populations and since science is culturally positioned as a source of authoritative knowledge, such institutions generally have an interest in scientific knowledge not only for the value of knowledge, for example, for facilitating economic growth or technical control but also for legitimation of its own interests. Science, including social science, is ideologically useful, in Philip Wexler's words, in "the generalization of the particular view of the ruling class as universal" (1983:24), in imposing that view on the population.

To such ends, *naturalization*—which we have encountered at numerous points in the foregoing chapters—is one of the most effective tools because it *reframes socially produced phenomena as natural*, thereby removing any thought or suspicion that they may be a product of the apparatus of dominant interests. This arrangement absolves the state and its institutions and practices of any responsibility for the well-being of citizens, even in those circumstances in which it has caused the problem in question. Examples of this are pervasive, familiar and often personal—as when children are slotted into age-graded classrooms that systematically disadvantage them by virtue of their pace of physical development or their month of birth or when an elder who resists subjection to the inhumane regimens of conventional nursing home life and is labeled a troublemaker, overmedicated with aggressively marketed drugs to the point of cognitive confusion, and then diagnosed as suffering from an organic decline that requires still additional drugs (recall Bengtson's "cycle of induced incompetence" discussed in earlier chapters). It is indeed apt to describe naturalization, as has Pierre Bourdieu (2001:3; see also Burawoy 2019:116–17), as entailing a logic of "reverse causality"—imagining the effect (located within the individual) of social forces to be the cause, and the actual causal force (located in social, interactional or other environmental dynamics) to be the effect.

THE MODERN STATE AND THE NATURALIZATION OF AGE

Among the reasons that age itself has taken central stage as a criterion of social organization over the past two centuries has been its value as a metric of state planning and population management (Chudacoff 1989; Hacking 1990; Katz 1996). Across an expanding number life-course domains, age has become naturalized. That is, when the cultural stock of knowledge includes the belief that someone's age predictably defines her "normal" and "natural" needs, such "knowledge" legitimates state institutions and practices in fields as diverse as education, management, mental health services, and medicine and health care, each of which has its own elaborated and age-graded institutional complex. In each of these cases, the "public" interests of the state (e.g., in managing pension benefits or access to specialized training, medical procedures, etc.) rely on naturalizing premises. Similarly, the private interests of corporate employers or pharmaceutical companies, and the professional self-interest of educators and health professionals, are often obscured by naturalization.

In the foregoing chapters we have seen numerous examples of evidence that scientific or pseudoscientific ideas about development and aging have interfaced not only with general public perceptions but also with political power and economic and cultural interests.

Recall the historical analyses reviewed in Chapter 4, demonstrating that the notion of "adolescence" as articulated by G. Stanley Hall at the opening of the 20th century provided an ideology for the management and control of teenagers—who had formerly been often considered an annoyance and perhaps a civic problem—as migratory and often vagrant youth. With Hall's opus, teenagers were plausibly defined enduring "storm and stress", and as psychically fragile, anxiety-ridden and in need of control—control which had as one of its aspects age-grading. Although the standard narrative assumes age-grading in schools is dictated by developmental needs of children, this practice apparently derived, at least in part, from budgetary pressures to use as few of the (more expensive) male teachers as possible, which meant limiting their use to the instruction of older children, where the physical strength required to impose order and threaten discipline on potentially unruly male students was needed (Kaestle and Vinovskis 1980; Kett 1977:123–4).

Within a few decades, age-grading in early life was complemented by a shift of developmental scholarship to focus also on later life. Disengagement theory (Cumming and Henry 1961) clearly gave scientific sanction to the idea of retirement, including compulsory retirement, as an almost morally obligatory developmental life stage, suggesting that those who continue to defy the stage imperative and continue to work as "unsuccessful disengagers" (Hochschild 1975:555). At the same time, it failed to provide a basis for progressive policies for older people, given that their main developmental tasks simply entail a withdrawal from society (Estes 1979:225–7).

After the expansion of age-graded schooling and then by mid–20th century the idea of "retirement at 65", a preoccupation with the "neglected" years of midlife then developed—as described earlier, leading to a rash of scholarly work that was voraciously consumed by mental health professionals and the wider public (e.g., Gould 1977; Levinson 1978; Weiss 1991), along with popularized versions (e.g., LeShan 1973; Sheehy 1977, 2011) and various life-stage arguments tailored specifically to women (Levinson 1994; Sangiuliano 1978; Sheehy 2010).

NATURALIZING MIDLIFE STRUGGLES

Such influential theories declared midlife to be a time of predictable transitions and perhaps crises, driven by individual developmental imperatives. Disruptive societal changes that were contemporaneously impacting midlife individuals (e.g., corporate cost-cutting and layoffs, welfare retrenchment) were accorded little attention in such work. As noted in Chapter 2, the emphasis on putatively universal stages of development—in this case midlife development—were used to interpret adult mental health struggles (e.g., S.C. Thomas 1996) and to design therapeutic treatments (e.g., Vogel-Scibilia et al. 2009).

In proposing an explanation for midlife discontent, such psychologistic theories of midlife development resonated with many powerful interests. For example, such theories allowed corporate leaders and professional experts to deflect attention from the consequences of downsizing and other impactful corporate policies at the same time that they served to placate employees and clients enduring a range of midlife adversities. For counselors as well as corporate spokespersons, such theories could be useful as a way of cooling out frustrated and anxious midlife employees who found themselves laid off or plateaued in a world where upward mobility is normative (e.g., Kanter 2008) or where promises of mobility are offloaded to the employees themselves, a practice presented to them in the upbeat framing of the chance to have a "do-it-yourself career" (e.g., Kunda 1992:75, 122).

Thus, the notion of midlife developmental transitions and crises could be used to reassure such employees or patients that their "private troubles" are not related to public issues but are "truly private"—having everything to do with the developmentally normal, internal midlife struggles—thereby eclipsing the framing of public issues such as the threats of unemployment and unemployability that expanded in the rapidly deindustrializing economies over the past several decades (e.g., Fineman 1983; Finley and Lee 1981; Little 1976; S.C. Thomas 1996) and with the "celebrating" of individual autonomy. This tendency is well illustrated in Gideon Kunda's study of a successful engineering firm where employees were informed that "the company is not responsible for creating your career path for you" (1992:75) in materials provided at a career workshop.

In medicine, reduction to the individual level was taken further with the expanding interest in biology and pharmacological interventions in the field of aging. In particular, in dealing with mental health issues, a convergent set of interests emerged as the profession of psychiatry sought to maintain its legitimacy and identified pharmaceuticals as key to its solution. "What's going to save us is that we're physicians" declared a keynote speaker at a late-70s professional meeting—physicians who could not only diagnose illness but also write prescriptions for drugs (Whitaker and Cosgrove 2015:268; see also E. Dannefer 1990). Similarly, counselors, social workers and other helping professionals became preoccupied with "third-party payments" and with the potentials of drug therapies, leading to complex organizational politics and the transformation of counseling and related professions (Douthit 2006; Douthit and Marquis 2006), and to the development of cooperative arrangements that would allow the clients of a broader spectrum of helping professionals access to prescription drugs.

Such developments have been reinforced by drug companies' reported efforts to work with the American Psychiatric Association to extend "the number and variety of diagnostic conditions and then formulating drugs to match them" (Rose and Rose 2012:259) and to seek to penalize foundations and stakeholders that are openly critical of their products (Healy 2004:242).

In sum, the force and significance of "age as ideology" is well illustrated by the alignment in the last quadrant of the 20th century of a constellation of interests and forces. These include: 1) adverse labor market trends associated with downsizing, globalization, and technological change; 2) neoliberal policies that include reduced support for public health and welfare and for individuals, of a social safety net; 3) an increasing medicalization of psychiatry and expanding cadres of competing "helping professionals", and 4) big pharma, promising effective treatments while eyeing expanding markets—with diagnoses and products for every age. It should not go unremarked that all four of these trends are related to corporate interests and agendas—saving money on labor costs, and then charging workers (both employed and unemployed) for mental health services and for medications, at a time when capital investment is driven to find new domains of profitability.

To the extent that such organismically based accounts are effective in obfuscating and neutralizing the social sources of private troubles, whether midlife women's stress levels

(McKinlay, McKinlay, and Brambilla 1987; Echouffo-Tcheugui et al. 2018; Thornton 2018) or depression resulting from an unwanted mandatory retirement (Gallo, Bradley, Siegel, and Kasl 2000; Mosca and Barrett 2016), they are essentially using *Biology as a Social Weapon* (Lewontin 1977) to encourage the placidity of the individuals affected and, above all, to sustain the invisibility of the social forces that maintain dominant interests and preserve the structure of power, ensuring that the understandings of the world that people operate with are again "the dominant material relationships grasped as ideas".

The use of developmental and related theories in naturalizing "private troubles" is not limited to age per se but has also been applied to making invidious distinctions in the developmental issues of various "othered" groups, including women (e.g., Warren 1987, 1996) and indigenous groups whose meaning structures and interests are neither understood nor respected by dominant interests. For example, it has been clearly demonstrated that the "developmental" significance of Sioux rituals was profoundly misunderstood and distorted in Erik Erikson's clinical and developmental assessment of the Sioux's psyche in ways that infantilized Sioux practices and traditions, and implicitly offered legitimation and cover to the Eurocentric understandings and the interests of the US government (Elrod 1997; see also Dunbar-Ortiz 2014). As a second example, sociobiological arguments have also been deployed to justify different patterns of conduct and pathology across different sectors of the population, promoting arguments that support racist ideas—again, reducing public issues to individual-level private troubles (e.g., Belsky, Steinberg, and Draper 1992; see Dannefer 1999; Duster 2003; Lerner 1992; Rose and Rose 2012).

In sum, the "expert" declaration of age and age-related capacities and patterns of conduct as natural has been used to justify age-graded schooling, adolescent "angst", mandatory retirement, midlife crises and associated mental health therapies, and the production of dependency and the infantilization of elders in long-term care. Moreover, as we have seen, the resultant, pervasive emphasis on "normal aging" and age-based generalizations systematically excludes consideration of intra-age stratification and the production of inequality over the life course.

NATURALIZATION IN THE SERVICE OF DOMINANT NARRATIVES

In what follows, I offer two brief examples to illustrate the value of naturalization to the dominant societal narrative: 1) the legitimation of institutions of long-term care, especially the contemporary nursing home, and 2) the use of genomics to sustain the biologization of individual characteristics (as reviewed in Chapter 7) even in the face of mounting empirical counter-evidence.

LONG-TERM CARE IN THE US

> The whole thing just got pulled out from under me and just left me bare naked, you might say, as far as having anything to do or anything to say or any way to feel like a person . . . I just feel like a nobody. . . . Now I'm here and I can't complain because they are very nice to me. . . . It's always clean and I probably should give thanks that

everything is so pleasant. Life for me, as far as being comfortable, couldn't be better. I don't have to worry about groceries or paying for whatever you pay for, you know, if I just wanted to sit around and do nothing. I'm told what to do and when to do it. I don't have nothing to say about anything, not even if they come in and clean my ears and they do and they do that. I know that they think they're doing good things, which they probably are. There's no privacy in my place. People walk in and they take my pulse and they do this. I don't know what they're doing or why because I'm healthy. I'm very well fed and I'm comfortable, but that's not living.

(nursing home resident, quoted in Stein 2005)

It is not without reason that older people in the US live in terror of being placed in a nursing home (Pleschberger 2007), in some cases threatening suicide as a preferred option to this state-designed and sanctioned institution of "civilized" modernity (Mezuk, Lohman, Leslie, and Powell 2015; Murphy, Bugeja, Pilgrim, and Ibrahim 2015). The damage done in the name of professional expertise and "humane" population management in the long-term care industry has been well documented in the US (e.g., Abramson 2015; Kayser-Jones 1990; Shura, Siders, and Dannefer 2011; Stein 2005; Thomas 1996) as in other societies (Cohen 1992, 1998).

This problem cannot be explained by the character of nursing home personnel. Both leadership and staff often have good intentions as they seek to meet resident needs with limited resources and within ill-designed institutional structures (Lustbader 2010). However, the structure of traditional nursing homes reflects an institutionalized ageism that legitimates assumptions that the rational way to treat residents is to corral them in regimented and disempowering conditions, in which they are structurally positioned as passive recipients of care, and that presumes that their primary conditions and health issues are medical and not psychosocial (e.g., Lustbader 2010; Stein 2005; W. H. Thomas 1996).

Diagnosed by a leading nursing home reformer, the chief "plagues" of nursing home life are not, e.g., Alzheimer's and arthritis; rather, they are social and existential – boredom, hopelessness and loneliness (Thomas 1996, 2004). When those plagues are dealt with by changing the structure, practices and/or routines of nursing home life, health improves and mortality declines (Dannefer and Stein 2001; Langer 2009; Langer and Rodin 1976; Thomas 1994, 1996).

In this case, the pervasive ageist impulses of modernity are mobilized in support of the long-term care industry's pressures for cost reduction and industrial efficiencies that benefit no one except, possibly, shareholders—yet are held in place by the complex of regulatory, legal and financial forces, all supported by the ideologies of ageism, individualism and scarcity.

Despite sustained criticism and well-documented adverse effects (see, e.g., Abramson 2015; Dannefer and Stein 2001, 2002; Kayser-Jones 1990; Stein 2005; W. H. Thomas 1996), the standard institutional model of care that has long governed the American nursing home and was greatly expanded after the 1960s continues to be based on the factory model of industrial mass production and efficiency.

While now complemented by the proliferation of institutions of "assisted living" as a stopover between adult retirement and nursing home entry, the nursing home itself remains largely unchanged as the next stop along what is normatively seen as an inevitable program of age-related decline in later life. Staff and leadership who seek ways to be more responsive to resident needs often find themselves frustrated by the financial, regulatory and cultural constraints under which they operate.

These routines have an adverse impact on more than "mood states" or "quality of life". The ways that legitimated institutions do damage to humans, including those they are intended to serve, is often revealed when taken-for-granted routines are disrupted and interrogated. The ways in which structural realities translate into destructiveness and the squelching of human potential in everyday life can often be vividly seen in the up-close observation of the front lines of interaction (Dannefer 2015; Stein 2005; W. H. Thomas 1996).

As an example of such disruption, consider the following interaction that occurred at mealtime at an excellent, traditional nursing home. The following account is from the field notes of my research associate, the late Janet Gelein, who was doing participant observation in the role of nursing home volunteer. As an experienced nurse practitioner herself, Janet was asked by lunchroom staff to help feed Emily, a stroke-impaired resident:

> Picking up Emily's spoon I filled it. . . . As I moved the spoon close to her mouth she opened it and accepted the food. . . . After she had finished several mouthfuls I initiated a conversation with other people. As we talked I concentrated on including Emily in the conversation. . . . After a while she began to shake her head 'no' to some spoons of food, and as the meal progressed I started to wonder if Emily really did need to be fed. 'You seem interested in this food, Emily', I said. 'I wonder if you can feed yourself?' She did not respond, but as I enclosed her hand within mine to use the spoon, Emily did not resist. After doing this several times, together, I complimented her efforts. Noticing that she seemed to like the pudding best, I moved it directly in front of her, saying: 'Why don't you go ahead and eat that on your own'. Reluctantly at first, but with increasing confidence, she continued feeding herself the entire dish of pudding. . . . She continued to feed herself. After a while, when almost everything was eaten she put down the spoon.
>
> (Dannefer, Stein, and Gelein 1998:11)

This episode occurred during our observations at a facility that was unusual in that it actively sought to make its regular practices more "resident-centered". Yet when we reported this and similar episodes at a meeting with nursing home leadership, they responded not with surprise but resignation. Acknowledging the tradeoffs between the efficiency requirements of the home and personalized attention to residents, they emphasized the constraints that govern lunchtime and resident care more generally in time-bound, short-staffed situations in which meeting medical, nutritional and regulatory requirements all must be prioritized by the institution. Given the naturalized expectation of resident decline, there is no risk of regulatory sanction for failure to pursue everyday opportunities to enable residents to regain function. Premised on an industrial "mass-production" model of service delivery, such priorities are understandable for the functioning and survival of such institutions.

Aides and other staff working in the setting were similarly unimpressed by the evidence from this and other similar efforts that showed some promise in possibly reversing trajectories of decline and regaining function. Their comments in this situation vividly reflected the standard interlocking narratives of resident decline and institutional imperatives: "You can't do that here—it will take too long" and "It won't really matter. After a while, they just give up anyway." Such everyday episodes demonstrate how the unrecognized potential for regaining strength is eclipsed by the taken-for-granted assumptions and dispositions that are shared by the staff and that pervade the nursing home culture.

An additional window on the extent to which the ideologies of modernity have naturalized the warehousing and dehumanizing of older citizens can be seen in the reaction of frontline nursing home staff who are US immigrants and grew up in indigenous societies of West Africa and the Caribbean. As noted in Chapter 1, such staff frequently expressed shock and distress at the segregated and dehumanized treatment of elders that constitutes the taken-for-granted "business as usual" in conventional US nursing homes. "We would never treat our elders like this", is a comment heard more than once from such employees. Parenthetically, it should also be noted here that in an effort to give more voice and agency to residents, leadership of this nursing home created a "residents' personnel committee" that would interview job applicants for frontline caregiving positions. The resident's top choice was just such an immigrant, selected precisely because of her manifest respect for elders. I hasten to add that it would be a mistake to use such comments to romanticize old age and intergenerational relations in such indigenous societies; these relations are often far from idyllic (e.g., Cohen 1992; Fry 2006; Glascock 1982). Nevertheless, many indigenous societies are characterized by a strongly internalized sense of respect for elderhood.

GENOMICS AND THE CENTRAL DOGMA: EPIGENOME/SOCIAL GENOMICS

> (Little has) hindered the spread of the evolutionary metaphor far outside its biological domains, above all in repeated attempts to at least tame and limit, and at worst to eradicate, the social in theorizing humanity, and thus to biologize human nature.
>
> (Rose and Rose 2012:79)

The 21st century began as a time of great expectations and hopes for the potentials of the mapping of the genome for understanding human behavior. In anticipation, a proliferation of scientific and pseudoscientific claims were advanced to claim genes for a remarkable array of characteristics and "behaviors'", ranging from voting to "criminal" predispositions to health outcomes (McQuaid, McInnis, Matheson, and Anisman 2016; Fowler and Dawes 2013; Settle, Dawes, Loewen, and Panagopoulos 2017). Such claims were aggressively advanced (e.g., Fowler, Baker, and Dawes 2008; Pinker 2003, 2010) and readily picked up and circulated in popular media, reaching comic proportions (e.g., Charney 2012). In science, the mapping of the genome was accompanied by the hope that gene-based therapies and neuropsychiatric interventions could be identified for a wide range of characteristics and "behaviors". It was hoped that the mapping of the genome and the identification of specific genes would facilitate new bodies of knowledge in relation to behavior, such as those that enable prediction not only of troublemaking in school (read ADHD—see Breggin and Scruggs 2001; Douthit and Marquis 2006; Douthit and Sullivan 2014), common mental illnesses and anti-social behavior, but also criminality, terrorist impulses and other domains of action of great concern to the state, as well as the development of pharmaceuticals to address a host of such problems (Rose and Rose 2012).

As is now well known, these "stellar expectations" for the human genome project have been largely unmet (see, e.g., Kolata 2013; Zwart 2015). The high expectations for advances in disease cures and diagnostic tools have not been realized. Instead, what has followed is the discovery of a simpler-than-expected genome (with only 22.5K genes rather than the hundreds of thousand that were envisioned) in which genes interact with each other and with the environment in much more complex ways than many anticipated.

This is not to say that the mapping of the genome has been without theoretical or practical value. It arguably facilitated greater understanding of functional genomics, including processes of gene regulation discussed in Chapter 7, and has been of use in the field of personalized medicine (Ventner 2008). Moreover, the basic knowledge provides important details about the structure of the human genome. Yet, especially in conjunction with contemporaneous discoveries about gene regulation, it is knowledge pointing to greater interactivity and complexity on the part of genes than was initially assumed. It is knowledge that points to relations conditioned on gene-gene interactions and environmental inputs.

Much like the reaction to discoveries of the importance of gene regulation and epigenetics discussed in Chapter 7, the reaction to this news has seemingly not been met with a reinvigorated interest in understanding the origins of problems in the social conditions with which they are often correlated.

Instead, many colleagues seem to be digging in more deeply—reducing their claims and expectations for the explanatory potentials of genetic variation while enlarging and expanding their genetic databases. This drop-back-and-punt logic seems roughly to be "if a magic bullet gene cannot be discovered, let us see how much variance can be explained using the huge samples of available GWAS data". Reacting to the miniscule amount of variance in the measure of educational achievement explained by such data, a respected economist engaged in research on these issues told me "the measures and the data are not very good, so what we need is to enlarge the sample".

I would like to suggest that the curious logic of this statement is a testament to the continuing appeal of the individual-reductionist holy grail implied by the Central Dogma and consistent with the logic of the functional-organismic nexus. It exposes a preoccupation with allowing "biology to shine through" (as reviewed in Chapter 7), despite its lack of explanatory promise, while ignoring immediately obvious and modifiable pathogenic social circumstances and dynamics. As a further indication of the continued popularity of this logic, consider the results of a content analysis that my research team conducted. We reviewed 85 articles published in major social science journals on G-E interactions from 2014 to 2020, finding that 82% of them were based on Central Dogma assumptions. Some leading researchers in this area remain skeptical about the value of exploring gene expression (through epigenetics and related mechanisms) but few question the perceived promises of the expanding domains of genome-wide association studies (GWAS) and Big Data (see., e.g., Freese 2018).

Thus, it appears that the yearning for magic, explanatory bullets remains alive and well, despite its reliance on the outmoded assumptions of the Central Dogma (see Chapter 7), and on the corollary that biology and genetics operate independent of social factors. While the appeal of this organismically based logic clearly resonates with the underlying impulses of an individualistic cultural ethos as discussed in Chapter 8 (e.g., anchored in the language of "development" and the invisibility of the social), it also has a more specific, added ideological relevance with both political and economic dimensions.

First, to the extent that the search for relevant causal factors remains focused at the level of the individual and the individual genome, scientific and public attention and energy are diverted away from consideration of humanly damaging aspects of existing social arrangements (e.g., exclusionary policies, economic inequality) and toward considerations with potential for political inconvenience.

This is a framing that leaves such issues entirely unnoticed and seeks to address the problem primarily in terms of treatment—specifically pharmacological treatment. Thus, it allows to go entirely unremarked the ways in which actual societal problems and public issues may generate deep and enduring private troubles and daunting ongoing challenges for individuals.

Second, of no less importance, is its economic appeal. It is a framing that envisions opportunities for profit-making while continuing to define problems at the individual level. Given the massive amounts of resources involved and the potentials for profit in marketing successful drugs, treatments, tests, and therapy techniques, it is not surprising that this set of forces exerts enormous force on the scientific work of academics. It is now well known, for example, that supposedly disinterested academics have been well paid by corporations to endorse their products (hence COI statements—see Healy 2004). In the US, the legitimating power of the Food and Drug Administration has long endured efforts at political intrusion and manipulation (see, e.g., Adashi, Rajan, and Cohen 2019).

As Hilary Rose and Steven Rose point out, the power of financial inducements is not limited to the private gain of individual scientists, corporate balance sheets or research programs but extends even to academic journals. Despite their dedication to reward sound research using strictly rational and "objective" criteria, journals—themselves often facing daunting financial challenges—are strongly incentivized to publish papers that would be purchased in huge volume, recirculated or otherwise featured by pharmaceutical companies or other interests of the medical-industrial complex (2012:259–60; see also Estes 2001).

The impact of such "disease-mongering" (LaMattina 2013) has been a topic of lively discussion within the pharmaceutical industry and among its critics (e.g., Angell 2011a,

2011b; Breggin and Scruggs 2001; Healy 2004; Rose and Rose 2012). It is an issue that has been the subject of particularly vigorous debate in the area of mental health, a concern that extends to gerontology.

In gerontology, mental health concerns are of particular relevance because of the major challenges with dementia, especially Alzheimer's disease and other forms of disabling cognitive impairment. For example, serious questions have been raised regarding the recently devised "stage" of "mild cognitive impairment", and regarding pharmaceutical incentives for its recognition and development (George and Whitehouse 2010; Whitehouse and Moody 2006).

SUMMARY

Across disciplines, the enterprise of science has generated knowledge with the potential to benefit human interests. With the continuing rise of anti-scientific sentiments over the past several years, it is perhaps worth making clear that the contextualizing of scientific work offered in this and the preceding chapter are not in any way intended to diminish the central value and importance of science for advancing and protecting human interests, including the interests of the planet.

Yet scientific activity is human activity and it occurs within the dialectics of everyday life, which are, necessarily, culturally, politically and economically situated.

Therefore, a key and distinctive task of the social sciences is to provide a reflexive moment. It is to assist in illuminating how paradigmatic assumptions maintain their dominance and, specifically, the extent to which their dominance is warranted by the advance of empirical evidence as opposed to extra-scientific interests. As we have now seen, such extra-scientific interests include not only the paradigmatically established and experientially anchored practices of the daily experiences of scientists but also the ideological interests of economically, politically and culturally powerful forces. As we have seen, such forces have an interest in promoting scientific ideas that frame realities in ways that legitimate their narratives. As the previous examples have sought to illustrate, this occurs in multiple areas, as disparate as the naturalization of long-term care institutions as beneficent overseers of individual decline (that is in part socially produced), and in the synergies between medicine and big pharma to identify new human problems for which genetic explanations can be found, or drugs can be developed.

Despite the dramatically disparate contents of such domains (as frontline long-term care and the continued appeal of traditional biological thinking in genetic and pharmaceutical research), one thing they have in common is the effect of obscuring entirely from view the question of the extent to which the human maladies they are intended to redress and that are in fact the justification of their activities are socially constituted.

The two examples offered—frontline service delivery in long-term-care settings and the enterprises of pharmaceutical and genetic research—could hardly be more disparate in terms of the nature and objectives of the everyday life of their practitioners. Yet one key thing they hold in common is their *effect*—which is to engage in the reverse causality of naturalization (Bourdieu 2001; Burawoy 2019; Dannefer 1999). It entails eclipsing entirely from view the recognition that the maladies and problems they are intended to redress and that are in fact the justification of their activities derive not only from organismic or biological problems but may often have their sources in the organization of social life. From the vantage point of such established interests, there is an understandable disinclination to want such possibilities interrogated; from the vantage point of thoughtful critical analysis and a sociological imagination, such interrogation is central to both scientific advance and human interests.

What difference can it make if sociological imagination is deployed as integral to the analysis of such issues? I will offer some thoughts on that question in the final chapter.

REFERENCES

Abramson, Corey M. 2015. *The End Game: How Inequality Shapes Our Final Years.* Cambridge, MA: Harvard University Press.

Adashi, Eli Y., Rohit S. Rajan, and L. Gleen Cohen. 2019. "When Science and Politics Collide: Enhancing the FDA." *Science* 364(6441): 628–30.

Angell, Marcia. 2011a. *The Epidemic of Mental Illness: Why?* Retrieved December 30, 2020 (www.nybooks.com/articles/2011/06/23/epidemic-mental-illness-why/)

Angell, Marcia. 2011b. *The Illusion of Psychiatry.* Retrieved December 30, 2020 (www.nybooks.com/articles/2011/07/14/illusions-of-psychiatry/)

Baars, Jan, Dale Dannefer, Chris Phillipson, and Alan Walker. 2006. *Aging, Globalization and Inequality: The New Critical Gerontology.* Amityville, NY: Routledge.

Baran, Paul, and Paul Sweezy. 1966. *Monopoly Capital: An Essay on the American Economic and Social Order.* New York: Monthly Review Press.

Beck, Ulrich. 1992. *Risk Society: Towards a New Modernity.* Thousand Oaks, CA: SAGE.

Bourdieu, Pierre. 1984. *Distinction: A Social Critique of the Judgement of Taste.* Cambridge, MA: Harvard University Press.

Bourdieu, Pierre. 2001 (1998). *Masculine Domination.* Stanford, CA: Stanford University Press.

Breggin, Peter R., and Dick Scruggs. 2001. *Talking Back to Ritalin: What Doctors Aren't Telling You about Stimulants and ADHD.* Revised edition. Cambridge, MA: Da Capo Press.

Broughton, John M., ed. 1987. *Critical Theories of Psychological Development.* New York, NY: Springer Publishing Company.

Burawoy, Michael. 2019. *Symbolic Violence: Conversations with Bourdieu.* Durham: Duke University Press Books.

Case, Anne, and Angus Deaton. 2020. *Deaths of Despair and the Future of Capitalism.* Princeton, NJ: Princeton University Press.

Charney, Evan. 2012. "Behavior Genetics and Postgenomics." *Behavioral and Brain Sciences* 35(5): 331–58.

Chudacoff, Howard P. 1989. *How Old Are You?: Age Consciousness in American Culture.* Princeton, NJ: Princeton University Press.

Cohen, Lawrence. 1992. "No Aging in India: The Uses of Gerontology." *Culture, Medicine and Psychiatry* 16(2): 123–61.

Cohen, Lawrence. 1998. *No Aging in India: Alzheimer's, the Bad Family, and Other Modern Things*. Berkeley, CA: University of California Press.

Couture, John, Aviva Cristy, and Douglas Duhaime. 2010. *Ideology*. Retrieved April 5, 2020 (https://keywords.ace.fordham.edu/index.php/Ideology)

Crystal, Stephen. 2018. "Cumulative Advantage and the Retirement Prospects of the Hollowed-out Generation: A Tale of Two Cohorts." *Public Policy & Aging Report* 28(1): 14–18.

Crystal, Stephen, and Dennis Shea. 2002. *Annual Review of Gerontology and Geriatrics (Volume 22): Economic Outcomes in Later Life: Public Policy, Health and Cumulative Advantage*. New York: Springer Publishing Company.

Crystal, Stephen, Dennis G. Shea, and Adriana M. Reyes. 2017. "Cumulative Advantage, Cumulative Disadvantage, and Evolving Patterns of Late-Life Inequality." *The Gerontologist* 57(5): 910–20. doi: 10.1093/geront/gnw056.

Cumming, Elaine, and William E. Henry. 1961. *Growing Old, the Process of Disengagement*. New York: Basic Books.

Dannefer, Dale. 1987. "Aging as Intracohort Differentiation: Accentuation, the Matthew Effect, and the Life Course." *Sociological Forum* 2(2): 211–36.

Dannefer, Dale. 1999. "Neoteny, Naturalization and Other Constituents of Human Development." Pp. 67–93 in *The Self and Society of Aging Processes*, edited by C. D. Ryff and V. W. Marshall. New York: Springer Publishing Company.

Dannefer, Dale. 2003. "Cumulative Advantage/Disadvantage and the Life Course: Cross-Fertilizing Age and Social Science Theory." *Journals of Gerontology Social Sciences* 58B: S327–37.

Dannefer, Dale. 2015. "Right in Front of Us: Taking Everyday Life Seriously in the Study of Human Development." *Research in Human Development* 12(3–4): 209–16. doi: 10.1080/15427609.2015.1068043.

Dannefer, Dale. 2020. "Systemic and Reflexive: Foundations of Cumulative Dis/Advantage and Life-Course Processes." *The Journals of Gerontology: Series B* 75(6): 1249–63. doi: 10.1093/geronb/gby118.

Dannefer, Dale, Jielu Lin, and George Gonos. 2021. "Age-Differentiated vs. Age-Integrated: Neoliberal Policy and the Future of the Life Course." *Journal of Elder Policy* 1(2).

Dannefer, Dale, and Paul Stein. 2001. "From the Top to the Bottom, From the Bottom to the Top: Systemically Changing the Culture of Nursing Homes." Unpublished final report prepared for the van Ameringen Foundation.

Dannefer, Dale, and Paul Stein. 2002. "Beyond Culture Change: Building the Living Learning Community." Final project report to funding agency, the New York State Department of Health.

Dannefer, Dale, Paul Stein, and Janet Gelein. 1998. "Microtemporal and Macrotemporal Linkages in Life Course Institutionalization: The Case of the Resident Career in Long Term Care." Paper presented at the XIV World Congress of Sociology Montreal (July).

Dannefer, Elaine F. 1990. *The Constitution of Professional Knowledge: A Study of the Transformation of Psychiatry*. Ph.D. Dissertation. University of Rochester, Rochester, NY.

Douthit, Kathryn Z. 2006. "The Convergence of Counseling and Psychiatric Genetics: An Essential Role for Counselors." *Journal of Counseling & Development* 84(1): 16–28.

Douthit, Kathryn Z., and A. Marquis. 2006. "Empiricism in Psychiatry's Post-Psychoanalytic Era: Contemplating DSM's Atheoretical Nosology?" *Constructivism in the Human Sciences*, 11(1): 32–59.

Douthit, Kathryn Z., and Tamara Sullivan. 2014. "Attention-Deficit/Hyperactivity Disorder." Pp. 564–671 in *Understanding Psychopathology: An Integral Exploration*, edited by R. E. Ingersoll and A. Marquis. Boston, MA: Pearson.

Dunbar-Ortiz, Roxanne. 2014. *An Indigenous Peoples' History of the United States*. Vol. 3. Boston, MA: Beacon Press.

Duster, Troy. 2003. *Backdoor to Eugenics*. New York: Routledge.

Echouffo-Tcheugui, Justin B., Sarah C. Conner, Jayandra J. Himali, Pauline Maillard, Charles S. DeCarli, Alexa S. Beiser, Ramachandran S. Vasan, and Sudha Seshadri. 2018. "Circulating Cortisol and Cognitive and Structural Brain Measures: The Framingham Heart Study." *Neurology* 91(21): e1961–70. doi: 10.1212/WNL.0000000000006549.

Elrod, Norman. 1997. *500 Years of Deception: A Classic Case in the 20th Century: Erik H. Erikson's Portrayal of the Native American*. Zurich: Althea Verlag.

Estes, Carroll L. 1979. *The Aging Enterprise*. San Francisco: Jossey-Bass.

Estes, Carroll L. 1991. "The New Political Economy of Aging: Introduction and Critique." Pp. 19–36 in *Critical Perspectives on Aging: The Political and Moral Economy of Growing Old*, edited by M. Minkler and C. L. Estes. Amityville, NY: Baywood.

Estes, Carroll L. 2001. *Social Policy and Aging: A Critical Perspective*. Thousand Oaks, CA: SAGE Publications.

Fineman, Stephen. 1983. *White Collar Unemployment: Impact and Stress*. New York: Wiley.

Finley, Murray H., and A. Terence Lee. 1981. "The Terminated Executive: It's Like Dying." *Personnel & Guidance Journal* 59(6): 382–4. doi: 10.1002/j.2164-4918.1981.tb00575.x.

Fowler, James H., Laura A. Baker, and Christopher T. Dawes. 2008. "Genetic Variation in Political Participation." *American Political Science Review* 102(2): 233–48. doi: 10.1017/S0003055408080209.

Fowler, James H., and Christopher T. Dawes. 2013. "In Defense of Genopolitics." *The American Political Science Review* 107(2): 362–74.

Freese, Jeremy. 2018. "The Arrival of Social Science Genomics." *Contemporary Sociology* 47(5): 524–36. doi: 10.1177/0094306118792214a.

Fry, Christine L. 2006. "Whatever Happened to Culture?" Pp. 159–76 in *Aging in Context: Socio-Physical Environments: Annual Review of Gerontology and Geriatrics*. Vol. 23, edited by H. W. Wahl, R. J. Scheidt, and P. G. Windley. New York: Springer Publishing Company.

Gallo, William T., Elizabeth H. Bradley, Michele Siegel, and Stanislav V. Kasl. 2000. "Health Effects of Involuntary Job Loss among Older Workers: Findings from the Health and Retirement Survey." *The Journals of Gerontology: Series B* 55(3): S131–40. doi: 10.1093/geronb/55.3.S131.

George, Danny, and Peter Whitehouse. 2010. "Dementia and Mild Cognitive Impairment in Social and Cultural Context." Pp. 343–56 in *The Sage Handbook of Social Gerontology*, edited by Dale Dannefer and Chris Phillipson. London: Sage Publications.

Gilleard, Chris, and Paul Higgs. 2014. *Cultures of Ageing: Self, Citizen and the Body*. New York: Routledge.

Glascock, Anthonoy P. 1982. "Decrepitude and Death-Hastening: The Nature of Old Age in Third World Societies." Pp. 43–66 in *Aging and the Aged in the Third World, Part 1: Studies in Third World Societies*, edited by J. Sokolovsky. Williamsburg, VA: College of William and Mary.

Gould, Stephen J. 1977. "Human Babies as Embryos." Pp. 70–5 in *Ever Since Darwin: Reflections on Natural History*, edited by S. J. Gould. New York: Norton.

Hacking, Ian.1990. *The Taming of Chance*. Cambridge, UK: Cambridge University Press.

Healy, David. 2004. "Shaping the Intimate: Influences on the Experience of Everyday Nerves." *Social Studies of Science* 34(2): 219–45.

Higgs, Paul. 2013. "Disturbances in the Field: The Challenge of Changes in Ageing and Later Life for Social Theory and Health." *Social Theory & Health* 11(3): 271–84.

Hochschild, Arlie Russell. 1975. "Disengagement Theory: A Critique and Proposal." *American Sociological Review* 40(5): 553–69. doi: 10.2307/2094195.

Horkheimer, Max, and Theodor W. Adorno.1972 (1947). *Dialectic of Enlightenment*. New York: Herder and Herder.

Jay, Martin. 1996. *The Dialectical Imagination: A History of the Frankfurt School and the Institute of Social Research, 1923–1950*. Berkeley, CA: University of California Press.

Kaestle, Carl F., and Maris A. Vinovskis. 1980. *Education and Social Change in Nineteenth Century Massachusetts*. Cambridge: Cambridge University Press.

Kail, Ben Lennox, Jill Quadagno, and Jennifer Reid Keene. 2009. "The Political Economy Perspective of Aging." Pp. 555–72 in *Handbook of Theories of Aging*, edited by V. L. Bengtson. New York: Springer Publishing Company.

Kanter, Rosabeth Moss. 2008 (1977). *Men and Women of the Corporation: New Edition*. New York: Basic Books.

Katz, Stephen. 1996. *Disciplining Old Age*. Charlottesville, VA: University of Virginia Press.

Kayser-Jones, Jeanie. S. 1990. *Old, Alone, and Neglected: Care of the Aged in the United States and Scotland*. Berkeley, CA: University of California Press.

Kett, Joseph F. 1977. *Rites of Passage: Adolescence in America, 1790 to the Present*. New York: Basic Books.

Kolata, Gina. 2013. "Human Genome, Then and Now: A Conversation with Eric Greene." *New York Times* April 15. Retrieved from www.nytimes.com/2013/04/16/science/the-human-genome-project-then-and-now.html

Kunda, Gideon. 1992. *Engineering Culture: Control and Commitment in a High-Tech Corporation*. Philadelphia: Temple University Press.

LaMattina, John L. 2013. *Devalued and Distrusted: Can the Pharmaceutical Industry Restore Its Broken Image?* 1st edition. Hoboken, NJ: Wiley.

Langer, Ellen J. 2009. *Counter Clockwise: Mindful Health and the Power of Possibility*. New York: Ballantine Books.

Langer, Ellen J., and Judith Rodin. 1976. "The Effects of Choice and Enhanced Personal Responsibility for the Aged: A Field Experiment in an Institutional Setting." *Journal of Personality and Social Psychology* 34(2): 191–8. doi: 10.1037/0022-3514.34.2.191.

Lerner, Richard. 1992. *Final Solutions: Biology, Prejudice and Genocide*. University Park, PA: Pennsylvania State University Press.

LeShan, Eda J. 1973. *The Wonderful Crisis of Middle Age: Some Personal Reflections*. Dysart, UK: David McKay Company.

Levinson, Daniel J. 1978. *The Seasons of a Man's Life*. New York: Random House.

Levinson, Daniel J. 1994. *Seasons of a Woman's Life*. New York: Knopf.

Lewontin, Richard C. 1977. "Biology as a Social Weapon." Pp. 6–20 in *The Ann Arbor Science for the People Editorial Collective*. Minneapolis: Burgess Publishing.

Little, Craig B. 1976. "Technical-Professional Unemployment: Middle-Class Adaptability to Personal Crisis." *The Sociological Quarterly* 17(2): 262–74. doi: 10.1111/j.1533-8525.1976.tb00978.x.

Lustbader, Wendy. 2010. *Counting On Kindness: The Dilemmas of Dependency*. New York: Free Press.

Marx, Karl, and Friedrich Engels. 1978 (1932). "The German Ideology Volume 1." Pp. 146–200 in *The Marx-Engels Reader*. 2nd edition, edited by R. C. Tucker. New York: Norton.

McKinlay, John B., Sonja M. McKinlay, and Donald Brambilla. 1987. "The Relative Contributions of Endocrine Changes and Social Circumstances to Depression in Mid-Aged Women." *Journal of Health and Social Behavior* 28(4): 345–63. doi: 10.2307/2136789.

McQuaid, Robyn J., Opal A. McInnis, Kimberly Matheson, and Hymie Anisman. 2016. "Oxytocin and Social Sensitivity: Gene Polymorphisms in Relation to Depressive Symptoms and Suicidal Ideation." *Frontiers in Neuroscience* 10: 1–9. doi: 10.3389/fnhum.2016.00358.

Meyer, Madonna Harrington. 2010. "Shifting Risk and Responsibility: The State of Inequality in Old Age." Pp. 21–41 in *The New Politics of Old Age Policy*, edited by R. B. Hudson. Baltimore, MD: Johns Hopkins University Press.

Mezuk, Briana, Matthew Lohman, Marc Leslie, and Virginia Powell. 2015. "Suicide Risk in Nursing Homes and Assisted Living Facilities: 2003–2011." *American Journal of Public Health* 105(7): 1495–502. doi: 10.2105/AJPH.2015.302573.

Morss, John R. 1996. *Growing Critical: Alternatives to Developmental Psychology*. Abingdon, UK: Routledge.

Mosca, Irene, and Alan Barrett. 2016. "The Impact of Voluntary and Involuntary Retirement on Mental Health: Evidence from Older Irish Adults." *The Journal of Mental Health Policy and Economics* 19(1): 33–44.

Murphy, Briony J., Lyndal Bugeja, Jennifer Pilgrim, and Joseph E. Ibrahim. 2015. "Completed Suicide among Nursing Home Residents: A Systematic Review." *International Journal of Geriatric Psychiatry* 30(8): 802–14. https://doi.org/10.1002/gps.4299.

Myles, John, and Jill S. Quadagno. 1991. *States, Labor Markets, and the Future of Old Age Policy*. Philadelphia: Temple University Press.

Phillipson, Chris. 1982. *Capitalism and the Construction of Old Age*. London: Macmillan.

Phillipson, Chris. 2013. *Ageing*. Cambridge, UK: Polity Press.

Phillipson, Christopher, and Allan Walker. 1986. *Ageing and Social Policy: A Critical Assessment*. London: Gower.

Piketty, Thomas, and Emmanuel Saez. 2003. "Income Inequality in the United States, 1913–1998." *The Quarterly Journal of Economics* 118(1): 1–41. doi: 10.1162/00335530360535135.

Pinker, Steven. 2003. "Are Your Genes to Blame?" *Time* 161(3).

Pinker, Steven. 2010. "The Cognitive Niche: Coevolution of Intelligence, Sociality, and Language." *Proceedings of the National Academy of Sciences* 107(suppl 2): 8993–9. doi: 10.1073/pnas.0914630107.

Pleschberger, Sabine. 2007. "Dignity and the Challenge of Dying in Nursing Homes: The Residents' View." *Age and Ageing* 36(2): 197–202. doi: 10.1093/ageing/afl152.

Raine, Adrian. 2002. "Biosocial Studies of Antisocial and Violent Behavior in Children and Adults: A Review." *Journal of Abnormal Child Psychology* 30(4): 311–26.

Rose, Hilary, and Steven Rose. 2012. *Genes, Cells, and Brains: The Promethean Promises of the New Biology*. New York: Verso Publishing.

Sangiuliano, Iris. 1978. *In Her Time*. New York: Morrow.

Settle, Jaime E., Christopher T. Dawes, Peter John Loewen, and Costas Panagopoulos. 2017. "Negative Affectivity, Political Contention, and Turnout: A Genopolitics Field Experiment." *Political Psychology* 38(6): 1065–82. https://doi.org/10.1111/pops.12379.

Sheehy, Gail. 1977. *Passages: Predictable Crises of Adult Life*. New York: Bantam.

Sheehy, Gail. 2010. *Passages in Caregiving: Turning Chaos into Confidence*. New York: William Morrow.

Sheehy, Gail. 2011. *New Passages: Mapping Your Life across Time*. New York: Ballantine Books.

Shura, Robin, Rebecca A. Siders, and Dale Dannefer. 2011. "Culture Change in Long-Term Care: Participatory Action Research and the Role of the Resident." *The Gerontologist* 51(2): 212–25. doi: 10.1093/geront/gnq099.

Stein, Paul. 2005. "Social Life under the Evacuation of Culture: Lost Minds, Demented Selves and Social Solidarity." Ph.D. Dissertation, University of Rochester.

Szasz, Thomas. 1993. *A Lexicon of Lunacy: Metaphoric Malady, Moral Responsibility and Psychiatry*. New Brunswick: Routledge.

Thomas, Sydney Carroll. 1996. "A Sociological Perspective on Contextualism." *Journal of Counseling and Development* 74(6): 529–36.

Thomas, William H.1994. *The Eden Alternative: Nature, Hope, and Nursing Homes*. Rochester, NY: Eden Alternative Foundation.

Thomas, William H. 1996. *Life Worth Living: How Someone You Love Can Still Enjoy Life in a Nursing Home*. Acton, MA: Wanderwyk & Burnham.

Thomas, William H. 2004. *What Are Old People For?: How Elders Will Save the World*. Acton, MA: Wanderwyk & Burnham.

Thornton, Michaella A. 2018. "Women at Mid-Life Have Higher Stress? Duh." *Common Reader*. Retrieved August 23, 2020 (https://commonreader.wustl.edu/women-at-mid-life-have-higher-stress-duh/)

Ventner, J. Craig. 2008. *A Life Decoded: My Genome: My Life*. London: Penguin Books.

Vogel-Scibilia, Suzanne E., Kathryn Cohan McNulty, Beth Baxter, Steve Miller, Max Dine, and Frederick J. Frese. 2009. "The Recovery Process Utilizing Erikson's Stages of Human Development." *Community Mental Health Journal* 45(6): 405–14. doi: 10.1007/s10597-009-9189-4.

Walker, Alan. 1980. "The Social Creation of Poverty and Dependency in Old Age." *Journal of Social Policy* 9(1): 49–75.

Walker, Alan. 1981. "Towards a Political Economy of Old Age." *Ageing and Society* 1(1): 73–94.

Walker, Alan, and Liam Foster. 2014. *The Political Economy of Ageing and Later Life: Critical Perspectives*. Cheltenham, UK: Edward Elgar.

Warren, Carol. 1987. *Madwives: Schizophrenic Women in the 1950s*. New Brunswick, NJ: Rutgers University Press.

Warren, Carol. 1996. "Older Women, Younger Men: Self and Stigma in Age-Discrepant Relationships." *Clinical Sociology Review* 14(1): 62–86.

Weiss, Robert S. (1991). *Staying the Course: The Emotional and Social Lives of Men Who Do Well at Work*. New York: Free Press.

Wexler, Philip. 1996. *Critical Social Psychology*. New York: Peter Lang.

Whitaker, Robert and Lisa Cosgrove. 2015. *Psychiatry under the Influence: Institutional Corruption, Social Injury, and Prescriptions for Reform*. New York, NY: Palgrave Macmillan.

Whitehouse, Peter J., and Harry R. Moody. 2006. "Mild Cognitive Impairment: A 'Hardening of the Categories'?" *Dementia* 5(1): 11–25.

Zwart, Hub. 2015. "Human Genome Project: History and Assessment." Pp. 311–17 in *International Encyclopedia of Behavioral and Social Sciences*, edited by J. D. Wright. Amsterdam: Elsevier.

CHAPTER 10
AGE, SOCIOLOGICAL IMAGINATION AND HUMAN POSSIBILITY

The popular understanding of age is anchored in the chronometrically defined material events of conception and birth. Given this anchorage, it is understandable that there is a widespread inclination to accept unquestioningly the idea that age-related change is mainly organismically driven. This inclination may be especially strong in cultural contexts that are both suffused by an ideology of individualism (as are Eurocentric and especially US culture) and relatively stable—permitting socialization into a world where "relative patterns are experienced as absolute" (Berger and Berger 1972). Under these conditions, scientists as well as the lay public are inevitably predisposed to views that ascribe a strong causal role to individual-level and biologically anchored processes.

The foregoing chapters have reviewed empirical evidence from biology as well as the social sciences and history, to demonstrate that social forces play a central constitutive role in human development and human aging. This includes of course matters like the meaning of age, the value associated with being of a particular age, and the legal implications of age. But much more than that, social forces are increasingly recognized as playing a constitutive role in shaping how individual aging occurs, biologically as well as psychologically and socially. And we have also seen that social forces shape the very awareness of age as a category of thought and the widely varying relevance of age in the consciousness in everyday life, across different social worlds, mobilizing it as a finely calibrated principle of social organization in the modern state.

In short, social forces *organize* age for individual persons and indeed, within individual human bodies, as socioenvironmental factors interact with physiology and organismic templates, and it also organizes and defines the role of age in shaping opportunity structures in society and culture.

We have also borne witness to the remarkably persistent *disinclination* of the dominant lines of discourse in life course, developmental and gerontological research, to embrace the implications of such discoveries for both advancing the science of aging and for apprehending new horizons of human possibility. Psychologist Robert Kastenbaum provocatively observed that rather than thinking of individual aging as inevitable decline, it might be better understood as a result of being subordinated to a routinized and unreflected set of entrenched activity routines, a condition he termed *hyperhabituation* (1981; see also Dannefer and Perlmutter 1990). I would suggest that gerontology itself—along with related fields—is similarly caught in a largely unexamined and hyperhabituated attachment to the entrenched but obsolete assumptions of the functional-organismic nexus, which has again and again sought to contain the implications of the social constitution of age, and hence to squelch or limit sociological imagination.

Even in the face of promising discoveries that keep pointing to an expanded explanatory role for social forces, the social science attachment to the paradigmatic assumptions of the functional-organismic nexus has proven to be remarkably resilient. As discussed in Chapters 8 and 9, some reasons for this resistance become more understandable when viewed from the analytic frames of the sociology of knowledge and science, which help to expose the wider ideological utility of functionalism and organismic theory. Yet for the field as a whole, there seems to be, at best, an ambivalent uncertainty regarding how to handle information that challenges its parameters.

This is especially so when the structures of research funding and other career-related rewards presuppose working with the premises of the functional-organismic paradigm (Falletta 2011; Healy 2004; Panofsky 2014; Rose and Rose 2012; Whitaker 2005). But where does all this leave us? So what?

Some readers might reasonably ask such questions. Does this all really matter? Whatever their limitations, the functional and organismic paradigms present a straightforward, easy to understand account of individual development occurring in a mostly beneficent social context. They are familiar, easy to grasp and they seem in many respects to "work" within the daily routines and reward structures to which many citizens and researchers are oriented. Is the added causal complexity really worth it? Why does this set of issues and concerns, even if valid, warrant so many words, so many pages, so much argument? And even if the critiques and concerns raised are warranted, can such analysis lead to any action steps to address them in a meaningful way, given the manifest strength of the dominant social apparatus and narrative, and the functional–organismic nexus that supports them?

WHY PARADIGM ASSUMPTIONS MATTER

In truth, it matters a great deal, for anyone who is 1) dedicated to the principles of science (for anyone who cares about empirical accuracy and sound bases for human knowledge) and 2) equally, for anyone who cares about understanding and enhancing the possibilities of human experience over the life course, and in childhood as well as later life. I will conclude by briefly discussing each of these.

If human development and age are subject matters worthy of study at all, it is essential that those who seek to understand these phenomena "get it right". As Herbert Blumer (1969:48) reminds us, the first task of science is to respect its subject matter, and we have seen in the foregoing chapters, again and again, how the empirical phenomena under study have been *disrespected*—reframed and/or distorted so they can be wedged into the categories of the functional–organismic nexus, with the result that the breakthrough insights are tossed off as incidental or curious side observations, and thereby ignored by its paradigmatic narrative. It is true, as noted, that mainstream accounts of "normal aging" present what for many is an intuitively appealing narrative. However, as we have seen, it is a narrative that implicitly legitimates and naturalizes existing arrangements, instead of interrogating the actual processes involved in the production of observed outcomes and their consequences. Respecting the subject matter must start with giving it careful scrutiny.

Getting the science right—getting our understanding of the forces that actually regulate and account for the phenomena we seek to understand right—is certainly a reason of fundamental importance. However, it is not the only reason the argument worked through in the preceding chapters is a consequential matter. It is also consequential because it has direct implications for how the possibilities of human lives are understood. How decision-makers think, how professional experts think, and how the general public thinks about age also have an impact on how to understand the limits and possibilities of human experience, both individually and collectively. In turn, those understandings unavoidably interact with age, both as physiological reality and as real ideology. Those understandings have a great deal to do with how individuals live, and also how they might aspire to live, which points to the second reason that this argument matters, the enhancement of human possibilites.

As we have seen, thanks to imaginative and rigorous empirical work across multiple disciplines, a great deal has been learned about the prospects for expanding human potentials over the life course, including in later life. In biology, an explosion of research on epigenetics and other mechanisms of gene regulation is making clear the complex yet powerful dynamics through which experience and context bear directly upon gene expression, with implications for development, aging and health. Other research has demonstrated the possibilities for physical regeneration, including brain plasticity and growth and the production of new neurons through the years of adulthood and into later life. In psychology, the centrality of positive mental health and stress modulation has long been acknowledged. However, science is only just beginning to appreciate the impact of experience on physiology, on the potentials for sustaining health and reversing the age-related declines assumed by disengagement theory and by the proponents of mild cognitive impairment and other age-related maladies.

Point by point, such work calls into question the rationality of existing age-graded and other institutional arrangements that regularly damage human beings, and their *naturalization* in ageist premises and other humanly destructive practices and institutions. Again, by naturalization I mean the reframing of socially produced outcomes and circumstances as though they are not human products and are rather misrecognized and assumed to be part of the natural order of things—a reversal of the order of causation (Bourdieu 2001; Burawoy 2019; Dannefer 1999).

NATURALIZATION AND THE ECLIPSE OF SOCIAL FORCES

Naturalization is the hallmark of the dominant narrative in age and life-course studies, which continues to be framed by the functional-developmental nexus. In the naturalized view, the role of the social is eclipsed, and individual human actors are assumed to be guided by some combination of "choice and fate"—volition on one hand and fateful individual attributes on the other. In this view, social institutions of every sort are generally accepted as taken-for-granted givens of everyday life, as the background and context of human activity, somewhat like climate, or weather. Questions of the coercive aspects of such institutions do not arise, nor do questions of their legitimacy or beneficence.

NATURALIZATION IN DEVELOPMENTAL THEORY: TURNING PUBLIC ISSUES INTO PRIVATE TROUBLES

As a now-familiar example of this, *organismic theories of development* have arguably done their part to propagate an unthinking acceptance of major institutions, including the naturalization of school grades and of childhood and the teenage years as age-graded "adolescence". In adulthood, increasing midlife precarity resulting from corporate downsizing or restructuring may be reframed as accommodations to "developmental stages"—the naturalization of private troubles in adulthood, deftly eclipsing public issues. When it comes to later life, the field of professional social gerontology is too often the uncritical bystander, observing with scant objection the naturalization of decline in later life, of which nursing homes are regarded as the beneficent overseers, as illustrated in the prior chapter. In some cases, such institutions may themselves produce the supposedly "natural" effects that legitimate their existence. Again, this is an efficacious form of sustaining entrenched societal power relations; it contributes to the manufacture of consent and can rightly be seen as a form of symbolic violence (Bourdieu 1984; Burawoy 1982, 2019).

NATURALIZATION AND FUNCTIONAL ANALYSIS: LEGITIMATING THE INSTITUTIONALIZED LIFE COURSE

The sociologically grounded concept of the *life course as a social institution* has a somewhat different relation to naturalization. Unlike stage theories predicting midlife crises or other such organismically propelled angst, the idea of the ILC (institutionalized life course) could never be used to justify and naturalize the personal crises induced by, for example, sudden unemployment due to corporate downsizing or relocation trauma within or between nursing homes because it is explicitly conceived as a historically specific and socially constructed apparatus, and one that provides security and predictability throughout the life course. However, a concomitant of the age-based uniformity and standardization that is part and parcel of the ILC brings its own naturalization by offering at least an implicit, Parsonian-style legitimation of powerful and potentially oppressive age-graded practices, rules and age norms that may become an added source of anxiety or social restraint (Hagestad and Uhlenberg 2005; Lawrence 1984; Riley, Kahn, and Foner 1994; Settersten and Hägestad 1996).

While it may be the case that, for many, the structure and accompanying normative expectations of the ILC offer certain existential comforts (Kohli 2007), the power of such norms can also be often oppressive—dictating "age-appropriate behavior" and providing negative sanctions, for example, for children whose developmental pace does not correspond to age-graded school expectations (e.g., Rogoff 2003; Stetsenko 2016), for students who would choose to take a break during college years or returning midlife students who feel out of place sitting in class or taking tests alongside 19-year-old students (e.g., Bell 2003), or when they are used for the policing of sexually frustrated and infantilized nursing home residents (Diamond 1992; Doll 2012; Gubrium 1975).

While one can point to examples of pushback against such expectations, and to ingenious efforts to deconstruct these age-based rigidities, the fact that such pushback is necessary is an index of the coercive power of such norms—a case of the exception proving the rule.

Those who teach returning "nontraditional" students—whether grad or undergrad—
frequently hear comments from such students of the form "Can I do this?" and "I
really don't feel like I belong here". The power of these perceptions and expectations is
remarkable when one considers the growing ranks of nontraditional students. For me, one
gratifying aspect of teaching *Sociology of the Life Course* to nontraditional graduate students
has been hearing comments like, "This course changed my life" and "All of a sudden
the possibilities seemed to get real big"—enabled by a base of evidence and knowledge
equipping them to challenge the oppressive hegemony of traditional normative thinking
about "age-appropriate roles" and life-course possibilities.

Thus, despite the sociological grounding of the ILC approach, its functionalist inclinations
lead it to endorse and legitimate the power of humanly arbitrary and specific age norms
by uncritically depicting age-graded social institutions, and positioning them as "normal"
and implicitly beneficent—thereby discounting and discouraging the interrogation of their
human value and human costs.

The naturalizing logic of both the ILC and the psychological approaches discussed earlier
is also manifested at the macro-level. At this level, they can be seen as offering a kind
of political and economic naturalization because—by their implicit characterization of
individuals as clustering in something like a normal distribution around a desirable "golden
mean" and of life-course patterns as homogeneous and undifferentiated—they allow to go
unnoticed the realities of human diversity and especially of intracohort inequality and its
systemic tendencies for life-course increase, discussed in Chapters 5 and 6. For the logic of
the functional-organismic nexus, systemic increases in inequality are of little interest and,
when noticed, tend to be viewed simply as an artifact of individual differences in talent
and industriousness, as illustrated by John Clausen's claims for the explanatory power of
planful competence (1991), or Moffitt's claims for decisiveness of early individual traits
(Moffitt 1993, 1994; Laub and Sampson 2003:84–85). Again the social is naturalized,
rendered irrelevant and invisible while individual differences are credited with producing
socioeconomic stratification. Again, "there is no such thing as society".

THEORY AND PRACTICE: REIMAGINING INSTITUTIONS TO CHALLENGE NATURALIZATION

For individuals in the real world, how can the critique of naturalization and related insights
be put to use? In practical terms, what can be done to address the humanly destructive
aspects of the naturalized logic that mistakes humanly produced patterns and requirements
for natural ones? And that imposes this definition of nature and human nature onto
citizens, encouraging them to resign themselves to such a social apparatus?

Indeed, what can be done? In actuality, a lot can be done. There are enough cases of human
efforts springing both from spontaneous social combustion and from organizationally
sponsored and planned progressive change efforts to fill the pages of another book. I
conclude with three brief examples which make clear the benefits and power of the form

that social interaction takes, including 1) social interactions with elders, and specifically with disabled elders: the example of culture change in long-term care in the US, 2) the implementation of a Vygotskian *transformative activist stance* in a group home for young boys and in other settings, and 3) The Intergenerational School—based on a theoretically grounded approach that deliberately creates linkages across age.

KNOWLEDGE AND HUMAN INTEREST IN LONG-TERM-CARE SETTINGS

One of the most straightforward examples of how expanded sociological imagination can matter in societies like the US is in the domain of long-term care. Earlier chapters reviewed what to many readers is a familiar fact—that the standard paradigm of long-term-care institutions comprises a template of human destructiveness and a prescription for ensuring human decline. Thus, nursing homes offer a particularly obvious example of a conflict between social practices and human benefits, and one in which—despite its blatant and manifest violations of human dignity and respect—it has proven challenging to align "knowledge and human interests" (Habermas 1972).

As I noted earlier, Langer, Rodin and others have experimentally demonstrated the energizing and sometimes juvenescent impacts of positive and meaningful experiences in later life, both in conventional everyday life experiences and in nursing home settings. Decades ago, they discovered that nursing home residents with a plant to care for live longer (Langer and Rodin 1976). "Hmmm, that's interesting", may say leadership subject to the bureaucratically driven matrix structuring everyday life in nursing homes (the apparatus of interlocking financial, legal, regulatory requirements and cultural support within which nursing home care is located, and within which nursing home residents appear mainly as "full beds" and malpractice risks), who go right on with the imperatives of these interdependent systems, which can function very well without regard to the decline and death of nursing home residents, since that is in any case what is expected of and predicted for such residents. Some nursing homes might even provide plants for residents to water. Of course, the implication of Rodin and Langer's work was not necessarily that the residents should have plants but that a less barren life might be, as reformer Bill Thomas puts it, "a life worth living" (1996).

The industrial model of conventional care, as noted earlier, has been challenged by reform efforts based on a refusal to accept the legitimacy of the dehumanizing and damaging conditions of the "legitimate" institutional form of the traditional nursing home (Barkan 2003; Dannefer, Stein, Siders, and Shura 2008; Thomas 1996, 2004). This challenge has found a groundswell of popular support that became a social movement in long-term care, guided by its own industry, and centered around the mantra of "culture change" in long-term care. This movement is manifested in nationally organized reform efforts, notably the Pioneer Network (www.pioneernetwork.net/about-us/overview/), and in the packaging of culture change practices in at least one brand-name franchise, the Eden Alternative (1996; www.edenalt.org) and related initiatives such as the Society for the Advancement of Gerontological Environments (SAGE, www.sagefederation.org/). Subsequently, arrangements for dependent elders and others have extended beyond the nursing home model into experimentation with residential and "mainstream" forms of living arrangement for dependent elders (Kane 2001; Kane and Kane 2001; Thomas 2004;

www.thegreenhouseproject.org/) as well as efforts devoted to more specific aspects of institutional living (e.g., Barkan 2003: Calkins 2018; Day and Calkins 2002; Rader 2019; Rader and Tornquist 1995; Rader et al. 2006).

REFORM AND ITS CHALLENGES

In general terms, these developments encourage successive degrees of "deindustrialization" of the nursing home setting. They have included several types of changes that, while seemingly pedestrian, translate into significant material improvements in quality of life. Nursing home insiders will recognize that these innovations, which sound surpassingly mundane, represent palpable changes in practice and sometimes in life possibilities for residents, and they are a reflection of how truly dehumanizing and debilitating is the everyday life structure imposed by standard nursing home regimes. Such changes include: resident control over when to go to bed and when to get up in the morning, some degree of control over food menu and in some cases opportunity to cook; dining in spontaneously arranged social groupings rather than assigned seating; aging in place (i.e., not having to move to a different ward if the type of care needs to change, thereby deconstructing the resident career); opportunities to interact with pets and also with children and fixed relationships with caregivers, which can nurture meaningful personal relationships. Such "liberation" from the rigid and impersonal routines of standard nursing home practices and experiences inevitably runs up against regulatory and legal hurdles, often creating a delicate balancing act (Brokaw 2002; Dannefer and Stein 2001; Kane 2001) that journalist Paula Span (2010) aptly calls a "safety dance". Where these and other such changes have been implemented, improvements in health and longevity as well as levels of social activity have been well documented (e.g., Calkins 2018; Dannefer and Stein 2001, 2002; McNees 1997; Thomas 1994, 1996).

Yet such salutary changes hardly herald the arrival of a "state of Eden" in long-term care, even in the most promising and progressive settings. The reasons for this are numerous, incuding 1) financial challenges, 2) bureaucratic resistance, 3) co-optation, and 4) unevenness in addressing the plagues of nursing home life.

FINANCIAL CHALLENGES

When seen from a national level, one overriding set of hurdles to moving long-term care in a more humanly responsive direction at the macro-level is of course financial—conventional nursing homes may lack resources to entertain ambitious possibilities of culture change. Moreover, for-profit institutions, often controlled by private equity, are perennially under added pressure to increase the bottom line for stockholders, representing a direct link between humanly counterproductive institutional arrangements and political economy.

However, the monetary bottom line is also intertwined with other risks and potential sanctions. Many homes, especially those with a proportion of public-pay residents, struggle for regulatory and fiscal survival, with little energy to expend on self-motivated reform efforts. And all long-term such facilities operate under continuous state surveillance and may be financially penalized for health and safety violations. As a result, financial challenges overlap with bureaucratic ones.

BUREAUCRATIC AND REGULATORY RESISTANCE
One of the change-oriented facilities my research team studied received a six-figure fine from the state because of a violation involving a resident with dementia who enjoyed walks outside every day in an area that was secured but not recognized by the state as "safe" for dementia residents (Brokaw 2002). The "safety dance" thus reveals itself as not merely a daily existential balancing act on the frontline of resident care but one that poses nontrivial existential risks for nursing home administrators.

For the successes demonstrated in what is still a tiny number of homes nationally to become a game-changer for the conventional paradigm of long-term care, the movement for culture change will have to capture political as well as popular imagination. To date, Edenized or other humanized and progressive care arrangements continue to expand but often in expensive "Cadillac homes" and have thus mostly been the privilege of well-resourced and well-informed families, bringing the matter of cumulative dis/advantage into individual and family efforts to sustain care and quality of life for elders in need of care.

CO-OPTATION
A growing awareness by the long-term care industry of the cache of "culture change" and innovations like "Edenization" have given these terms a street value for individuals and families shopping for long-term care options, especially those with "private pay" resources. This situation creates a strong incentive for nursing homes with the potential to attract clients who can afford an expensive per diem rate to attain some credential of culture change legitimacy. This arrangement, inevitably, raises the inevitable danger of co-optation of reform efforts—of the risk that a facility may succeed in presenting itself as a place in the vanguard of culture change primarily because of the associated market value, especially with a high-end clientele, while engaging in "window dressing"—advertising some trappings of reform, yet only in a limited or superficial way embracing the resident-centered and humanizing principles called for by the culture change movement.

As is the case with any emancipatory effort or project, all such efforts represent an ongoing dialectic of change, especially when the product of labor that is in question is the daily production of quality human care and attendant social relations in everyday life. Even those who have taken seriously the challenge of humanizing long-term care and implementing some degree of culture change cannot claim that they have "arrived". Indeed, one prescient principle of the culture change endeavor is the explicit recognition that the work is never finished.

UNEVENNESS IN THE ABILITY TO DEAL WITH THE "THREE PLAGUES"
In our research on culture change efforts, my colleagues and I found that—across several facilities we studied in two states—the institutionally imposed "plagues" described previously were unevenly addressed. Facilities had often made demonstrable strides in expanding social events and options for other kinds of activity, relating to Thomas' plagues of loneliness and boredom. The same could not be said, however, for residents' sense of helplessness.

"What I miss most is the doing something of value for someone else" is a modal comment of contemporary nursing home residents (Siders 2016; Dannefer and Stein 2001, 2002;

McNees 1997) and one reflected in the observations of a nursing home resident observed earlier (Stein 2005). In the long-term care (LTC) context, this can be a tall order. Nursing home entry is implicitly defined by the ageist narrative of decline as part of the life course, as a move from independence to dependence, from competence to incompetence, from activity to passivity. Even if the pre-admission experience of an incoming resident has been one of eroding independence and autonomy, nursing home entry entails a degradation ceremony that institutes a new order of magnitude of social and existential invisibility and irrelevance and unilaterally impose control, as illustrated earlier.

This occurs, of course, while the health and comfort of the new resident are ostensibly the center of attention and foregrounded in everyone's experience, and the anxiety-induced poor performance on mental status tests that are routinely imposed on incoming residents prompts added well-intentioned but increasingly patronizing concern (Stein 2005). In such a situation, it is easy even for "critical", "self-critical", "humanistic" and "person-centered" reformers to overlook the demolition of selfhood that attends such a situation. It is a demolition that is likely to be internalized and sustained because traditional nursing home routines, even culture-change inspired activities and sociality, offer no escape from it, comprising a classic example of Bengston's "cycle of induced incompetence". Yet many of these individuals are not only keenly aware of what is occurring around them but have had life experiences that provide a useful perspective and enable them to take the measure of what they encounter in daily life in LTC.

PARTICIPATORY ACTION RESEARCH: ENGAGING RESIDENTS' SKILLS AND INSIGHTS

With the leadership of my colleague Paul Stein, our research team sought to address this important problem by introducing *participatory action research* (PAR) into our research program. PAR recognizes that when the goal of research is a defined direction of change in a social context, "subjects" or "respondents" often possess knowledge and ongoing observations and perspectives that may be uniquely valuable to those goals—and should be considered co-researchers.

Thus, we began with the premise that long-term-care residents are the true experts of LTC life—not only because their lives are the *raison d'etre* of these institutions but also because they are the persons and the only persons who inhabit the facility 24/7. In addition, many of them possess skills and insights seasoned with the experience of decades of living and working that can offer heretofore unarticulated insights, perspectives and creative ideas.

To access that knowledge, we undertook research that invited residents as well as staff and family members to participate in research groups (RGs) that met weekly to discuss issues of concern to them, and especially to invite ideas for what might be done to improve the functioning of the home and their quality of life within it. In the RGs, an array of problems, needs and solutions were identified by residents. In one facility, more than a dozen imaginative strategies for improvement were initiated and many were implemented, ranging from practical matters (e.g., enlarging fonts on posted material and lowering bulletin boards to make them more accessible to wheelchair users) to relationship-building (on one unit, residents initiated a personalized "staff picture book" to assist residents in knowing their staff). Other resident-driven activities included publishing a resident newspaper and arranging for residents to provide on-site volunteer assistance for nearby charities with mailings and other such tasks (see Shura, Siders, and Dannefer 2011 for a detailed discussion). In other facilities, a diverse array of other innovations were proposed—ranging from having the social worker obtain her CDL so she could transport residents to funerals/wakes of deceased friends (implemented) to inviting striptease dancers (both female and male) to perform for the unit (not implemented, at least not during the period of our on-site research projects).

For many residents, one of the more telling benefits of the RG was not the product but the process—it was the regular weekly event of the RG meetings themselves that was valued by the resident participants. More than once, RG members frustrated staff by refusing to keep other appointments if they conflicted with the scheduled weekly meetings, and residents often described these RG meetings as the "high point of the week".

While localized, this small-scale set of projects are useful in demonstrating the possibilities for a radically different kind of daily experience and a different structural position, or role, for those residing within long-term-care facilities. It is a radical change that may matter little to most citizens who hurry past such facilities on a daily basis, until the time comes that they or someone close to them find themselves being admitted. Then the quality of experience will likely make a difference for them as well. It will suddenly become one of the things, if not THE thing, that matters most.

The potentials of PAR for research on age and development have been demonstrated at every point in the life course, and in an array of settings. Its value for elders is not limited to nursing home life; their mobilization as co-researchers has also been effectively deployed in community settings (Buffel 2019; Greenfield, Black, Buffel, and Yeh 2019). In addition, it has proven fruitful for facilitating positive, participatory change at other points in the life course, as the next example illustrates.

IMPLEMENTING A TRANSFORMATIVE-ACTIVIST STANCE IN THE EARLY LIFE COURSE

PAR has been extensively deployed as a strategy for transforming life chances and life-course possibilities at earlier points in the life course. One example of this can be seen in the work of developmental psychologist Anna Stetsenko (2016) and her efforts to apply a "transformative ontology" grounded in Vygotskian psychology. This approach is premised on a recognition of personhood as resulting not from socialization that expects conformity to a normative apparatus of an imposed social order but from "an active project of historical becoming" that involves a reflexive interrogation of and a critical, agentive uptake on one's circumstances, possibilities and interests—an *encounter with*, sometimes a confrontation with, those circumstances (Stetsenko 2018). This perspective is applied in everyday life situations using what Stetsenko terms a *transformative activist stance* (TAS):

> The central premise is that people come to know themselves and their world and ultimately come to be human in and through (not in addition to) the processes of collaboratively transforming their world in view of their goals and purposes.
>
> (Vianna, Hougaard, and Stetsenko 2014:62)

Here, the basic formulations of social scientists describing the dialectic of experience involving both action and co-construction of self and society are deliberately mobilized in everyday life practices, with deliberate individual and collective life-course intentions giving new dimensions to the idea of "linked lives".

Grounded in this perspective, action research has been used to promote human interests and fruitfully interrogate their relation to institutional arrangements, including child welfare programs (Vianna and Stetsenko 2011), community-college classrooms (Vianna, Hougaard and Stetsenko 2014) and juvenile group home settings (Vianna and Stetsenko 2014). Action research using the TAS begins by cultivating among all participants the fundamental insight of the sociology of knowledge discussed earlier, that "knowledge is contingent on the position from which it is produced", and simultaneously, in keeping with the premises of action research, that it is also

> strongly contingent on the destination toward which those producing knowledge are oriented, hence the term "endpoint epistemology". . . . Such endpoints have to be worked out by researchers and participants together, through explorations into the presently existing conflicts and contradictions.
>
> (Vianna and Stetsenko 2014:584; see also Stetsenko 2008, 2012)

Such work is intended to enable co-participants

> not just to define significant, investigable questions. Instead, it also demands that we ask, 'From whose perspective is the question significant? What phenomena are worth studying? Who decides? For what goals are the questions we ask significant?' and 'What kind of a future are answers to our questions likely to contribute to?'
>
> (Vianna and Stetsenko 2014:585)

The resultant activity is simultaneously intended to be a project of personal development and social change.

I will briefly review Eduardo Vianna's efforts to implement a program of action research while working as a staff psychologist in a teenage group home. Readers may suspect that while this work has a well-articulated and critically reflexive theoretical grounding, its abstraction can offer little insight in to the realities of group home life—where the implicit motto seems to be "all talk and no action". However, the account of the research process and results provided by Vianna and Stetsenko make clear that the application of these theoretical notions had a practical payoff, especially as the boys who lived in the group home came to recognize the potential power of their own actions and their relevance in everyday experience—the sense that they themselves mattered in their own lives and the life of their institution.

At the beginning of this work, the social world of the group home and the boys' sense of themselves and their possibilities were typical of such settings. They were rebellious and frustrated, one stating that "he refused to spend his life asking 'paper or plastic', referring to work in grocery stores". Another, not surprisingly, said that he "would rather sell drugs than be poor" (Vianna and Stetsenko 2014:589).

Such views are of course understandable. They were premised on an understanding of the boys' life chances that both staff and the boys themselves fully shared—that since college "was virtually out of reach vocational education or entry into the low-wage job market were . . . the most favorable outcomes" (Vianna and Stetsenko 2014:589).

Much as in the nursing home example recounted earlier, Vianna (who was initially regarded by the boys with the same suspicion and hostility as were other staff) proceeded by recognizing certain domains of expertise and insight possessed by the boys themselves, connecting their insights with their interests and respecting their plight. As Vianna and Stetsenko describe Vianna's work with the boys:

> [I]n his efforts to address the thematic universe of the boys, he began to create opportunities for them to expand their agency through novel collaborative activities devised with them (e.g., collective video project, films, trips). These activities responded to the boys' desire to participate in the decisions involving them, no matter how small. Due to its democratic character . . . (this) work bypassed the need to resort to the type of authority typically invoked. . . . [Vianna's] success in engaging boys in these activities convinced the program administration to support them. This, in turn, opened the way to negotiate a radical departure from the researcher's initial clinically oriented job description. The project goal to develop an alternative learning context was accepted.
>
> (2014:591)

The authors report that through this process, the boys began to recognize the effects of systemic oppression and also the ways that their own actions contributed to their oppression, not just in the group home setting but in the wider society—by, for example, buying into consumerist preoccupations with jewelry and clothes, accepting the staff's limited appraisal of their potentials and ignoring opportunities that could advance their own learning.

When their own understandings changed along with their actions and conduct, their relations with the staff moved in a more positive direction:

> Gradually, the boys' desire for a comfortable, more peaceful and democratic home, where they were respected and their voices heard, began to be realized. Increasingly, staff and boys began to see each other more as allies, which strengthened their sense of community. The number of incidents of noncompliance with program rules started to go down and punitive actions by the staff sharply decreased too, leading to fewer conflicts. A new daily routine was established, and boys stopped running away from the program. . . . A novel and more democratic community practice took root. . . Boys

and staff together dismantled the hierarchical power structure based on authoritarian control and its corollary system of favoritism and spurious alliances. In this process, the vicious cycle was broken as the contradiction between control and resistance gave way to a new power dynamic based on solidarity and collaboration.

(Vianna and Stetsenko 2014: 594)

In such situations, as these authors recount elsewhere, participants come to realize the costliness involved in "the collective impact of their individualist stance" (Vianna, Hougaard and Stetsenko 2014:74). By disrupting the humanly damaging cycles operating in everyday interaction, this case offers another example of how Bengtson's *cycle of induced incompetence* can be reversed and potentially turned into a "cycle of induced solidarity" (Dannefer and Siders 2013). Such cases illustrate how sociological imagination can be mobilized on behalf of human development.

Thus, the insights gained were not just for new dynamics and new possibilities for individual students but for the group process as well. The authors report that, as a result of this "paradoxical moment", the boys "also began to realize that even by passively accepting the status quo they were contributing to perpetuating it" (Vianna, Hougaard, and Stetsenko 2014:74), and that these constructive innovations were institutionally sustained.

AGE INTEGRATION AT THE INTERGENERATIONAL SCHOOL

A third example comes from an innovative and impactful educational initiative deliberately designed to combat both age segregation and ageism by enlisting the strengths and skills of elders, even elders facing significant health and memory challenges, in nurturing and teaching.

Founded in 2000 in Cleveland, Ohio, The Intergenerational School (TIS) was originally housed in a senior services facility. The original school has since moved to larger quarters and has been joined by several other schools in Cleveland and elsewhere in the US and other countries including Canada, Ghana and Scotland.

The TIS program simultaneously provides a progressively designed, interactive and learning-based pedagogy while attacking age segregation on multiple fronts (Whitehouse 2005). Nursing home residents as well as community volunteers, many of them seniors, serve as mentors or "learning partners", interacting regularly and spontaneously with TIS students. In addition, the curriculum (as in Stetsenko's case, also founded on Vygotskian principles) bases learning plans and needs on developmental progression rather than age per se. Learning is arguably enhanced for both teachers and senior mentors by its bidirectional character. Cohort differences in familiarity with new gadgets and electronic devices positions children to be teachers of senior mentors at the same time they are learning, enabling a role flexibility and partial role reversal that can itself be a growth experience and a source of empowerment (see Dannefer 2005).

Initially, the idea of elders in schools, particularly elders with dementia, was strange to some. But success stories made many converts once we had been up and running for

a few years. For example, the 'Volunteer of the Year' award was given two years ago
to a woman who was a gifted teacher, although she could not remember why she was
being given the award because of her short-term memory problem. She literally could
not remember that she volunteered in the school every week, but was much beloved
and recognised for her many achievements with children.

(Whitehouse 2013:85–6)

Like all complex and cutting-edge programs, TIS has had its struggles. Yet it has been, by any
objective measure, a straightforward success—earning honors year after year as one of the top
charter schools in its state, and numerous other honors and national awards. Such recognition
does not adequately apprehend the scope of the program's success, either in the depth of
learning of standard classroom material or in the broader contextual value of interactive
learning, and age-integrated relationships. Nevertheless, it is recognized as a promising model
of effective education that begins from premises that immediately break barriers of age
segregation, and one that continues to expand its reach, nationally and internationally.

SUMMARY: BEYOND THE LIFE-COURSE COMFORT ZONE

In each of these examples, it should be clear how a rational critique of taken-for-granted but
humanly destructive institutional forms can lead to fresh and innovative configurations of
life course possibilities. Whether the critique entails a rejection of the imposed control of old
age as a "natural" decline, a rejection of youth management by hierarchical "bureaucratic
control", or a rejection of schooling as "naturally" age-segregated and unidirectional
instruction, in each case we have seen that it can lead to innovative configurations, and can
energize a sociological imagination that mobilizes the design of alternative arrangements
that serve human interests instead of private interests or the established comfort zone of
hyperhabituated and taken-for-granted institutional arrangements.

Despite their success both in human terms and in organizational terms, these are, of course,
highly specific cases. Even though they are in some instances having a national impact and
international reach and have great potential, they remain, effectively, demonstration projects. I
offer them in the hope of encouraging broad consideration of the unrealized potential of the
social and gerontological sciences for advancing human interests and imaginative thinking about
possibilities that do not yet exist to advance quality of life over the life course. As we have seen,
this cannot be adequately done without exposing and opposing institutional and other power
arrangements that are indifferent or hostile toward human potentials and interests, and especially
those that tend to undermine human interests while claiming to serve them. But it also cannot
be done without using human and sociological imagination to envision alternatives.

In some respects, each of the cases discussed here may appear to entail a rejection of
foundational premises of the logic of modernity—a "repersonalization" of bureaucratically
instituted rationalities and efficiencies and a supplanting of universalism with personal, and
sometimes arguably particularistic, concerns. However, this is driven not by a nostalgia
for the past but rather, as Harry Braverman (1998:7) wrote in introducing his critique of

monopoly capital, by "nostalgia for an age that has not yet come into being"—a time in which human expressivity driven by possibilities for constructive and meaningful action combines with positive innovation in organizational design as in science and technology to advance individual and collective human interests. Implicit in this vision is a structuring of resources in ways that prioritize human interests—allocating resources to quality whether in schooling, in health care or in long term care, rather than prioritizing corporate profits or governmental cost-cutting while ignoring the needs and silencing the voices of human want and vulnerability.

POSSIBILITIES OF THE LIFE COURSE: LINKED LIVES, HUMAN INTERESTS AND HUMAN POSSIBILITY

In the study of the life course, much has been made of the concept of linked lives, which is one of Glen Elder's foundational principles of his approach to the life course (Elder, Johnson, and Crosnoe 2003; Elder and Shanahan 2006). Although *"linked lives"* has been a fruitful concept for researchers within and beyond age and life-course studies, its usage has been almost entirely in the domain of micro-level relationships of families, friendship convoys and other personal relations located in the private sphere—an example of microfication (Hagestad and Dannefer 2001). I have suggested that the limitation of linked lives to such usage overlooks other linkages of lives that reflect equally if not more profound dimensions of experience, such as the linkage between 12-year-old factory workers in Hong Kong or elsewhere who work overtime under grueling conditions to satisfy the holiday demand of the 12-year-olds of affluent Western families for Christmas toys (Dannefer 2003). Such a connection illustrates how both life-course opportunities and experiences and many of the micro-level interactions featured in life-course research are shaped by macro-level forces—in this case, consumerism and child labor—exposing exploitative realities that support of consumerist impulses of affluent modern lifestyles. While such an analysis may move beyond microfication, it remains at the level of the analysis of the reproduction of existing social arrangements—again, functionalism in a minor key.

Why has a consideration of linked lives not included any attention to the potentials of linked lives for transformation? Why has it not been applied, for example, to the work of the Gray Panthers and or other activist groups who seek to challenge prevailing institutional arrangements and sometimes succeed in changing the reality (as in the elimination of mandatory retirement in the US)? Such accomplishments set the frame within which the properties for which life-course scholars have a fondness—for example, "agency" and "resilience"—may be nourished, not to mention reflecting prime examples of those properties.

Perhaps driven in part by the increasing precarity and the expansion of social exclusion that is becoming more evident with the erosion of public and state power in relation to the influence of private interests, recent work by researchers in related fields provides numerous examples of the potential for social science research to explore *collective* agency and *community* resilience (White 2017; see also Stetsenko 2018). Why should not the potentials of such collective efforts be considered in the efforts of life-course scholars to envision the life course?

If science is generally understood to be worthy of public investment because it can contribute to an enriched understanding of human potentials and the conditions for their realization, then social science must—like other sciences—be a science of human possibility, not just a chronicler and implicit legitimator of (and apologist for) existing social arrangements. Of course, it is essential—as a first step—to understand and analyze existing arrangements and causal relationships; it is only by such analysis that scientists across disciplines have discovered the often-invisible power of social forces to shape the biophysical as well as social realities of human experience and existence. Yet to stop at the exposition of existing arrangements and connections, without exploring the horizon of possibilities that such knowledge reveals, is an abdication both of both sociological imagination and of science as vocation, in the best Weberian sense.

Sociological imagination both invites and requires social scientists to focus on human possibilities—what *might be* as well as what *is*. It is very interesting that pioneering sociologist Matilda White Riley—a close personal friend of both Talcott Parsons and Robert Merton, and a lifelong devotee of Parsonian functionalism—titled her last major book *Age and Structural Lag: **Society's Failure** to Provide Meaningful Opportunities in Work, Family and Leisure* (Riley, Kahn, and Foner 1994, emphasis mine). It is remarkable that the final decades of her own life, encountering the power of ageism as an insidious social force and perhaps also as a personal one, added to Riley's longstanding critique of age segregation and prompted her to challenge further the functionalist template of the three-box linear life-course sequence (school/work/retirement) as legitimate and desirable. In this work, Riley and colleagues proposed as an alternative what they term the "integrated life course" in which the experiences of education, worklife and free time are all blended across the life course.

Such an idea obviously moves beyond the naturalized acceptance of the institutionalized life course and attendant age norms and expectations, and invites other such innovative proposals and questions. Why should age and life-course studies not be a forum for elaborating efforts like the German *Bildungsurlaub* (literally, "education vacation") federally mandated for many workers, or acknowledge respected scholarly critiques of the "one-life, one-career imperative" (e.g., Sarason 1977). Why not try to imagine alternative arrangements—for example, what if careers lasted 12 years (after which time one would be expected to learn a new field) instead of 50 or 60? Why not model the effects on late-life inequality of a universal basic income or a 30-hour work week at a living wage? It is interesting that such notions are seen as "unaffordable" in a powerful and affluent society in which families can no longer make it on the income of one full-time earner, while almost 90% of private equity is owned by 10% of the population (Wigglesworth 2020). Similar arguments were made a century ago, when the idea of a 40-hour work week seemed radical and unattainable (Sahlins 1976; Standing 2014).

In his important essay, "The Moral Equivalent of War" (2015 [1910]), William James, a pacifist, acknowledges candidly the developmental benefits for human beings of learning military discipline and cooperation and enduring the vicissitudes of wartime adversity.

Indeed, other life-course research has also pointed to the positive life-course consequences of military experience for many veterans (e.g., Laub and Sampson 2003; Wilmoth, London, and Parker 2010). James makes a compelling case for universal conscription to combat not other humans but rather, perennial, unnamed enemies such as poverty and disease. In a similar vein, the recent pandemic illustrated the potential social and collective value of such notions, as it prompted suggestions from some quarters that Americorps volunteers might be pressed into service to deal with the resultant societal challenges.

If James is correct that military-style discipline and focus are of general educational and developmental value, why not explore it at the societal level, as an extension of schooling, as a developmentally valuable new component of life-course institutionalization? And again, rather than limiting such beneficial experiences to young people, why not encourage such an option for midlife adults as well, modeled by initiatives such as the *Bildungsurlaub* or worker sabbaticals (see, e.g., Burkus 2017)?

Especially in view of the mounting evidence of the developmental potentials and health impacts of midlife experience, thinking about the possibilities for reconfiguring the life course brings to mind Marx's famous vision (albeit constrained by a 19th-century view of gender—see Brown 2013) that, in a world of emancipated human possibilities,

> nobody has one exclusive sphere of activity but each can become accomplished in any branch he (sic) wishes, society regulates the general production and thus makes it possible for me to do one thing today and another tomorrow, to hunt in the morning, fish in the afternoon, rear cattle in the evening, criticise after dinner, just as I have a mind, without ever becoming hunter, fisherman, herdsman or critic.
>
> (Marx and Engels 1932:160)

Sociological imagination is being increasingly applied to understanding the ways human interests and potentials are squelched by both oppressive and habituated institutional regimens and corporate and private interests, whether through the oppression of age norms or the obdurate realities of cumulative dis/advantage, systemic racism and other forms of opression that contribute to the reproduction of adversity. But that is only a first step.

Applying such imagination to everyday life also requires careful attention to the matter of what emancipation might mean, which unavoidably takes the discussion into the realm of values, including issues of social justice, meaning and spiritual grounding (Baars 2010, 2012, 2017; Joas, 2021). Even here, empirical evidence continues to be centrally relevant. It now can be taken as well established that inequality itself has far-reaching adverse effects, affecting even those most well off (Daniel, Kennedy, Kawachi, Cohen, and Rogers 2001; Marmot 2005; Wilkinson and Pickett 2011). The continuing concentration of wealth in the 21st century makes clear that the precarity of such concentrated means may threaten the fundamental structures of social order on which everyone depends, including the affluent.

Yet beyond such utilitarian arguments, questions of values remain. One is reminded of Daniel Callahan's (1987, 1995) notorious suggestion that life-saving health care be denied to those over 70 (although he seemed to exempt from this guideline those with the means to pay for good care, and himself had an expensive, life-saving hospital visit at age 79 [Callahan 2013; Pinkerton 2009]). Whatever the difficulties with Callahan's argument (see Smith 2002), these issues have been given an ominous new vividness throughout the advanced postindustrial world by political and institutional responses to the COVID-19 crisis. Under what assumptions could one agree with politicians who argue that older people should be willing to die to save the largely pointless and one-dimensional consumerism of a capitalist economy? Or with those who justify the stratification of exposure, disease and death it has made even more visible (Kelley, Yu, Oladimeji, and Dahal 2021). Especially under conditions where relatively few supports exist for those most vulnerable, such tendencies will be further aggravated. For example, the pandemic of 2020 clearly amplified dramatically the power of the socioeconomic gradient of health.

Under what conditions could one accept the actions of leaders who, beyond the level of rhetoric, fail to move proactively to protect the safety of frail elders in nursing homes and other high-contact settings? Age is a value on the chopping block, it seems. Yet age peers do not share a common risk.

HUMAN INTERESTS AND THE FUTURE OF LIFE-COURSE POSSIBILITIES

In sum, we have learned that the internal constraints of the developing human organism do dictate certain delimited features of development and aging but far fewer than are generally assumed. We have learned that we generally take for granted the patterns of age that we observe in a way that provides coherence—albeit often oppressive coherence—to the mainstream social order. To push beyond the rigidity of the existing order quickly raises a host of other value questions: Can a diverse population agree on how much freedom is to be tolerated, on how to reconceive age as truly "irrelevant", as Bernice Neugarten called for, or how much age diversity should be encouraged in, say, cohort-bound hangouts and bars or in age-targeted audiences for TV shows? Matilda Riley once predicted that polygamy might again emerge as a later-life norm, given the growing imbalance in numbers of men and women. The cougar phenomenon is more than offset by the tendency for available older men to partner with relatively younger women (Alarie and Carmichael 2015). What kind of values are needed to accommodate and encourage a full array of fulfilling human possibilities? Can we really endorse Harold marrying Maude as acceptable? While exciting for some, such prospects can be unnerving for many others.

Because of the normative and other restrictions within which the modern life course is continuously reconstituted, and because so little exploration has been done on the horizon of open life-course possibilities, the answers to many such questions remain unclear and can only be clarified by critical self-reflexiveness, both individual and collective (Baars 2012, 2017; Baars and Dohmen, forthcoming; Dannefer, Stein, Siders, and Patterson, 2008). Such questions, it seems, fall within the scope of what C. Wright Mills wrote, as I noted at the beginning of Chapter 1, that the sociological imagination involves "a magnificent lesson, but also a terrible one" (Mills 1961). It is, indeed, a lesson that makes us aware of the tentativeness of the world-taken-for-granted, which is simultaneously frightening and potentially emancipatory. It is a lesson that implies that there is hard work to be done for scholars of age and the life course, and also for citizens living their individual and collective lives, in rethinking assumptions and envisioning possibilities that may extend well beyond the comfort zone of existing practices and relationships.

Those of us concerned with the true meaning of the concept of agency might consider the oft-noted paradox that human actors, while feeling vulnerable, may be even more afraid of their individual and collective power because it is often unclear to what new domains the exercise of that power might take us.

Thus, although it is now clear that the taken-for-granted patterning of the life course is not dictated by the imperatives of organismic development, nor by the inevitability of current institutional and normative imperatives, confronting this realization does not by itself bring emancipation. It does little, for example, to remove the very real economic strictures that limit and define experience, and the normative sanctions for venturing into novel lifestyle or age-based territory. It does little to resolve the vexing existential, ethical and spiritual issues that many find increasingly challenging.

Nevertheless, clarifying the dimensions of the empirical realities of human experience is an essential first step. Illuminating these fundamental human interests and identifying the kinds of social conditions that would support them and what kinds of change would be required to realize those conditions is a central and fundamental task and promise of sociological imagination.

Moreover, it may begin to remove the alienation of failing to recognize that the social relationships in which we participate and the social institutions we inhabit are themselves the products of our own collective human labor—of human activity (see Marx 1978 [1932]:85). It may invite the question of the extent to which these forms of relationship serve human interests over the life course, and what kinds of change can facilitate modes of relating that will enable a fuller realization of developmental potentials and more fully serve human interests. Under what conditions can those potentials be realized?

Clearly, this is not a problem that admits an individual-level solution. No amount of resolve, talent or resilience activated on behalf of individual agents can change the defining aspects of this situation. Even in the most open societies, individual life chances are not a matter of individual choice but of structured power relations—relations that are sustained by an ideological apparatus that operates in part through symbolic violence. Moreover, evidence is robust that the interests of even the most affluent members of such societies are ill served by high levels of inequality (Daniels, Kennedy, Kawachi, Cohen, and Rogers 2001; Remington, Catlin, and Gennuso 2015; Wilkinson and Pickett 2011).

It is ironic that especially in the most individualistically oriented societies such as the US, individuals are not necessarily well served by taken-for-granted social arrangements. The US currently ranks 48th among nations in life expectancy (flanked by Lebanon and Cuba) and has high rates of poverty and inequality, and some evidence suggests that inequality tends to increase with age more than in other advanced societies. Moreover, inequality not only persists but is on a steady historic trend of dramatic increase. Given the life-course impact of these developments as individuals age and given their clear social sources, it seems clear that those in life-course studies and gerontology who are concerned with the well-being of aging human individuals must confront these questions, and can only do so by nurturing the sociological imagination.

At the same time, it must also be recognized that the assault on material inequality is not the final measure of individual or societal health. It is necessary, but only as a foundation for the free interrogation of the kinds of social relations, interests and values that human beings might seek to realize, and how those intersect with life-course realities. Such questions have dimensions that are both individual and collective, both existential and political. They entail a focus on the synergies of the material and spiritual, and ultimately may take us beyond the scope of social science per se. However, there can be no question that a vigorous sociological imagination is an essential foundational element if such questions are to be pursued honestly and fruitfully.

REFERENCES

Alarie, Milaine, and Jason T. Carmichael. 2015. "The 'Cougar' Phenomenon: An Examination of the Factors That Influence Age-Hypogamous Sexual Relationships among Middle-Aged Women." *Journal of Marriage and Family* 77(5): 1250–65. https://doi.org/10.1111/jomf.12213.

Baars, Jan. 2010. "The Meaning of Age: Cultures Meet Biology." Pp. 3–14 in *Times of Our Lives*, edited by H. Blatterer and J. Glahn. Oxford: Inter-Disciplinary Press.

Baars, Jan. 2012. *Aging and the Art of Living*. Baltimore: Johns Hopkins University Press.

Baars, Jan. 2017. "Aging: Learning to Live a Finite Life." *The Gerontologist* 57(5): 969–76. doi: 10.1093/geront/gnw089.

Baars, Jan and Joseph Dohmen. Forth. *Towards an Art of Aging: A Rediscovery of Forgotten Texts*. Baltimore: Johns Hopkins University Press.

Barkan, Barry. 2003. "The Live Oak Regenerative Community." *Journal of Social Work in Long Term Care* 2: 197–221.

Bell, James A. 2003. "Statistics Anxiety: The Nontraditional Student." *Education* 124(1): 157–62.

Berger, Peter L., and Brigitte Berger. 1972. *Sociology: A Biographical Approach*. New York: Basic Books.

Blumer, Herbert. 1969. *Symbolic Interactionism: Perspective and Method*. Englewood Cliffs, NJ: Prentice-Hall.

Bourdieu, Pierre. 1984. *Distinction: A Social Critique of the Judgement of Taste*. New York: Routledge.

Bourdieu, Pierre. 2001 (1998). *Masculine Domination*. Stanford, CA: Stanford University Press.

Braverman, Harry. 1998 (1974). *Labor and Monopoly Capital: The Degradation of Work in the Twentieth Century*. New York: Monthly Review Press.

Brokaw, Garth. 2002. "Physical Environments as a Tool to Culture Change." In Rosalie Kane (organizer) Symposium, *What a Difference a Place Makes! How Physical Environments in Nursing Homes Affect Quality of Life*. Annual Meeting of the Gerontological Society of America, Boston.

Brown, Heather. 2013. *Marx on Gender and the Family: A Critical Study*. Chicago: Haymarket Books.

Buffel, Tine. 2019. "Older Coresearchers Exploring Age-Friendly Communities: An 'Insider' Perspective on the Benefits and Challenges of Peer-Research." *The Gerontologist* 59(3): 538–48. doi: 10.1093/geront/gnx216.

Burawoy, Michael. 1982. *Manufacturing Consent: Changes in the Labor Process Under Monopoly Capitalism.* Chicago, IL: University of Chicago Press.

Burawoy, Michael. 2019. *Symbolic Violence: Conversations with Bourdieu.* Durham: Duke University Press Books.

Burkus, David. 2017. "Research Shows That Organizations Benefit When Employees Take Sabbaticals." *Harvard Business Review Digital Articles* 2–4.

Calkins, Margaret P. 2018. "From Research to Application: Supportive and Therapeutic Environments for People Living with Dementia." *The Gerontologist* 58(suppl 1): S114–28. doi: 10.1093/geront/gnx146.

Callahan, D. 1987. "Terminating Treatment: Age as a Standard." *The Hastings Center Report* 17(5): 21–5.

Callahan, Daniel. 1995. *Setting Limits: Medical Goals in an Aging Society with "A Response to My Critics."* Washington, DC: Georgetown University Press.

Callahan, Daniel. 2013. "Opinion | On Dying after Your Time (Published 2013)." *The New York Times* November 30. Retrieved from www.nytimes.com/2013/12/01/opinion/ sunday/on-dying-after-your-time.html

Clausen, John S. 1991. "Adolescent Competence and the Shaping of the Life Course." *American Journal of Sociology* 96(4): 805–42.

Daniels, Norman, Bruce Kennedy, Ichiro Kawachi, Joshua Cohen, and Joel Rogers. 2001. *Is Inequality Bad for Our Health?* Boston, MA: Beacon Press.

Dannefer, Dale. 1999. "Neoteny, Naturalization and Other Constituents of Development." Pp. 67–93 in *The Self and Society of Aging Processes*, edited by C. D. Ryff and V. W. Marshall. New York: Springer Publishing Company.

Dannefer, Dale. 2003. "Whose Life Course Is It, Anyway? Diversity and 'Linked Lives' in Global Perspective." Pp. 259–68 in *Invitation to the Life Course: Toward New Understandings of Later Life*, edited by R. A. Settersten. Amityville, NY: Baywood Publishing.

Dannefer, Dale. 2005. "Practicing the Best of Theory: Age Integration at the Intergenerational School." *Intercom: Aging in Focus* 12: 22–3.

Dannefer, Dale, and Marion Perlmutter. 1990. "Development as a Multidimensional Process: Individual and Social Constituents." *Human Development* 33(2–3): 108–37. doi: 10.1159/000276506.

Dannefer, Dale, and Rebecca A. Siders. 2013. "Social Structure, Social Change and the Cycle of Induced Solidarity." Pp. 284–92 in *Kinship and Cohort in an Aging Society: From Generation to Generation*, edited by M. Silverstein and R. Giarusso. Baltimore, MD: John Hopkins University Press.

Dannefer, Dale, and Paul Stein. 2001. "From the Top to the Bottom, From the Bottom to the Top." Final project report to van Ameringen Foundation.

Dannefer, Dale, and Paul Stein. 2002. "Beyond Culture Change: Building the Living Learning Community." Final project report to funding agency, the New York State Department of Health.

Dannefer, Dale, Paul Stein, Rebecca Siders, and Robin Shura Patterson. 2008. "Is That All There Is? The Concept of Care and the Dialectic of Critique." *Journal of Aging Studies* 22(2): 101–8. doi: 10.1016/j.jaging.2007.12.017.

Day, Kristen, and Margaret P. Calkins. 2002. "Design and Dementia." Pp. 374–93 in
    Handbook of Environmental Psychology, edited by R. B. Bechtel and A. Churchman.
    Hoboken, NJ: John Wiley & Sons, Inc.

Diamond, Timothy. 1992. *Making Grey Gold: Narratives of Nursing Home Care*. Chicago,
    IL: University of Chicago Press.

Doll, Gayle Appel. 2012. *Sexuality & Long-Term Care: Understanding and Supporting the
    Needs of Older Adults*. Baltimore, MD: Health Professions Press.

Elder, Glen H., Monica Kirkpatrick Johnson, and Robert Crosnoe. 2003. "The Emergence
    and Development of Life Course Theory." Pp. 3–19 in *Handbook of the Life Course*,
    Handbooks of Sociology and Social Research, edited by J. T. Mortimer and M. J.
    Shanahan. Boston, MA: Springer.

Elder, Glen H., Jr., and Michael J. Shanahan. 2006. "The Life Course and Human
    Development." Pp. 665–715 in *Handbook of Child Psychology: Theoretical Models of
    Human Development*. Vol. 1, 6th edition. Hoboken, NJ: John Wiley & Sons Inc.

Falletta, Lynn, 2011. *'It's Not Just Pure Science': Federal Funding of Children's Mental
    Health Research through the Request for Applications (RFA) Process*. Doctor of
    Philosophy Dissertation, Case Western Reserve University, Cleveland, OH.

Greenfield, Emily A., Kathy Black, Tine Buffel, and Jarmin Yeh. 2019. "Community
    Gerontology: A Framework for Research, Policy, and Practice on Communities and
    Aging." *The Gerontologist* 59(5): 803–10. doi: 10.1093/geront/gny089.

Gubrium, Jaber F. 1975. *Living and Dying at Murray Manor*. Charlottesville, VA: University
    of Virginia Press.

Habermas, Jurgen. 1972. *Knowledge and Human Interests*. Boston: Beacon Press.

Hagestad, Gunhild, and Dale Dannefer. 2001. "Concepts and Theories of Aging."
    Pp. 3–21 in *Handbook of Aging and the Social Sciences*. 5th edition, edited by R. H.
    Binstock and L. K. George. San Diego, CA: Academic Press.

Hagestad, Gunhild O., and Peter Uhlenberg. 2005. "The Social Separation of Old
    and Young: A Root of Ageism." *Journal of Social Issues* 61(2): 343–60. https://doi.
    org/10.1111/j.1540-4560.2005.00409.x.

Healy, David. 2004. *Let Them Eat Prozac: The Unhealthy Relationship between the
    Pharmaceutical Industry and Depression*. New York: New York University Press.

James, William. 2015 (1910). *The Moral Equivalent of War*. Plano, TX: Obscure Press.

Joas, Hans. 2021. *The Power of the Sacred: An Alternative to the Narrative of
    Disenchantment*. New York: Oxford.

Kane, Rosalie A. 2001. "Long-Term Care and a Good Quality of Life: Bringing Them
    Closer Together." *The Gerontologist* 41(3): 293–304. doi: 10.1093/geront/41.3.293.

Kane, Robert L., and Rosalie A. Kane. 2001. "What Older People Want from Long-Term Care,
    and How They Can Get It." *Health Affairs* 20(6): 114–27. doi: 10.1377/hlthaff.20.6.114.

Kastenbaum, R. J. 1981. "Habituation as a Model of Human Aging." *International Journal
    of Aging & Human Development* 12(3): 159–70. doi: 10.2190/br5f-h8b7-2b9x-53u8.

Kelley, Jessica, Jiao Yu, Abolade Oladimeji, and Poshan Dahal. 2021. "States of Infection:
    Evidence Supporting the Relative Income Hypothesis in COVID-19 Infection and
    Death Rates Among OECD Nations." Unpublished manuscript.

Kohli, Martin. 2007. "The Institutionalization of the Life Course: Looking Back to Look Ahead."
    Research in Human Development 4(3–4): 253–71. doi: 10.1080/15427600701663122.

Langer, Ellen J., and Judith Rodin. 1976. "The Effects of Choice and Enhanced Personal
    Responsibility for the Aged: A Field Experiment in an Institutional Setting." *Journal
    of Personality and Social Psychology* 34(2): 191–8. doi: 10.1037/0022-3514.34.2.191.

Laub, John H., and Robert J. Sampson. 2003. *Shared Beginnings, Divergent Lives: Delinquent Boys to Age 70.* Cambridge, MA: Harvard University Press.

Lawrence, Barbara S. 1984. "Age Grading: The Implicit Organizational Timetable." *Journal of Organizational Behavior* 5(1): 23–35. https://doi.org/10.1002/job.4030050104.

Marmot, Michael. 2005. *The Status Syndrome.* New York, NY: Owl Books.

Marx, Karl. 1978 (1932). "Economic and Philosophic Manuscripts of 1844." Pp. 66–125 in *The Marx-Engels Reader.* 2nd edition, edited by R. C. Tucker. New York: Norton.

Marx, Karl, and Friedrich Engels. 1978 (1932). *The German Ideology, Part I.* Pp. 146–200 in *The Marx-Engels Reader.* 2nd edition, edited by R. C. Tucker. New York: Norton.

McNees, Patrick. 1997. "A Day in the Life of a Nursing Home Resident, or the Lack Thereof." Paper presented at the Century Circle Conference on Nursing Home Innovation, Rochester, NY (March).

Mills, C. Wright. 1961. *The Sociological Imagination.* New York: Grove Press.

Moffitt, Terrie E. 1993. "Adolescence-Limited and Life-Course-Persistent Antisocial Behavior: A Developmental Taxonomy." *Psychological Review 100*: 674–701.

Moffitt, Terrie E. 1994. "Natural Histories of Delinquency." Pp. 3–61 in *Cross-National Longitudinal Research on Human Development and Criminal Behavior,* edited by E. Weitekamp and H. Kerner. Dordrecht: Kluwer Academic.

Panofsky, Aaron. 2014. *Misbehaving Science: Controversy and the Development of Behavior Genetics.* Chicago: University of Chicago Press.

Pinkerton, James P. 2009. "Are All 'Bioethicists' This Hypocritical? Or Just Daniel Callahan?" *Cure Strategy.* Retrieved December 15, 2020 (http://seriousmedicinestrategy.blogspot.com/2009/08/are-all-bioethicists-this-hypocritical.html)

Rader, Joanne. 2019. "Do We Need To Keep Repeating the Past: Is Bathing Still a Battle?" *Pioneer Network.* Retrieved December 17, 2020 (www.pioneernetwork.net/do-we-need-to-keep-repeating-the-past-is-bathing-still-a-battle/)

Rader, Joanne, Ann Louise Barrick, Beverly Hoeffer, Philip D. Sloane, Darlene McKenzie, Karen Amann Talerico, and Johanna Uriri Glover. 2006. "The Bathing of Older Adults with Dementia: Easing the Unnecessarily Unpleasant Aspects of Assisted Bathing." *American Journal of Nursing* 106(4): 40–8.

Rader, Joanne, and Elizabth M. Tornquist. 1995. *Individualized Dementia Care: Creative, Compassionate Approaches.* New York: Springer Publishing Company.

Remington, Patrick L., Bridget B. Catlin, and Keith P. Gennuso. 2015. "The County Health Rankings: Rationale and Methods." *Population Health Metrics* 13: 11. doi: 10.1186/s12963-015-0044-2.

Riley, Matilda White, Robert L. Kahn, and Anne Foner. 1994. *Age and Structural Lag: Society's Failure to Provide Meaningful Opportunities in Work, Family, and Leisure.* New York: Wiley.

Rogoff, Barbara. 2003. *The Cultural Nature of Human Development.* New York: Oxford University Press.

Rose, Hilary, and Steven Rose. 2012. *Genes, Cells, and Brains : The Promethean Promises of the New Biology.* London: Verso.

Sahlins, Marshall. 1976. *Culture and Practical Reason.* Chicago: University of Chicago Press.

Sarason, Seymour B. 1977. *Work, Aging, and Social Change: Professionals and the One Life-One Career Imperative.* New York: Free Press.

Settersten, Richard A. and Gunhild O. Hägestad. 1996. "What's the Latest? Cultural Age Deadlines for Family Transitions." *The Gerontologist* 36(2): 178–88. doi: 10.1093/geront/36.2.178.

Shura, Robin, Rebecca A. Siders, and Dale Dannefer. 2011. "Culture Change in Long-Term Care: Participatory Action Research and the Role of the Resident." *The Gerontologist* 51(2): 212–25. doi: 10.1093/geront/gnq099.

Siders, Rebecca. 2016. *Voices from the Inside: Gender and the Meaning of Care.* Doctor of Philosophy Dissertation, Case Western Reserve University, Cleveland, OH.

Smith, Wesley J. 2002. *Culture of Death: The Assault on Medical Ethics in America.* New York: Encounter Books.

Span, Paula. 2010. "The Safety Dance." *New York Times.* Retrieved December 17, 2020 (https://newoldage.blogs.nytimes.com/2010/06/16/the-safety-dance/)

Standing, Guy. 2014. *A Precariat Charter: From Denizens to Citizens.* London: Bloomsbury Academic.

Stein, Elizabeth M., Keith P. Gennuso, Donna C. Ugboaja, and Patrick L. Remington. 2017. "The Epidemic of Despair among White Americans: Trends in the Leading Causes of Premature Death, 1999–2015." *American Journal of Public Health* 107(10): 1541–7. doi: 10.2105/AJPH.2017.303941.

Stein, Paul. 2005. *Social Life under the Evacuation of Culture: Lost Minds, Demented Selves and Social Solidarity.* Doctor of Philosophy Dissertation. University of Rochester, Rochester, NY.

Stetsenko, Anna. 2008. "From Relational Ontology to Transformative Activist Stance on Development and Learning: Expanding Vygotsky's (CHAT) Project." *Cultural Studies of Science Education* 3(2): 471–91. doi: 10.1007/s11422-008-9111-3.

Stetsenko, Anna. 2012. "Personhood: An Activist Project of Historical Becoming through Collaborative Pursuits of Social Transformation." *New Ideas in Psychology* 30(1): 144–53. doi: 10.1016/j.newideapsych.2009.11.008.

Stetsenko, Anna. 2016. *The Transformative Mind: Expanding Vygotsky's Approach to Development and Education.* Cambridge, UK: Cambridge University Press.

Stetsenko, Anna. 2018. "Agentive Creativity in All of Us: An Egalitarian Perspective from A Transformative Activist Stance." Pp. 41–60 in *Vygotsky and Creativity: A Cultural-Historical Approach to Play, Meaning Making, and the Arts.* 2nd edition, edited by M. C. Connery, V. John-Steiner, and A. Marjanovic-Shane. New York: Peter Lang.

Thomas, William H. 1994. *The Eden Alternative: Nature, Hope, and Nursing Homes.* New Berlin, NY: Eden Alternative Foundation.

Thomas, William H. 1996. *Life Worth Living: How Someone You Love Can Still Enjoy Life in a Nursing Home: The Eden Alternative in Action.* Acton, MA: Wanderwyk & Burnham.

Thomas, William H. 2004. *What Are Old People For? How Elders Will Save the World.* Acton, MA: Wanderwyk & Burnham.

Vianna, Eduardo, Naja Hougaard, and Anna Stetsenko. 2014. "The Dialectics of Collective and Individual Transformations: Transformative Activist Research in a Collaborative Learning Community Project." Pp. 59–88 in *Collaborative Projects: An Interdisciplinary Study*, edited by A. Blunden. Boston, MA: Brill Publishing.

Vianna, Eduardo, and Anna Stetsenko. 2011. "Connecting Learning and Identity Development through a Transformative Activist Stance: Application in Adolescent Development in a Child Welfare Program." *Human Development* 54(5): 313–38. doi: 10.1159/000331484.

Vianna, Eduardo, and Anna Stetsenko. 2014. "Research with a Transformative Activist Agenda: Creating the Future through Education for Social Change." *National Society for the Study of Education* 113(2): 575–602.

Whitaker, Robert. 2005. "Anatomy of an Epidemic: Psychiatric Drugs and the Astonishing Rise of Mental Illness in America." *Ethical Human Psychology and Psychiatry* 7(1): 23–35.

White, M. M. 2017. "Collective Agency and Community Resilience: A Theoretical Framework to Understand Agricultural Resistance." *Journal of Agriculture, Food Systems and Community Development* 7(4): 17–21.

Whitehouse, Catherine. 2005. "Creating an Empowering Intergenerational Learning Environment." *Intercom: Aging in Focus* 12: 13–15.

Whitehouse, Peter J. 2013. "InterWell: An Integrated School-Based Primary Care Model." *London Journal of Primary Care* 5(2): 83–7.

Wigglesworth, Robin. 2020. "How America's 1% Came to Dominate Stock Ownership." *Financialpost*. Retrieved December 22, 2020 (https://business.financialpost.com/investing/how-americas-1-came-to-dominate-stock-ownership)

Wilkinson, Richard, and Kate Pickett. 2011. *The Spirit Level: Why Greater Equality Makes Societies Stronger*. New York: Bloomsbury Press.

Wilmoth, Janet M., Andrew S. London, and Wendy M. Parker. 2010. "Military Service and Men's Health Trajectories in Later Life." *The Journals of Gerontology: Series B* 65B(6): 744–55. doi: 10.1093/geronb/gbq072.

INDEX

Note: Page numbers in *italic* indicate a figure and page numbers in **bold** indicate a table on the corresponding page.

For Product Safety Concerns and Information please contact our EU
representative GPSR@taylorandfrancis.com
Taylor & Francis Verlag GmbH, Kaufingerstraße 24, 80331 München, Germany

www.ingramcontent.com/pod-product-compliance
Lightning Source LLC
Chambersburg PA
CBHW081737270326
41932CB00020B/3309